Critical Pedagogy and Race

Critical Pedagogy and Race

Edited by

Zeus Leonardo

Blackwell
Publishing

First published as a special issue of *Educational Philosophy and Theory*, 2005, except for: '*The Social Construction of Difference and the Quest for Educational Equality*' (Association and Curriculum Development), '*Maintaining Social Justice Hopes within Academic Realities*' (William S. Hein & Co., Inc), '*Anti-Racism*' (Routledge), '*An Apartheid of Knowledge in the Academy*' (Routledge), '*Race, Class and Gender in Education Research*' (Sage) and '*Introduction*' by Eduardo Bonilla-Silva (Eduardo Bonilla-Silva).

BLACKWELL PUBLISHING
350 Main Street, Malden, MA 02148-5020, USA
9600 Garsington Road, Oxford OX4 2DQ, UK
550 Swanston Street, Carlton, Victoria 3053, Australia

The right of Zeus Leonardo to be identified as the Author of
the Editorial Material in this Work has been asserted in accordance with
the UK Copyright, Designs, and Patents Act 1988.

First published 2005 by Blackwell Publishing Ltd

Library of Congress Cataloging-in-Publication Data has been applied for

ISBN 1-4051-2968-9

A catalogue record for this title is available from the British Library.

The publisher's policy is to use permanent paper from mills that operate a sustainable forestry policy, and which has been manufactured from pulp processed using acid-free and elementary chlorine-free practices. Furthermore, the publisher ensures that the text paper and cover board used have met acceptable environmental accreditation standards.

For further information on
Blackwell Publishing, visit our website:
www.blackwellpublishing.com

Contents

Critical Race Matters

One of the aims of our journal *Educational Philosophy and Theory* is to promote debate outside our comfort zone and territory. The special issue edited by Zeus Leonardo, which has since expanded into this book project, surely does this: it is, if I may say, basically an American collection, by which I mean not only are most of the contributors American in the wider sense of the term (belonging to the Americas), but also the concept itself is American (in the more narrow sense of the term). Except for Valerie Scatamburlo-D'Annibale, who teaches at the University of Windsor in Ontario, Canada, and David Gillborn, who teaches at the University of London, UK, all contributors teach at universities in the United States of America. The concept itself of 'critical race theory' is also American in origin, although its reference and articulation in terms of issues of race, whether in relation to 'whiteness', 'anti-racist education', 'critical pedagogy' or 'postcolonial studies' has a much wider acceptance, intellectually speaking.

The term 'critical race theory', thus, may well be unfamiliar to our readers and to education philosophers and theorists outside the USA. It originated in the Civil Rights movement in the US, or at least its early intellectual precursors can be found there, and especially in school desegregation litigation (e.g. the famous case of *Brown vs. Board of Education*) and anti-discrimination law. It can be traced to the early works of Derrick Bell, an NAACP lawyer, and Alan Freeman, who in the mid 1970s were concerned with the slow pace of racial reform and the fact that civil rights gains of the 1960s were being eroded (Delgado, 1995). Bell and the other founders of critical race theory broke away from the critical legal studies movement because, while the liberal system of civil rights was characterised by faith in a better future, it was colour-blind and too wedded to the notion of incremental change. Bell and others like Richard Delgado, Mari Matsuda, Kimberlé Crenshaw and Patricia Williams challenged the liberal consensus in part through the introduction of storytelling into legal scholarship and methodology, which powerfully demonstrated the way in which racism was lived as part of the daily lives of black and Latino American citizens.

Education was a focus from the beginning and from the early days there emerged a strong coalition of critical race theory and critical legal studies that drew inspiration from the reconstructive theology of Dr Martin Luther King, Jr, the NAACP and an emerging race consciousness. The history of critical race theory, then, is tied closely not only to critical legal studies and the search for an oppositional voice that questioned deeply held beliefs about the US Constitution and the nature of equality in American society, but also sought to anchor itself in a kind of racial realism based on the actual lives or life stories of its subjects. As the movement matured it also became less focused on black struggles alone; it became both more inclusive and more pluralistic, seeking to oppose the many faces of racism at the intersection of race and cultures, race and gender, and more carefully theorising the politics of identity in relation to territory, geography, history, community and nation.

Critical race theory, historically associated with critical legal studies, worked with the notion of rights, where the right to education was fundamental. We should remind ourselves that rights achieved through school litigation did not exist before 1954 and still remain to be clearly defined despite hundreds of legal opinions (Crenshaw *et al.*, 1995). The movement has diversified and now covers a lot of ground. While 'critical race theory' still does not exist as an official subject heading in the *Library of Congress Subjects Headings*, it can be accessed in relation to topics such as Culture and law; Critical legal studies; Discrimination in education; Freedom of speech; and, of course, Race; Race discrimination—law and legislation; Racism in language; Racism—United States; Sociologial jurisprudence; and Race relations—philosophy (see *Critical Race Theory Resource Guide* at http://www.pages.drexel.edu/~jp49/). Scholars in education employed critical race theory in the 1990s to evaluate and research educational policies (e.g. Tate, 1996; Parker, 1998). Its development and inclusion in educational philosophy and theory is therefore very recent, which is an important reason for this excellent collection of essays.

In the United Kingdom, the notions of institutional racism and anti-racist education emerged in the 1970s, leading to the 1976 Race Relations Act (and its 2003 Amendment) and yet deep institutional racism has been revealed recently in the police force, prison service and public services more generally (for details see the Commission for Racial Equality website at http://www.cre.gov.uk/). In Britain, racism is mixed with forms of neo-Nazism and fascism, and often clearly evident in city race riots and football hooliganism (but also see the list of anti-racist organisations at http://www.magenta.nl/crosspoint/uk.html). It is also deeply institutionalised in schools and universities. Moreover, it has taken on a different hue in light of the Iraqi war. This should remind us that racism takes different society, state and historical formations. Certainly, the experience of Aotearoa/New Zealand and Australia as white-settler colonies would bear out this bold assertion. In all cases mentioned, significant progress has been made through the courts, although this experience has also varied. One of the questions educational theorists reading this collection might pose is the extent to which US critical race theory applies in their own context and whether the coalition of it with critical pedagogy requires situation adjustments and country-specific developments.

I wish to thank Zeus Leonardo publicly and personally for taking the editorial responsibility for such an important project, and also his contributors, for a challenging and thought-provoking collection.

MICHAEL A. PETERS
University of Illinois,
Montana-Champaign

References

Crenshaw, K., Gotanda, N., & Thomas, K. (1995) *Critical Race Theory: The key writings that formed the movement* (New York, New Press).

Delgado, R. (1995) Legal Storytelling: Storytelling for oppositionists and others: A plea for narrative, in: R. Delgado (ed.), *Critical Race Theory: The cutting edge* (Philadelphia: Temple University Press).

Parker, L. (1998) Race Is ... Race Ain't: An explanation of the utility of critical race theory in qualitative research in education, *International Journal of Qualitative Studies in Education*, 11:43–57.

Tate, W. F. (1996) Critical Race Theory, *Review of Research in Education*, 22, pp. 201–247.

Foreword

ZEUS LEONARDO

California State University, Long Beach and University of Washington, Seattle

Since the publication of Paulo Freire's seminal work *Pedagogy of the Oppressed* in 1970, the academic scene has benefited from the innovations in critical pedagogy. Scholarship in critical pedagogy led the search for ways to explain educational domination and a language of possibility to resist it and transform the schooling process. Informed by the writings of Marx, the Frankfurt School, neo-Marxism, cultural studies, and post-foundational critiques, critical pedagogy found itself engaging the class debate, and for important reasons. No doubt because Marxian influence has been so great, critical pedagogy began its ascendance as a critique or problematization of class relations. This focus means that critical pedagogy has evolved in a particular direction that centers the critique on the problem of capitalism.

This book finds that the question of race has played a secondary role in the development of critical pedagogy and argues for a deeper engagement of it.[1] Race has been interwoven into critical pedagogy but often in relation to a prioritized engagement with class struggle. The essays represented in this collection privilege the concept of race as the point of departure for critique, not the end of it. It represents scholars whose ideas engage the race question in critical pedagogy from various theoretical orientations, such as whiteness studies, critical race theory, multiculturalism, anti-racism, LatCrit theory, historical materialism, and cultural studies. The particular articulations of critical pedagogy in national as well as global contexts cannot afford to neglect the structures of race, especially in these times of terrorism and counter-strategies to curtail terrorist activities. We have a new chapter in the history of race relations that critical educators are under pressure to understand. Education becomes a site for its interrogation and testing ground for tolerance because critics suggest that increased civil rights violations loom large in the discourse of patriotism popularized by Bush's administration and its respective allies.

The concept of race is an important node in the analysis of the triumvirate between capitalism, racism, and patriarchy. Its primacy differs between scholars and pedagogy is critical to the extent that it has made sincere efforts to confront it. This is the expressed goal of the book: to confront race. Although critical pedagogists have supported intersectional arguments linking structures of race, class, and gender, the essays concentrate on the first of these relations in order to deepen our understanding of the evolution of race critique within critical pedagogy. As a result, the place of race in critical pedagogy is established, problematized, and in the end enriched. The collection represented here promotes multiple perspectives in an effort to map the contours of race and racism, which will advance the field of educational philosophy and theory, strengthen engagement with critical pedagogy, and increase dialogue on race matters.

In chapter 1, 'The Color of Supremacy: Beyond the discourse of "white privilege",' I begin the book by problematizing the concept of 'white privilege' and building a case for a closer look at 'white supremacy.' I find that a critical pedagogy of white supremacy analyzes the actions, decisions, and structures that make white privilege possible. By returning to the concept of supremacy, I clarify the subject and object of racial domination. Although the two processes are related, the conditions of white supremacy make white privilege possible. In order for white racial hegemony to saturate everyday life, it has to be secured by a process of domination, or those acts, decisions, and policies that white subjects perpetrate on people of color. As such, a critical pedagogy of white racial supremacy revolves less around the issue of unearned advantages, or a state of being dominant, and more around direct processes that secure domination and the privileges associated with it.

In chapter 2, 'Whiteness and Critical Pedagogy,' Ricky Lee Allen rethinks critical pedagogy from a race-radical perspective that contextualizes social relations within a white supremacist totality. He argues for an anti-racist critical pedagogy that draws from critical whiteness studies, critical race theory, and Paulo Freire's *Pedagogy of the Oppressed*. Whites exhibit all the characteristics of an oppressor group mentioned by Freire, but they do so in race-specific ways that a Freirean lens fails to capture. Extending Freire's notions for transforming the oppressor, whites can become anti-racist to the extent that they achieve solidarity with race-radical people of color. This essay seeks to assist in the transformation of whites by offering a critical dialogical theory for intervening in whiteness in the classroom. It also seeks to problematize and transform the white identity politics of critical pedagogy.

In chapter 3, 'Maintaining Social Justice Hopes within Academic Realities: A Freirean approach to critical race/LatCrit pedagogy,' Daniel Solórzano and Tara Yosso continue Allen's appropriation of Freire's philosophy by merging it with critical race theory and LatCrit frameworks. They argue that just as Freirean pedagogy 'names the problem,' critical race and LatCrit theories 'name the injury.' This is done in order to bring out the voice of oppressed groups, to promote social justice for the victims of racism, and to remind us that 'the dynamic nature of oppression requires dynamic response.' They use the methodology of (counter)storytelling established by critical race theory, told through the narratives of a senior scholar, Professor Sanchez, and her former doctoral student and junior scholar, Professor Leticia Garcia. Through the stories of Professors Sanchez and Garcia, Solórzano and Yosso expose the challenges and contradictions of oppositional consciousness in the context of institutional realities, such as tenure, and ideals of social justice. Searching for justice requires that diversity become real insofar as it affirms equality and *dignidad humana*, rather than merely difference.

In chapter 4, 'The Social Construction of Difference and the Quest for Educational Equality,' James Banks lends support to Solórzano and Yosso's project with critical thoughts on the social construction of race, mental retardation, and giftedness as well as how the victims of such constructions contest their institutional forms. Writing from a sociological framework, Banks focuses on the latent, rather than manifest, function of knowledge construction about social groups. Central in his analysis is the relationship between power, knowledge, and group membership.

In this context, difference means reconceptualizing the nature of power as something shared rather than centralized. In agreement with Omi and Winant (1994), Banks notes the shifting terrain of race relations and the challenges forged by oppositional racial groups to change its meanings. To Wilson's (1978) chagrin, Banks argues for the 'continuing significance of race' but marries an analysis of its constructions with the multiplying effects of relations of (dis)ability. Just as students of color have been pathologized in education, the same can be said of students with disabilities. In asserting this synthesis, Banks makes a case for a racialized analysis of ability and giftedness, and an ability-conscious study of race.

Chapter 5 takes the book across the ocean from North America as David Gillborn surveys the ebb and flow of anti-racist work in England. In 'Anti-racism: From policy to praxis,' Gillborn documents the history of anti-racist pedagogy in the UK, a matter not only about power but of praxis. Gillborn notes that the decade of the 1980s featured the height of British concern with anti-racism as evidenced by a variety of overt practices, including mobilization against the Nazi League, the National Front, and later the British National Party. However, anti-racist struggles faced criticisms from both the Right *and* Left, the first leveling a common complaint about the end of merit and democracy as we know it, the second questioning the essentialist tendencies in anti-racist discourses. In particular, scholars and activists influenced by the cultural studies movement were quick to note the 'racial dualism' (Modood's phrase) that splits society into Whites and Blacks, not to mention leaving the question of culture in the back of the anti-racist bus. Gillborn notes that one of the most significant weaknesses of 1980s anti-racism in England was its penchant for rhetoric over practical application. Gillborn advises that for anti-racism to remain vital, it must remain critical not only of others, but of ourselves in our efforts to understand and curtail racism.

Chapter 6, 'Critical Race Theory, Afrocentricity, and their Relationship to Critical Pedagogy,' introduces the main innovations of a critical race theory of education. In this essay, Marvin Lynn argues for a serious engagement of a 'critical race pedagogy,' which makes race a central structuring principle in schooling processes and complements critical pedagogy's search for social justice. More important, he also provides a synthesis between critical race theory and Afrocentrism, building a dialogue between two schools of thought that have remained relatively separate, the first concerned with what Du Bois (1989/1903) earlier called 'the color line,' the second with culture and cultural imperialism. Lynn asserts that if critical pedagogy is going to intervene in relations of oppression, then it must draw more heavily from the 'race-based epistemologies' of people of color.

In chapter 7, Valerie Scatamburlo-D'Annibale and Peter McLaren argue for a historical materialist analysis of racism and race relations. In 'Class Dismissed? Historical materialism and the politics of "difference",' Scatamburlo-D'Annibale and McLaren note that in their rush to avoid the 'capital' sin of 'economism,' many post-Marxists have fallen prey to an ahistorical form of culturalism which holds that cultural struggles external to class organizing provide the cutting edge of emancipatory politics. This essay contends that cultural arguments about difference (which includes race) are deeply problematic because they de-emphasize the totalizing power and function of capital and for their attempts to diminish the centrality of class. They assert that the advocates of difference cannot pose a substantive challenge to capitalism, which is able to accommodate a vast pluralism of ideas and cultural practices. Therefore, Scatamburlo-D'Annibale and McLaren believe that it is necessary to (re)conceptualize 'difference' by drawing upon Marx's materialist and historical formulations because 'difference' needs to be understood as the product of political and economic organization.

In chapter 8, Laurence Parker and David Stovall continue the engagement with critical race theory and the apparent permanence of racism. In 'Actions Following Words: Critical race theory connects to critical pedagogy,' Parker and Stovall expose the gaps within critical pedagogy with respect to the problem of color-blind positions in various post-discourses and Marxist engagements of political economy. In this essay, which uses critical race narrative as methodology, Parker and Stovall discuss some of the ways that critical race theory could be linked to critical pedagogy in order to provide a more comprehensive analytical framework to analyze the role of race–class dynamics. They also raise more issues of concern related to critical pedagogy and race in educational research and practice, especially in light of African American/black ambivalence toward critical pedagogy. Consistent with the findings of critical race scholars in this collection, Parker and Stovall question the value-neutral assumptions of mainstream research. Finally, they speculate about what lies ahead regarding possible points of agreement and conflict between critical race theory and critical pedagogy.

Chapter 9 takes the collection into a critical scrutiny of the racialized production of knowledge in academic publishing. In 'Race, Class, and Gender in Education Research: Surveying the political terrain,' Michèle Foster documents the racial, economic, and gender politics of academic journal publishing and citation. Here she finds a decisive advantage for white and male scholars, who publish more frequently in general, and in high-status journals in particular. Women academics and scholars of color have challenged this hegemony in their own publications. Foster offers several explanations for this uneven development. First, the lower numbers of doctoral students of color at top institutions affects their status and rate of acceptance into elite networks. Second, they are often excluded from granted research projects that produce high-status research knowledge. Third, mainstream journals are not accepting of subjugated perspectives, especially when these commitments pose a threat to white, middle-class, and male sensibilities. Foster suggests that, in order to 'right the wrong,' academics must broaden their readings to include knowledge from the margins, assign non-mainstream texts in education courses, and halt the 'colonial mentality of citation' whereby the Other's work is not cited unless it conforms to the established paradigms.

Chapter 10 continues Foster's investigation of uneven knowledge valuation by building a framework for understanding 'knowledge apartheid.' In 'An Apartheid of Knowledge in Academia: The struggle over the "legitimate" knowledge of faculty of color,' Dolores Delgado Bernal and Octavio Villalpando argue that a certain 'epistemological racism' (Scheurich & Young, 1997) sustains a segregation of knowledge that fails to legitimate the perspectives of scholars of color. Drawing both from national trend data concerning the status of faculties of color and storytelling about a composite Chicana scholar, Patricia Avila, Bernal and Villalpando demystify the 'race-neutral' tenure process that faculties of color navigate in the academy. First, the authors present a backroom discussion of Professor Avila's file through the majoritarian perspective, where colleagues question the appropriateness of her journal publication venues, her (in)ability to remain 'objective' when teaching about multiculturalism, and her 'special interest' involvement in 'political organizations' for her service. Second, Bernal and Villalpando re-present the same situation through a counterstory as embodied by Professor Avila and a sympathetic colleague to showcase the often unrecognized or unlegitimized cultural resources that scholars of color bring to the academy. In the end, their essay debunks the Eurocentric assumptions about a neutral and objective (i.e. non-racial) formal process in higher education.

In the final chapter, 'Postcolonial Literature and the Curricular Imagination: Wilson Harris and the pedagogical implications of the carnivalesque,' Cameron McCarthy and Greg Dimitriadis argue that contemporary debates around multiculturalism have typically been driven by notions of 'inclusion.' Postcolonial artists, however, give us no such easy referents, which can best be captured in the concept of the 'carnivalesque,' or the notion of unpredictable patterns of association, inversions of hierarchies of powers, and the playful flourishing of multiplicity that has taken over the modern city and metropolis. In this last essay, the authors take the literature on critical pedagogy and race in new directions by focusing on a new racial identity through the postcolonial works of Wilson Harris, including *Carnival* (1985), *The Palace of the Peacock* (1960), and *Companions of the Day and Night* (1975). The carnivalesque postcolonial writing of novelists, such as Harris, offers pedagogues new models of thoughtfulness that challenge the tendency toward intellectual isolationism and cultural insularity currently evident in education.

References

Du Bois, W. E. B. (1989/1903) *The Souls of Black Folk* (New York, Penguin Books).

Freire, P. (1993/1970). *Pedagogy of the Oppressed*, trans. M. Ramos (New York, Continuum).

Omi, M. & Winant, H. (1994) *Racial Formation in the United States: From the 1960s to the 1990s*, 2nd edn (New York and London, Routledge).

Scheurich, J. & Young, M. (1997) Coloring Epistemologies: Are our research epistemologies racially biased?, *Educational Researcher*, 26:4, pp. 4–16.

Wilson, W. J. (1978). *The Declining Significance of Race: Blacks and changing American institutions* (Chicago, University of Chicago Press).

Acknowledgements

This book would not have been possible without help and encouragement from Michael Peters. The project began in 2001 when I discussed the idea with Peters after the AERA Conference in Seattle, Washington. It started as a special issue of the journal, *Educational Philosophy and Theory*, and has since evolved into a larger project in its current form. Special thanks goes to Michael Peters, a comrade in the political and intellectual search for democracy. For all the hard work and faith that they put into the book, the contributors were central in making it a powerful collection of ideas and perspectives. Each contribution was unique and made an impact on my own thinking. Last, I dedicate this book to my wife, Maggie Hunter, who taught me everything I know about race.

Further Acknowledgements

The original versions of the following papers were first printed in the following publications:

Banks, James A (2000), 'The Social Construction of Difference and the Quest for Educational Equality', in Ronald S. Brandt (Editor), *Education in a New Era* (ASCD 200 Yearbook) (pp. 21–45), Alexandria, VA: Association for Supervision and Curriculum Development.

Solorzano, Daniel & Yosso, Tara (2001), 'Maintaining Social Justice Hopes within Academic Realities: A Freirean Approach to Critical Race/LatCrit Pedagogy', *Denver Law Review*, 78, 595–621, William S. Hein & Co., Inc.

Gillborn, David (2000), 'Anti-Racism: from policy to praxis', in Bob Moon, Sally Brown & Miriam Ben-Peretz (eds) *Routledge International Companion to Education*, pp. 476–488, London Routledge.

Delgado Bernal, Dolores & Villalpando, Octavio (2002), 'An Apartheid of Knowledge in the Academy: The Struggle over "Legitimate" Knowledge for Faculty of Color', *Equity and Excellence in Education*, 35(2), 169–180, Routledge.

Foster, Michèle (1999), 'Race, Class, and Gender in Education Research: Surveying the Political Terrain', *Educational Policy*, 13(January), 77–85, SAGE.

INTRODUCTION

'Racism' and 'New Racism': The contours of racial dynamics in contemporary America

EDUARDO BONILLA-SILVA
Duke University

> The habit of considering racism as a mental quirk, as a psychological flaw, must be abandoned.
>
> —Frantz Fanon

> Race and racism are not figments of demented imaginations, but are central to the economics, politics, and culture of this nation.
>
> —Robert Blauner

In this Introduction I criticize mainstream and even radical scholars from a variety of perspectives (e.g. Marxism, internal colonialism, etc.) for conceiving of racism in a fundamentally psychological and individualistic manner. After this critique, I introduce my own structural interpretation anchored around a materialist understanding of race relations; that is, based on the idea that the races have dissimilar interests stemming from their different group position in the *racialized social system*. Furthermore, I describe the most current form of racialization in what I call the 'New Racism.' I conclude the Introduction by highlighting the advantages of my framework over the mainstream and alternative approaches to interpret racial matters.

The area of race and ethnic studies lacks a sound theoretical apparatus. To complicate matters, many analysts of racial matters have abandoned the serious theorization and reconceptualization of one of their central concepts: racism. Too many social analysts researching racism assume that the phenomenon is self-evident, and therefore either do not provide a definition or provide an elementary definition (Schuman *et al.*, 1985, 1997; Sniderman & Piazza, 1993). Nevertheless, whether implicitly or explicitly, most analysts regard racism as a purely ideological phenomenon.

Although the concept of racism has become a central analytical category in contemporary social scientific discourse on racial phenomena, the concept is of recent origin (Banton, 1970; Miles, 1989, 1993). It was not employed at all in the classic works of Thomas and Znaiecki (1918), Edward Reuter (1934), Gunnar Myrdal (1944), and Robert Park (1950).[1] Benedict (1945) was one of the first scholars to use the notion of racism in her book *Race and Racism*. She defined racism as 'the dogma that one ethnic group is condemned by nature to congenital

Discrimination—*Actions* against members of races	Example: Lynching a black male
Prejudice—Negative *attitudes* toward races	Example: Believing that all black men are oversexed
Racism—Stereotypical *beliefs* about races	Example: Believing that blacks are inferior to whites

Figure 1: Mainstream Conceptual Framework on Racism

inferiority and another group is destined to congenital superiority' (p. 87). Despite some refinements, current use of the concept of racism in the social sciences is similar to Benedict's. Thus van den Berghe (1967) states that racism is 'any *set of beliefs* that organic, genetically transmitted differences (whether real or imagined) between human groups are intrinsically associated with the presence or the absence of certain socially relevant abilities or characteristics, hence that such differences are a legitimate basis of invidious distinctions between groups socially defined as races' (p. 11; emphasis added). Schaefer (1990) provides a more concise definition of racism: 'a *doctrine* of racial supremacy, that one race is superior' (p. 16).

This idealist view is still held widely among social scientists. Its narrow focus on ideas has reduced the study of racism mostly to social psychology, and this perspective has produced a schematic view of the way racism operates in society. First, racism is defined as a set of ideas or beliefs. Second, those beliefs are regarded as having the potential to lead individuals to develop prejudice, defined as 'negative attitudes towards an entire group of people' (Schaefer, 1990, p. 53). Finally, these prejudiced attitudes may induce individuals to real actions or discrimination against racial minorities. This conceptual framework, graphically illustrated in Figure 1 above, with minor modifications, prevails in the social sciences.

Some alternative perspectives on racism have closely followed the prevailing ideological conceptualization in the social sciences. For example, orthodox Marxists (Cox, 1948; Perlo, 1975; Szymanski, 1981, 1983), who regard class and class struggle as the central explanatory variables of social life, reduce racism to a legitimating ideology used by the bourgeoisie to divide the working class. Other scholars have advanced non-ideological interpretations of racism but have stopped short of developing a structural conceptualization of racial matters. From the institutionalist perspective (Alvarez *et al.*, 1979; Carmichael, 1971; Carmichael & Hamilton, 1967; Chesler, 1976; Knowles & Prewitt, 1969; Wellman, 1977) racism is defined as a combination of prejudice and power that allows the dominant race to institutionalize its dominance at all levels in a society. Similarly, from the internal colonialism perspective (Barrera, 1979; Blauner, 1972; Moore, 1970), racism is viewed as an institutional matter based on a system in which the white majority 'raises its social position by exploiting, controlling, and keeping down others who are categorized in racial or ethnic terms' (Blauner, 1972, p. 22). The main difference between these two perspectives is that the latter regards racial minorities as colonial subjects in the United States; this view leads unequivocally to nationalist solutions.[2] Both perspectives contribute greatly to our understanding of racial phenomena by stressing the social and systemic nature of racism and the structured nature of white advantages. Furthermore, the effort of the institutionalist perspective to uncover contemporary mechanisms and practices that reproduce white advantages is still empirically useful (e.g. Knowles and Prewitt, 1969). Yet neither of these perspectives provides a rigorous conceptual framework that allows analysts to study the operation of racially stratified societies.

The racial formation perspective (Omi & Winant, 1986, 1994; Winant, 1994) is the most recent theoretical alternative to mainstream idealist approaches. Omi and Winant (1994) define racial formation as 'the sociohistorical process by which racial categories are created, inhabited, transformed, and destroyed' (p. 55). In their view, race should be regarded as an organizing principle of social relationships that shapes the identity of individual actors at the micro level and shapes all spheres of social life at the macro level.

Although I regard this perspective as a theoretical breakthrough, I contend that it still gives undue attention to ideological/cultural processes,[3] does not regard races as truly social collectivities, and over-emphasizes the racial projects (Omi & Winant, 1994; Winant, 1994) of certain actors (neoconservatives, members of the far right, liberals), thus obscuring the *social* and *general* character of racialized societies.

Because of the analytical relevance of these alternative interpretations of racism, I offer below a more substantive and formal review of each of these approaches.

Limitations of Mainstream Idealist Views and of Some Alternative Frameworks

I describe below some of the main limitations of the idealist conception of racism. Because not all limitations apply to the Marxist, institutionalist, internal colonialist, and racial formation perspectives, I point out the ones that do apply, and to what extent.

1. Racism is excluded from the foundation or structure of the social system

When racism is regarded as a baseless ideology ultimately dependent on other, 'real' forces in society, the structure of the society itself is not classified as racist. The Marxist perspective is particularly guilty of this shortcoming. Although Marxists have addressed the question of the historical origin of racism, they explain its reproduction in an idealist fashion. Racism, in their accounts, is an ideology that emerged with chattel slavery and other forms of class oppression to justify the exploitation of people of color and survives as residue of the past. Although some Marxists have attempted to distance their analysis from this purely ideological view (Solomos, 1986; Wolpe, 1988) and to ground racial phenomena, they do so by ultimately subordinating racial matters to class matters.

Even though the institutionalist, internal colonialism, and racial formation perspectives regard racism as a structural phenomenon and provide some useful ideas and concepts, they do not develop the theoretical apparatus necessary to describe how this structure operates.

2. Racism is ultimately viewed as a psychological phenomenon to be examined at the individual level

The research agenda that follows from this conceptualization is the examination of individuals' attitudes to determine levels of racism in society (Schuman *et al.*, 1985; Sears, 1988; Sniderman & Piazza, 1993). Given that the constructs used to measure racism are static—that is, that there are a number of standard questions which do not change significantly over time—this research usually finds that racism is declining in society. Those analysts who find that racist attitudes are still with us usually leave unexplained why this is so (Sniderman & Piazza, 1993).

This psychological understanding of racism is related to the limitation I cited above. If racism is not part of a society but is a characteristic of individuals who are 'racist' or 'prejudiced'—that is, is a phenomenon operating at the individual level—then (a) social institutions cannot be racist and (b) studying racism is simply a matter of surveying the proportion of people in a society who hold 'racist' beliefs.

Orthodox Marxists (Cox, 1948; Perlo, 1975; Szymanski, 1983) and many neo-Marxists (Miles, 1993; Miles & Phizaclea, 1984; Solomos, 1986) conceive of racism as an ideology that may affect members of the working class. Although the authors associated with the institutionalist, internal colonialist, and racial formation perspectives focus on the ideological character of racism, they all emphasize how this ideology becomes enmeshed or institutionalized in organizations and social practices.

3. Racism is treated as a static phenomenon

The phenomenon is viewed as unchanging; that is, racism yesterday is like racism today. Thus, when a society's racial structure and its customary racial practices are rearticulated, this rearticulation is characterized as a decline in racism (Wilson, 1978), a natural process in a cycle (Park, 1950), an example of increased assimilation (Rex, 1973, 1986), or effective 'norm changes' (Schuman *et al.*, 1985). This limitation, which applies particularly to social psychologists and Marxist scholars, derives from not conceiving racism as possessing an independent structural foundation. If racism is merely a matter of ideas that have no material basis in contemporary society, then those ideas should be similar to their original configuration, whatever that was. The ideas may be articulated in a different context, but most analysts essentially believe that racist ideas remain the same. For this reason, with notable exceptions (Kinder & Sears, 1981; Sears, 1988), their attitudinal research is still based on responses to questions developed in the 1940s, 1950s, and 1960s.

4. Analysts defining racism in an idealist manner view racism as 'incorrect' or 'irrational thinking'; thus they label 'racists' as irrational and rigid

Because racism is conceived of as a belief with no real social basis, it follows that those who hold racist views must be irrational or stupid (Adorno *et al.*, 1950;

Allport, 1958; Santa Cruz, 1977; Sniderman & Piazza, 1993. For a critique, see Blauner, 1972; Wellman, 1977). This view allows for a tactical distinction between individuals with the 'pathology' and social actors who are 'rational' and racism-free. The problem with this rationalistic view is twofold. First, it misses the rational elements on which racialized systems were originally built. Second, and more important, it neglects the possibility that contemporary racism still has a rational foundation. In this account, contemporary racists are perceived as Archie Bunker type individuals (Wellman, 1977). Among the alternative frameworks reviewed here, only orthodox Marxism insists on the irrational and imposed character of racism. Neo-Marxists and authors associated with the institutionalist, internal colonialist, and racial formation perspectives insist, to varying degrees, on the rationality of racism. Neo-Marxists (e.g. Bonacich, Wolpe, Hall) and authors in the racial formation tradition acknowledge the short-term advantages that workers gain from racism; the institutionalist and internal colonial paradigms emphasize the systematic and long-term character of these advantages.

5. Racism is understood as overt behavior

Because the idealist approach regards racism as 'irrational' and 'rigid,' its manifestations should be quite evident, usually involving some degree of hostility. This does not present serious analytical problems for the study of certain periods in racialized societies when racial practices were overt (e.g. slavery and apartheid), but problems in the analysis of racism arise in situations where racial practices are subtle, indirect, or fluid. For instance, many analysts have suggested that in contemporary America racial practices are manifested covertly (Bonilla-Silva & Lewis, 1997; Wellman, 1977) and racial attitudes tend to be symbolic (Pettigrew, 1994; Sears, 1988). Therefore it is a waste of time to attempt to detect 'racism' by asking questions such as 'How strongly would you object if a member of your family wanted to bring a black friend home to dinner?'[4] Also, many such questions were developed to measure the extent of racist attitudes in the population during the Jim Crow era of race relations; they are not suitable for the post-1960s period.

Furthermore, this emphasis on overt behavior limits the possibility of analyzing racial phenomena in other parts of the world such as Brazil, Cuba, and Puerto Rico where race relations do not have an overt character. The form of race relations—overt or covert—depends on the pattern of racialization that structured a particular society (Cox, 1948; Harris, 1964; Rex, 1983; van den Berghe, 1967) and on how the process of racial contestation and other social dynamics affected that pattern (see the following section).

6. Contemporary racism is viewed as an expression of 'original sin'—as a remnant of past historical racial situations

In the case of the United States, some analysts argue that racism preceded slavery and/or capitalism (Jordan, 1968; Marable, 1983; Robinson, 1983). Others regard racism in the United States as the result of slavery (Glazer & Moyniham, 1970). Even in promising new avenues of research, such as that presented by Roediger (1991) in

The Wages of Whiteness, contemporary racism is viewed as one of the '*legacies* of white workerism' (p. 176; italics in original). By considering racism as a legacy, all these analysts downplay the significance of its contemporary materiality or structure.

Again the Marxist perspective shares this limitation. Marxists believe that racism developed in the sixteenth century and has been used since then by capitalists or white workers to further their own class interests. All other models recognize the historic significance of this 'discovery' but associate contemporary racial ideology with contemporary racially based inequalities.

7. Racism is analyzed in a circular manner

'If racism is defined as the behavior that results from the belief, its discovery becomes ensnared in a circularity—racism is a belief that produces behavior, which is itself racism' (Webster, 1992, p. 84). Racism is established by racist behavior, which itself is proved by the existence of racism. This circularity results from an insufficient grounding of racism in social relations among the races. If racism, viewed as an ideology, were seen as possessing a *structural*[5] foundation, its examination could be associated with racial practices rather than with mere ideas and the problem of circularity would be avoided.

Some Alternative Frameworks to Interpret Racial Matters

The Marxist Perspective

For Marxists, *class* is the central explanatory variable of social life and *class struggle* is viewed as the main societal dynamic. In Marx's succinct words: 'The history of all hitherto existing society is the history of class struggles' (Marx & Engels, 1977, p. 222). Hence, for Marxists other types of social divisions and possible sources of collective conflict (e.g. gender or race-based struggles) are necessarily viewed as secondary contradictions or regarded as derivations of the class structure (Aronowitz, 1992). The orthodox[6] Marxist position on race is simple and straightforward: racism is an *ideology* used by the bourgeoisie to divide workers. In the words of Albert Szymanski, racism or racialism is:

> a legitimating ideology for an exploitative structure. Racist ideology propagated in the media, educational system, and other institutions, together with the actual distribution of relative petty advantage within the working class serves to disorganize the entire working class including the ethnic majority, thereby allowing capital to more effectively exploit most majority group workers. (Szymanski, 1983, p. 402)

Although some Marxists suggest that a racial structure exists and can be observed in job allocations, wealth, housing, and other larger allocation of resources (Szymanski, 1981; Wolpe, 1986), they all underscore the 'capitalist nature of racist structures, racialist ideology, and interpersonal racism' (Szymanski, 1983, p. 431).

One of the first Marxist-inspired analysts to deal with racial matters in a systematic way was black sociologist Oliver C. Cox in his impressive *Caste, Class, and Race*

(1948).[7] There he defined racism or *race prejudice* as 'a social attitude propagated among the public by an exploiting class for the purpose of stigmatizing some group as inferior so that the exploitation of either the group itself or its resources or both may be justified' (Cox, 1948, p. 393). This social attitude or *ideology* emerged in the fifteenth century as a practical consequence of the labor needs of European imperialists. In Cox's words:

> The socioeconomic matrix of racial antagonism involved the commercialization of human labor in the West Indies. In the East Indies, and in America, the intense competition among businessmen of different western European cities for the capitalist exploitation of the resources of this area, the development of nationalism and the consolidation of European nations, and the decline of the influence of the Roman Catholic Church with its mystical inhibitions to the free exploitation of economic resources. Racial antagonism attained full maturity during the latter half of the nineteenth century, when the sun no longer set on British soil and the great nationalistic powers of Europe began to justify their economic designs upon weaker European peoples with subtle theories of racial superiority and masterhood. (Cox, 1948, p. 330)

But does Cox view the race relations and racial antagonisms that emerged out of European imperialism as racial? Does he recognize that certain aspects of social structure are racial in nature? Cox, as all Marxists, argues that race relations are not truly racial. Thus for Cox European imperialists justified their exploitation of the people and resources of the New World in racial terms but essentially established 'labor–capital profit relationships' or 'proletarian bourgeois relations' (Cox, 1948, p. 336). Racial exploitation is viewed as a special form of *class* exploitation (Cox, 1948, p. 344). The racial component of these class-based relations stems from the fact that blacks were proletarianized in their entirety (as a people) in contrast to whites who experienced a *partial* proletarianization. Given that the racial aspects of societies is not deemed as real, Cox concludes his *Caste, Class, and Race* by suggesting that racial minorities should strive towards *assimilation*, follow white working-class leadership, and ultimately struggle for socialism alongside white workers. The lack of any critical race viewpoint is amazing considering that Cox, a black writer, wrote this book at a time of great white working-class hostility toward black and minority workers.[8]

Another popular Marxist interpretation of racism is that of Edna Bonacich (1980). The twist in Bonacich's approach is that instead of regarding race relations and racism as fundamentally orchestrated by the bourgeoisie, she suggests that they are the product of intra-working-class frictions resulting from the *split labor market*. For Bonacich a split labor market exists when there is 'a difference in the price of labor between two or more groups of workers holding constant their efficiency and productivity' (Bonacich, 1980, pp. 343–344). According to Bonacich, the United States has had a split labor market since slavery, with blacks as the cheaply priced labor segment. After the abolition of slavery, Bonacich claims, the black laborers remained at the bottom of the labor market due to a 'difference in labor militance' compared to white workers (ibid., p. 345). For Bonacich, white workers—whether old stock or immigrants—had a 'greater ... recognition of class conflict with the capitalist class' (ibid., p. 346). Although Bonacich is aware of the fact 'that a number of "white" unions openly excluded blacks while many others discriminated more covertly,' she insists that the lesser degree of black involvement in labor unions was the reason for their utilization as cheap laborers by capitalists in the post-World War I period (ibid., p. 347).[9]

What about the well-known and abundantly documented history of white working-class racism? Bonacich reinterprets this racist history as white workers' resistance to the threats (e.g. strike-breakers, displacement, lowering the wage rate, etc.) posed by blacks. In Bonacich's opinion, this 'resistance'[10] involved the total exclusion of blacks from unions and caste-like occupational divisions. Significantly, Bonacich says little about the labor threats posed by the millions of European immigrants to white American workers. Although Bonacich believes that black and white workers coalesced between 1940 and 1960, she argues that the counter-offensive launched by the bourgeoisie (plant relocations and automation in the past and downsizing today) extended the life of the split labor market. Since blacks were very vulnerable at the outset of the coalition period, the policies of the capitalists disproportionally hurt blacks and contributed to the creation of a 'class of hard-core unemployed in the ghettos' (ibid., p. 358).[11]

The limitations of the orthodox Marxist views on racial matters are many. However, rather than criticizing *each* analyst, I offer below some limitations common to all orthodox Marxists. First, as I suggested above, these analysts regard racism and racial antagonism as products of class dynamics. Regardless of whether the antagonism is viewed as fostered by the bourgeoisie (Cox, 1948; Szymanski, 1981) or as the product of intra-working-class strife (Bonacich, 1980) or as the outcome of contingent historical processes (Saxton, 1990), *racial strife* is viewed as not having a *real* racial component—that is, as not having its own racial base. Second, racial strife is conceived as emanating from *false* interests. Because the unity of the working class and the impending socialist revolution are *a priori* Marxist axioms, racial (or gender-based) struggle is not viewed as having its own material basis (that is, as based on the different interests of the actors involved).[12] Consequently racism is explained as 'ideological' or 'irrational.' Although Bonacich views many of the black–white workers' struggles as 'rational,' she interprets them as 'rational' in *class* but not in *racial* terms. Finally, given that racial phenomena are not deemed as independent and are essentially classified as 'ideological,' most Marxists shy away from performing an in-depth analysis of the politics and ideologies of race (see Omi & Winant, 1986).

Recently some Marxist analysts—many of them inspired by the pivotal work of Stuart Hall (1980)—have attempted to develop more flexible interpretations of racial phenomena (Carchedi, 1987; Cohen, 1989; Miles, 1989, 1993; Miles & Phizaclea, 1984; Solomos, 1986, 1989; Wolpe, 1986). John Solomos, for instance, after critically reviewing several Marxist approaches to racial matters, concludes that:

> (a) there is no problem of 'race relations' which can be thought of
> separately from the structural (economic, political, and ideological)

features of capitalist society; (b) there can be no general Marxist theory of racism, since each historical situation needs to be analyzed in its own specificity; and (c) 'racial' and 'ethnic' divisions cannot be reduced to or seen as completely determined by the structural contradictions of capitalist societies. (Solomos, 1986, p. 104)

Harold Wolpe has suggested that what is needed to adequately grasp issues of race is a non-reductionist conception of class. Class, for Wolpe, should be regarded as a process rather than as an abstract category. In his own words, class 'is constituted, not as unified social force, but as a patchwork of segments which are differentiated and divided on a variety of bases and by varied processes' (Wolpe, 1986, p. 121; cf. Rose, 1997). This conceptualization allows classes to have fragments with unique interests based on ethnicity, race, or gender.

Yet despite providing some honest indictments of the class-reductionist reading of racial phenomena, both analysts share many of the limitations of the orthodox view. First, both Solomos and Wolpe conceive the *context*—the *structure*—of the social system as fundamentally capitalist in nature and see 'racialism' as something that *may* affect its character. Although this represents a theoretical and political break with the orthodox Marxist position, it still precludes the possibility that racial phenomena have their own structure (albeit articulated with capitalism and patriarchy).[13] That is why, for example, Wolpe's (1970) focus has been examining within class stratification and, in his more recent work, how race has been 'interiorized' into the class struggle (1986, p. 111). Analogously, Solomos has examined in his work how racism has affected class politics and ideology in Britain (1986, 1989). Second, they stress *a priori* class as the central organizing principle of social systems and hence regard race as a secondary element that *fractures* or *stratifies* class. Third, in their analysis (particularly that of Solomos) racism is still viewed in fundamentally ideological terms. Finally, and despite their poignant criticism of class-reductionist views on racial matters, they have not provided any new theoretical tools with which to analyze the relative autonomous structural character of race and racism in social systems.

The Racial Formation Perspective

The recent work of Howard Winant and Michael Omi represents a theoretical breakthrough in the area of race relations. In their *Racial Formation in the United States* (1986, 1994) the authors provide a thorough critique of previous theoretical approaches and suggest a new approach for the study of racial phenomena: the *racial formation* perspective. They define racial formation as the 'process by which social, economic, and political forces determine the content and importance of racial categories, and by which they are in turn shaped by racial meanings' (Omi & Winant, 1986, p. 61) The essence of this approach is the idea that race 'is a phenomenon whose meaning is contested throughout social life' (Winant, 1994, p. 23). The very existence of the category race is viewed as the outcome of *racialization* or 'the extension of racial meaning to a previously unclassified relationship, social practice or group ... [it] is an ideological process, an historically specific one (Omi & Winant, 1986, p. 64). In their view, race should be regarded as an organizing principle of social relationships which, at the micro level, shapes the identity of individual actors, and, at the macro level, shapes all spheres of social life. Although racialization affects all social spheres, Omi and Winant assign a primary role to the political level,[14] particularly to the 'racial state' which they regard in Poulantzian fashion (1981) as the factor of cohesion of any racial order. Hence racial conflict, particularly in the post-civil rights era, is viewed as playing itself out at the state level (Omi & Winant, 1986, pp. 68–69).

Equipped with these categories, Omi and Winant review the recent history of racial formation in the United States. They argue that as the civil rights movement expanded to include the masses of black people, it rearticulated and radicalized the collective meaning of black subjectivity. The new subjectivity, symbolized at the cultural level by the transition from being 'Negros' to 'blacks,' involved a change in the tactics to challenge the racial order. *Direct* and *collective* strategies replaced *individual* and *indirect* forms of contestation. According to Omi and Winant, the first phase of the civil rights movement produced real although limited reforms (e.g. enactment of the 1964 Civil Rights Act, the 1965 Voting Rights legislation, and registration of millions of Southern black voters). However, the economic status of most blacks was left unaffected by these reforms. This produced the radicalization of a segment of the movement which manifested itself in the politics of black power. Despite the amorphous character of this political movement—from self-help to revolutionary nationalists—it involved a further rearticulation of the political and cultural agenda of blacks. For many black power politicians the question became not so much gaining 'rights' but gaining 'power.'

The racial state's response to the demands of the racial social movement of the sixties was twofold. On the one hand, it *absorbed* some demands (state guarantees for civil and political rights) and actors (some 'militant' leaders were coopted) and, on the other hand, it *insulated* crucial areas of state activity (e.g. tax policy) from any contestation by defining them as non-racial. As the movement fragmented in the late sixties, the state was able to repress some of the most radical segments and coopt the reformist leadership. Moreover, the state's acquiescence to the demands of racial minorities for civil and political rights entailed recasting the racial movement into another 'interest group' and channeling its activities through 'normal' politics.

This demise of the racial movement coincided with the profound economic and political dislocations of the seventies. As in other periods in U.S. history, these dislocations were blamed on racial minorities (e.g. the expansion of the welfare state was viewed as the cause of the economic demise of the U.S.). This set the stage for the rearticulation of racial ideology and politics carried out by neoconservatives and the new right around the notion of 'reverse racism.' Although this rearticulation has not rolled back the historical clock by arguing against the principle of racial equality and advocating the resegregation of America, it has been successful in challenging *all* the *means* to achieve equality (from state spending, to busing, to affirmative action).

The racial formation perspective, as evident from the numerous scholars who have been inspired by it (e.g. Roediger, Frankenberg, etc.), has provided very useful tools for the analysis of racialized societies and a mine of clues for further research. Nonetheless, this perspective still has some significant limitations. First, Omi and Winant's (1986, 1994) concepts of *racial formation* and *racialization* give undue emphasis to ideological processes. Although both concepts are helpful in grasping how racial meanings are formed and *rearticulated*, they do not help analysts understand how it is that racial orders are structured. Arguing that racial classifications are permanently contested and malleable is a reaffirmation of the old idea in sociology and anthropology that race is a socially constructed category (Boas, 1928, 1936; Weber, 1978). However, this affirmation does not make clear whether or not they believe that race is or can become an *independent basis of group association and action*.[15] Second, although in their book there are hints of a conception of races as social collectivities with *different interests* (e.g. race is a concept which signifies and symbolizes social conflicts and interests by referring to different types of human bodies (1994, p. 55)), Omi and Winant stop short of making such a claim. Without due regard to races as collectivities with different interests, their analysis of political contestation over *racial projects* seems like quarrels over *meanings* rather than *positions* in the racial order.[16] In their approach it is unclear why people fight over racial matters and why they endorse or contest *racial projects* (see chapters 4 and 7 in 1996 edition). Third, Omi and Winant's analysis of the most recent rearticulation of racial ideology in the U.S. leaves out a comprehensive or systemic view of the process. The change is described as singularly carried out by the right wing and neoconservatives instead of reflecting a *general* change in the U.S. racial structure (Bonilla-Silva & Lewis, 1997; Brooks, 1990; Smith, 1995). In order to make this claim, Omi and Winant would have to include the agency of *all* the members of the dominant race—rather than privileging some actors—and conceive the change as affecting *all* the levels of the social formation—rather than privileging the political level. Finally, although I am sympathetic to the idea of regarding race as 'a fundamental *organizing principle* of social relationships' (Omi & Winant, 1986, p. 66), their theoretical framework comes close to race-reductionism in many areas. For instance, their conceptualization of the state as the 'racial state,' although borrowed from structuralist Marxism, leaves out the capitalist—as well as the patriarchal—character of the state (Goldfield, 1997).[17]

Racialized Social Systems: An alternative framework for understanding racial phenomena

Because all kinds of racial matters have been explained as a product of racism, I propose the more general concept of *racialized social systems* as the starting point for an alternative framework. This term refers to societies in which economic, political, social, and ideological levels are partially structured by the placement of actors in racial categories or races. Races typically are identified by their phenotype, but (as we see later) the selection of some human traits to designate a racial group is always *socially* rather than *biologically* based. I use the term *white supremacy* as an efficient and powerful (politically speaking) shorthand for racialized social systems since they emerged as part of the momentous expansion of the world-system in the fifteenth and sixteenth centuries which included the developement of *global white supremacy* (Balibar & Wallerstein, 1991; Mills, 1998).

These systems are structured partially by race because modern social systems articulate two or more forms of hierarchical patterns (Hall, 1980; Williams, 1990; Winant, 1994).[18] Although processes of racialization are always embedded in other structurations (Balibar & Wallerstein, 1991), they acquire autonomy and have 'pertinent effects' (Poulantzas, 1982) in the social system. This implies that the phenomenon which is coded as racism and is regarded as a free-floating ideology in fact has a structural foundation.

In all racialized social systems the placement of people in racial categories involves some form of hierarchy[19] that produces definite social relations between the races. The race placed in the superior position tends to receive greater economic remuneration and access to better occupations and/or prospects in the labor market, generally occupies a primary position in the political system, is granted higher social estimation (e.g. is viewed as 'smarter' or 'better looking'), often has the license to draw physical (segregation) as well as social (racial etiquette) boundaries between itself and other races, and receives what Du Bois (1939) called a 'psychological wage' (Marable, 1983; Roediger, 1991).[20] The totality of these racialized social relations and practices constitutes the racial structure of a society.

Although all racialized social systems are hierarchical, the particular character of the hierarchy, and thus of the racial structure, is variable. For example, domination of blacks in the United States was achieved through dictatorial means during slavery, but in the post-civil rights period this domination has been hegemonic (Omi & Winant, 1994; Winant, 1994).[21] Similarly, the racial practices and mechanisms that have kept blacks subordinated changed from overt and eminently racist to covert and indirectly racist (Bonilla-Silva & Lewis, 1997). The unchanging element throughout these stages is that blacks' life chances are significantly lower than those of whites. Ultimately a racialized social order is distinguished by the difference in the races' life chances. Generally, the more dissimilar the races' life chances, the more racialized a social system, and vice versa.

Insofar as the races receive different social rewards at all levels, they develop dissimilar objective interests, which can be detected in their struggles either to transform or to maintain a particular racial order. These interests are collective rather than individual, are based on relations between races rather than on particular group needs, and are not structural but practical; that is, they are related to concrete struggles rather than derived from the location of the races in the racial structure. In other words, although the races' interests can be detected from their practices, they are not subjective and individual but collective and shaped by the field of real practical alternatives, which is itself rooted in the power struggles betweeen the races.[22] Although the races' objective general interests may ultimately lie in the complete elimination of a society's racial structure, the array of alternatives may not include that possibility. For instance, the historical struggle against chattel slavery led not to the development of race-free societies but to the establishment of social systems with a different kind of racialization. Race-free societies were not among the available alternatives because the non-slave populations had the capacity to preserve some type of racial privilege. The historical 'exceptions' occurred in racialized societies in which the non-slaves' power was almost completely superseded by that of the slave population.[23]

A simple criticism of the argument advanced so far would be that it ignores the internal divisions of the races along class and gender lines. Such criticism, however, does not deal squarely with the issue at hand. The fact that not all members of the superordinate race receive the same level of rewards and (conversely) that not all members of the subordinate race or races are at the bottom of the social order does not negate the fact that races, as social groups, are in either a superordinate or a subordinate position in a social system. Historically the racialization of social systems did not imply the exclusion of other forms of oppression. In fact, racialization occurred in social formations also structured by class and gender. Hence, in these societies, the racial structuration of subjects is fragmented along class and gender lines.[24] The important question—which interests move actors to struggle?—is historically contingent and cannot be ascertained *a priori* (Anthias & Yuval-Davis, 1992; Wolpe, 1988). Depending on the character of racialization in a social order, class interests may take precedence over racial interests as in contemporary Brazil, Cuba, and Puerto Rico. In other situations, racial interests may take precedence over class interests as in the case of blacks throughout U.S. history.

In general, the systemic salience of class in relation to race increases when the economic, political, and social distance between races decreases substantially. Yet this broad argument generates at least one warning: the narrowing of within-class differences between racial actors usually causes more rather than less racial conflict, at least in the short run, as the competition for resources increases (Blalock, 1967; Olzak, 1992). More significantly, even when class-based conflict becomes more salient in a social order, the racial component survives until the races' life chances are equalized and the mechanisms and social practices that produce those differences are eliminated. Hence, societies in which race has declined in significance, such as Brazil, Cuba, and Mexico, still have a racial problem insofar as the racial groups have different life chances.

Because racial actors are also classed and gendered, analysts must control for class and for gender to ascertain the material advantages enjoyed by a dominant race. In a racialized society such as ours, the independent effects of race are assessed by analysts who (1) compare data between whites and non-whites in the same class and gender positions, (2) evaluate the proportion as well as the general character of the races' participation in some domain of life, and (3) examine racial data at all levels—social, political, economic, and ideological—to ascertain the general position of racial groups in a social system.

But what is the nature of races or, more properly, of racialized social groups? Omi and Winant (1986; also see Miles, 1989) state that races are the outcome of the racialization process, which they define as 'the extension of racial meaning to a previously racially unclassified relationship, social practice or group' (p. 64). Historically the classification of a people in racial terms has been a highly political act associated with practices such as conquest and colonization, enslavement, peonage, indentured servitude, and, more recently, colonial and neocolonial labor immigration. Categories such as 'Indians' and 'Negroes' were invented (Allen, 1994; Berkhoffer, 1978; Jordan, 1968) in the sixteenth and seventeenth centuries to justify the conquest and exploitation of various peoples. The invention of such categories entails a dialectical process of construction; that is, the creation of a category of 'other' involves the creation of a category of 'same.' If 'Indians' are depicted as 'savages,' Europeans are characterized as 'civilized'; if 'Blacks' are defined as natural candidates for slavery, 'Whites' are defined as free subjects (Gossett 1963; Roediger 1991, 1994; Todorov 1984). Yet, although the racialization of peoples was socially invented and did not override previous forms of social distinction based on class or gender, it did not lead to imaginary relations but generated new forms of human association with definite status differences. After the process of attaching meaning to a 'people' is instituted, race becomes a real category of group association and identity.[25]

Because racial classifications partially organize and limit actors' life chances, racial practices of opposition emerge. Regardless of the form of racial interaction (overt, covert, or inert), races can be recognized in the realm of racial relations and positions. Viewed in this light, races are the effect of racial practices of opposition ('we' versus 'them') at the economic, political, social, and ideological levels.[26]

Races, as most social scientists acknowledge, are not biologically but socially determined categories of identity and group association.[27] In this regard, they are analogous to class and gender (Amott & Matthaei, 1991). Actors in racial positions do not occupy those positions because they are of X or Y race, but because X or Y has been socially defined as a race. Actors' phenotypical (i.e. biologically inherited) characteristics, such as skin tone and hair color and texture, are usually, although not always (Barth, 1969; Miles, 1993), used to denote racial distinctions. For example, Jews in many European nations (Miles, 1989, 1993) and the Irish in England have been treated as racial groups (Allen, 1994). Also, Indians in the United States have been viewed as one race despite the tremendous phenotypical and cultural variation among tribes. Because races are socially constructed, both the meaning and the position assigned to races in the racial structure are always contested (Gilroy, 1991). What and who is to be black or white or Indian reflects and affects the social, political, ideological, and economic struggles between the races. The global effects of these struggles can change the meaning of the racial categories as well as the position of a racialized group in a social formation.

This latter point is illustrated clearly by the historical struggles of several 'white ethnic' groups in the United States in their efforts to become accepted as legitimate whites or 'Americans' (Litwach, 1961; Saxton, 1990; Roediger, 1991; Williams, 1990). Neither light-skinned nor, for that matter, dark-skinned immigrants necessarily come to this country as members of X or Y race. Light-skinned Europeans, after brief periods of 'not-yet white' (Roediger, 1994), became 'white' but did not lose their 'ethnic' character. Their struggle for inclusion had specific implications: racial inclusion as members of the white community allowed Americanization and class mobility. On the other hand, among dark-skinned immigrants from Africa, Latin America, and the Caribbean, the struggle was to avoid classification as 'black.' These immigrants challenged the reclassification of their identity for a simple reason: in the United States 'black' signified a subordinate status in society. Hence many of these groups struggled to keep their own ethnic or cultural identity, as denoted in expressions such as 'I am not black; I am Jamaican,' or 'I am not black; I am Senegalese' (Kasinitz & Freidenberg-Herbstein, 1987; Rodríguez, 1991; Sutton & Makiesky-Barrow, 1987). Yet eventually many of these groups resolved this contradictory situation by accepting the duality of their social classification as black in the United States while retaining and nourishing their own cultural or ethnic heritage—a heritage deeply influenced by African traditions.

Although the content of racial categories changes over time through manifold processes and struggles, race is not a secondary category of group association. The meaning of black and white, the 'racial formation' (Omi & Winant, 1986), changes within the larger racial structure. This does not mean that the racial structure is immutable and completely independent of the action of racialized actors. It means only that the social relations between the races become institutionalized (form a structure as well as a culture) and affect their social life whether individual members of the races want it or not. In Barth's words (1969), 'Ethnic identity implies a series of constraints on the kinds of roles an individual is allowed to play [and] is similar to sex and rank, in that it constrains the incumbent in all his activities' (p. 17). For instance, free blacks during the slavery period struggled to change the meaning of 'blackness,' and specifically to dissociate it from slavery. Yet they could not escape the larger racial structure that restricted their life chances and their freedom (Berlin, 1975; Franklin, 1974; Meir & Rudwick, 1970).

The placement of a group of people in a racial category stemmed initially[28] from the interests of powerful actors in the social system (e.g. the capitalist class, the planter class, colonizers). After racial categories were employed to organize social relations in a society, however, race became an independent element of the operation of the social system (Stone, 1985). Here I depart from analysts such as Jordan (1968), Robinson (1983), and Miles (1989, 1993), who take the mere existence of a racial discourse as manifesting the presence of a racial order. Such a position allows them to speak of racism in medieval times (Jordan, 1968) and to classify the anti-peasant views of French urbanites (Miles, 1989, 1993) or the prejudices of the aristocracy against peasants in the Middle Ages (Robinson, 1983) as expressions of racism. In my view, we can speak of racialized orders only when a racial discourse is accompanied by social relations of subordination and superordination between the races. The available evidence suggests that the racialization of the world-system emerged after the imperialist expansion of Europe to the New World and Africa (Boggs, 1970; Cox, 1948; Furnivall, 1948; Magubane, 1990; Williams, 1944; Williams, 1990). Furthermore, this racialization led to the development of what Charles W. Mills calls *global white supremacy* (racial orders structured along the axis of white/European and non-white/non-European) in the world-system (Mills, 1997, 1998). To those who object to the white and, by extent, the global in *global white supremacy* because they doubt that all post-fifteenth-century social orders are fractured along this white/non-white line, the following argument by Mills (1998) should suffice for now.

The color and shade hierarchies in many Latin American countries have been established by global white supremacy, in that ascent up the ladder is strongly correlated with a greater degree of white ancestry and a greater degree of assimilation of European culture, so that these systems are essentially derivative and still need to be related to it. And—it needs to be underlined—against the widespread myth of Latin racial democracy they *are* hierarchies. Though differently structured than the bipolar northern model, they privilege the lighter-skinned, with the official ideology of a race-transcendent *mestizaje*, race mixture, being undercut in practice by the ideal of *blanqueamiento*, whitening. (pp. 102–103)

What are the dynamics of racial issues in racialized systems? Most important, after a social formation is racialized, its 'normal' dynamics always include a racial component. Societal struggles based on class or gender contain a racial component because both of these social categories are also racialized; that is, both class and gender are constructed along racial lines. In 1922, for example, white South African workers in the middle of a strike inspired by the Russian revolution rallied under the slogan 'Workers of the world unite for a white South Africa.' One of the state's 'concessions' to this 'class' struggle was the passage of the Apprenticeship Act of 1922, 'which prevented Black workers acquiring apprenticeships' (Ticktin, 1991, p. 26). In another example, the struggle of women in the United States to attain their civil and human rights has always been plagued by deep racial tensions (Caraway, 1991; Giddens, 1984).

Nonetheless, some of the strife that exists in a racialized social formation has a distinct racial character; I call such strife racial contestation—the struggle of racial groups for systemic changes regarding their position at one or more levels. Such a struggle may be social (Who can be here? Who belongs here?), political (Who can vote? How much power should they have? Should they be citizens?), economic (Who should work, and what should they do? They are taking our jobs!), or ideological (Black is beautiful! The term designating people of African descent in the United States has changed from Negro to black to African American).

Although much of this contestation is expressed at the individual level and is disjointed, sometimes it becomes collective and general, and can effect meaningful systemic changes in a society's racial organization. The form of contestation may be relatively passive and subtle (e.g. in situations of fundamental overt racial domination such as slavery and apartheid) or more active and more overt (e.g. in quasi-democratic situations such as the contemporary United States). As a rule, however, fundamental changes in racialized social systems are accompanied by struggles that reach the point of overt protest.[29] This does not mean that a violent racially based revolution is the only way of accomplishing effective changes in the relative position of racial groups. It is a simple extension of the argument that social systems and their supporters must be 'shaken' if fundamental transformations are to take place.[30] On this structural foundation rests the phenomenon labeled racism by social scientists.

I reserve the term *racism* (racial ideology) for the segment of the ideological structure of a social system that crystallizes racial notions and stereotypes. Racism provides the rationalizations for social, political, and economic interactions between the races (Bobo, 1988). Depending on the particular character of a racialized social system and on the struggles of the subordinated races, racial ideology may be developed highly (as in apartheid) or loosely (as in slavery) and its content expressed in overt or covert terms (Bobo & Smith, 1994; Jackman, 1994; Kinder & Sears, 1981; Pettigrew, 1994; Sears, 1988).

Although racism or racial ideology originates in race relations, it acquires relative autonomy in the social system and performs practical functions.[31] In Gilroy's (1991) words, racial ideology 'mediates the world of agents and the structures which are created by their social praxis' (p. 17; also see Omi & Winant, 1994; van Dijk, 1984, 1987, 1993). Racism crystallizes the changing 'dogma' on which actors in the social system operate (Gilroy, 1991), and becomes 'common sense' (Omi & Winant, 1994); it provides the rules for perceiving and dealing with the 'other' in a racialized society. In the United States, for instance, because racial notions about what blacks and whites are or ought to be pervade their encounters, whites still have difficulty in dealing with black bankers, lawyers, professors, and doctors (Cose, 1993; Graham, 1995). Thus, although racist ideology is ultimately false, it fulfills a practical role in racialized societies.

At this point it is possible to sketch the elements of the alternative framework presented here. First, racialized social systems are societies that allocate differential economic, political, social, and even psychological rewards to groups along racial lines; lines that are socially constructed. After a society becomes racialized, a set of social relations and practices based on racial distinctions develops at all societal levels. I designate the aggregate of those relations and practices as the racial structure of a society. Second, races historically are constituted according to the process of racialization; they become the effect of relations of opposition between racialized groups at all levels of a social formation. Third, on the basis of this structure, there developed a racial ideology (what analysts have coded as racism). This ideology is not simply a 'superstructural' phenomenon (a mere reflection of the racialized system) but becomes the organizational map that guides actions of racial actors in society. It becomes as real as the racial relations it organizes. Fourth, most struggles in a racialized social system contain a racial component, but sometimes they acquire and/or exhibit a distinct racial character. Racial contestation is the logical outcome of a society with a racial hierarchy. A social formation that includes some form of racialization will always exhibit some form of racial contestation. Finally, the process of racial contestation reveals the different objective interests of the races in a racialized system.

The New Racism: The U.S. racial structure since the 1960s

The (white) common-sense view on racial matters is that racists are few and far between, that discrimination has all but disappeared since the 1960s, and that most whites are color-blind. Although this new common sense is not totally without foundation (e.g. traditional forms of racial discrimination and exclusion as well as Jim Crow-based racist beliefs have decreased in significance) it is ultimately false.

What has happened is that white supremacy in the United States (i.e. the racial structure of America) has changed. Today a new racism has emerged that is more sophisticated and subtle than Jim Crow racism and yet is as effective as the old in maintaining the (contemporary) racial status quo. In the following, I describe the central features and the new social, political, economic, and social control practices associated with this new racism.

Some analysts claim that race and racism have decreased in importance in contemporary America (Wilson, 1978, 1987). This view is consistent with survey data on white attitudes since the early sixties (Hyman & Sheatsley, 1964; Greeley & Sheatsley, 1971; Schuman *et al.*, 1985; Sniderman & Piazza, 1993), as well as with many demographic and economic studies comparing the status of whites and blacks in terms of income, occupations, health, and education which suggest that a remarkable reduction in racial inequality has occurred in America (Duncan, 1968; Palmore & Whittington, 1970; Farley & Hermalin, 1972; Freeman, 1973, 1978; Farley, 1984, 1993; Farley & Allen, 1987; Smith & Welch, 1986).

A smaller number of social scientists, on the other hand, believe that race continues to play a role similar to the one it played in the past (Pinkney, 1984; Fusfeld & Bates, 1984; Willie, 1989; Bell, 1992). For these authors, little has changed in America in terms of racism and there is a general pessimism in the prospects of changing the racial status of minorities. Although this is a minority viewpoint in academia, it represents the perception of many members of minority communities, especially of the black community.

These opinions about the changes in the significance of race and racism in the United States are based on a narrowly defined notion of racism. For these analysts, racism is fundamentally an ideological or attitudinal phenomenon. In contrast, I regard racism as a *structure*; that is, as a network of social relations at social, political, economic, and ideological levels that shapes the life chances of the various races. What social scientists define as racism is conceptualized in this framework as racial ideology. Racism (racial ideology) helps to glue and, at the same time, organize the nature and character of race relations in a society. From this vantage point, rather than arguing about whether the significance of race has declined, increased, or not changed at all, the real issue is assessing if a transformation has occurred in the *racial structure* of the United States. It is my contention that, despite the profound changes that occurred in the 1960s, a new racial structure— the New Racism for short—is operating which accounts for the persistence of racial inequality.

The elements that comprise this new racial structure are: (1) the increasingly *covert* nature of racial discourse and racial practices; (2) the avoidance of racial terminology and the ever-growing claim by whites that they experience 'reverse racism'; (3) the elaboration of a racial agenda over political matters that eschews direct racial references; (4) the invisibility of most mechanisms to reproduce racial inequality; and, finally, (5) the rearticulation of some racial practices characteristic of the Jim Crow period of race relations.

During the Jim Crow period of race relations blacks were kept in a subordinate position through a variety of bluntly racist practices. At the economic level, blacks were restricted to menial[32] jobs by the joint effort of planters, corporations, and unions. The economic position of blacks did not change much until well into the twentieth century (Spero & Harris, 1974; Higgs, 1977; Foner, 1981; Marable, 1983). It was not until after World War I, which created a labor shortage in the industrial north, that many blacks migrated from the south and joined the ranks of the working class (Myrdal, 1944; Foner, 1981). Yet, this transition from agricultural to industrial jobs did not break the Jim Crow pattern of employment. Spero and Harris (1974; see also Woodson, 1947) contend that although there was no wage discrimination[33] between blacks and whites in the north, blacks earned less than whites because they were concentrated in low-skill jobs: the jobs into which the Negroes went were usually those which native Americans and Americanized foreign-born white labor did not want. This largely accounts for the almost spectacular increase in the proportion of Negroes in the iron and steel foundaries, where the work is dirty, hot, and unpleasant (Spero & Harris, 1974, pp. 155–156). Racial ideology during the Jim Crow period of race relations was explicitly racist. Without question, most whites believed that minorities were intellectually and morally inferior, that they should be kept apart, and that whites should not mix with any of them (Gossett, 1963).

The apartheid that blacks experienced in the United States was predicated on (1) keeping them in rural areas, mostly in the south, (2) maintaining them as agricultural workers, and (3) excluding them from the political process. However, as blacks successfully challenged their socioeconomic position by migrating initially from rural areas to urban areas in the south and later to the north and west (Henri, 1975; Harrison, 1991), by pushing themselves by whatever means necessary[34] into non-agricultural occupations (Tuttle, 1970; Foner, 1981; Leiman, 1992), and by developing political organizations and movements like Garveyism, the NAACP, CORE, the National Urban League, the Southern Regional Council, and the CIC (Woodward, 1966; McAdam, 1982; Morris, 1984), the infrastructure of apartheid began to crumble.

What industrialization and urbanization did for blacks was to provide a new context for struggle that made the Southern Jim Crow system impossible to maintain in the face of black opposition. These demographic, social, political, and economic factors and the actions of blacks made change almost inevitable. But ripe conditions are not enough to change any structural order. Hence, the racial order had to be *directly* challenged if it was going to be effectively transformed. That was the role fulfilled by the civil rights movement and the other forms of mass protest by blacks (so-called race riots) that took place in the sixties and seventies. Organized and spontaneous challenges were the catalysts that brought down overt segregation.

Yet the demise of Jim Crow did not end racial discrimination in America. Many analysts (Caditz, 1976; Wellman, 1977; Kinder & Sears, 1981; Sears, 1988; Pettigrew, 1994) have noted that 'racism' (as usually defined) and race relations have acquired a new character since the sixties. They point to the increasingly covert nature of racial discourse and racial practices; the avoidance of racial terminology in racial conflicts by whites; and the elaboration of a racial agenda over political matters (state intervention, individual rights, responsibility, etc.) that eschews any direct racial reference. In the following sections I detail discriminatory practices of the post-civil rights era and assess their character.

The history of black–white education in this country is one of substantive inequities maintained through public institutions. While today many of the traditional barriers to black advancement have been outlawed, the situation is by no means one of equity. Although scholars have documented the narrowing of the gap in the *quantity* of education attained by blacks and whites (Farley, 1984; Farley & Allen, 1987; Jaynes & Williams, 1989), little has been said about the persisting gap in the *quality* of education received. Still remaining (and in some cases worsening) high levels of *de facto* segregation are at least partly to blame for the gap in quality (Rivken, 1994). However, tracking, differential assignment to special education, and other informal school practices are important factors too.

Over 30 percent of black students attend schools that are 95 percent or more non-white and over 30 percent of white students attend schools that are less than 95 percent white (Booker *et al.*, 1992; Orfield, 1993).[35] Despite some progress during the period immediately after 1964, the level of school segregation for black students remains relatively high in all regions and has deteriorated in the northeast and midwest regions (Orfield & Monfort, 1992). The relevance of this fact is that, as Gary Orfield has noted, 'Segregated schools are still profoundly unequal' (Orfield, 1993, p. 235). Inner-city minority schools, in sharp contrast to white suburban schools, lack decent buildings, are overcrowded, have outdated equipment—if they have equipment at all, do not have enough textbooks for their students, lack library resources, are technologically behind and pay their teaching and administrative staff less, which produces, despite exceptions, a low level of morale. These 'savage inequalities' (Kozol, 1991) have been directly related to lower reading achievement and learning attained by black students (Dreeben & Gamoran, 1986) and their limited computer skills (Booker *et al.*, 1992).

In integrated schools, blacks still have to contend with discriminatory practices. Oaks and her co-authors (1992) have found clear evidence of discriminatory practices in tracking within schools. Whites (and Asians) are considerably (and statistically significantly) more likely to be placed in the academic track than comparably achieving African American and Latino students (Oaks *et al.*, 1992). Another study found that of the 1985 students who took the SAT, 65.1 percent of blacks compared to 81.2 percent of whites were enrolled in an academic track. No wonder black students tend to score lower on the SAT than white students.

Conclusion

My central argument in this Introduction has been that racism, as defined by mainstream social scientists, or as viewed by authors in the Marxist, internal colonialist, institutionalist, or racial formation perspectives, does not provide an adequate theoretical foundation for understanding racial phenomena. With notable exceptions (Bobo *et al.*, 1997; Jackman, 1994), analysts in academia are still entangled in ungrounded ideological views of racism. Lacking a structural view, they tend to reduce racial phenomena to a derivation of the class structure (as Marxist interpreters do) or as the result of an irrational ideology (as mainstream social scientists do).

In the alternative framework developed here, I suggest, as Omi and Winant (1986, 1994), that racism should be studied from the viewpoint of racialization. I contend that after a society becomes racialized, racialization develops a life of its own.[34] Although it interacts with class and gender structurations in the social system, it becomes an organizing principle of social relations in itself (Essed, 1991; Omi & Winant, 1986; Robinson, 1983; van Dijk, 1987). Race, as most analysts suggest, is a social construct, but that construct, like class and gender, has independent effects in social life. After racial stratification is established, race becomes an independent criterion for vertical hierarchy in society. Therefore different races experience positions of subordination and superordination in society and develop different interests.

The alternative framework for studying racial orders presented here has the following advantages over traditional views of racism:

Racial phenomena are regarded as the 'normal' outcome of the racial structure of a society. Thus we can account for all racial manifestations. Instead of explaining racial phenomena as deriving from other structures or from racism (conceived of as a free-floating ideology), we can trace cultural, political, economic, social, and even psychological racial phenomena to the racial organization of that society.

The changing nature of what analysts label 'racism' is explained as the normal outcome of racial contestation in a racialized social system. In this framework, changes in racism are explained rather than described. Changes are due to specific struggles at different levels among the races, resulting from differences in interests. Such changes may transform the nature of racialization and the global character of racial relations in the system (the racial structure). Therefore, change is viewed as a normal component of the racialized system.

The framework of racialization allows analysts to explain overt as well as covert racial behavior. The covert or overt nature of racial contacts depends on how the process of racialization is manifested; this in turn depends on how race was originally articulated in a social formation and in the process of racial contestation. This point implies that rather than conceiving of racism as a universal and uniformly orchestrated phenomenon, analysts should study 'historically-specific racisms' (Hall, 1980, p. 336). This insight is not new; Robert Park (1950), Oliver Cox (1948), and Marvin Harris (1964) described varieties of 'situations of race relations' with distinct forms of racial interaction.

Racially motivated behavior, whether or not the actors are conscious of it, is regarded as 'rational'—that is, as based on the races' different interests.[35] This framework accounts for Archie Bunker type racial behavior as well as for more 'sophisticated' varieties of racial conduct. Racial phenomena are viewed as systemic; therefore all actors in the system participate in racial affairs. Some members of the dominant racial group tend to exhibit less virulence toward members of the subordinated races because they have greater control over the form and the outcome of their racial interactions. When they cannot control that interaction—as in the case of revolts, general threats to whites, blacks moving into 'their' neighborhood—they behave much like other members of the dominant race.

The reproduction of racial phenomena in contemporary societies is explained in this framework not by reference to a long-distant past but in relation to its contemporary structure. Because racism is viewed as systemic (possessing a racial structure) and as organized around the races' different interests, racial aspects of social systems today are viewed as fundamentally related to hierarchical relations between the races in those systems. Elimination of the racialized character of a social system entails the end of racialization, and hence of races altogether. This argument clashes with social scientists' most popular policy prescription for 'curing' racism, namely education. This 'solution' is the logical outcome of defining racism as a belief. Most analysts regard racism as a matter of individuals subscribing to an irrational view; thus the cure is educating them to realize that racism is wrong. Education is also the choice 'pill' prescribed by Marxists for healing workers from racism. The alternative theorization offered here implies that because the phenomenon has structural consequences for the races, the only way to 'cure' society of racism is by eliminating its systemic roots. Whether this can be accomplished democratically or only through revolutionary means is an open question, and one that depends on the particular racial structure of the society in question.

A racialization framework accounts for the ways in which racial/ethnic stereotypes emerge, are transformed, and disappear. Racial stereotypes are crystallized at the ideological level of a social system. These images ultimately indicate—although in distorted ways—and justify the stereotyped group's position in a society. Stereotypes may originate out of (1) material realities or conditions endured by the group, (2) genuine ignorance about the group, or (3) rigid, distorted views on the group's physical, cultural, or moral nature. Once they emerge, however, stereotypes must relate— although not necessarily fit it perfectly—to the group's true social position in the racialized system if they are to perform their ideological function. Stereotypes that do not tend to reflect a group's situation do not work and are bound to disappear: for example, notions of the Irish as stupid or of Jews as athletically talented have all but vanished since the 1940s, as the Irish moved up the educational ladder and Jews gained access to multiple routes to social mobility. Generally, then, sterotypes are reproduced because they reflect the group's distinct position and status in society. As a corollary, racial or ethnic notions about a group disappear only when the group's status mirrors that of the dominant racial or ethnic group in the society.

The framework developed here is not a universal theory explaining racial phenomena in societies. It is intended to trigger a serious discussion of how race shapes social systems. Moreover, the important question of how race interacts and intersects with class and gender has not yet been addressed satisfactorily. Provisionally I argue that a nonfunctionalist reading of the concept of social system may give us clues for comprehending societies 'structured in dominance' (Hall, 1980). If societies are viewed as systems that articulate different structures (organizing principles on which sets of social relations are systematically patterned), it is possible to claim that race—as well as gender—has both individual and combined (interaction) effects in society.

To test the usefulness of racialization as a theoretical basis for research, we must perform comparative work on racialization in various societies. One of the main objectives of this comparative work should be to determine whether societies have specific mechanisms, practices, and social relations that produce and reproduce racial inequality at all levels—that is, whether they possess a racial structure. Unlike analysts who believe that racism has withered away, I argue that the persistent inequality experienced by blacks and other racial minorities in the United States today is due to the *continued*, albeit *changed*, existence of a racial structure (Bonilla-Silva & Lewis, 1997). In contrast to race relations in the Jim Crow period, however, racial practices that reproduce racial inequality in contemporary America (1) are increasingly covert, (2) are embedded in normal operations of institutions, (3) avoid direct racial terminology, and (4) are invisible to most whites. *Thus today whites all over the Western world seem to be saying the same thing about their countries (This is a white country!) and expressing the same fears (Why are* THEY *taking* MY *job!).*

To sum up, blacks through their struggle have been able to gain access to the political system but that access has not translated itself into a significant influence. More blacks are elected to office and appointed to various positions than at any other time but that has a very limited impact on the status of the black masses. Moreover, a series of indirect barriers to the election of blacks, the rules of the game in Congress, and conditions in the cities of America where blacks have seemingly had more political success help to maintain them at bay and to preserve white political power almost intact.

The changes in the racial dynamics at all levels which we have documented in this Introduction seem to amount to a reorganization—still incomplete and somewhat partial—of the racial structure of this country. This reorganization of the racial structure is incomplete because (1) not all the mechanisms and practices have settled—that is, have become institutionalized—and (2) we still have many legacies of the previous period affecting the life chances of blacks. On the first point, discrimination in the realm of education, for example, has not taken a definite institutional pattern in the contemporary period. Instead, there are various means (resegregation through white flight to the suburbs and to private schools, within school segregation, tracking, etc.) to guarantee white advantages. On the second point, we still have old-fashioned racists, extra-legal violence, and an undeclared apartheid in the housing arena. Although many of these practices are manifestations of the legacies of slavery and Jim Crow in this country (Winant, 1994), the evidence reviewed here suggests that blacks and other minorities should fear less the angry men with white hoods and their traditional discriminatory practices than the men with suits and their 'smiling discrimination' (Brooks, 1990).

I agree with Pettigrew and Martin when they claim that:

> the greater subtlety of these new forms [of racial discrimination] pose new problems of remedy. They act at both the structural-institutional level focused on by sociologists, and the face-to-face situational level focused on by social psychologists. (Pettigrew & Martin, 1987, p. 42)

Some of these problems that require remedy are:

1. Detection of racial discrimination is extremely difficult for the party being discriminated against. Furthermore, too many progressive whites tend to explain away many of the claims of contemporary discrimination because:

   > Often the black is the only person in a position to draw the conclusion that prejudice is operating in the work situation. Whites have usually observed only a subset of the incidents, any one of which can be explained away by a nonracial account. Consequently, many whites remain unconvinced of the reality of subtle prejudice and discrimination, and come to think of their black co-workers as 'terribly touchy' and 'overly sensitive' to the issue. For such reasons, the modern forms of prejudice frequently remain invisible even to its perpetrators. (Pettigrew & Martin, 1987, p. 50)

2. The standards that the Supreme Court has enacted recently on discrimination cases (plaintiffs carrying the burden of proof in discrimination cases and the denial of statistical evidence as valid proof of discrimination)[36] help to preserve intact the contemporary forms for reproducing racial inequality in America. Unless the Court becomes cognizant of the new character of racial discrimination and changes its current practice of requiring the 'smoking gun' in discrimination cases, the Court itself will be participating in covering up the far-reaching effects of racism in America.
3. Black leaders who continue to focus on the 'old racism' will miss the most important manners by which racial inequality is being reproduced in America. It is vital that studies documenting the pervasive and comprehensive character of the New Racism are done systematically.
4. Research that is still focused on the old racism will invariably find a decline in the significance of race. Research on racial practices has to become as sophisticated as the New Racism. The studies carried out by the Urban Institute and HUD in which testers are sent out to various settings and organizations are an example of what can be done. Unfortunately, that type of research does not enjoy the sympathy of our disciples and has ever been deemed as 'unethical.'[37]

The web of discriminatory practices in the contemporary period is still not complete. Hence it is still possible to mount an offensive to change its course. However, at the moment that we write this paper, the prospects for such an offensive look bleak. At a time when many of the achievements of the civil rights movement (e.g. affirmative action, the real possibility of bringing claims against organizations for discrimination, efforts to desegregate schools) are being rapidly eroded, the civil rights movement and many of its organizations are in a state of disarray, there is a serious crisis in leadership in minority communities (Marable, 1983; Lusane, 1994), and many traditional allies have moved to the right. Recently, the Supreme Court imposed 'formidable standards' for government-sponsored affirmative action programs (Greenhouse, 1995) and the Board of Regents of the University of California system decided to eliminate its affirmative action programs.[38] Unless this situation is reversed, the new racial practices will be institutionalized.

As the Supreme Court ruling involving the University of Michigan affirmative action case signaled, race is very much a continuing consideration in education.

Notes

1. Yet they employed the very similar notion of ethnocentrism as developed by William Graham Sumner (1906). According to Sumner (1906) ethnocentrism was the belief that 'one's own group is at the center of everything, and all others are scaled and rated with reference to it' (p. 13).
2. Carmichael and Hamilton (1967) also advocated nationalist strategies. Unlike other institutionalists, however, they insisted on the colonial relationship of minorities to the majority in the United States.
3. In the most recent edition of *Racial Formation in the United States* (1994), Omi and Winant move closer to a structural view, but they still retain the ideological and juridico-political focus that characterizes the original edition.
4. This question is used by NORC and has been employed by Schuman *et al.* (1985).
5. By *structure* I mean, following Whitmeyer (1994), 'the networks of (interactional) relationships among actors as well as the distributions of socially meaningful characteristics of actors and aggregates of actors' (p. 154). For similar but more complex conceptions of the term, which are relational and which incorporate the agency of actors, see Bourdieu (1984) and Sewell (1992). I reserve the term *material* to refer to the economic, social, political, or ideological rewards or penalties received by social actors for their participation (whether willing, unwilling, or indifferent) in social structural arrangements.
6. One of the best representatives of the orthodox Marxist view on race and racism is Victor Perlo, *Economics of Racism U.S.A.: Roots of Black Inequality*. But alongside this orthodox view, some African American Marxists like W. E. B. Dubois, C. L. R. James, and, more recently, Manning Marable, Cornel West, and Robin G. Kelley, have questioned the simplistic analysis of racism of their white counterparts. For particularly biting criticisms of the traditional Marxist view on racial matters, see James Boggs, *Racism and the Class Struggle*; Robert L. Allen, *Reluctant Reformers* and Harold Cruse, *Rebellion or Revolution*.
7. Despite my multiple disagreements with Cox's (1948) work, I regard his *oeuvre* as phenomenal, particularly considering that he did most of his work under Jim Crow. In his *Caste, Class, and Race*, Cox developed a competent class analysis of post-World War II class matters in the U.S. and elsewhere. Although I disagree with the essence of his race analysis, I agree with much of his critique of Myrdal's work, of the caste-school of race relations, and think that his analysis of lynching is simply brilliant.
8. For an extended discussion of this view, see ch. 25, 'The Race Problem in the United States,' in Cox's *Caste, Class, and Race* (1948).
9. This argument strikes me as blaming the victim in disguise. For two excellent alternative readings of why blacks did not join unions with their 'brothers and sisters,' see Philip Foner's excellent *Organized Labor and the Black Worker, 1619–1981* (1981) and David Roediger's *The Wages of Whiteness: Race and the Making of the American Working Class* (1991). For a more recent book showing the racialized character of working-class politics, see Michael Goldfield's *The Color of Politics: Race and the Mainsprings of American Politics* (1997).
10. Bonacich downplays interpretations of this 'resistance' based on racial prejudice against blacks. Therefore, she explains the race riots that occurred in the 1919–1940 period as expressions of class protectionism from whites facing 'threats' from black workers. This interpretation naturalizes the racist white view symbolized in the statement '*they* are taking *our* jobs' and ignores the racial aspect of class formation

(Roediger, 1991). On this point, black historian Carter G. Woodson (1947) commmented a long time ago that:

> As Negroes in the North and West, therefore, were pitted against the trades unions, they engendered much feeling between the races by allying themselves with the capitalists to serve as strikebreakers. In this case, however, *the trades unions themselves were to be blamed.* The only time the Negroes could work under such circumstance was when the whites were striking, and it is not surprising that some of them easily yielded then to the temptation. In those unions in which the Negroes were recognized, they stood with their white co-workers in every instance of making a reasonable demand of their employers. Some of these unions, however, accepted Negroes merely as a subterfuge to prevent them from engaging in strikebreaking. When the Negroes appealed for work, identifying themselves as members of the union in control, they were turned away with the subterfuge that no vacancies existed, while at the same time white men were gladly received. (Woodson, 1947, p. 439; my emphasis)

11. For a more nuanced analysis of race in the post-1930s, see Jill Quadagno's *The Color of Welfare* (1994).

12. For a similar critique of the Marxist myopia to gender oppression and the materiality of patriarchy, see Christine Delphy, *Close to Home: A Materialist Analysis of Women's Oppression.*

13. On this point Italian Marxist Guglielmo Carchedi (1987), after acknowledging that there are special groups in society who are subject to specific forms of *domination* (e.g. women, blacks, young people, 'sexual deviants'), ends up devaluating the *specificity* of their domination. This is accomplished by arguing that although these forms of domination are not class-specific they are class-determined; that is, 'they are functional for the domination of the capitalist class' (Carchedi, 1987, p. 110). Thus, Carchedi concludes, in typical Marxist fashion, that 'socialism is in the interest, and must be the result of the struggle, *of all those subjected to a type of domination functional for the reproduction of the capitalist system*' (p. 11; emphasis in original). Similarly, British Marxist Gerry A. Cohen, after recognizing the failure of Marxism to appreciate that 'divisions of identity are as deep as those of class' reduces 'racial exploitation' (his term) to class exploitation. In his words, 'racial exploitation is (largely) relegation to an exploited class because of race' (Cohen, 1989, p. 159). Finally, Erik Wright, a premier U.S. Analytical Marxist, believes that racial minorities are *oppressed* but claims that only workers are *exploited* (Wright, 1985).

14. In Winant's recent book *Racial Conditions*, the fundamentally political character of racialization is attributed to the fact that 'elites, popular movements, state agencies, cultural and religious organizations, and intellectuals of all types develop *racial projects*, which interpret and reinterpret the meaning of race ... These projects are often explicitly, but always implicitly, political' (Winant, 1994, p. 24).

15. In Winant's *Racial Conditions* (1994) he comes close to enunciating a structural conception of race. He criticizes the purely ideological conception of race because it fails to: (1) appreciate the significance that a construct can acquire over 1,000 years of existence and (2) recognize that race shapes our identity and everyday experiences (Winant, 1994, p. 16). However, Winant eschews a truly structural reading of race because he thinks such a reading would *reify* the category. Below I suggest that an *objective* understanding of race (similar to the case of class or gender) based upon the notion that these social groups have *different* interests does not necessarily entail *freezing* the content or meaning of the category.

16. Omi and Winant define *racial projects* as 'simultaneously an interpretation, representation, or explanation of racial dynamics, and an effort to reorganize and redistribute resources along particular racial lines' (1994, p. 56).

17. This problem is partially addressed in Howard Winant's recent *Racial Conditions* (1994) through the Gramscian concept of *hegemony*, which he defines as 'a form of rule that operates by constructing its subjects and incorporating contestation' (p. 113). According to Winant this form of rule prevails in most 'modern' societies and organizes, among other things, cleavages based on class, race, and gender.

18. For some potentially useful conceptions about the interaction of race, class, and gender (the primary axes of social hierarchy in modern societies), see Segura's (1990) 'triple oppression' and Essed's (1991) analysis of 'gendered racism.' See also Andersen and Hill Collins (1995) and Fraser (1989).

19. This argument applies only to racialized social systems. In contrast, the basis of *ethnic* situations need not be based on relations between superiors and subordinates, as is the case between the Fur and the Baggara in western Sudan (Barth, 1969), the various ethnic groups in Switzerland (Hunt & Walker, 1974), the Tungus and the Cossacks in Siberia (Berry, 1965), the Lake Zwai Laki and the Arsi in Ethiopia (Knutson, 1969), and certain mountain tribes and the Thai in Laos (Izikowitz, 1969). Certainly, ethnic situations can be conflictual and hierarchical, as illustrated by the Tutsis and the Hutus in Rwanda or the conflict between Serbians, Croatians, and Bosnians in what was once Yugoslavia. The point is that ethnicity and race are different bases for group association. Ethnicity has a primarily sociocultural foundation, and ethnic groups have exhibited tremendous malleability in terms of who belongs (Leach, 1964; Barth, 1969); racial ascriptions (initially) are imposed externally to justify the collective exploitation of a people and are maintained to preserve status differences. Hence scholars have pointed out that, despite the similarities between race and ethnicity, they should be viewed as producing different types of structurations (Balibar & Wallerstein, 1991; Cox, 1948; Rex, 1973; van den Berghe, 1967; Wilson, 1973). On this point see Horowitz (1985), Schemerhorn (1970), and Shibutani and Kwan (1965).

20. Herbert Blumer was one of the first analysts to argue that races at the top of a racial order receive systemic privileges. Blumer summarized his views in his essay 'Reflections on Theory of Race Relations' (1955). See also the works of Shibutani and Kwan (1965), van den Berghe (1967), Blalock (1967), and Schermerhorn (1970).

21. *Hegemonic* means that domination is achieved more through consent than by coercion.

22. *Power* is defined here as a racial group's capacity to push for its racial interests in relation to other races.

23. I am referring to cases such as Haiti. Nonetheless, recent research has suggested that even in such places, the abolition of slavery did not end the racialized character of the social formation (Trouillot, 1990).

24. Some authors have developed notions combining racial/ethnic positions with class. Gordon (1964) developed the concept of 'ethclass' but assumed that this was a temporary phenomenon. Geschwender (1977) transformed the notion into the concept of race-class, defined as 'a social collectivity comprised of persons who are simultaneously members of the same class and the same race' (p. 221; also see Barrera, 1979, pp. 174–279). Geschwender, however, views racial interests as somewhat less 'objective' and less 'fundamental' than class interests.

25. This point has been stressed by many social analysts since Barth's (1969) crucial work conceiving of ethnicity as a form of social organization.

26. This last point is an extension of Poulantzas's view on class. Races—as classes—are not an 'empirical thing'; they denote racialized social relations or racial practices at all levels (Poulantzas, 1982, p. 67).

27. One of the earliest statements of this view was made by Max Weber (1978/1920). He regarded race and ethnicity as 'presumed identities' in which the actors attached subjective meanings to so-called common traits. Leach (1964), in his study of the Kachin in highland Burma, was one of the first social scientists to illustrate the malleability of ethnic boundaries.

28. The motivation for racializing human relations may have originated in the interests of powerful actors, but after social systems are racialized, all members of the dominant race participate in defending and reproducing the racial structure. This is the crucial reason why Marxist analysts (Cox, 1948; Reich, 1976, 1981) have not succeeded in analyzing racism. They have not been able to accept the fact that after the phenomenon originated with the expansion of European capitalism into the New World, it acquired a life of its own. The subjects who were racialized as belonging to the superior race, whether or not they were members of the dominant class, became zealous defenders of the racial order.

29. This argument is not new. Analysts of the racial history of the United States have always pointed out that most of the significant historical changes in this country's race relations were accompanied by some degree of overt violence (Cruse, 1968; Franklin, 1974; Marable, 1983; Button, 1989).

30. This point is important in literature on revolutions and democracy. On the role of violence in the establishment of bourgeois democracies, see Moore (1966). On the role of violence in social movements leading to change, see Piven and Cloward (1979) and Tilly (1978).

31. The notion of relative autonomy comes from the work of Poulantzas (1982) and implies that the ideological and political levels in a society are partially autonomous in relation to the economic level; that is, they are not merely expressions of the economic level.

32. See also Herman Fellman, *Racial Factors in American Industry* (1931). Historian Eugene Genovese (1971) made a similar argument. Although he still regarded racism as an ideology, he stated that once it 'arises it alters profoundly the material reality and in fact becomes a partially autonomous feature of that reality' (p. 340).

33. The data on whether or not northern employers engaged in wage discrimination is not clear-cut. Although Spero and Harris (1974) believed that it was not widespread, they reported some wage discrimination in several northern cities (pp. 176–177).

34. These numbers include only those students attending public schools; since a greater proportion of white students than black attend private schools (Blackwell, 1991), it is likely that these numbers underestimate the real extent of segregation experienced by blacks.

35. Actions by the Ku Klux Klan have an unmistakably racial tone, but many other actions (choosing to live in a suburban neighborhood, sending one's children to a private school, or opposing government intervention in hiring policies) also have racial undertones.

36. The sole exception is in the area of jury selection where statistical evidence is still deemed acceptable.

37. Recently, we tried to launch an investigation to uncover contemporary racial practices by sending testers to various social interactions (renting apartments, trying to find jobs, attempting to get a loan, etc.). To our surprise, the board that reviews all research proposals dealing with human subjects at our institution did not approve our research design because it deemed it 'unethical.' Why? Because we were not eliciting the informed consent of the subjects. Of course, asking for the consent of the 'subjects' would have doomed our research.

38. This chapter was drafted before the most recent Supreme Court decision (the Michigan decision). However, I contend that this decision has not changed substantially the troublesome status of affirmative action programs. And, with the re-election of George W. Bush in 2004, and the impending change in the composition of the Supreme Court (i.e. the selection of more conservative judges to replace retiring liberal ones), I predict that affirmative action programs will be abolished in the near future.

References

Adorno, T. W., Frenkel-Brunswick, E., Levenson, D. J. & Sanford, R. N. (1950) *The Authoritarian Personality* (New York, NY, Harper and Row).

Allen, R. L. (1994) *Reluctant Reformers* (Washington, DC, Howard University Press).

Allport, G. W. (1958) *The Nature of Prejudice* (New York, NY, Doubleday/Anchor Books).

Alvarez, R., Lutterman, K. G. & Associates (1979) *Discrimination in Organizations: Using social indicators to manage social change* (San Francisco, Jossey-Bass Inc.).

Amott, T. & Mathhaei, J. A. (1991) *Race, Gender, and Work: A multicultural economic history of women in the United States* (Boston, MA, South End Press).

Anderson, M. & Collins, P. H. (1995) *Race, Class, and Gender: An anthology* (New York, NY, Thomson Learning).

Anthias, F. & Yuval-Davis, N. (1992) Racialized Boundaries: Race, nation, gender, colour and class and the anti-racist struggle (New York, NY, Routledge).

Aronowitz, S. (1992) *False Promises: The shaping of American working class consciousness* (Durham, NC, Duke University Press).

Balibar, E. & Wallerstein, I. (1991) *Race, Nation, Class: Ambiguous identities* (New York, NY, Verso).

Banton, M. (1970) The Concept of Racism, in: S. Zubaida (ed.), *Race and Racialism* (London, Tavistock Publications), pp. 17–34.

Barth, F. (1969) Introduction, in: F. Barth (ed.), *Ethnic Groups and Boundaries: The social organization of culture difference* (Bergen, Oslo, Tromso: Universitetsforlaget), pp. 9–38.

Barrera, M. (1979) *Race and Class in the Southwest: A theory of racial inequality* (Notre Dame and London: University of Notre Dame Press).

Bell, D. (1992) *Race, Racism, and American Law* (Boston, MA, Little, Brown, and Company).

Benedict, R. F. (1945) *Race and Racism* (London, UK, Routledge and Kegan Paul Ltd).

Berkhoffer, R. F., Jr (1978) *The White Man's Indian: Images of the American Indian from Columbus to the present* (New York, NY, Vintage Books).

Berlin, I. (1975) *Slaves Without Masters: The free Negro in the antebellum South* (New York, NY, Random House, Inc).

Berry, B. (1965) *Race and Ethnic Relations* (Boston, MA, Houghton Mifflin).

Blackwell, T. A. (1991) *The Black Community: Diversity and unity* (New York, NY, Harper and Collins).

Blalock, H. M., Jr. (1967) *Toward a Theory of Minority-Group Relations* (New York, London and Sidney, John Wiley & Sons, Inc).

Blauner, R. (1972) *Racial Oppression in America* (New York, NY, Harper and Row Publishers).

Blumer, H. (1955) Reflections on Theory of Race Relations, in: A. W. Lind (ed.), *Race Relations in World Perspective* (Honolulu, HI, University of Hawaii Press), pp. 3–21.

Boas, F. (1928) *Anthropology and Modern Life* (New York, NY, W. W. Norton and Co., Inc).

Boas, F. (1936) *Race, Language, and Culture* (New York, NY, Macmillan Company).

Bobo, L. D. (1988) Group Conflict, Prejudice, and the Paradox of Contemporary Racial Attitudes, in: P. A. Katz and D. A. Taylor (eds), *Eliminating Racism: Profiles in controversy* (New York, NY, Plenum Press), pp. 85–114.

Bobo, L. D., Kluegel, J. A. & Smith, R. A. (1997) Laissez-Faire Racism: The crystallization of a kinder, gentler, antiblack ideology, in: S. A. Tuch & J. K. Martin (eds), *Racial Attitudes in the 1990s: Continuity and Change* (Westport, CT, Praeger), pp. 15–44.

Bobo, L. D. & Smith, R. A. (1994) From Jim Crow to Racism to *Laissez-Faire* Racism: An essay on the transformation of racial attitudes in America, paper presented at the annual meeting of the American Sociological Association, Los Angeles, 26 August 1994.

Boggs, J. (1970) *Racism and the Class Struggle* (New York, NY, Monthly Review Press).

Bonacich, E. (1980) Advanced Capitalism and Black/White Relations in the United States: A split labor market interpretation, in: T. Pettigrew (ed.), *The Sociology of Race Relations: Reflection and reform* (New York, NY, Free Press), pp. 341–362.

Bonilla-Silva, E. & Lewis, A. E. (1997) The 'New Racism': Toward an analysis of the U.S. racial structure, 1960–1990s, in: Paul Wong (ed.), *Race, Nation, and Citizenship* (Boulder, CO, Westview), pp. 100–150.

Booker, M. A., Krueger, A. B. & Wolkon, S. (1992) Race and School Quality Since *Brown v. Board of Education*, Brookings Papers on Economic Activity: Microeconomics (Washington, DC, Brookings Institution).

Bourdieu, P. (1984) *Distinction* (Cambridge, MA, Harvard University Press).

Brooks, R. L. (1990) *Rethinking the American Race Problem* (Berkeley, LA, and Oxford, University of California Press).

Button, J. W. (1989) *Blacks and Social Change: Impact of the Civil Rights Movement in Southern communities* (Princeton, NJ, Princeton University Press).

Caditz, J. (1976) *White Liberals in Transition: Current dilemmas of ethnic integration* (New York, Spectrum).

Caraway, N. (1991) *Segregated Sisterhood: Racism and the politics of American feminism* (Knoxville, TN, University of Tennessee Press).

Carchedi, G. (1987) *Class Analysis and Social Research* (New York, NY, Blackwell Publishing Co.).

Carmichael, S. (1971) *Stokely Speaks: Black power to Pan-Africanism* (New York, Vintage Books).

Carmichael, S. & Hamilton, C. (1967) *Black Power: The politics of liberation in America* (New York, NY, Vintage Books).

Chesler, M. (1976) Contemporary Sociological Theories of Racism, in: P. A. Katz (ed.), *Towards the Elimination of Racism* (New York, NY, Pergamon Press, Inc.), pp. 21–71.

Cohen, G. A. (1989) Reconsidering Historical Materialism, in: A. Gallinicos (ed.), *Marxist Theory* (Oxford, UK: Oxford University Press), pp. 84–104.

Cose, E. (1993) *Rage of a Privileged Class* (New York, NY, HarperCollins).

Cox, O. C. (1948) *Caste, Class, and Race* (New York, NY, Doubleday and Company).

Cruse, H. (1968) *Rebellion or Revolution* (New York, NY, William Morrow & Company, Inc.).

Delphy, C. (1984) *Close to Home: A materialist analysis of women's oppression* (Amherst, MA, University of Massachusetts Press).

Dreeben, R. & Gamoran, A. (1986) Race, Instruction, and Learning, *American Sociological Review*, 51, pp. 660–669.

Du Bois, W. E. B. (1939/1909) *Black Folk, Then and Now: An essay in the history and sociology of the Negro race* (New York, NY, Henry Holt).

Duncan, O. (1968) Patterns of Occupational Mobility Among Negro Men, *Demography*, 5, pp. 11–22.

Essed, P. (1991) *Understanding Everyday Racism: An interdisciplinary approach* (London, UK, Sage Publications).

Farley, R. (1984) *Blacks and Whites: Narrowing the gap?* (Cambridge, MA, Harvard University Press).

Farley, R. (1993) The Common Destiny of Blacks and Whites: Observations about the social and economic status of the races, in: H. Hill & J. E. Jones, Jr. (eds), *Race in America: The struggle for equality* (Madison, WI, University of Wisconsin Press), pp. 197–223.

Farley, R. & Allen, W. R. (1987) *The Color Line and the Quality of Life in America* (New York, NY, Oxford University Press).

Farley, R. & Hermalin, A. (1972) The 1960s: A decade of progress for Blacks? *Demography*, 9, pp. 353–370.

Feldman, H. & Lasker, B. (1931) *Racial Factors in American Industry* (New York & London, Harper & Bros.).

Foner, P. (1981) *Organized Labor and the Black Worker, 1619–1981* (New York, NY, International Publishers).

Franklin, J. H. (1974) *From Slavery to Freedom: A history of Negro Americans* (New York, NY, Alfred A. Knopf).

Fraser, N. (1989) *Unruly Practices: Power, discourse and gender in contemporary social theory* (Minneapolis, MN, University of Minnesota Press).

Freeman, R. B. (1973) Black Economic Progress Since 1964, *The Public Interest*, Summer.

Freeman, R. B. (1978) Decline in Labor Market Discrimination and Economic Analysis, *American Economic Review*, 63, pp. 280–286.

Furnivall, J. S. (1948) *Colonial Policy and Practice: A comparative study of Burma and Netherlands India* (Cambridge, UK, Cambridge University Press).

Fusfeld, D. R. & Bates, T. T. (1984) *The Political Economy of the Urban Ghetto* (Carbondale, Southern Illinois University Press).

Genovese, E. D. (1971) *In Red and Black: Marxian explorations in Southern and Afro-American History* (New York, NY, Pantheon).

Geschwender, J. A. (1977) *Class, Race, and Worker Insurgence: The League of Revolutionary Black Workers* (Cambridge, MA, Cambridge University Press).

Giddens, P. (1984) *When and Where I Enter: The impact of black women on race and sex in America* (New York, NY, Bantam).

Gilroy, P. (1991) *'There Ain't No Black in the Union Jack:' The cultural politics of race and nation* (Chicago, IL, University of Chicago Press).

Glazer, N. & Moynihan, P. (1970) *Beyond the Melting Pot: The Negroes, Puerto Ricans, Jews Italians, and Irish of New York City* (Cambridge, MA, MIT Press).

Goldfield, M. (1997) *The Color of Politics: Race and the mainsprings of American politics* (New York, NY, New Press, distributed by W. W. Norton & Co.).

Gordon, M. M. (1964) *Assimilation in American Life: The role of race, religion, and national origins* (New York, NY, Oxford University Press).

Gossett, T. F. (1963) *Race: The history of an idea in America* (New York, NY, Random House, Inc.).

Graham, O. L. (1995) *Member of the Club: Reflections on life in a racially polarized world* (New York, NY, HarperCollins).

Greeley A. M. M. & Sheatsley, P. B. (1971) Attitudes Toward Racial Integration, *Scientific American*, 225, pp. 13–19.

Greenhouse, L. (1995) Ruling Elite: A big shift, *New York Times*, 13 June.

Hall, S. (1980) Race Articulation and Societies Structured in Dominance, in: UNESCO (ed.), *Sociological Theories: Race and Colonialism* (Paris, France, UNESCO).

Harris, M. (1964) *Patterns of Race in the Americas* (New York, NY, Walker).

Harrison, A. (1991) *Black Exodus: The great migration from the American South* (Jackson, MS, University Press of Mississippi).

Henri, F. (1975) *Black Migration: Movement north, 1900–1920* (New York, NY, Anchor Press/Doubleday).

Higgs, R. (1977) *Competition and Coercion: Blacks in the American economy, 1865–1914* (Cambridge, UK, Cambridge University Press).

Horowitz, D. (1985) *Ethnic Groups in Conflict* (Berkeley, CA, University of California Press).

Hunt, C. L. & Walker, L. (1974) *Ethnic Dynamics: Patterns of intergroup relations in various societies* (Homewood, IL, Dorsey).

Hyman, H. H. & Sheatsley, P. B. (1964) Attitudes Toward Desegregation, *Scientific American*, 211, pp. 16–23.

Izikowitz, K. G. (1969), Neighbors in Laos, in: F. Barth (ed.), *Ethnic Groups and Boundaries: The social organization of culture difference* (Bergen, Norway, Universitetsforlaget), pp. 135–144.

Jackman, M. R. (1994) *Velvet Glove: Paternalism and conflict in gender, class, and race relations* (Berkeley, CA, University of California Press).

Jaynes, G. D. & Williams, R. M. (1989) *A Common Destiny: Blacks in American society* (Washington, DC, National Academy Press).

Jordon, W. D. (1968) *White Over Black: American attitudes toward the Negro, 1550–1812* (New York, NY, Norton).

Kasinitz, P. & Freidenberg-Herbstein, J. (1987) The Puerto Rican Parade and West Indian Carnival: Public celebrations in New York City, in: C. R. Sutton & E. M. Channey (eds), *Caribbean Life in New York City: Sociocultural dimensions* (New York, NY, Center for Migration Studies of New York), pp. 305–325.

Kinder, D. R. & Sears, D. O. (1981) Prejudice and Politics: Symbolic racism versus racial threats to the good life, *Journal of Personality and Social Psychology*, 40:1, pp. 414–431.

Knowles, L. L. & Prewitt, K. (1969) *Institutional Racism in America* (Englewood Cliffs, NJ, Prentice-Hall, Inc.).

Knutson, E. (1969) Dichotomization and Integration, in: F. Barth (ed.), *Ethnic Groups and Boundaries: The social organizations of culture difference* (Bergen, Norway, Universitetforlaget), pp. 86–100.

Kozol, J. (1991) *Savage Inequalities: Children in America's Schools* (New York, NY, HarperPerennial).

Leach, E. R. (1964) *Political Systems of Highland Burma: A study of Kachin social structure* (London, UK, G. Bell and Sons).

Leiman, M. M. (1992) *Political Economy of Racism* (London, UK, Pluto Press).

Litwach, L. F. (1961) *North of Slavery: The Negro in the Free States* (Chicago, IL, University of Chicago Press).

Lusane, C. (1994) *African Americans at the Crossroads: The restructuring of black leadership and the 1992 elections* (Boston, MA, South End Press).

Magubane, B. M. (1990) *The Political Economy of Race and Class in South Africa* (New York, NY, Monthly Review Press).

Marable, M. (1983) *How Capitalism Underdeveloped Black America* (Boston, MA, South End Press).

Marx, K. & Engles, F. (1977) *The Communist Manifesto* (New York, NY, Penguin USA).

McAdam, D. (1982) *Political Process and the Development of Black Insurgency, 1930–1970* (Chicago, IL, University of Chicago Press).

Meir, A. & Rudwick, E. (1970) *From Plantation to Ghetto* (New York, NY, Hill and Wang).

Miles, R. (1989) *Racism* (London and New York, Routledge).

Miles, R. (1993) *Racism After 'Race Relations'* (London, UK, Routledge).

Miles, R. & Phizaclea, A. (1984) *White Man's Country* (London, UK, Pluto).

Mills, C. W. (1997) *The Racial Contract* (Ithaca and London, Cornell University Press).

Mills, C. W. (1998) *Blackness Visible* (Ithaca, NY, Cornell University Press).

Moore, B., Jr. (1966) *Social Origins of Dictatorship and Democracy* (Boston, MA, Beacon Press).

Moore, J. W. (1970) Colonialism: The case of the Mexican-Americans, *Social Problems*, 17, pp. 463–472.

Morris, A. (1984) *The Origins of the Civil Rights Movement: Black communities organizing for change* (New York, NY, Free Press).

Myrdal, G. (1944) *An American Dilemma: The Negro problem and modern democracy* (New York and London, Harper and Brothers Publishers).

Oaks, J., Selvin, M., Karoly, L. & Guiton, G. (1992) *Educational Matchmaking: Academic and vocational tracking in comprehensive high schools* (Santa Monica, CA, RAND).

Olzak, S. (1992) *The Dynamics of Ethnic Competition and Conflict* (Stanford, CA, Stanford University Press).

Omi, M. & Winant, H. (1986) *Racial Formation in the United States: From the 1960s to the 1980s* (New York, NY, Routledge and Kegan Paul).

Omi, M. & Winant, H. (1994) *Racial Formation in the United States: From the 1960s to the 1980s*, 2nd edn (New York, NY, Routledge).

Orfield, G. (1993) School Desegregation after Two Generations: Race, schools, and opportunity in urban society, in: H. Hill & J. E. Jones (eds), *Race in America* (Madison, WI, University of Wisconsin Press).

Orfield, G. & Monfort, F. (1992) *Status of School Desegregation: The next generation* (Alexandria, VA, National School Boards Association).

Palmore, E. & Whittington, F. T. (1970) Differential Trends Towards Equality Between Whites and Nonwhites, *Social Forces*, 49, pp. 108–117.

Park, R. E. (1950) *Race and Culture* (Glencoe, IL, Free Press).

Perlo, V. (1975) *Economics of Racism U.S.A.: Roots of Black Inequality* (New York, NY, International Publishers).

Pettigrew, T. (1994) New Patterns of Prejudice: The different worlds of 1984 and 1964, in: F. L. Pincus & H. J. Erlich (eds), *Race and Ethnic Conflict* (Boulder, CO, Westview), pp. 53–59.

Pettigrew, T. F. & Martin, J. (1987) Shaping the Organizational Context for Black American Inclusion, *Journal of Social Issues*, 43:1, pp. 41–78.

Pinkney, A. (1984) *The Myth of Black Progress* (Cambridge, UK, Cambridge University Press).

Piven, F. F. & Cloward, R. A. (1979) *Poor People's Movements: Why they succeed, how they fail* (New York, NY, Vintage).

Poulantzas, N. (1982) *Political Power and Social Classes* (London, UK, Verso).

Quadagno, J. (1994) *The Color of Welfare: How racism undermined the war on poverty* (New York, NY, Oxford University Press).

Reich, M. (1976) The Economics of Racism, in: W. Barclay, K. Kumar & R. P. Simms (eds), *Racial Conflict, Discrimination, and Power: Historical and Contemporary Studies* (New York, NY, AMS Press).

Reich, M. (1981) *Racial Inequality: A political-economic analysis* (Princeton, NJ, Princeton University Press).

Reuter, E. B. (1934) Introduction: Race and culture contacts, in E. B. Reuter (ed.), *Race and Culture Contacts* (New York, NY, McGraw Hill), pp. 1–12.

Rex, J. (1973) *Race, Colonialism and the City* (London, UK, Routledge and Kegan Paul).

Rex, J. (1983) *Race Relations in Sociological Theory* (London, UK, Weidenfeld and Nicolson).

Rex, J. (1986) *Race and Ethnicity* (Philadelphia, PA, Open University Press).

Rivken, S. (1994) Residential Segregation and School Integration, *Sociology of Education*, 67, pp. 279–292.

Robinson, C. J. (1983) *Black Marxism: The making of the black radical tradition* (London, UK, Zed Press).

Rodriguez, C. E. (1991) *Puerto Ricans: Born in the U.S.A.* (Boulder, CO, Westview Press).

Roediger, D. R. (1991) *The Wages of Whiteness: Race and the making of the American working class* (London and New York: Verso).

Roediger, D. R. (1994) *Towards the Abolition of Whiteness: Essays on race, politics, and working class history* (London and New York: Verso).

Rose, S. O. (1997) Class Formation and the Quintessential Worker, in: J. R. Hall (ed.), *Reworking Class* (Ithaca, NY, Cornell University Press), pp. 133–166.

Santa Cruz, H. (1977) *Racial Discrimination: Special rapporteur of the sub-commission on prevention of discrimination and protection of minorities* (New York, NY, United Nations).

Saxton, A. (1990) *The Rise and Fall of the White Republic: Class politics and mass culture in nineteenth century America* (New York, NY, W. W. Norton and Co., Inc.).

Schaefer, R. T. (1990) *Racial and Ethnic Gourps*, 4th edn (CITY, IL, Scott Foresman/Little Brown Higher Education).

Schemerhorn, R. A. (1970) *Comparative Ethnic Relations: A framework for theory and research* (New York, NY, Random House).

Schuman, H., Steeh, C. & Bobo, L. (1985) *Racial Attitudes in America: Trends and interpretations* (Cambridge, MA, Harvard University Press).

Schuman, H., Steeh, C., Bobo, L. & Krysan, M. (1997) *Racial Attitudes in America: Trends and interpretations* (Cambridge, MA, Harvard University Press).

Sears, D. O. (1988) Symbolic Racism, in: P. Katz & D. Taylor (eds), *Eliminating Racism: Profiles in controversy* (New York, NY, Plenum), pp. 53–84.

Segura, D. A. (1990) Chicanas and the Triple Oppression in the Labor Force, in: National Association for Chicano Studies (ed.), *Chicana Voices: Intersection of class, race, and gender* (Albuquerque, NM, University of New Mexico Press), pp. 47–65.

Sewell, W. H., Jr. (1992) A Theory of Structure: Duality, agency, and transformation, *American Journal of Sociology*, 98, pp. 1–29.

Shibutani, T. & Kwan, K. (1965) *Ethnic Stratification* (New York, NY, MacMillan).

Smith, R. (1995) *Racism in the Post-Civil Rights Era: Now you see it, now you don't* (New York, NY, State University of New York Press).

Smith, J. P. & Welch, F. R. (1986) *Closing the Gap: Forty years of economic progress for blacks* (Santa Monica, CA, RAND).

Sniderman, P. M. & Piazza, T. (1993) *The Scar of Race* (Cambridge, MA, Harvard University Press).

Solomos, J. (1986) Varieties of Marxist Conceptions of 'Race,' Class, and the State: A critical analysis, in: J. Rex & D. Mason (eds), *Theories of Race and Ethnic Relations* (Cambridge, UK, Cambridge University Press), pp. 84–109.

Solomos, J. (1989) *Race and Racism in Contemporary Britain* (London, UK, Macmillan).

Spero, S. D. & Harris, A. L. (1974) *The Black Worker: The Negro and the Labor Movement* (New York, NY, Atheneum).

Stone, J. (1985) *Racial Conflict in Contemporary Society* (Cambridge, UK, Cambridge University Press).

Sumner, W. G. (1906) *Folkways* (New York, NY, New American Library, Mentor Book).

Sutton, C. R. & Makiesky-Barrow, S. R. (1987) Migration and West Indian Racial and Ethnic Consciousness, in: C. R. Sutton & E. M. Channey (eds), *Caribbean Life in New York City: Socioecultural dimensions* (New York, NY, Center for Migration Studies of New York), pp. 86–107.

Szymanski, A. (1981) The Political Economy of Racism, in: S. G. McNall (ed.), *Political Economy: A critique of American society* (Dallas, TX, Scott, Foresman and Company).

Szymanski, A. (1983) *Class Structure: A critical perspective* (New York, NY, Praeger Publishers).

Thomas, W. I. & Znaiecki, F. (1996/1918) *The Polish Peasant in Europe and America*, vol. 1 (New York, NY, Knopf).

Ticktin, H. (1991) *The Politics of Race: Discrimination in South Africa* (London, UK, Pluto).

Tilly, C. (1978) *From Mobilization to Revolution* (Reading, MA, Addison-Wesley).

Todorov, T. (1984) *The Conquest of America: The question of the Other* (New York, NY, Harper Colophon).

Trouillot, M.-R. (1990) *Haiti, State Against Nation: Origins and legacy of Duvalierism* (New York, NY, Monthly Review Press).

Tuttle, W. M., Jr. (1970) *Race Riot: Chicago in the Red Summer of 1919* (New York, NY, Atheneum).

van den Berghe, P. (1967) *Race and Racism: A comparative perspective* (New York, NY, John Wiley & Sons, Inc.).

van Dijk, T. A. (1984) *Prejudice in Discourse: An analysis of ethnic prejudice in cognition and conversation* (Amsterdam, John Benjamins Publishing Company).

van Dijk, T. A. (1987) *Communicating Racism: Ethnic prejudice in thought and talk* (Newbury Park, CA, Sage Publications).

van Dijk, T. A. (1993) *Elite Discourse and Racism* (Newbury Park, CA, Sage Publications).

Weber, M. (1978/1920) *Economy and Society: An outline of interpretive sociology*, ed. G. Roth & C. Wittich (Berkeley, CA, University of California Press).

Webster, Y. O. (1992) *The Racialization of America* (New York, NY, St Martin's).

Wellman, D. (1977) *Portraits of White Racism* (Cambridge and London, UK, Cambridge University Press).

Whitmeyer, J. (1994) Why Actors are Integral to Structural Analysis, *Sociological Theory*, 12, pp. 153–165.

Williams, E. (1944) *Capitalism and Slavery* (New York, NY, Capricorn).

Williams, R. (1990) *Hierarchical Structures and Social Value: The creation of Black and Irish identities in the United States* (Cambridge, UK, Cambridge University Press).

Willie, C. V. (1989) *Caste and Class Controversy on Race and Poverty: Round two of the Willie/ Wilson debate* (New York, NY, General Hall).

Wilson, W. J. (1973) *Power, Racism, and Privilege: Race Relations in Theoretical and Sociohistorical Perspectives* (New York, NY, MacMillan).

Wilson, W. J. (1978) *The Declining Significance of Race: Blacks and changing American institutions* (Chicago, IL, University of Chicago Press).

Wilson, W. J. (1987) *The Truly Disadvantaged: The inner city, the underclass, and public policy* (Chicago, IL, University of Chicago Press).

Winant, H. (1994) *Racial Conditions: Politics, theory, comparisons* (London and Minneapolis, University of Minnesota Press).

Wolpe, H. (1970) Industrialism and Race in South Africa, in: S. Zubaida (ed.), *Race and Racialism* (London, UK, Tavistock Publications), pp. 151–179.

Wolpe, H. (1986) Class Concepts, Class Struggle, and Racism, in: J. Rex & D. Mason (eds), *Theories of Race Relations* (Cambridge, MA, Cambridge University Press), pp. 110–130.

Wolpe, H. (1988) *Race, Class, and the Apartheid State* (Paris, UNESCO Press).

Woodson, C. G. (1947) *The Mis-Education of the Negro* (New York, NY, Hakims Bookstore).

Woodward, C. V. (1966) *The Strange Career of Jim Crow.* 2nd edn (New York, NY, Oxford University Press).

Wright, E. O. (1985) *Classes* (New York, NY, W. W Norton and Co., Inc.).

1

The Color of Supremacy: Beyond the discourse of 'white privilege'

ZEUS LEONARDO

California State University, Long Beach and University of Washington, Seattle

In the last decade, the study of white privilege has reached currency in the educational and social science literature. In April 2002, the city of Pella, Iowa, hosted the Third Annual Conference on White Privilege. Concerned with the circuits and meanings of whiteness in everyday life, scholars have exposed the codes of white culture, worldview of the white imaginary, and assumptions of the invisible marker that depends on the racial other for its own identity (Frankenberg, 1993, 1997; Hurtado, 1996; Kidder, 1997; Rothenberg, 2002). In particular, authors like Peggy McIntosh (1992) have helped educators understand the taken for granted, daily aspects of white privilege: from the convenience of matching one's skin color with bandages, to opening up a textbook to discover one's racial identity affirmed in history, literature, and civilization in general. In all, the study of white privilege has pushed critical pedagogy into directions that account for the experiences of the 'oppressor' identity (Hurtado, 1999).

This essay takes a different approach toward the study of whiteness. It argues that a critical look at white privilege, or the analysis of white racial hegemony, must be complemented by an equally rigorous examination of white supremacy, or the analysis of white racial domination. This is a necessary departure because, although the two processes are related, the conditions of white supremacy make white privilege possible. In order for white racial hegemony to saturate everyday life, it has to be secured by a process of domination, or those acts, decisions, and policies that white subjects perpetrate on people of color. As such, a critical pedagogy of white racial supremacy revolves less around the issue of unearned advantages, or the *state* of being dominant, and more around direct processes that secure domination and the privileges associated with it.

Racial privilege is the notion that white subjects accrue advantages by virtue of being constructed as whites. Usually, this occurs through the valuation of white skin color, although this is not the only criterion for racial distinction. Hair texture, nose shapes, culture, and language also multiply the privileges of whites or those who *approximate* them (Hunter, 2002). Privilege is granted even without a subject's (re)cognition that life is made a bit easier for her. Privilege is also granted despite a subject's attempt to dis-identify with the white race. 'Race treason' or the renunciation of whiteness is definitely a choice for many whites (Ignatiev & Garvey, 1996), but without the accompanying structural changes, it does not choke off the flow of institutional privileges that subjects who are constructed as white enjoy.

During his summative comments about racial privilege at a 1998 American Educational Research Association panel, James Scheurich described being white as akin to walking down the street with money being put into your pant pocket without your knowledge. At the end of the day, we can imagine that whites have a generous purse without having worked for it. Scheurich's description is helpful because it captures an accurate portrayal of the unearned advantages that whites, by virtue of their race, have over people of color; in addition, it is symptomatic of the utter sense of oblivion that many whites engender toward their privilege. However, there is the cost here of downplaying the active role of whites who take resources from people of color all over the world, appropriate their labor, and construct policies that deny minorities' full participation in society. These are processes that students rarely appreciate because their textbooks reinforce the innocence of whiteness. As a result, the theme of privilege obscures the subject of domination, or the agent of actions, because the situation is described as happening almost without the knowledge of whites. It conjures up images of domination happening behind the backs of whites, rather than on the backs of people of color. The study of white privilege begins to take on an image of domination without agents. It obfuscates the historical process of domination in exchange for a state of dominance *in medias res*.

Describing white privilege as the process of having money put in your pocket comes with certain discursive consequences. First, it begs the question: if money is being placed in white pockets, who places it there? If we insert the subject of actions, we would conclude that racial minorities put the money in white pockets. It does not take long to realize that this maneuver has the unfortunate consequence of inverting the real process of racial accumulation, whereby whites take resources from people of color; often they also build a case for having earned such resources. Second, we can invoke the opposite case. This is where Scheurich's narrative gives us some direction, but only if we put the logic back onto its feet and reinsert the subject of domination. It might sound something like this. The experience of people of color is akin to walking down the street having your money taken from your pocket. Historically, if 'money' represents material, and even cultural, possessions of people of color then the agent of such taking is the white race, real and imagined. The discourse on privilege comes with the unfortunate consequence of masking history, obfuscating agents of domination, and removing the actions that make it clear who is doing what to whom. Instead of emphasizing the process of appropriation, the discourse of privilege centers the discussion on the advantages that whites receive. It mistakes the symptoms for causes. Racial advantages can be explained through a more primary history of exclusions and ideological practices.

At the annual meeting of the National Association of Multicultural Education (NAME) in 2001 in Las Vegas, Nevada, 'privilege' was a hot topic. During a workshop led by Victor Lewis, Hugh Vasquez, Catherine Wong, and Peggy McIntosh, the audience was treated to poignant personal histories of people coming to terms with their male, heterosexual, adult, and white privilege, respectively. We might recall that Lewis and Vasquez were two central figures in the excellent film on race, *Color of Fear*. Known for her work in whiteness studies and anthologized in multiple books for having produced the essay with a list of forty-six privileges whites enjoy (see McIntosh, 1992), at the workshop McIntosh spoke clearly about her coming to terms with white skin advantage. Admitting that the gender lens was at first more convenient for her academic work and teaching, she describes her own engagement with race as seeing fin-like figures dancing out of the water before submerging and disappearing from sight, a scene taken from Virginia Woolf's *To the Lighthouse*. Speaking personally about her process of becoming conscious of white skin privilege, McIntosh describes the process as similar to having glimpsed a fin, not sure what to make of it but knowing that beneath the surface something great was attached to it. In short, McIntosh had seen something significant and it became the work of a critical scholar to make sense of it.

Ostensibly addressing a white audience at the NAME workshop, McIntosh continued by saying that coming to terms with white privilege is 'not about blame, shame, or guilt' regarding actions and atrocities committed by other whites in their name. Likewise, in a recent invited lecture, titled 'Race, Class, and Gender: The problem of domination,' I was tempted to begin my talk with the same sentiment. Upon reflection, I decided against the strategy because I wanted my audience to understand that despite the fact that white racial domination precedes us, whites daily recreate it on both the individual and institutional level. On this last point, there are several issues that I want to bring up, which I believe are coterminous with the discourse on privilege.

Domination is a relation of power that subjects enter into and is forged in the historical process. It does not form out of random acts of hatred, although these are condemnable, but rather out of a patterned and enduring treatment of social groups. Ultimately, it is secured through a series of actions, the ontological meaning of which is not always transparent to its subjects and objects. When early Americans, or what patriots fondly refer to as 'founding fathers,' drafted the Constitution, they proclaimed that people were created equal. Of course, slavery, patriarchy, and industrial capitalism were inscribing forces surrounding their discourse of freedom. In short, 'humanity' meant male, white, and propertied. For this reason, any of their claims to universal humanity were betrayed by the inhumanity and violation of the 'inalienable rights' of people of color, women, and the working class. In this case, domination means that the referents of discourse are particulars dressed up as universals, of the white race speaking for the human race.

In another instance, the case of African slaves in the U.S. literally reduced them to a fraction of a human being when the government reduced slave representation to three-fifths of a person. Fearing a northern-controlled Congress, the south struck the 'Great Compromise', thereby effectively increasing their population while controlling the taxation on importation of slaves. We bracket this process of reduction as a reminder that claims to literation always contain a process of figuration; that is, a representation. The literal reduction of blacks to three-fifths invokes the parasitic figure of whites, the representation of masculinity, and the specter of the bourgeois class. It is easy to see that the white supremacist, patriarchal, capitalist subject represents the standard for human, or the figure of a whole person, and everyone else is a fragment. In this way, policies of domination are betrayed by their accompanying contradictions and tropes.

Although McIntosh's essay enters its second decade since first appearing, it is worthwhile to re-examine it because of its currency. In fact, I include it in one of my course syllabi. To the extent that domination represents a process that establishes the supremacy of a racial group, its resulting everyday politics is understood as 'dominance.' McIntosh superbly maps this state of privilege by citing the many forms of racial advantage whites enjoy in daily life. However, domination can be distinguished from dominance where the former connotes a process and the latter a state of being, the first a material precondition that makes possible the second as a social condition. It is possible to discuss conferred dominance (McIntosh, 1992, pp. 77–78) because there are existing structures of domination that recognize such benefits, albeit unearned as McIntosh correctly points out. Otherwise, it is meaningless to construct perceived notions of advantage when social structures do not recognize them.

Although they clearly benefit from racism in different ways, whites as a racial group secure supremacy in almost all facets of social life. The concept of race does not just divide the working class along racial lines and compromise proletarian unity. Racism divides the white bourgeoisie from the black bourgeoisie (a mythical group, according to Marable, 1983), and white women from women of color (hooks, 1984). In other words, race is an organizing principle that cuts across class, gender, and other imaginable social identities. This condition does not come about through an innocent process, let alone the innocence of whiteness.

When educators advise white students to avoid feelings of guilt, we are attempting to allay their fears of personal responsibility for slavery and its legacies, housing and job discrimination, and colonialism and other generalized crimes against racial minorities. Indeed, white guilt can be a paralyzing sentiment that helps neither whites nor people of color. White guilt blocks critical reflection because whites end up feeling individually blameworthy for racism. In fact, they become overconcerned with whether or not they 'look racist' and forsake the more central project of understanding the contours of structural racism. Anyone who has taught racial themes has witnessed this situation. Many whites subvert a structural study of racism with personalistic concerns over how they are perceived as individuals. In a society that denies whites access to a sociological and critical understanding of racism, this is not a surprising outcome. Stephen Small (1999) advises,

> it is not useful to approach ideologies by asking whether they are 'racist' or 'non-racist.' It is more useful to acknowledge the varied ideologies, and to examine them for their 'racialized' intentions, content and consequences. In other words, it is more useful to consider all ideologies and the outcomes they have or are likely to have, for different 'racialized' groups. (p. 56)

Looking racist has very little to do with whites' unearned advantages and more to do with white treatment of racial minorities. Said another way, the discourse on privilege comes with the psychological effect of personalizing racism rather than understanding its structural origins in interracial relations. Whites have been able to develop discourses of anti-racism in the face of their unearned advantages.

Whites today did not participate in slavery but they surely recreate white supremacy on a daily basis. They may not have supported South African apartheid, but many whites refuse interracial marriage(see Alcoff, 2000), housing integration (Massey & Denton, 1993), and fully desegregated schools (Kozol, 1991).

Teaching, addressing, and writing for a white audience is necessary insofar as whites require inroads into discourses about race and racism. Certain slices of the literature on whiteness, for example, are an attempt to create a discourse that centers on white subjectivity, psychology, and everyday life. Frequently employing ideological critique of white worldview, whiteness studies expose white lies, maneuvers, and pathologies that contribute to the avoidance of a critical understanding of race and racism. As these authors correctly point out, none of these strategies of whiteness is innocent or harmless. They frequently serve to perpetuate white racial supremacy through color-blindness, ahistorical justifications, and sleights-of-mind. However, we arrive at one of the limitations of writings or teachings based on an imagined white audience.

Countless authors from Freire to Fanon have suggested that oppression is best apprehended from the experiences or vantage point of the oppressed. This is not to suggest that oppressed people, as individual subjects of domination, somehow possess the correct or true understanding of racial oppression. Many of them are just as confused as whites when it comes to an organic understanding of racism. Many people of color have shown their inability to perform critical analyses of the causes of their own oppression (Leonardo, 2000). That said, critical analysis begins from the objective experiences of the oppressed in order to understand the dynamics of structural power relations. It also makes sense to say that it is not in the interest of racially dominated groups to mystify the process of their own dehumanization. Yet the case is ostensibly the opposite for whites, who consistently mystify the process of racial accumulation through occlusion of history and forsaking structural analysis for a focus on the individual. This is not to go down the road of essentialized racial subjects, be they black or otherwise, and an equally essentialized white subject, as Stuart Hall (1996a) has pointed out. The advantage of beginning our analysis of domination from the objective position of those who receive policies of domination puts educators on the side of the oppressed, or at least an understanding of history from their conditions. Even when critical analysis takes white experience as its unit of analysis, this must be subjected to the rigors of the analytics of the oppressed. That is, there is a difference between analyzing whiteness with an imagined white audience against an imagined audience of color.

When scholars and educators address an imagined white audience, they cater their analysis to a worldview that refuses certain truths about race relations. As a result, racial understanding proceeds at the snail's pace of the white imaginary (Leonardo, 2002). When McIntosh listed her privileges as a white woman, she came to terms with unearned advantages. White confessionals are helpful insofar as they represent a discursive strategy to recognize the insidiousness of structural privileges. They also articulate an attempt to side with racial minorities through their sympathetic appeal to undo the said privileges. Tim Wise (2002) is insistent on pointing out the pathologies and flights from reason in white rationalizations of the American race situation. Wise's Center at Fiske University links our current assault on whiteness with the avatar of Du Bois, who taught at the same university. However, we must also recognize that recent white attacks on whiteness appeal mainly to a liberal white audience, the content of which has been previously articulated by scholars and activists of color, as Cornel West (1999a) is quick to remind us.

Ruminations on whiteness are not new to many people of color and have been available for white readership. Black women know that their skin color does not match store-bought bandages, Latinos know their language is not spoken by management in most business places, and Asians know that their history rarely achieves the status of what Apple (2000) calls 'official knowledge' in schools. White audiences have had access to these traditions of criticism for over a century. As such, radical writings on the topic of white privilege are new to white audiences *who read mainly white authors.* Much like the popularization of black R & B music by Elvis and Pat Boone, critiques of white privilege are given credence by white authors whose consumers are white readers. Rap music has now reached mainstream U.S.A. through its all-time best selling artist, white rapper Eminem. None of this disregards their contributions, which are helpful for students interested in 'pedagogies of whiteness' (Kincheloe & Steinberg, 1997). When Roediger (1991) launched his critique of the 'wages of whiteness,' he expressed his debt to scholars of color, such as Du Bois. That said, the literature on white privilege is indicative of the lag in white uptake of radical racial thought.

Ultimately this same lag limits the racial analysis in the popular film *Color of Fear.* Although it is one of the most graphic films on the topic of race relations, it suffers from the tethers of white imagination. Throughout much of the ninety minutes, the men of color labor to convince a white participant, David, that white supremacy exists. After a while, one senses that it is a bit like convincing neo-Nazis that the Jewish holocaust happened. Despite the great and memorable lines from the film participants, race conscious viewers are frustrated by David's discourse of refusals when he discredits black people's fear of white rage as 'unfounded,' and claims that individual hard work (or lack thereof) explains the history of groups, and that being white is essentially like being black. When I have shown the film to my class, students of color felt a sense of vindication when Victor, an assertive black man, lashes out at David. They experience their history articulated with a rage they have often felt toward white supremacy and white people. However, the discourses of color expressed in the film are familiar to my students of color; the information is not new to them.

The newness comes in the form of its publicity, of its coming to voice for them through the film participants. Victor, Hugh, and the other men of color become surrogates for the centuries of oppression experienced by many people of color, which rarely gets articulated in public life. By contrast, the same information is new to many of my white students, some of whom feel attacked, others enlightened. Thus, the majority of the film's discourse is spent on the question, 'What does it mean to be white?' and forsakes a deeper engagement with 'What does it mean to be black, Latino, or Asian?' David's consciousness drives the discussion and frames the issues because he needs to be convinced of the first fact of racial analysis: mainly, that white domination is a reality. In short, even the progressive discourse of *Color of Fear* caters to the white imagination. It is inscribed by the rudimentary aspects of racial analysis incarnated through David.

There is a double bind at work here. Although it is crucial that whites 'buy into' racial justice since they arguably possess the strongest form of investment in race (Lipsitz, 1998), they also have the most to give up in terms of material resources. Consequently, convincing them to appropriate racial analysis for their own lives runs into difficulties. This is what McIntosh inevitably attempts with her honest appraisal of her own privilege. However, she is led to construct her narrative in such a way as to obscure some of the real processes of racial domination. This strategy might be necessary insofar as she avoids threatening her (white) audience to the point that they discredit her message. Anyone who has performed a radical racial analysis has faced a similar scenario where the messenger is dismissed because the message produces psychological dissonance between a white subject's desire for racial justice and her inability to accept radical change. Nevertheless, there are certain discursive costs.

Throughout her essay, McIntosh repeats her experience of having been taught to ignore her privilege, to consider her worldview as normal, and to treat race as the problem of the other. Deserving to be quoted at length, she writes,

> whites are carefully taught not to recognize white privilege ... about which I was 'meant' to remain oblivious ... My schooling gave me no training in seeing myself as an oppressor ... I was taught to see myself as an individual whose moral state depended on her individual moral will ... [A] pattern of assumptions that were passed on to me as a white person ... I was taught to recognize racism only in individual acts of meanness by members of my group, never in invisible systems conferring racial dominance on my group from birth. (pp. 71, 72, 77, 81)

First, notice the passage's passive tone. White racist thoughts are disembodied, omnipresent but belonging to no one. White racist teachings, life lessons, and values are depicted as actions done or passed on to a white subject, almost unbeknownst to him, rather than something in which he invests. Second, the passage is consistent with McIntosh's advice for whites to avoid feelings of personal blame for racism. But white domination is never settled once and for all; it is constantly reestablished and reconstructed by whites *from all walks of life*. It is not a relation of power secured by slavery, Jim Crow, or job discrimination alone. It is not a process with a clear beginning or a foreseeable end (Bell, 1992). Last, it is not solely the domain of white supremacist groups. It is rather the domain of average, tolerant people, of lovers of diversity, and of believers in justice.

If racist relations were created only by people in the past, then racism would not be as formidable as it is today. It could be regarded as part of the historical dustbin and a relic of a cruel society. If racism were only problems promulgated by 'bad whites,' then bad whites today either outnumber 'good whites' or overpower them. The question becomes: Who are these bad whites? It must be the position of a good white person to declare that racism is always about 'other whites,' perhaps 'those working-class whites.' This is a general alibi to create the 'racist' as always other, the self being an exception. Since very few whites exist who actually believe they are racist, then basically no one is racist and racism disappears more quickly than we can describe it. We live in a condition where racism thrives absent of racists (Bonilla-Silva, 2003). There must be an alternative explanation: in general, whites recreate their own racial supremacy, despite good intentions.

There is the other half of domination that needs our attention: white investment. To the extent that racial supremacy is taught to white students, it is pedagogical. Insofar as it is pedagogical, there is the possibility of critically reflecting on its flows in order to disrupt them. The hidden curriculum of whiteness saturates everyday school life and one of the first steps to articulating its features is coming to terms with its specific modes of discourse. In an interview with Grossberg, Stuart Hall (1996b) defines 'articulation' as 'the connection that *can* make a unity of two different elements, under certain conditions. It is a linkage which is not necessary, determined, absolute, and essential for all time' (p. 141; italics in original). Articulating the possibility of 'universal' white supremacy necessitates strategies that unpack discourses in particular school places. One of its features that critical educators confront is the notion of investment. The forces of racial amnesia daily threaten both white and non-white students. School curricula are able to describe racial disparities but are often limited to their testable forms and standardized lessons. Critical discourse on the continuity between past and present, institutional arrangements, and the problems of color-blind discourses are forsaken for 'correct' forms of knowledge.

Communities of color have constructed counter-discourses in the home, church, and informal school cultures in order to maintain their sense of humanity. They know too well that their sanity and development, both as individuals and as a collective, depend on alternative (unofficial) knowledge of the racial formation. By contrast, white subjects do not forge these same counter-hegemonic racial understandings because their lives also depend on a certain development; that is, color-blind strategies that maintain their supremacy as a group. Like their non-white counterparts, white students are not taught anti-racist understandings in schools; but, unlike non-whites, whites invest in practices that obscure racial processes. State sponsored curricula fail to encourage students of all racial backgrounds to critique white domination. In other words, schools may teach white students to naturalize their unearned privileges, but they also willingly participate in such discourses, which maintains *their* sense of humanity. White humanity is just that: humanity of whites. So it is not only the case that whites are taught to normalize their dominant position in society; they are susceptible to these forms of teachings because they benefit from them. It is not a process that is somehow done to them, as if they were duped, are victims of manipulation, or lacked certain learning opportunities. Rather, the color-blind discourse is one that they fully endorse.

White domination is the responsibility of every white subject because her very being depends on it. A discourse of absolution misses the mark on the actual processes of white supremacy, a process that benefits every white individual, albeit in different degrees. Poor or working-class whites may be beneficiaries of white supremacy, but they are not signatories of it (Mills, 1997). That said, if whites do not assume responsibility for the history of white supremacy, then who can? The strategy of race treason asks whites to take personal and group responsibility for the predicament we know as structural racism (Ignatiev & Garvey, 1996). This is undoubtedly an unpopular option because the situation is admittedly 'more complex' than that. It is true that people of color add to or participate in their own oppression, but at most this is annoying, not oppressive, to whites. Often, it is a psycho-social result of the degradation of a whole race of people and the way it compromises their self-confidence and produces apoliticized forms of resistance. We can also speak of maltreatment between minorities, or what I call 'inter-minoritarian politics,' which is different from white racism. It is even possible that non-whites act or speak in ways that rearticulate and reinforce racist relations.

When Stephen Steinberg (1998) criticizes William Julius Wilson for his 'retreat from race,' Steinberg, who brands Wilson as former New York Senator Patrick Moynihan's academic reincarnation, calls into question any universal or color-blind social policy as a backlash of liberal thought since the 1960s. Wilson's (1987) popular and generalist proposals for raising black educational skills and credentials puts the onus on blacks to disrupt the cycle or culture of poverty, rather than centering the problem of white racism and its legacy of school segregation and Eurocentric curricula, just to name a few. Steinberg also takes Cornel West to task when the otherwise insurgent philosopher attempts to uplift the spirit of the race by noting its nihilistic tendencies and rampant materialism (see West, 1994), thus deflecting the focus away from white supremacy. One should not confuse Steinberg for suggesting that these afflictions, as West describes them, are not real or that the black community does not have its *own* problems. It also may sound strange to pair two scholars with seemingly divergent political commitments, Wilson being a social democrat of a Weberian persuasion and West (1999b) a self-proclaimed 'democratic and libertarian socialist' (p. 256). Wilson and West's political similarity ends with the alliteration of their names. In fact, one senses West discursively distancing himself from his former Harvard colleague who advocates a 'bourgeois perspective' with respect to Afro-American oppression (West, 1988, p. 21).

Steinberg interrogates West, like Wilson and Moynihan before him, for a 'politics of conversion' that announces black nihilism as 'a problem *sui generis*, with an existence and momentum independent of the forces that gave rise to it in the first place' (p. 37), a cultural politics with a life of its own independent of political economy and white domination. Is this a return to the culture of poverty argument? Indeed, it is a bit telling that the trade book *Race Matters*, arguably West's least radical compendium on race and racism, should strike such an enchanting chord with the public. Because *Race Matters* resonates with a white audience's imagery of blacks as pathological and nihilistic, its discursive consequences are such that the text becomes coffee table reading for the white imagination, despite its best intentions. This is the power of discourse to be inserted into the historical flow out of the hands of its creator. West also receives added criticism from Miles and Torres (1999) who question if 'race matters,' preferring a return to class struggle. On this note, West (1999a) does not negate the importance of class struggle in tandem with race struggle. That said, he seems less concerned that the economy assume a determining effect on race and other relations, let alone an originary point of struggle.

The sheer amount of acts of violence or terror by whites toward racial minorities is overwhelming. However, following the format used by McIntosh, it is helpful to create a selective list of acts, laws, and decisions, if only to capture a reliable portrait of white supremacy.

1. In order to promote the 'purity' of the white race, anti-miscegenation laws prevent diversification of the gene pool (Davis, 2001; Alcoff, 2000). White racism's claims to purity are an instance of its problematic humanist essentialism (Balibar, 1990).
2. Housing segregation limits black mobility and access to jobs and other kinds of networks. Abandoned in inner cities, blacks suffer the most enduring and complete ghettoization in American history (Massey & Denton, 1993).
3. The rule of hypodescent, or the 'one drop rule,' allows the creation of more blacks and hence more slaves, increases scarcity of white identity, and provides an 'out' for white rapists of black women to disclaim responsibility for their children (Davis, 2001; hooks, 1981).
4. Segregated education for students of color creates substandard schools, lack of resources, and inferior education (Spring, 2000). Even after the 1954 decision following Brown vs. Board of Education in Topeka, Kansas ruled that 'separate is inherently unequal,' second generation, or *de facto*, segregation still mars the educational experience of many students of color in the U.S. (Kozol, 1991).
5. Anti-immigrant Laws and Exclusion Acts curtail the rights of many Asian immigrants on U.S. soil and place limitations or quotas on immigration from their home nation (Takaki, 1993). These laws negatively affect family development and life, psychological wellness, and increase experiences of exile in Asian immigrants.
6. Colonization of third world nations establishes white global supremacy and perceived white superiority (Fanon, 1963; Memmi, 1965). Much of the continents of Africa, South America, North America, Australia, frigid Greenland and New Zealand, and large chunks of tropical Asia and the Pacific Islands succumbed to the expansion of the white race (see Jordan, 1968).
7. The Occident creates its infantilized other through methods of cultural imperialism whereby the other is constructed, controlled, and written into inferiority (Said, 1979, 1994). Through cultural imperialism, ideologies of the West make their way to the shores of the 'heart of darkness' (Conrad's terminology), where the culture of the white race is consolidated into a dominant frame of reference for civilization, moral development, and rationality.
8. Job discrimination limits the upward mobility of workers of color and their access to productive networks (Feagin & Vera, 1995; Feagin, 2000).
9. Whites' genocidal efforts against Native Americans facilitated takeover of Northern American soil and the attempt to eliminate its indigenous population. Where a policy of elimination was not possible, whites produced a form of education violent to Native Americans (Dog & Erdoes, 1999).

10. Global enslavement of Africans produced profit for white slave owners, compromised African collective development, and established centuries of the master–slave relationship between whites and blacks (Jordan, 1968; Fanon, 1967).

11. U.S. internment camps for Japanese target an Asian group as 'traitors' of the nation state and brand them as 'forever foreigners' on American soil. The same treatment did not fall on other 'enemies of the state' during World War II, such as Germans or Italians (Houston & Houston, 1973).

12. Exoticization of the other, which masks the colonial policy of the degradation of indigenous culture, has turned colonial posts into commercial artifacts to be enjoyed by the white imagination. Colonized lands, like Hawaii, are now places thoroughly 'tourified' for the pleasure of visitors to partake in its stereotypical, prostituted, cultural forms (Trask, 1999).

13. California's Proposition 227, and others like it, impose English as the only legitimate language in schools and the workplace, thereby devaluing non-white cultures (Nieto, 2000). Although other European languages, such as French and German, are also unofficial, groups associated with them are not conveniently constructed as 'aliens,' or the common insult for Mexicans and other Latinos.

14. Appropriation of third world labor exploits the global work force for the profit of (post)industrial first world nations and the benefit of the white global bourgeoisie. This increases alienation for both groups, with the third world suffering the brutal structures of exploitation, unsafe work conditions, and an imbalance in relations of power between nations (Davis, 1997).

15. Military installation of naval and army bases to 'protect' third world nations from external aggression promotes a condescending and patronizing relationship between the protectorate first world nation and third world nation whose sovereignty is compromised (Enloe, 2001).

16. Welfare reform legislation in the U.S., reaching its height during the Clinton era, works against the interests of people of color (Neubeck & Cazenave, 2001).

17. Forced sterilization of women of color continues the curtailment of their human and reproduction rights (Roberts, 1999).

18. The Tuskegee syphilis study, and other unethical medical research projects like it, use minority bodies for medical experimentations without the participants' full awareness and consent. In this case, the U.S. government deceived 400 blacks by promising free treatment for their syphilis. Between 1932 and 1972, the researchers conducted their disguised study of *untreated* syphilis, from which 100 black men died (Spina, 2000).

19. Jim Crow laws create American apartheid whereby blacks and whites are treated unequally under the auspices of the judicial system (Morris, 1984).

20. Inheritance laws favor whites, whose families benefited from free black labor during slavery. Centuries later, their children retain their parents' wealth. In general, whites bequeath wealth onto their children, whereas blacks often bequeath debt to theirs (Oliver & Shapiro, 1997).

21. IQ-intelligence testing, eugenics, and phrenology construct the genetic inferiority of people of color (Stepan, 1990). Herrnstein and Murray's recent popular book, *The Bell Curve* (1994), revisits and reasserts eugenics assumptions.

22. Tracking practices in schools limit the educational mobility, curricular offerings, and positive interactions with teachers of black and Latino students (Oakes, 1985).

23. The systematic lynching of African Americans served as a tool of social control. Often couched in the fears of miscegenation, lynching was thought to be justified because African Americans violated the racial and social etiquettes of the South or in order to deter their civil rights activism, such as registering to vote (Davis, 1981).

24. Race riots against blacks were used as tools by whites to destroy black property and business districts, especially when they were flourishing. Riots were also used to enforce neighborhood boundaries that maintained racial segregation. Reparations to blacks, who lost their property during the riots, were never made. Moreover, city governments often did not officially acknowledge that the riots occurred (Massey & Denton, 1993; Roediger, 1991).

25. Women of color are more likely to be raped than white women, but less likely to be believed. The U.S. has a long history of sexual abuse of women of color, largely because of their lack of power and whites' hypersexualization of them. Sexual abuse and rape of women of color create a culture of violence (Davis, 1981).

26. Imposition of Christian religion and forceful conversion of non-Christian peoples (Spring, 2000).

27. Whites subverted community reading programs and other educational practices by blacks, forcing them to create clandestine literacy programs (Holt, 1990).

28. Union exclusion of blacks from the working-class movement or from leadership positions in proletarian groups (West, 1999b).

29. Many blacks and Latinos live in forsaken neighborhoods with high levels of toxic pollution. As a result, they suffer from diseases related to these forms of environmental racism (Lipsitz, 1998).

Privilege is the daily cognate of structural domination. Without securing the latter, the former is not activated. A few examples should suffice. Whites have 'neighbors ... [who] are neutral or pleasant' (McIntosh, 1992, p. 73) to them because redlining and other real estate practices, with the help of the Federal Housing Agency, secure the ejection of the black and brown body from white spaces. Whites can enter a business establishment and expect the ' "person in charge" to be white' (McIntosh, 1992, p. 74) because of a long history of job discrimination. Whites are relatively free from racial harassment from police officers because racial profiling strategies train U.S. police officers that people of color are potential criminals. Finally, whites 'can choose blemish cover or bandages in "flesh" color' to match their skin (McIntosh, 1992, p. 75) because of centuries of denigration of darker peoples and images associated with them, fetishism of the color line, and the cultivation of the politics of pigmentation. We can condense the list under a general theme: whites enjoy privileges largely because they have created a system of domination under which they can thrive as a group. The volumes of writing on the issue of domination testify that the process is complex and multi-causal. But the enactment is quite simple: set up a system that benefits the group, mystify the system, remove the agents of actions from discourse, and when interrogated about it, stifle the discussion with inane comments about the 'reality' of the charges being made.

When it comes to official history, there is no paucity of representation of whites as its creator. From civil society, to science, to art, whites represent the subject for what Matthew Arnold once called the best that a culture has produced. In other words, white imprint is everywhere. However, when it concerns domination, whites suddenly disappear, as if history were purely a positive sense of contribution. Their previous omnipresence becomes a position of nowhere, a certain politics of undetectability. When it comes to culture, our students learn a benign form of multiculturalism, as if culture were a purely constructive notion free of imperialist histories and examples of imposition. Encouraging white students to reinsert themselves into the underbelly of history does not always have to occur in a self-destructive context. There are ways to address domination that require very little from people who benefit from it.

A white student in one of my courses admitted that whites possess the ultimate power in the U.S. and it does not threaten him much as an individual to recognize this fact. He explained that he can take this first step and often wonders why other whites find it so hard to join him. After all, admission does not necessarily mean ending domination; yet, many whites find even this act of enunciation impossible. In a brave attempt to ameliorate historical wounds between Japan and the Philippines, Professor Tsuyoshi Amemiya of Aoyama Gakuin University in Tokyo, Japan, works with his students to accept personal responsibility for Japan's imperialist past (Walfish, 2001). None of these students occupied the Philippines during World War II; none of them was involved in the killings during this military invasion; and none of them appropriated the Filipinos' labor. But they all have one thing in common: an inherited sense of history that belongs to, rather than is taken from, them. These students are not admitting that they created Japan's imperialist past and current Asian hegemony. Far from it. However, they recognize that their daily taken-for-granted benefits are legacies from the decades of Japanese imperialist policies.

Likewise, Australians have discussed instituting a national day of grieving, a day of atonement for crimes against the aboriginal population. White Australians are encouraged to sign a 'sorry book' to apologize to indigenous people and acknowledge responsibility for the history of colonization and its continuing legacies, like the lost generation of aboriginal people whom the Australian government took from their families and tried to assimilate into white culture. Such a gesture does not represent a radical solution but an official attempt to recognize white racial domi-nation. In the United States, the effort to provide former slaves 'forty acres and a mule' failed during Reconstruction. Whites resisted this expression of atonement, one that would have changed the landscape of race relations. Free blacks would have come closer to Booker T. Washington's (1986) dream of economic independence and a rebuilding of black America. In the new millennium, the U.S. government is no closer to an official apology or plans for reparations.

The discourse on privilege has pushed critical pedagogy to ask crucial questions about the nature of 'white experience' and the psychological and material benefits from an unearned position in society. To the extent that white audiences need a discursive space they can negotiate as safe participants in race critique, discourses on privilege provide the entry. However, insofar as white feelings of safety perpetuate a legacy of white refusal to engage racial domination, or acts of terror toward people of color, such discourses rearticulate the privilege that whites already enjoy when they are able to evade confronting white supremacy. As long as whites ultimately feel a sense of comfort with racial analysis, they will not sympathize with the pain and discomfort they have unleashed on racial minorities for centuries. Solidarity between whites and non-whites will proceed at the reluctant pace of the white imagination, whose subjects accept the problem of racism without an agent.

A discourse on supremacy offers whites and minority students a progressive starting point because it does not cater to white racial thinking. Racial minorities comprise its projected audience, whether or not this is literally the case. As a result, it recognizes the existence of minority subjects and affirms their history. It begins from their starting point, one which needs little convincing about the reality of white domination. Discourses of supremacy acknowledge white privileges, but only as a function of whites' actions toward minority subjects and not as mysterious accumulations of unearned advantages. In our post-September 11 global village, racism reaches into the hearts of more people, into the hearths of their homes and schools. Through discourses of supremacy the racial story unfolds, complete with characters, actions, and conflicts. More important, resolution of the plot transforms into a discreet and pedagogical possibility.

References

Alcoff, L. (2000) Mestizo Identity, in: R. Bernasconi & T. Lott (eds), *The Idea of Race* (Indianapolis and Cambridge, Hackett Publishing Company, Inc).

Apple, M. (2000) *Official Knowledge: Democratic education in a conservative age* (New York, Routledge and Kegan Paul).

Balibar, E. (1990) Paradoxes of Universality, in: D. T. Goldberg (ed.), *Anatomy of Racism* (Minneapolis, University of Minnesota Press).

Bell, D. (1992) *Faces at the Bottom of the Well: The permanence of racism* (New York, Basic Books).

Bonilla-Silva, E. (2003) *Racism Without Racists: Color-blind racism and the persistence of racial inequality in the United States* (Lanham, Rowman & Littlefield).

Davis, A. (1981) *Women, Race, and Class* (New York, Random House).

Davis, A. (1997) *The-Prison-Industrial-Complex* (Audio-CD) (San Francisco and Edinburgh, UK, AK Press Audio).

Davis, F. J. (2001) *Who is Black?: One nation's definition* (University Park, PA, Penn State University Press).

Dog, M. & Erdoes, R. (1999) Civilize Them With a Stick, in: S. Ferguson (ed.), *Mapping the Social Landscape* (Mountain View, CA, London, and Toronto, Mayfield Publishing Company).

Enloe, C. (2001) *Bananas, Bases, and Beaches: Making feminist sense of international politics* (Berkeley and Los Angeles, University of California Press).

Fanon, F. (1963) *The Wretched of the Earth*, trans. C. Farrington (New York, Grove Press).

Fanon, F. (1967) *Black Skin White Masks*, trans. C. Markmann (New York, Grove Weidenfeld).

Feagin, J. (2000) *Racist America: Roots, current realities, and future reparations* (New York, Routledge).

Feagin, J. & Vera, H. (1995) *White Racism: The basics* (New York, Routledge).

Frankenberg, R. (1993) *White Women, Race Matters: The social construction of whiteness* (Minneapolis, University of Minnesota Press).

Frankenberg, R. (ed.) (1997) *Displacing Whiteness* (Durham, NC, and London, Duke University Press).

Hall, S. (1996a) What Is This 'Black' in Black Popular Culture?, in: D. Morley & K. Chen (eds), *Stuart Hall* (New York and London, Routledge).

Hall, S. (1996b) On Postmodernism and Articulation: An interview with Stuart Hall, in: D. Morley & K. Chen (eds), *Stuart Hall* (New York and London, Routledge).

Herrnstein, R. & Murray, C. (1994) *The Bell Curve* (New York, Free Press).

Holt, T. (1990) 'Knowledge Is Power': The black struggle for literacy, in: A. Lunsford, H. Moglen & J. Slevin (eds), *The Right to Literacy* (New York, Modern Language Association).

hooks, b. (1981) *Ain't I a Woman?: Black women and feminism* (Boston, South End Press).

hooks, b. (1984) *Feminist Theory: From margin to center* (Boston, South End Press).

Houston, J. W. & Houston, J. (1973) *Farewell to Manzanar* (New York, Toronto, London, Sydney, Auckland, Bantam Books).

Hunter, M. (2002) 'If You're Light You're Alright': Light skin color as social capital for women of color, *Gender & Society*, 16:2, pp. 171–189.

Hurtado, A. (1996) *The Color of Privilege: Three blasphemies on race and feminism* (Ann Arbor, MI, University of Michigan Press).

Hurtado, A. (1999) The Trickster's Play: Whiteness in the subordination and liberation process, in: R. Torres, L. Miron & J. Inda (eds), *Race, Identity, and Citizenship* (Malden, MA, and Oxford, UK, Blackwell).

Ignatiev, N. & Garvey, J. (1996) Abolish the White Race, in: N. Ignatiev & J. Garvey (eds), *Race Traitor* (New York and London, Routledge).

Jordan, W. (1968) *White over Black* (Chapel Hill, University of North Carolina Press).

Kidder, L. (1997) Colonial Remnants: Assumptions of privilege, in: M. Fine, L. Weis, L. Powell & L. Wong (eds), *Off White* (New York and London, Routledge).

Kincheloe, J. & Steinberg, S. (1997) Addressing the Crisis of Whiteness: Reconfiguring white identity in a pedagogy of whiteness, in: J. Kincheloe, S. Steinberg, N. Rodriguez & R. Chennault (eds), *White Reign* (New York, St Martin's Griffin).

Kozol, J. (1991) *Savage Inequalities* (New York, Harper Perennial).

Leonardo, Z. (2000) Betwixt and Between: Introduction to the politics of identity, in: C. Tejeda, C. Martinez & Z. Leonardo (eds), *Charting New Terrains of Chicana(o)/Latina(o) Education* (Cresskill, NJ, Hampton Press).

Leonardo, Z. (2002) The Souls of White Folk: Critical pedagogy, whiteness studies, and globalization discourse, *Race Ethnicity & Education*, 5:1, pp. 29–50.

Lipsitz, G. (1998) *The Possessive Investment in Whiteness* (Philadelphia, Temple University Press).

Marable, M. (1983) *How Capitalism Underdeveloped Black America* (Boston, South End Press).

Massey, D. & Denton, N. (1993) *American Apartheid* (Cambridge, MA, and London, Harvard University Press).

McIntosh, P. (1992) White Privilege and Male Privilege: A personal account of coming to see correspondences through work in women's studies, in: M. Andersen & P. H. Collins (eds), *Race, Class, and Gender: An anthology* (Belmont, CA, Wadsworth Publishing).

Memmi, A. (1965) *The Colonizer and the Colonized* (Boston, Beacon Press).

Miles, R. & Torres, R. (1999) Does 'Race' Matter?: Transatlantic perspectives on racism after 'race relations', in: R. Torres, L. Miron & J. Inda (eds), *Race, Identity, and Citizenship* (Malden, MA, and Oxford, Blackwell).

Mills, C. (1997) *The Racial Contract* (Ithaca and London, Cornell University Press).

Morris, A. (1984) *The Origins of the Civil Rights Movement* (New York, Free Press).

Neubeck, K. & Cazenave, N. (2001) *Welfare Racism: Playing the race card against America's poor* (New York and London, Routledge).

Nieto, S. (2000) *Affirming Diversity*, 3rd edn (New York, Longman).

Oakes, J. (1985) *Keeping Track* (New Haven, Yale University Press).

Oliver, M. & Shapiro, T. (1997) *Black Wealth, White Wealth: A new perspective on racial inequality* (New York and London, Routledge).

Roberts, D. (1999) *Killing the Black Body: Race, reproduction, and the meaning of liberty* (New York, Vintage Books).

Roediger, D. (1991) *The Wages of Whiteness* (London and New York, Verso).

Rothenberg, P. (ed.) (2002) *White Privilege: Essential readings on the other side of racism* (New York, Worth Publishers).

Said, E. (1979) *Orientalism* (New York, Random House).

Said, E. (1994) *Culture and Imperialism* (New York, Vintage Books).

Small, S. (1999) The Contours of Racialization: Structures, representations and resistance in the United States, in: R. Torres, L. Miron & J. Inda (eds), *Race, Identity, and Citizenship* (Malden, MA, and Oxford, Blackwell).

Spina, S. (2000) The Psychology of Violence and the Violence of Psychology, in: S. Spina (ed.), *Smoke & Mirrors: The hidden context of violence in schools and society* (Lanham, Boulder, New York and Oxford, Rowman & Littlefield).

Spring, J. (2000) *Deculturalization and the Struggle for Equality*, 3rd edn (Boston, McGraw-Hill).

Steinberg, S. (1998) The Liberal Retreat from Race during the Post-Civil Rights Era, in: W. Lubiano (ed.), *The House that Race Built* (New York, Vintage Books).

Stepan, N. (1990) Race and Gender: The role of analogy in science, in: D. T. Goldberg (ed.), *Anatomy of Racism* (Minneapolis and Oxford, University of Minnesota Press).

Takaki, R. (1993) *A Different Mirror* (Boston, New York, and London, Little, Brown and Co.).

Trask, H. (1999) Lovely Hula Hands: Corporate tourism and the prostitution of Hawaiian culture, in: S. Ferguson (ed.), *Mapping the Social Landscape* (Mountain View, CA, London and Toronto, Mayfield Publishing Company).

Walfish, D. (2001) Tracing the Echoes of the Bataan Death March, *The Chronicle of Higher Education*, A56 (11 May 2001).

Washington, B. T. (1986) *Up from Slavery* (New York, Penguin Books).

West, C. (1988) Marxist Theory and the Specificity of Afro-American Oppression, in: C. Nelson & L. Grossberg (eds), *Marxism and the Interpretation of Culture* (Urbana and Chicago, University of Illinois Press).

West, C. (1994) *Race Matters* (New York, Vintage Books).

West, C. (1999a) The Indispensability Yet Insufficiency of Marxist Theory, in: C. West (ed.), *The Cornel West Reader* (New York, Basic Books).

West, C. (1999b) Race and Social Theory, in: C. West (ed.), *The Cornel West Reader* (New York, Basic Books).

Wilson, W. J. (1987) *The Truly Disadvantaged* (Chicago, University of Chicago Press).

Wise, T. (2002) Membership Has Its Privileges: Thoughts on acknowledging and challenging whiteness, in: P. Rothenberg (ed.), *White Privilege: Essential readings on the other side of racism* (New York, Worth Publishers).

2
Whiteness and Critical Pedagogy

RICKY LEE ALLEN
University of New Mexico

> No revolt of a white proletariat could be started if its object was to make
> black workers their economic, political and social equals. It is for this
> reason that American socialism has been dumb on the Negro problem,
> and the communists cannot even get a respectful hearing in America
> unless they begin by expelling Negroes.
>
> —Du Bois, 1995/1933, p. 542

During the 1930s, W. E. B. Du Bois criticized the racial exclusion that was being
practiced, and that had been practiced, in the name of Marxism and unionism. Du
Bois challenged the common notion of Marxist thought that class relations first and
foremost explain the motivations of racial groups. His epic *Black Reconstruction in
America* (1935) illuminated the role that racial identity played in the political
practices of poor whites during slavery. Du Bois argued that poor whites chose
receiving the benefits of the 'public and psychological wages of whiteness' over
joining with Blacks to undo the plantation system. Within a system of white
supremacy, whites received both material and psychological benefits for surveilling
the racialized system that had made the US into an opportunity structure for
European ethnics, who were able to become white. Poor whites understood that
there were more social rewards for those who were poor and white than for those
who were people of color. In contrast to the common refrain of Marxist discourse,
it was whites, not people of color, whose racial focus blinded them to the possibilities of class struggle. Thus, Du Bois suggested that the central obstacle to solidarity on the left, and, for that matter, all of society, was the problem of race relations
within a white supremacist context. Put another way, no social and economic
changes were likely to occur unless whites were willing to deal directly with how
their own racism prevented cross-racial solidarity. To this day, the public and
psychological wages of whiteness continue to shape the racial politics of the US.
The problem of race relations is primarily—but not solely—a white problem, and
it has spilled over into the movements that we whites have created and led, no
matter how well intentioned we may have been.

Critical pedagogy is one such movement. It has been normalized around a
discourse that sees class as the principal determinant of social and political life, while
assigning race to a subordinate position (Allen, 2001; Ladson-Billings, 1997; Leonardo,
2002). Instead of naturalizing critical pedagogy's fixation with class, I suggest
that a closer examination of its initial assumptions is needed. We need to delve into

the implications of basing critical pedagogy upon class rather than race. For instance, what would critical pedagogy look like if it had been founded upon the belief that white supremacy, not capitalism, is the central problem of humankind? What would be its main tenets if, say, Du Bois had been its originator rather than Paulo Freire? Would it have gained wider acceptance in the US had it been based upon a more race-conscious framework that matches our own history? Critical pedagogy has had a difficult time gaining acceptance among people of color on the US educational left, who are more likely to be concerned about white power and privilege and suspicious of critical theory (Ladson-Billings, 1997). Meanwhile, we white critical pedagogists continue to scratch our heads as we try to figure out why darker-skinned groups in the US, particularly Blacks and Indians, have been reluctant to join our educational movement. We seem to be unable to realize that our diminution of race has alienated those who do not have the privilege to ignore white supremacy—no matter what economic form it takes.

Can a discourse that pays so little attention to race be anti-racist? Historically speaking, critical pedagogy has constructed an illuminating political discussion around concepts like hegemony, domination, empowerment, and solidarity (see Allen, 2002a; McLaren, 1994). These are all concepts that are vital to organizing struggles against white supremacy. However, critical pedagogy itself has not taken the next step and applied these terms to a significant race-radical project. For example, how do domination and hegemony work in a system of global white supremacy? What are the racialized barriers to solidarity both within and between racial groups? How can critical education act as a form of empowerment within and against a white supremacist context? On these key anti-racist questions, critical pedagogy has been amazingly reticent. For critical pedagogy to become anti-racist, it will need to be much more serious about the race-radical philosophies of people of color around the world and move away from the comforts and constrictions of a Marxist Eurocentricity (Allen, 2001; Means, 1983; Larson & Churchill, 1983; West, 1999).

In the 1990s, some critical pedagogists did in fact take on the problem of whiteness (see Giroux, 1997; Kincheloe & Steinberg, 1998; McLaren, 1997). Notably, Giroux (1997) entered into the debate about the possibility for white anti-racist agency, arguing for the transformation of white identity rather than its complete abolition (see Garvey & Ignatiev, 1997). Likewise, Kincheloe and Steinberg (1998) explained that a 'critical white identity' must be offered in order to give whites a more radical alternative to the neo-white supremacist identities that are part and parcel of the post-Civil Rights conservative agenda. Unfortunately, this race-focused period of scholarship ended as quickly as it came and seemed like a tack on to preexisting critical pedagogy. Moreover, these critical pedagogists neither questioned why whiteness had been previously omitted from the discourse nor did they significantly retheorize the base assumptions of critical pedagogy in light of this historical blindness.

There were scholars who did take critical pedagogy to task for its inattention to anti-racism. Ladson-Billings (1997) stated that critical pedagogy has 'failed to address adequately the question of race' and that scholars of color were beginning to challenge the assumption that critical theory/pedagogy has 'universal applicability.' She argued for a 'culturally relevant pedagogy' that is more in tune with the racialized realities of US classrooms. Ellsworth (1989) challenged the liberatory capacity of concepts like empowerment, student voice, and dialogue, referring to them as 'repressive myths.' She based her critique on the failure of critical pedagogy to deal with the concrete specificities of race, class, and gender. For example, white students sometimes use 'student voice' as a way to ignore the claims of students of color, asserting that a critique of whiteness minimizes their voice. But, the criticisms of Ladson-Billings and Ellsworth seem to have gone unheeded and the class-based political foundations of critical pedagogy have remained intact.

The purpose of the remainder of this essay is to rethink critical pedagogy by imagining it from a race-radical perspective that owes its lineage to scholars like Du Bois. I assemble a critical pedagogy that hopes to contribute to both the transformation of white identity and the abolition of white supremacy. I draw from the roots of critical pedagogy, but I also re-racialize those root elements that have unfortunately given support to the often blasé or color-blind racial attitudes of many critical pedagogists. For many, the roots of critical pedagogy mean returning to the work of Paulo Freire, and, most specifically, to *Pedagogy of the Oppressed* (1970/1993), which of course has provided the primary foundation for critical pedagogical praxis. The reader should note that I am not concerned in this essay with discussing the corpus of Freire's work. Instead, I am concerned with incorporating and critiquing the ideas from this one book because they have become central to the curriculum of critical pedagogy. Certainly, *Pedagogy of the Oppressed* has significantly shaped the normative, moral and political philosophy of critical pedagogy, and thus, of critical pedagogists themselves. It is for this reason that this single book warrants such close and careful scrutiny.

Although *Pedagogy of the Oppressed* does not mention racism, it does have very important things to say about the general nature of oppression. Readers tend to overlook Freire's deep and crucial discussion concerning the *oppressor*, opting instead to focus only on what the text says about the *oppressed*. This is probably due to the fact that people have a much easier time thinking of themselves as the oppressed rather than the oppressor (Collins, 2000). Most humans are oppressors because they are members of groups that have *relative* privilege over those of other groups with even less power. At the same time, most humans are oppressed in that there are those of other groups who have more relative privilege. The trick, then, is to dig into the specificities of a particular oppressor–oppressed relationship. For instance, even though elite white capitalists oppress white middle-class men, like myself, we are nevertheless the oppressors of white middle-class women and white working-class people. Moreover, all of us white folks are the oppressors of people of color of all economic classes since race operates as a caste system in the US (Guinier & Torres, 2002) and throughout the world (Kelley, 2000). Wealthy and middle-class people of color are only a step away from being the object of white supremacist activities and are never fully included into their alleged class status (Ladson-Billings, 1997). But rather than siding with those we oppress, our tendency as humans is to do the bidding of those who oppress us. We middle-class whites frame working-class whites as the embodiment of white supremacy when we are really its truer form. And we blame people of color for tainting our 'civilization' when the fact is that we have yet to learn what the word really means. That said, Freire's pedagogical theory of the oppressor must be woven with a critique of whiteness in order to guide whites towards a race-radical white identity.

To start, Freire (1993) asserts, 'It would be a contradiction in terms if the oppressors not only defended but actually implemented a liberating education' (p. 36). This is because those of the primary oppressor group, which in the case of race are whites, are highly invested in a mentality and an ethics geared towards the daily process of dehumanizing people of color. A plan for humanization that is led by whites will always be fraught with problems due to the limited consciousness of whites, even if the plans arise from those who are well meaning. Thus, in a Freirean perspective people of color must provide the major source of knowledge, inspiration, and sacrifice in humanity's collective liberation from white racism.

> Although the situation of oppression is a dehumanized and dehumanizing totality affecting both the oppressors and those whom they oppress, it is the latter who must, from their stifled humanity, wage for both the struggle for a fuller humanity; the oppressor, who is himself dehumanized because he dehumanizes others, is unable to lead this struggle. (Freire, 1993, p. 29)

As people of color around the world engage in the struggle against global white supremacy, they should work to humanize both themselves and whites, *when strategic*. They should avoid the pull to follow the white model of humanity and instead replace oppression with radical love. They are the ones who must be the main instigators in releasing a world incarcerated by white supremacy. This is not a new role for people of color. They have played this role on various levels for centuries, often operating outside the consciousness of even radical whites. As the oppressed within global white supremacy, people of color are the only ones who are able to see, at least with any primacy and certitude, the various ways that whiteness operates (Allen, 2001, 2002b; Mills, 1997). Whites can also learn to see how whiteness functions, but they require the spark of knowledge that comes from people of color. And this racial knowledge is the essential source of liberation for us all.

Freire (1993) reminds us that we should not confuse oppression with dehumanization. They are dialectical siblings, not synonyms. White supremacy gives whites greater protections and material advantages (Lipsitz, 1998; McIntosh, 1997) as we perpetually dehumanize others and ourselves through white territorial practices (Allen, 2002b). In stark contrast, people of color must spend a significant part of their lives trying to survive and resist white supremacy. This is what it means to live as the oppressed. Now, one could argue that anti-racist whites experience the wrath of white dominance as well. The difference, however, is that this wrath comes as a choice that the white person makes. Due to white privilege, the white person could opt to fall back into the graces of the white community if he so wished.

However, people of color experience the wrath of whiteness regardless of whether they choose to be vocal about white racism or not, although being a vocal critic is much more likely to make one a target of severe retaliation than if one remains silent or joins the oppressor.

Whites seem almost incapable of trusting the leadership of people of color. Even seemingly radical white anti-racist movements are often unable to break free of white tendencies. Take for instance the neo-abolitionist movement spearheaded by the journal *Race Traitor*. Its editors, John Garvey and Noel Ignatiev (1997), have declared that whites should commit 'treason to whiteness' as a way of showing their 'loyalty to humanity.' They call upon whites to practice anti-white behaviors that will disrupt the ability to predict the certainty of a white person's politics, thus causing white kinship bonds—which, as the norm, often go unrecognized—to ultimately splinter and disintegrate. They also ask whites to reject being called 'white' as part of the process. But, however well intentioned, theirs is a white-led plan of 'opting out' of whiteness, which, despite the sentiments contained in their slogans, says little about how to awaken whites to love and respect people of color. Becoming a white anti-racist is a long, involved process that requires a critical acceptance of one's racial identity, not a denial of it (Leonardo, 2002; Thompson, 2001). The race traitor strategy also does little to make whites aware of our tendency to take over social movements. Ultimately, the *Race Traitor* strategy lacks a theory of cross-race relations.

Becoming more fully human requires love for the oppressed (Freire, 1993), and whites do not possess it. Our current condition is such that we whites do not have what it takes to facilitate projects of humanization because we are more likely to have disdain or pity, certainly not love, for people of color. Whites operate from a neurotic mentality and act individually and collectively to silence and subvert the counternarratives of people of color. We can only be awakened and released from our neurosis to the extent that some person of color somewhere will take the time to help us do so, whether directly or indirectly. One such person of color is James Baldwin, a famous African American writer and scholar. Baldwin (2000) captures the predicament of whites when he says:

> people who imagine that history flatters them (as it does, indeed, since they wrote it) are impaled on their history like a butterfly on a pin and become incapable of seeing or changing themselves, or the world. (p. 321)

Instead of choosing love, whites have chosen to fear people of color (Wah, 1994). We have chosen to write histories that see whites as the creators of civilization and people of color as a drag on, if not a threat to, it (Mills, 1997). And, though we pretend that we do not know what we have done, we know the basic truth all too well since, after all, the greatest fear we whites have of people of color is that they will do to us what we have done to them (Baldwin, 2000). It is this fear that we have created for ourselves out of our phobic reluctance to face the real situation of our own role in history. In effect, we are Baldwin's metaphorical butterfly, having inserted the pin ourselves.

Freire (1993) contends that oppressors have the dehumanizing characteristic of making the world into a place that perpetuates their own false consciousness and confuses the image of 'human' with their own. In more race-focused terms, whites dehumanize all people by turning the world into a place for the sustainment of white subjectivity (McLaren, Leonardo & Allen, 2000; Mills, 1997). Within global white supremacy, the definition of 'humanity' takes on a white face, a white gate, a white sound, and a white mentality. 'White,' 'normal,' and 'human' converge into a disturbing synonymous relationship that serves to mystify the actual particularities of white existence and white dysfunction. As Freire (1993) says,

> Humanity is a 'thing,' and they possess it as an exclusive right, as inherited property. To the oppressor consciousness, the humanization of the 'others,' of the people, appears not as the pursuit of full humanity, but as subversion. (p. 41)

Whites spend a lot of energy defending the myth that whites are the model humans—kind, caring, and benevolent—even though many people of color do not see whites this way (Gallagher, 1997). Whites dedicate much of their daily activity to figuring out how to manage their interactions with people of color in order to maintain whiteness as both the image of humanity and a thing to be inherited (Harris, 1995). We accomplish this by normalizing social space in a way that perpetuates white power and privilege while also making it look like this is not what is happening.

Freire (1993) seems to imagine the oppressor's state of mind as a form of mental dysfunction that is required for the oppressor to be seen as sane by others in the oppressor group. Freire (1993) informs us of this point when he says, 'One of the characteristics of the oppressor consciousness and its necrophilic view of the world is thus sadism' (p. 41). The oppressor turns others into inanimate objects, rendering their symbolic death as human subjects and producers of emancipatory knowledge. Given that whites do not value people of color as considerers of the world, it is no wonder that whites have little or no awareness that people of color, those 'inanimate objects' of the white supremacist mind, actually do think about and scrutinize white people (hooks, 1992). When people of color point out to whites that our white skin gives us special privileges (see McIntosh, 1997), whites act as though this were an attack on humanity itself.

Furthermore, many whites now think of themselves as the oppressed group (Gallagher, 1997). In fact, conservative whites have twisted the racial discourse in their favor such that the word 'racist' can now be used to describe anti-racist people who publicly contest white racism. But, since society is premised on white supremacy, conservative whites have a lot of public support for such a move. In the post-Civil Rights Era, whites keep racial dialogue at the level of colorblindness, unless, of course, there is an opening to argue that affirmative action discriminates against whites. As we have seen recently in California, both liberal and conservative whites have unified in powerful ways against people of color through a series of voter propositions driven by white identity politics (McLaren, Leonardo & Allen, 2000; Lipsitz, 1998). As Freire (1993) reminds us, the unity of the oppressors, despite claims of their staunch individualism, is swift, vicious, and, above all else, cohesive when they are threatened by what they perceive to be an outside force. Recent political events in California suggest that whites display a strong sense of racial unity when feeling politically and economically threatened by Latinos and African Americans (Gallagher, 1997).

Another trait is that oppressors blame victims for their own victimization (Freire, 1993). This holds especially true for whites. Whites seem to know very little about the world that we ourselves have created (Mills, 1997). Yet, despite our efforts to hide from our history, we know enough to sense that there is something wrong with the world and that we are somehow responsible. As James Baldwin (2000) contends,

> They are dimly, or vividly, aware that the history they have fed themselves
> is mainly a lie, but they do not know how to release themselves from it,
> and they suffer enormously from the resulting personal incoherence. (p. 321)

The personal incoherence that whites experience, multiplied a million times over, creates a structural effect as it scripts white interactions with other races. We can see evidence of this dysfunctional structure when whites blame people of color for their own victimization under white supremacy. Throughout modern history, whites have projected all sorts of unfounded negative attributes onto people of color, and all sorts of unfounded positive attributes onto whites, as a way of diverting attention from white culpability and white terrorism. Whites have depicted people of color as non-human, savage, child-like, dangerous, genetically inferior, ugly, stupid, lazy, depraved, deprived, merely different, totally dominated, and angry. These terms cast people of color as outsiders to civilization, as violators of an alleged social contract who must be dragged out into the light of white rationality (Kincheloe & Steinberg, 1998; Mills, 1997). Rarely, however, do whites ever depict people of color as the ingenious survivors of 500 years of white supremacy and, as a result, the upholders of true humanity. Instead, whites—as oppressors will do—construct powerful myths that cast people of color as fundamentally inept participants in an allegedly just, fair, and meritocratic society based on individual competition and reward. These myths and the social experience they create are so overwhelming that people of color often come to believe in the myth of their own inferiority.

We whites project our own guilt and repressed selves onto people of color. We treat them as racialized objects because they remind us of our complicity with the immorality and dehumanization of white supremacy. To treat them as subjects means that whites would have to face the horror within themselves rather than projecting it onto the other. And, whites are reminded of this horror through the sensations of guilt that they experience when they look into a Black person's face, as if it is a 'most disagreeable mirror' (Baldwin, 2000). Freire (1993) contends that oppressors often resort to resolving their guilt through acts of generosity, which only perpetuate an oppressive condition. Generosity is a kind of alibi in that it makes the oppressor look like a caring person at the same time it absolves the oppressor from being responsible for eliminating structural oppression. White guilt is rarely dealt with in truly transformative ways (Kincheloe & Steinberg, 1998) that emphasize cross-racial solidarity against white supremacy. For example, public schooling allows whites to feel generous. We should not be surprised that white educators working in urban communities act out roles as 'white knights,' whose mission is to rescue people of color from oppression (McIntyre, 1997; Titone, 1998). White guilt and misguided generosity only serve to create an environment where people of color must pledge allegiance to the meritocracy myth. White educators and administrators do very little to form cross-racial solidarity against the larger problem of white supremacy.

Oppressors use divide and conquer strategies to weaken the collective resolve of the oppressed (Freire, 1993). Whites are especially adept at dividing people of color. Internalized racism is a tool that whites deploy to keep those within a racial group at odds with each other and distracted from organizing against white supremacy. Internalized racism occurs when people of color internalize the white model of humanity and the stereotypes of their own group (Tatum, 1997). It is a condition that causes people of color to aspire to whiteness, measure success and human worth relative to white standards, and put down the capabilities of their own race (Baldwin, 2000; Fanon, 1967; Fordham, 1988). As the primary gatekeepers of society, whites instigate this situation by giving more privilege to those people of color who assimilate to the white model—only as long as they serve the larger political interests of whites (Bell, 1992). Conversely, whites reject people of color who openly question white privilege. A critical pedagogy that directly intervenes in internalized racism should empower students of color to see the specific ways that whiteness causes them to think less of their individual and collective selves. Also, it should develop within whites a desire to examine how we perpetuate internalized racism through both our privileging of more assimilated people of color and our devaluation of internalized racism as a critical area of study.

Inter-ethnic racism is another divide and conquer strategy. It constructs barriers between non-white racial groups, pitting Asians against Blacks, Chicanos against Native Americans, and so on. Leonardo (2002) contends that whereas whites benefit from racism in absolute ways, racial privilege between communities of color should be seen more as relative, depending on where a minority group is located in the racial hierarchy. Tensions are created when whites elevate some non-white groups to a 'model minority' or 'honorary white' status so as to create a middle-level buffer against the race-radical politics of those at the bottom of the racial order (Tuan, 1998; Wu, 2002). A colorscale from light to dark assigns social status and group standing; those who are lighter receive more relative privilege (both from whites and other people of color) than do those who are darker (Hunter, 1998; Wade, 1993). Despite being oppressed themselves, those in the buffer groups cooperate with the exclusion and denigration of those who are darker-skinned and imagined as less human (Gans, 1999; Helg, 1990; Muhammad, 1995). Those in the buffer groups are fearful of groups located at the bottom and chastise them for not living up to a white measuring stick. In the US, inter-ethnic racism contributes to a racial hierarchy where darker-skinned caste groups like African Americans, Native Americans, and Filipinos are at the bottom (Bonilla-Silva & Glover, 2002).

The combination of white, buffer, and caste groups within a system of pigmento-cracy exists not just in the US but in many regions around the world (Dolby, 2001; Prashad, 2000; Wade, 1993). For example, race is considered a relatively unimportant topic of study in Latin America, even though pigmentocracy thoroughly structures everyday life (Skidmore, 1990). The buffer group in many Latin American nations is referred to as *mestizos*, or those of mixed European, Indian, and African ancestry (Anzaldúa, 1999). *Mestizos* collaborate with whites through both overt racism and colorblind ideologies to exclude Indians and Blacks from higher status levels. In fact, one of the ways in which lower strata (i.e., darker-skinned people of Indigenous and African descent) can become socially mobile is to marry someone who is white, or at least whiter (Guinier & Torres, 2002; Wade, 1993). Historically, colonizers from Iberia believed that they could improve the alleged inferior genetic stock of Indians and Africans by mating them with whites. The aesthetic eugenics of whitening sought to render away darker traits. It produced the *mestizo* group, and it is a way of life that continues to this day. Whiteness in Latin America is a desired form of social capital that is protected and aspired to, even by many of those it oppresses. *Mestizos*, as the buffer group, are invested in a solidification of the racial order and resist siding politically with darker groups in challenging the *mestizaje* myth about the absence of structural racism.

With all of this complexity and struggle among people of color, it is very difficult to develop a cross-racial collectivity. Public schools contribute to this dilemma in that they function to silence and separate people of color by not identifying inter-ethnic racism as an obstacle to democracy. This lack of attention allows whites to maintain the status quo as people of color continue to push each other further down. Critical pedagogy must deal with inter-ethnic racism if it is to have any chance of playing a role in uniting people of color against white supremacy. It must work to facilitate the desires of people of color to name those groups who have more power and privilege and describe how members of those groups perpetuate white privilege vis-à-vis inter-ethnic racism. Conversely, people of color who have power over other groups of color must be willing to both strategically consider themselves as the relational oppressor within a racial order of varied power levels and closely reflect upon the claims of those who are lower in status (Hurtado, 1996; Prashad, 2000). And whites need to learn how we create the context for inter-ethnic racism by how we assign more value to those who we believe are more like us. Whites must learn the deeper structural and political make-up of the racial order that we have created.

Let us now shift from the condition of the white oppressor to the necessary pedagogical counter-conditions for transforming him. Freire is hopeful that the oppressor can be converted, but he is not naïve about the intense challenge. As he states, 'Conversion to the people requires a profound rebirth' (Freire, 1993, p. 43). The rebirth of the white person to solidarity with people of color is a long and hard road, but it is certainly possible.

The first step in this process is that the white person needs to accept and admit that he is the oppressor, that is, he is necessarily racist as a consequence of his structural and epistemological standing as a member of the white race (Tatum,

1997). Freire (1993) contends that oppressors 'do not wish to consider themselves as an oppressive class' (p. 124). Though a member of the oppressor group, the typical white person would hate to think of himself as a racist, let alone as a white supremacist. Yet, this is the case. Whiteness functions as a system that bestows unearned power and privilege onto those who approximate as white (Allen, 2002b; McIntyre, 1997). White privilege is structural and cannot be erased unless the structure that creates it is erased. There is no neutral position to take; one either decides to work against it or to go along for the ride (Tatum, 1997). All whites gain power, status, and privilege from this system, even if we are actively anti-racist. The best a white person can be is a white anti-racist racist. As white anti-racist racists, reborn whites work against white supremacy by working with race-radical people of color and remembering that we will always have blindspots to our own whiteness.

White people who take the first step of moving past denial by admitting complicity with white supremacy need to do more, however, than merely offer public admissions. Reborn whites must also become comfortable with this fact, much like the alcoholic who has developed a new sense of self around his admittance of being an alcoholic. The white person needs to unlearn a lifetime of problematic white subjectivity, ideology, and behavior. He needs to learn how to see the world through new eyes that reveal the complexities and problematics of whiteness.

Rather than gauging rebirth on some abstract, absolute scale of anti-racist consciousness, reborn whites are to be judged on the level of anti-racist solidarity that we achieve with race-radical people of color. As Freire (1993) reminds us, 'Discovering himself to be an oppressor may cause considerable anguish, but it does not necessarily lead to solidarity with the oppressed' (p. 31). In other words, whites can admit to complicity with white racism and learn to articulate anti-racist concepts, yet continue to be oppressors. Oppressors bring with them into the process of rebirth the 'marks of their origins,' which include distorted negative beliefs about the capabilities of the oppressed and false positive beliefs about the superiority of the oppressor (Freire, 1993). In order for we whites to be truly in solidarity with race-radical people of color, it is essential that we unlearn the marks of our origins, which include our belief in the myths of colorblindness, racial meritocracy, and white superiority, to name a few.

Beyond cognitive changes, reborn whites must situate ourselves in opposition to whiteness and risk our standing in the white community by becoming traitors to the normative functioning of our group. As we attempt to do so, we must also remember that we cannot rely solely upon our own epistemologies for the ultimate verification of the worth of our actions (Guinier & Torres, 2002). Rather than asserting only our own politics, we must work to be welcomed to the side of people of color, whether as colleagues working for change in an institutional setting or as comrades in a social movement.

> Solidarity requires that one enter into the situation of those with whom one is solidary; it is a radical posture. If what characterizes the oppressed is their subordination to the consciousness of the master, as Hegel

affirms, true solidarity with the oppressed means fighting at their side to transform the objective reality which has made them these 'beings for another'. (Freire, 1993, p. 31)

In other words, whites who are in solidarity with people of color need to appropriate our white power and privilege as a way of subverting that same power and privilege. We must push to make ourselves into beings for the struggle against white supremacy, so as to demonstrate to others our love for humanity.

No matter how radical whites may claim to be, we are nevertheless complicitous with white supremacy if race-radical people of color do not condone our efforts.

A real humanist can be identified more by his trust in the people, which engages him in their struggle, than by a thousand actions in their favor without that trust. (Freire, 1993, p. 42)

Whites must be able to engage in strategic and solidarity discussions with people of color about the dismantling of white supremacy in order to avoid acting without their trust. We who enter into communion with race-radical people of color need to continue to grow in our understanding of whiteness as a system and our own white identity development. There may be times in the process of rebirth when whites need to form discursive circles with other whites for 'white only' discussions about our complicity with white racism (Tatum, 1997), and there is currently a growing movement of all-white groups with this focus. However, these groups are of little use if the individuals in them are not also close and active comrades of people of color because, ultimately, whites need their solidarity. Whites have the least to lose in this struggle, so we should also be the least in charge.

In educational institutions, from kindergartens to doctoral programs, whiteness is pervasive and constitutive. For instance, the typical curriculum is tied up in the production, valuation, and distribution of structural, or scientific, knowledge in ways that privilege whiteness. Instead of fully rejecting scientific knowledge, as do many reactionary postmodernists, Freire (1993) sees critical possibilities for those forms of scientific knowledge that depict the meanings and consequences of structural realities within oppressive regimes. He even suggests that the notion of authority is an acceptable component of revolutionary pedagogy, if couched in the proper political context.

In this process [of dialogue], arguments based on 'authority' are no longer valid; in order to function, authority must be *on the side of* freedom, not *against it*. Here, no one teaches another, nor is anyone self-taught. (Freire, 1993, p. 61)

Scientific knowledge that is 'on the side of freedom' has not been the legacy of white-dominated discourses in the social sciences (Harding, 1991). Rather, white scholars, researchers, and educators have played, and continue to play, a major role in reproducing whiteness through the dismissal and devaluation of knowledge that places a critique of white supremacy at the center of analysis (Deloria, 1999; Harding, 1991; Scheurich & Young, 1997).

For whites to be transformed, we need to be engaged in a curriculum that decenters whiteness as a favored epistemological vantage point (Hunter & Nettles, 1999). Unbeknownst to most white academics, scientific endeavors that seek to intervene in white supremacy can have, and have had, the effect of creating racial unification, promoting psychological well-being, and organizing collective action (Guinier & Torres, 2002). The epistemological, ontological, and axiological concerns of people of color, as they relate to life within white supremacy, must move from the margins and take center stage (Delgado Bernal, 1998; Scheurich & Young, 1997). And we should continue to structure these more race-radical concerns into critical theoretical and analytical paradigms that reflect larger patterns of experience and reality (Solorzano & Yosso, 2002) within global white supremacy.

For example, critical race theory and critical whiteness studies are paradigms that have been developed primarily by people of color. Unlike critical pedagogy, they staunchly take the side of liberation from white supremacy (Bell, 1992). When engaging in anti-racist education, critical pedagogists need to employ discourses such as these as strategic forms of scientific authority, as no one is 'self-taught' when it comes to race. Being self-taught leads to individualism and a lack of a structural analysis. Without a guiding structural analysis, a collective race-radical politics is unlikely to emerge. Conversely, discourses that propagate white mythologies through avoidance of or antagonism against race-radical theory are not on the side of liberation from white supremacy, and should be vigorously challenged. Research that transforms the empirical knowledge of people of color into a structural understanding of whiteness needs to be developed, encouraged, and funded, as well as utilized in the classroom as curricular content and critical pedagogical praxis.

Another way that whiteness manifests itself in schools is through its influence on the dialogical process. In courses that present a critique of whiteness, we whites tend to get defensive about so much focus on the oppressiveness of our group (Hunter & Nettles, 1999; McIntyre, 2002; Sleeter, 1993). But the ire of the oppressor should not be mistaken for the determination of the oppressed. Critical dialogue between members of oppressor and oppressed groups does not occur on equal grounds. Oppression creates a communicative illusion where it appears as though the oppressor is using common sense and the oppressed is irrational. To maintain this illusion, oppressors will do whatever it takes to prevent the oppressed from naming their oppression. Freire (1993) says that:

> dialogue cannot occur between those who want to name the world and those who do not wish this naming—between those who deny others the right to speak their word and those whose right to speak has been denied them. (p. 69)

Classrooms are very rarely a place where students of color can name whiteness and whites, in turn, learn to be accountable for their complicity with racial dehumanization. Critical dialogues on internalized and inter-ethnic racism are at least as rare, if not more so. White educators and students act—sometimes with the assistance of people of color—to ensure that such critical dialogues are quashed.

But the situation is not hopeless. Those in the oppressor position can change if they are willing to enter into a cross-racial dialogue as a humble learner courageously seeking to be humanized.

> Dialogue, as the encounter of those addressed to the common task of learning and acting, is broken if the parties (or one of them) lack humility. How can I dialogue if I always project ignorance onto others and never perceive my own? (Freire, 1993, p. 71)

Freire is primarily referring to those of the oppressor group. They need to actually believe that the oppressed have a more intimate understanding of the situation. It follows that humanizing dialogue between whites and people of color cannot occur without the humility of whites. Whites who are uncomfortable with race-radical people of color naming and critiquing whiteness have not yet been reborn into solidarity. In the intercultural communication process between whites and people of color, we whites tend to have more of a problem hearing than speaking. Our possessive investment in whiteness and our programmed surveillance of daily white privileges prevent us from really hearing people of color. In fact, whites who have yet to be reborn tend to have little trouble telling people of color how they are wrong about the existence of white privilege.

Finally, administrators and educators need to understand that acts that are meant to stop whites from perpetuating white supremacy are not the same as acts perpetrated by whites in the name of furthering white supremacy. Freire (1993) is quite insightful when he says that:

> the restraints imposed by the former oppressed on their oppressors, so that the latter cannot reassume their former position, do not constitute *oppression*. An act is oppressive only when it prevents people from being more fully human. Accordingly, these necessary restraints do not *in themselves* signify that yesterday's oppressed have become today's oppressors. (pp. 38–39)

It seems as though far too many educators who think of themselves as critical have forgotten this very radical element of critical pedagogy. They have succumbed to a type of postmodernism of voice, as though the mere sharing of experiences will ultimately lead to self-motivated transformation. However, the need for change is immediate and people of color do not have time to wait for whites to take some slow, bourgeois journey of white self-discovery (Kincheloe & Steinberg, 1998). Through text and dialogue, critical educators need to create an environment of dissonance that brings white students to a point of identity crisis. In order for the crisis to result in a race-radical white identity, white students must be shown other ways of being white (see Helms, 1990).

In closing, critical pedagogy has offered important and radical alternatives to functionalist teaching. Critical pedagogy has struggled to crack the normalcy of educational institutions while refusing to capitulate to capitalist hegemony. It has called attention to the essential political nature of curriculum and instruction. And, all of these efforts have made contributions to anti-racist activities. However, the contribution could have been much more significant had critical pedagogy not relegated race to the back of the bus. The problem of race relations has been wrongly theorized as a mere output of capitalistic desires and tendencies. The investment that whites have in the white polity, and its supporting and determining social structure, has been understated and overlooked (Bonilla-Silva, 1996). What critical pedagogy needs is an internal revolution that embraces the old beliefs in love, humanization, and solidarity, but leaves behind the unwillingness to significantly address race.

It was never appropriate to theorize critical pedagogy separate from a thorough, if not predominant, critique of white supremacy. Paulo Freire, by his own admission, was greatly influenced by Frantz Fanon (Freire, 1994), for whom white supremacy was key to understanding colonization (Fanon, 1967). But, Freire also repeatedly indicated that he was greatly influenced by Gilberto Freyre, a famous white Brazilian sociologist who was educated in the US. Gilberto Freyre promoted the notion of Brazil as a 'racial utopia,' which has since enabled white Brazilians to deny the existence of white domination in their own country (Skidmore, 1990). It is obvious that Freire, as well as other early critical pedagogists, chose to selectively hear what race-radical scholars, such as W. E. B. Du Bois and Frantz Fanon, were saying, as if racial politics were not a significant story. In the process, many moments of possible racial solidarity have been lost. Hopefully, critical pedagogy can now rectify this error and, thus, transform its epistemological exclusion of those at the bottom of the racial order. From here, the first step is to admit that white identity politics has structured critical pedagogy from its inception, regardless of its anti-colonial intentions. Its rebirth can only be had through a new focus on white supremacy, not just within society and schooling, but also within critical pedagogy itself.

Acknowledgements

I would like to thank Professor Zeus Leonardo for his insightful suggestions.

References

Allen, R. L. (2001) The Globalization of White Supremacy: Toward a critical discourse on the racialization of the world, *Educational Theory*, 51:4, pp. 467–485.

Allen, R. L. (2002a) Wake up, Neo: White consciousness, hegemony, and identity in *The Matrix*, in: J. Slater, S. Fein & C. Rossatto (eds), *The Freirean Legacy* (New York, Peter Lang Publishers).

Allen, R. L. (2002b) Whiteness as Territoriality: An analysis of white identity politics in society, education, and theory (unpublished diss., University of California, LA).

Anzaldúa, G. (1999) *Borderlands/La Frontera*, 2nd edn (San Francisco, Aunt Lute Books).

Baldwin, J. (2000) White Man's Guilt, in: D. Roediger (ed.), *Black on White: Black writers on what it means to be white* (New York, Schocken Books).

Bell, D. (1992) *Faces at the Bottom of the Well: The permanence of racism* (New York, Basic Books).

Bonilla-Silva, E. & Glover, K. (2002) 'We are all Americans': The Latin Americanization of race relations in the U.S. (paper presented at the annual meeting of the American Sociological Association, Chicago, IL).

Collins, P. H. (2000) *Black Feminist Thought*, 2nd edn (New York, Routledge).

Delgado Bernal, D. (1998) Using a Chicana Feminist Epistemology in Educational Research, *Harvard Educational Review*, 68:4, pp. 555–577.

Deloria, V. (1999) If You Think About It, You Will See That It Is True, in: B. Deloria, K. Foehner & S. Scinta (eds), *Spirit & Reason: The Vine Deloria, Jr. Reader* (Golden, CO, Fulcrum Publishing).

Dolby, N. (2001) *Constructing Race: Youth, identity, and popular culture in South Africa* (Albany, SUNY Press).

Du Bois, W. E. B. (1995/1933) Marxism and the Negro Problem, in: D. L. Lewis (ed.), *W. E. B. Du Bois: A reader* (New York, Henry Holt and Company, Inc).

Du Bois, W. E. B. (1935) *Black Reconstruction in America* (New York, Simon & Schuster).

Ellsworth, E. (1989) Why Doesn't This Feel Empowering? Working through the repressive myths of critical pedagogy, *Harvard Educational Review*, 59:3, pp. 297–324.

Fanon, F. (1967) *Black Skin, White Masks*, trans. C. L. Markmann (New York, Grove Press).

Fordham, S. (1988) Racelessness as a Factor in Black Students' School Success: Pragmatic strategy or pyrrhic victory? *Harvard Educational Review*, 58:1, pp. 54–84.

Freire, P. (1993) *Pedagogy of the Oppressed*, trans. M. B. Ramos (New York, Continuum).

Freire, P. (1994) *Pedagogy of Hope: Reliving Pedagogy of the Oppressed*, trans. R. R. Barr (New York, Continuum).

Gallagher, C. (1997) White Racial Formation: Into the twenty-first century, in: R. Delgado & J. Stefancic (eds), *Critical White Studies: Looking behind the mirror* (Philadelphia, Temple University Press).

Gans, H. (1999) The Possibility of a New Racial Hierarchy in the Twenty-first Century United States, in: M. Lamont (ed.), *The Cultural Territories of Race: Black and white boundaries* (Chicago, University of Chicago Press).

Garvey, J. & Ignatiev, N. (1997) Toward a New Abolitionism: A *Race Traitor* manifesto, in: M. Hill (ed.), *Whiteness: A critical reader* (New York, New York University Press).

Giroux, H. (1997) White Squall: Resistance and the pedagogy of whiteness, *Cultural Studies*, 11:3, pp. 376–389.

Guinier, L. & Torres, G. (2002) *The Miner's Canary: Enlisting race, resisting power, transforming democracy* (Cambridge, Harvard University Press).

Harding, S. (1991) *Whose Science? Whose Knowledge?: Thinking from women's lives* (Ithaca, NY, Cornell University Press).

Harris, C. (1995) Whiteness as Property, in: K. Crenshaw, N. Gotanda, G. Pellar & K. Thomas (eds), *Critical Race Theory: The key writings that formed the movement* (New York, The New Press).

Helg, A. (1990) Race in Argentina and Cuba, 1880–1930, in: R. Graham (ed.), *The Idea of Race in Latin America, 1870–1940* (Austin, University of Texas Press).

Helms, J. (1990) *Black and White Racial Identity: Theory, research, and practice* (Westport, CT, Greenwood).

Hooks, B. (1992) *Black Looks: Race and representation* (Boston, South End Press).

Hunter, M. (1998) Colorstruck: Skin color stratification in the lives of African American women, *Sociological Inquiry*, 68, pp. 517–535.

Hunter, M. & Nettles, K. (1999) 'What About the White Women?': Racial politics in a women's studies classroom, *Teaching Sociology*, 27, pp. 385–397.

Hurtado, A. (1996) *The Color of Privilege: Three blasphemies on race and feminism* (Ann Arbor, University of Michigan Press).

Kelley, R. (2000) 'But a Local Phase of a World Problem': Black history's global vision, 1883–1950, *Journal of American History*, 86:3, pp. 1045–1077.

Kincheloe, J. & Steinberg, S. (1998) Addressing the Crisis of Whiteness: Reconfiguring white identity in a pedagogy of whiteness, in: J. Kincheloe, S. Steinberg, N. Rodriguez & R. Chennault (eds), *White Reign: Deploying whiteness in America* (New York, St Martin's Press).

Ladson-Billings, G. (1997) I Know Why This Doesn't Feel Empowering: A critical race analysis of critical pedagogy, in: P. Freire (ed.), *Mentoring the Mentor: A critical dialogue with Paulo Freire* (New York, Peter Lang).

Larson, D. L. & Churchill, W. (1983) The Same Old Song in Sad Refrain, in: W. Churchill (ed.), *Marxism and Native Americans* (Boston, South End Press).

Leonardo, Z. (2002) The Souls of White Folk: Critical pedagogy, whiteness studies, and globalization discourse, *Race, Ethnicity & Education*, 5:1, pp. 29–50.

Lipsitz, G. (1998) *The Possessive Investment in Whiteness: How white people profit from identity politics* (Philadelphia, Temple University Press).

McIntosh, P. (1997) White Privilege and Male Privilege: A personal account of coming to see correspondences through work in women's studies, in: R. Delgado & J. Stefancic (eds), *Critical White Studies: Looking behind the mirror* (Philadelphia, Temple University Press).

McIntyre, A. (1997) *Making Meaning of Whiteness: Exploring racial identity with white teachers* (Albany, State University of New York Press).

McIntyre, A. (2002) Exploring Whiteness and Multicultural Education with Prospective Teachers, *Curriculum Inquiry*, 32:1, pp. 31–49.

McLaren, P. (1994) *Life in Schools: An introduction to critical pedagogy in the foundations of education*, 2nd edn (White Plains, NY, Longman).

McLaren, P. (1997) *Revolutionary Multiculturalism: Pedagogies of dissent for the new millennium* (Boulder, CO, Westview Press).

McLaren, P., Leonardo, Z. & Allen, R. L. (2000) Epistemologies of Whiteness: Transforming and transgressing pedagogic knowledge, in: R. Mahalingham & C. McCarthy (eds), *Multicultural Curriculum: New directions for social theory, practice, and policy* (New York, Routledge).

Means, R. (1983) The Same Old Song, in: W. Churchill (ed.), *Marxism and Native Americans* (Boston, South End Press).

Mills, C. (1997) *The Racial Contract* (Ithaca, NY, Cornell University Press).

Muhammad, J. (1995) Mexico and Central America: Mexico, in: Minority Rights Group (ed.), *No Longer Visible: Afro-Latin Americans today* (London, Minority Rights Publications).

Prashad, V. (2000) *The Karma of Brown Folk* (Minneapolis, University of Minnesota Press).

Scheurich, J. & Young, M. (1997) Coloring Epistemologies: Are our research epistemologies racially biased?, *Educational Researcher*, 26:4, pp. 4–16.

Skidmore, T. (1990) Racial Ideas and Social Policy in Brazil, 1870–1940, in: R. Graham (ed.), *The Idea of Race in Latin America, 1870–1940* (Austin, University of Texas Press).

Sleeter, C. (1993) How White Teachers Construct Race, in: C. McCarthy & W. Crichlow (eds), *Race, Identity, and Representation in Education* (New York, Routledge).

Solorzano, D. & Yosso, T. (2002) Critical Race Methodology: Counter-storytelling as an analytical framework for education, *Qualitative Inquiry*, 8:1, pp. 23–44.

Tatum, B. D. (1997) *'Why Are All the Black Kids Sitting Together in the Cafeteria?' And Other Conversations About Race* (New York, Basic Books).

Tuan, M. (1998) *Forever Foreigners or Honorary Whites?* (New Brunswick, NJ, Rutgers University Press).

Thompson, B. (2001) *A Promise and a Way of Life: White antiracist activism* (Minneapolis, University of Minnesota Press).

Titone, C. (1998) Educating the White Teacher as Ally, in: J. Kincheloe, S. Steinberg, N. Rodriguez & R. Chennault (eds), *White Reign: Deploying whiteness in America* (New York, St Martin's Press).

Wade, P. (1993) *Blackness and Race Mixture* (Baltimore, Johns Hopkins Press).

Wah, L. M. (producer/director) (1994) *The Color of Fear* (Video) (Oakland, CA, Stir-Fry Productions).

West, C. (1999) Race and Social Theory, in: C. West (ed.), *The Cornel West Reader* (New York, Basic Books).

Wu, F. (2002) *Yellow: Race in America Beyond Black and White* (New York, Basic Books).

3

Maintaining Social Justice Hopes within Academic Realities: A Freirean approach to critical race/LatCrit pedagogy

DANIEL G. SOLÓRZANO & TARA J. YOSSO
University of California, Los Angeles; University of California, Santa Barbara

Introduction

Scholars have commented that by the time of his death in 1997, Paulo Freire had moved well beyond his early work in *Pedagogy of the Oppressed* (1970b). We understand that position, but we also argue that Freire's early work (1970a) continues to provide a critical framework for educators struggling for social justice (see hooks, 1994). Freire's early work provides a powerful tool because of its parsimony and simplicity, and because it is 'not less complex ... but simply more accessible' (hooks, 1989, p. 39). In this essay, we merge the critical pedagogical work of Freire with the critical race and LatCrit frameworks.

Critical Race Theory and Critical Race Pedagogy

How can we better understand the role of critical pedagogy in higher education? One theoretical framework that can be used to help answer this question is critical race theory. Critical race theory draws from and extends a broad literature base that is often termed critical theory. In paraphrasing Brian Fay (1987), William Tierney (1993) has defined critical theory as 'an attempt to understand the oppressive aspects of society in order to generate societal and individual transformation' (p. 4). Indeed, for our purpose here, critical race theory is a framework or set of basic perspectives, methods, and pedagogy that seeks to identify, analyze, and transform those structural and cultural aspects of society that maintain subordinate and dominant racial positions in and out of the classroom (see Matsuda *et al.*, 1993; Tierney, 1993).

Mari Matsuda (1991) views critical race theory as

> the work of progressive legal scholars of color who are attempting to develop a jurisprudence that accounts for the role of racism in American law and that works toward the elimination of racism as part of a larger goal of eliminating all forms of subordination. (p. 1331)

Therefore, the overall goal of a critical race pedagogy in higher education is to develop a pedagogical strategy that accounts for the central role of race and racism in higher education, and works toward the elimination of racism as part of a larger goal of opposing or eliminating other forms of subordination such as gender, class, and sexual orientation in and out of the classroom.

Critical race pedagogy in education has at least five elements that form the basic perspectives, research methods, and pedagogy (see Solórzano, 1997, 1998). They are: (1) the centrality and intersectionality of race and racism; (2) the challenge to dominant ideology; (3) the commitment to social justice; (4) the importance of experiential knowledge; and (5) the use of interdisciplinary perspectives.[1]

1. The Centrality of Race and Racism and their Intersectionality with Other Forms of Subordination

A critical race pedagogy starts from the premise that race and racism are endemic, permanent, and in the words of Margaret Russell (1992), 'a central rather than marginal factor in defining and explaining individual experiences of the law' (pp. 762–763). Although race and racism are at the center of a critical race analysis, we also view them at their intersection with other forms of subordination such as gender and class discrimination (see Crenshaw, 1989, 1993). As Robin Barnes (1990) has stated, 'Critical Race scholars have refused to ignore the differences between race and class as basis of oppression ... Critical Race scholars know that class analysis alone cannot account for racial oppression' (p. 1868). We argue further that class and racial oppression cannot account for gender oppression. This intersection of race, gender, and class is where one can find some answers to the theoretical, conceptual, methodological, and pedagogical questions related to the experiences of People of Color.[2] We also concur with John Calmore (1997) in that what is noticeably missing from the discussion of race is a substantive discussion of racism. Indeed, in moving beyond a discussion of race, we must name, define, and focus on racism. For our purpose here, we use Manning Marable (1992) to define racism as 'the system of ignorance, exploitation, and power used to oppress African Americans, Latinos, Asians, Pacific Americans, American Indians and other people on the basis of ethnicity, culture, mannerisms, and color' (p. 5). Marable's definition of racism is important because it shifts the discussion of race and racism from a Black/White discourse to one that includes multiple faces, voices, and experiences.

2. The Challenge to Dominant Ideology

A critical race pedagogy challenges the traditional claims that the educational system and its institutions make toward objectivity, meritocracy, color-blindness, race neutrality, and equal opportunity. Critical race educators argue that these traditional claims act as a camouflage for the self-interest, power, and privilege of dominant groups in U.S. society (Calmore, 1992; Solórzano, 1997). In addition to challenging the way we examine race and racism, Kimberlé Crenshaw and her colleagues have argued that critical race theory also tries 'to piece together an intellectual identity and a political practice that would take the form both of a left intervention into race discourse and a race intervention into left discourse' (Crenshaw *et al.*,

1995, p. xix). Anthony Cook (1992) also stated that 'It is this profound critique of norms, background assumptions and paradigms, within which Black progress and regress take place, that gives Critical Race Theory its critical bite' (p. 1010).

3. The Commitment to Social Justice

A critical race pedagogy is committed to social justice and offers a liberatory or transformative response to racial, gender, and class oppression (Matsuda, 1991). We envision social justice education as the curricular and pedagogical work that leads toward (1) the elimination of racism, sexism, and poverty, and (2) the empowering of underrepresented minority groups. Critical race educators acknowledge that educational institutions operate in contradictory ways, with their potential to oppress and marginalize coexisting with their potential to emancipate and empower.

4. The Centrality of Experiential Knowledge

Critical race pedagogy recognizes that the experiential knowledge of Faculty of Color is legitimate, appropriate, and critical to understanding, analyzing, and teaching about racial subordination. In fact, critical race pedagogy views this knowledge as a strength and draws explicitly on the lived experience of People of Color by including such methods as storytelling, family histories, biographies, scenarios, parables, *cuentos*, chronicles, and narratives (Bell, 1987; Carrasco, 1996; Delgado, 1989, 1993, 1995a, 1996, 1999, 2003; Olivas, 1990). In our analysis, we incorporate the experiential knowledge of Faculty and Students of Color by drawing from interview data, the research literature, biographical and autobiographical data, and other literary sources to create a counterstory (Delgado, 1989).

5. The Transdisciplinary Perspective

A critical race pedagogy challenges ahistoricism and the unidisciplinary focus of most analyses and insists on analyzing race and racism by placing them in both an historical and a contemporary context (Delgado, 1984, 1992, 1995b; Garcia, 1995; Harris, 1994; Olivas, 1990). Critical race pedagogy utilizes the transdisciplinary knowledge base of ethnic studies, women's studies, sociology, history, law, and other fields to better understand racism, sexism, and classism in and out of the classroom.

In this essay, we take each of these five themes and apply them to Freirean pedagogy. These themes are not new in and of themselves, but collectively they represent a challenge to the existing modes of scholarship. Indeed, a critical race pedagogy is critical and different from other frameworks because: (1) it challenges the traditional paradigms, methods, texts, and discourse on race, gender, and class; (2) it helps us to bring to the forefront and focus on the racialized and gendered experiences of People of Color; (3) it offers a liberatory or transformative method to racial, gender, and class oppression; and (4) it utilizes the interdisciplinary knowledge base of ethnic studies, women's studies, sociology, history, and the law to better understand the various forms of oppression.

Indeed, critical race pedagogy names racist injuries and identifies their origins. In examining the origins, critical race pedagogy finds that racism is often well disguised in the rhetoric of shared values and neutral social scientific and educational principles and practices (Matsuda *et al.*, 1993). However, when the ideology of racism is examined and racist injuries named, victims of racism can find their voice. Further, the injured discover that they are not alone in their subordination. They become empowered participants, hearing their own stories and the stories of others, listening to how the arguments are framed, and learning to make the arguments themselves. It is at this point where the pedagogy of Paulo Freire is most useful for critical race scholars. Indeed, evidenced in the following counterstory, Freirean pedagogy begins with 'naming the problem' or, as critical race theorists say, 'naming the injury.'

Critical Race Pedagogy and Counterstorytelling

In order to integrate critical race theory with critical pedagogy, we use a technique that has a long tradition in the social sciences, humanities, and the law—storytelling. Richard Delgado (1989) uses a technique called counterstorytelling. Delgado argues that counterstorytelling is both a method of telling the story of those experiences that have not been told (i.e. those on the margins of society) and a tool for analyzing and challenging the stories of those in power and whose story is a natural part of the dominant discourse—the majoritarian story.[3] These counterstories serve five pedagogical functions: (1) they build community among those at the margins of society; (2) they challenge the perceived wisdom of those at society's center; (3) they open new windows into the reality of those at the margins of society by showing the possibilities beyond the ones they live and that they are not alone in their position; (4) they teach others that, by combining elements from both the story and the current reality, one can construct another world that is richer than either the story or the reality alone; and (5) they provide a context to understand and transform established belief systems (Delgado, 1989; Lawson, 1995). Storytelling has a rich and continuing tradition in the African American (Bell, 1987, 1992, 1996; Berkeley Art Center, 1982; Lawrence, 1992), Chicana/o (Delgado, 1989, 1995a, 1996, 1999, 2003; Olivas, 1990; Paredes, 1977) and Native American (Deloria, 1969; Williams, 1997) communities, and as Delgado (1989) has stated, 'Oppressed groups have known instinctively that stories are an essential tool to their own survival and liberation' (p. 2436).

We add to this tradition by illuminating the lives of critical educators, who may at times be at the margins of higher education (see Solórzano & Villalpando, 1998; Solórzano & Yosso, 2000, 2001; Solórzano & Delgado Bernal, 2001). As a way of raising various issues in critical pedagogy, we offer the following counterstory about two professors engaged in a dialogue. One is Professor Sanchez, a tenured male professor at a southwestern university and the other is Professor Leticia Garcia, an untenured female professor at another western college campus. We ask the reader to suspend judgement, listen for the story's points, test them against her/his own version of reality (however conceived), and use the counterstory as a pedagogical case study (see Barnes *et al.*, 1994). The two professors meet at the annual meeting of the American Sociological Association (see Solórzano & Yosso, 2000).[4] Their story begins here.

***

In an Elevator of the Hotel Sheraton

It was about 5:30 in the afternoon and I was attending a national sociology conference. The day's sessions were winding down and I was heading to my room for a quick nap. As I was standing in the elevator, the door opened at the mezzanine level and Leticia stepped in. 'Professor! You're just the person I wanted to see.' We exchanged greetings and Leticia continued, 'Can we talk? I have so much to tell you. I just finished my first year as a faculty member and I have so many questions.' I was pleased to see her. Leticia was my graduate student, and I chaired her dissertation committee. We coauthored two articles, and I had not heard from her in a couple of months. I replied, 'I figured you were really busy with your first-year adjustments, and I was actually hoping to catch up with you here. Would you like a cup of coffee? It's been a long day and I need something to get me started again.'

'Sounds great,' she replied. 'It will remind me of graduate school, discussing theory, research, and practice over coffee. You know, compared to now, those days seem relaxing. It sure is different with my own classes and research, let alone my family life.'

As we made our way to a coffee shop, we were able to catch up on the months we hadn't talked to each other. Leticia began to describe her first year in a tenure track position at her university. She was struggling to establish her research program, as well as teach five classes a year. 'You know my daughter Victoria is in the first grade, and she's reading a book a week,' beamed Leticia.

I responded, 'She has her mother's gifts.' Leticia smiled as I continued, 'How's your husband Frank doing?' She replied, 'He's still working for MALDEF (Mexican American Legal Defense and Education Fund) and is looking to set up his own law practice with a group of old community activists.' I wanted to ask her to define 'old,' but I figured I would wait until another time.

Institutional Confines versus Critical Pedagogy

We stopped at a small café. Leticia found us a table and I ordered a Colombian blend and a maple scone. 'Did you get me a baguette?' Leticia wanted to know. I nodded my head with a smile, 'You haven't changed a bit.' Leticia just smiled and I grabbed a stirrer so she could mix more cream and sugar into her French Roast. 'This bread reminds me of the *bolillos* I used to buy at the *panaderia* near my mom's house,' said Leticia. I sighed as I sat down at the table. It really did feel like it had been a long day.

Leticia started right away, 'Professor, did you hear the question raised at the opening plenary session yesterday?' 'Which one?' I asked. Leticia continued, 'Sorry,

I guess for me it was the only question. You know, when the panel was discussing critical pedagogy and the article by Stephen Sweet (1998), "Radical Curriculum and Radical Pedagogy: Balancing Political Sympathies with Institutional Constraints?" Well, remember when someone asked the panel, "How do we as critical educators maintain a sense of integrity as we attempt to work for social change within the confines of the academy?" '

I responded, 'I think I was just getting there when that happened, because I remember the moderator of the panel saying, "We'll answer that question throughout the conference." And I was confused by her statement.'

'Yes, that was the question she was referring to, and that was her response in the interest of time. But the panel never really got back to it. I appreciated the question because it raises some very important issues for new professors, and it really hit home for me in my first year of teaching.'

I replied, 'In the part of the panel I heard, they were responding to Sweet's article looking at the dismal state of critical pedagogy in sociology, which raised some important issues that I think educators need to be discussing. What did you think of his article? Does it address any part of the question?'

'Not really,' Leticia admitted, 'Sweet lays out three tactics for dealing with the tensions that arise for critical educators between the institutional demands on hiring, promotion, and tenure, and one's belief in the tenets of critical pedagogy. The first response to these tensions was to subordinate institutional demands to your own radical philosophy. The second response was to subordinate your radical philosophy to institutional demands, and the third response was to continue to struggle to achieve a balance between your radical philosophy and your institutions demands.' She paused for a moment and then continued, 'I was feeling something missing from those alternatives. Maybe because I don't see myself fitting into those three response options? Or maybe because the options sound so antiseptic?'

Merging Critical Race and Freirean Pedagogy

As I started my first cup of coffee, I began, 'I've read the article, and I agree the alternatives seem to be missing something. Maybe it's uncomfortable for us that Sweet seems to talk about critical pedagogy in the absence of the context of real students, struggling with racism, classism, sexism, and other forms of oppression every day. There are some important frameworks that link everyday struggle with critical pedagogy in the classroom and we should draw on those frameworks. Still, I believe Sweet raises two important issues that critical educators struggle with on a continuing basis: (1) the intersection of the personal history that each of us brings to the teaching enterprise, and (2) the contextual obstacles and opportunities that lie in our path.'

Puzzled, Leticia asked, 'Professor, I'm not sure I follow you. What do you mean by personal history in a critical pedagogical context?' I thought for a moment and then continued, 'Each of us brings to our research and teaching an accumulation of experiences that have had a profound impact on our work. For instance, I was an undergraduate during the 1960s and was influenced by and participated in the civil rights, anti-war, and farmworker movements. My beliefs and values for social justice were being applied right outside the classroom door, in the communities just off campus, and in the community that I grew up and lived in. We could see the contradictions and connections between what our professors were telling us and having us read, and what was happening in these very active struggles. On the other hand, you were an undergraduate in the late 1980s and a graduate student in the early 1990s and probably didn't have that experience with an active, broad-based civil rights movement.'

Leticia cut in, 'You're probably right. Just as the overt racism of the 1960s has given way to more covert, insidious forms, activism to challenge racism has also changed forms. Most of my activism was on campus and related to student issues. When I left campus, it wasn't to engage in an organized "civil rights" struggle *per se*, but to tutor high school students in East Los Angeles.'

I waited until she paused and then responded, 'Those are very important activities and are crucial to the continuing civil rights struggle. There has to be a place for people to participate in any way they can. Today, the struggles to maintain the skeletons of affirmative action, bilingual education, and immigrant rights are very important and ongoing.'

Leticia thought for quite a while and then continued, 'Professor, you bring up another issue: the struggle for social justice is a continuing one and it has a long history. I try to explain the struggles of the past with my students, and maybe I don't link those struggles enough with today's struggles.' 'Perhaps,' I said, 'your students would benefit from seeing themselves as part of this tradition of resistance. We have to see this as a long-term struggle. If we don't come to grips with that reality along with the further reality that civil rights gains are never completely won, then we can't deal with the continuous pattern of setbacks, short gains, setbacks, and short gains.'

Leticia said, 'That's a hard reality to come to grips with. I've been doing readings of legal scholars whose work outlines how civil rights gains are only allowed to the extent that they benefit Whites. They call it the "interest-convergence theory" (Bell, 1995). We should talk more about this. Actually, I've been working on an article that examines the linkages between a theoretical framework in the law—critical race theory—and its relation to education and the problem-posing pedagogy of Paulo Freire. I think I've been struggling in my writing because I have had a hard time coming to terms with some of these issues myself.'

I replied, 'That is going to be an important piece of work, Leticia. As you continue doing the research for it, look up Charles Lawrence (1992). He tells us that "Searching history to retrieve collective strengths is part of the work that must be done by law teachers engaged in liberating pedagogy" (p. 2259). We must continue to search for that history and bring it to our classrooms. Mari Matsuda (1987) argues that "Critical commentators should look to the bottom and acknowledge the richness there" ' (p. 344). Leticia responded, 'Sounds like she's referring to individual, family, and community histories, stories, and struggles in Communities of Color.' 'Yes and so much more,' I added.

Leticia continued, 'So far in my article, I've outlined how I utilize Freire's (1970b, 1973) work, exposing the banking method of education, and how I try to use the problem-posing process in my own curriculum and pedagogy. I walk with my students through this problem-posing method of naming the problem, finding the cause of the problem, developing an action-plan to remedy the problem, and finally reflecting on the whole process and renaming the problem to start the process over again.' 'Sounds like you're off to a solid start,' I said. 'The problem-posing method has two interrelated goals: (1) to teach the student certain educational skills, and (2) to develop a critical consciousness in the student. Have you outlined with them the different levels of Freirean consciousness?' 'Yes,' said Leticia, 'and I have them try to relate it to their own experiences and use examples that come from their experiences to describe each level. I'll explain that part in a minute.' 'Good,' I replied, 'those are necessary discussions to have with your students. As educators, we need to find out how people develop critical consciousness and our role in that development. For instance, can a person have an uneven consciousness development? Can there be growth in some areas and not in others? Indeed, one could be at the critical consciousness level as it relates to class, but be at the magical or naïve level in his/her gender and/or race consciousness. In our pedagogy, we need to look at the development of a critical race, gender, and class-consciousness. In fact, as we develop what Freire called "generative codes," to facilitate a critical reading of the word and the world, we must make sure to identify those examples that depict the intersection of race, gender, and class oppression and engage our students in a dialogue at that location.'

'Well Professor, I'd like to bring us back to the question during the panel session. How do we, as critical educators, maintain a sense of integrity as we attempt to work for social change within the confines of the academy? I have this diagram that I've adapted from some work of my colleagues, and I want to include it in my article. What do you think? Can it help us address the question?'

An Algebraic Approach to Resistance?

'Now, I hope you know that math, especially algebra, was never my strong suit, but …' Leticia pulled a piece of paper from her bag, unfolded it, and placed it on the table. 'Oh,' I said, 'I recognize some of this.' 'Yes,' said Leticia, 'my colleagues have really taken the idea of resistance and pushed the envelope to look at resistance as not just a self-defeating, destructive cycle (Delgado Bernal, 1997; Solórzano & Delgado Bernal, 2001). What I'm trying to do is understand these types of resistance within a Freirean approach to education.' 'Can you talk me through the diagram?' I asked. Leticia flashed a smile and said, 'Of course.'

'This figure replicates my colleagues' chart with the only change being the labels along the y-axis (Solórzano & Delgado Bernal, 2001, p. 318). My colleagues label the y-axis at the bottom 'no critique of the system' and the top of the y-axis, 'critique of the system.' I utilize Freire (1973) to label the y-axis from bottom to top, magical, naïve, and critical consciousness, each indicating the extent of an individual's critique of the system.

Letty's Figure in Progress
Resistance, Consciousness, and Motivation toward Social Justice[5]

CRITICAL CONSCIOUSNESS

Self-Defeating Resistance   **Transformative Resistance**

NAÏVE CONSCIOUSNESS

Not Motivated   *Moderately Motivated*   *Motivated by*
by Social Justice   *by Social Justice*   *Social Justice*

Reactionary Behavior   **Conformist Resistance**

MAGICAL CONSCIOUSNESS

'OK,' I said, 'now allow me to try and describe what I see. Like you said, the y-axis identifies Freire's (1973) three levels of consciousness. The bottom of the y-axis is the magical stage, where students may blame inequality on luck, fate, or God. Whatever causes the inequality seems to be out of the student's control, so he/she may resign to not do anything about it. For example, a person at a magical stage of consciousness may explain, "In the U.S., if Chicanas do not get a good education it is because God only helps those who help themselves."'

'Exactly,' said Leticia. She continued, 'in the middle of the y-axis is the naïve stage, where students may blame themselves, their culture, or their community for inequality. Because they're informed by a naïve consciousness, students may try to change themselves, assimilate to the White, middle-class, mainstream culture, or distance themselves from their community in response to experiencing inequality. For instance, a person at a naïve stage of consciousness may say, "In the U.S., if Chicanos do not do well in life, it is because culturally, they focus only on today rather than planning for tomorrow."'

'I like this tag team thing,' I replied. 'So the top of the y-axis is the critical stage, where students look beyond fatalistic or cultural reasons for inequality to focus on structural, systemic explanations. A student with a critical level of consciousness looks toward changing the system and its structures as a response to inequality. For example, a person at a critical stage of consciousness may explain, "In the U.S., if Chicanas and Chicanos don't go to college, it is because from kindergarten through high school they are being socialized for working-class occupations that don't require a college degree" ' (see Bowles & Gintis, 1976).

'OK, now we're cooking,' said Leticia. 'The x-axis is where I've been struggling the most, so I'll describe it and then we can get back to it later?' 'OK,' I said. She continued, 'The x-axis addresses various levels of motivation toward social justice. I'm defining social justice as working toward "the elimination of racism, sexism, and poverty, and the empowering of underrepresented minority groups" (Solórzano & Delgado Bernal, 2001, p. 313). A person who is *not motivated* by social justice would be on the left side of the x-axis. Someone who is not motivated by social justice perpetuates the status quo and upholds systems of inequality because he/she believes the system works ("if it ain't broke, don't fix it"). Someone who is *moderately motivated* by social justice looks to reform the current system by reforming him/herself and his/her community. This person would be in the middle of the x-axis. Someone who is *motivated* by social justice looks to transform the system by changing the structures of the system, which disempower underrepresented minority groups. A person motivated toward social justice would be on the right side of the x-axis.' I took out my automatic pencil and began to take notes on my coffee coaster.

Leticia went on, 'The four quadrants of the figure depict various forms of oppositional behavior. My colleagues adapt and extend the work of Henry Giroux (1983) to write about various forms of oppositional behavior, yet they differentiate reactionary or defiant behavior from the three methods of student resistance, which they identify and describe as (a) self-defeating, (b) conformist, and (c) transformative. Each of these three forms of resistance are based on two intersecting dimensions: (a) critique of domination (consciousness), and (b) motivation by an interest in individual or societal transformation (motivation toward social justice).' 'Now I see the reason for the x and y axes!' I exclaimed. 'Yes, Professor, pretty exciting work, huh!' I grinned, as I continued to listen to Leticia.

She explained, 'The upper left-hand quadrant is *self-defeating resistance*, which infers that one holds a critique of the structured nature of inequality but is not motivated by social justice and thus responds to oppression in ways that perpetuate inequality for him/herself and others. For example, a Chicano who complains to his teacher about being misplaced in a remedial class may be conscious of the structures of inequality that benefits from him being miseducated. However, if this Chicano drops out of school in defiance of being treated poorly, not only does he reinforce the school's notion that he was not able to do well in a "regular" class, but he also limits his own socioacademic opportunities. Even though this Chicano had a strong critique of the inequality perpetuated by society's institutions, he is now a high school drop-out, which adds to negative statistics and ideas about Chicanas/os.'

I interjected, 'Even if he is a "push out," meaning the system pushes him out and he leaves, it's still the student who ends up with limited options and resources.'

'Good point Professor,' Leticia continued, 'the lower right-hand quadrant, *conformist resistance*, can be seen when one does not critique the systemic nature of inequality, and although moderately motivated to create change for society, looks to create changes within the system (conforming to the system) by changing individuals, communities, cultures, etc. For example, a Chicana who begins to speak only English at school and home, in order to succeed in education, changes herself and may not question the system that privileges English and downgrades Spanish. This Chicana may try to assimilate linguistically to the dominant culture, but her individual sacrifice leaves the structures of domination intact. As she tries to conform (fit in) to the system, she may even start to look down on other Chicanas/os who speak Spanish as inferior, thereby strengthening the oppressive power of the system.'

Leticia continued, 'The upper right-hand quadrant, *transformative resistance*, means one critiques the structures of domination and is motivated toward social justice. *Transformative resistance* to oppression necessitates liberatory changes to the system. For example, the Chicana/o students who organized against California's anti-youth Proposition 21 held a strong critique of the structural nature of social inequality and were highly motivated to abolish racism, classism, and sexism and empower minority groups. These Chicana/o high school students protested along-side other Youth of Color to transform the social dialogue about juvenile crime and to transform the hypocritical California system that structures injustice through multiple means—such as being number one in the U.S. on prison spending and number forty-one on education spending.'[6]

'Whew!' I sighed. 'That's a lot in one figure. But it makes sense. I think your examples are helpful; make sure you include them in your article.' 'Thanks Professor, but how do I facilitate my students' movement through the stages of consciousness, through levels of motivation toward social justice, and still get promoted to tenure? How do I maintain my ideal for social justice and still get tenure at my institution?' Leticia paused and looked at her watch, realizing it was 7:30 in the evening and then made the suggestion, 'I think the panel moderator was right, this question looks like it's going to take awhile, would you like to have dinner and continue this conversation?' 'I'd like that,' I replied, 'but I have to make a phone call first.'

Toward a LatCrit Theory of Education

I returned to the table and Leticia was browsing through the dinner menu, and talking in Spanish to a man busing tables. I picked up my menu and began to peruse the salad selections, finally settling on one with chicken, wontons, and sesame sauce. I nodded 'hello' to the man as he left and Leticia said, 'He was an engineer and his wife was a professor in Mexico. He was joking with me about how his kids are like ones in the Tigres del Norte song, "Jaula De Oro."[7] Have you heard it?' 'No,' I replied, 'I don't think so.' Leticia continued, 'It talks about an undocumented worker whose children were born in the U.S. and the pain he feels because he wants to go back to Mexico but his children have become so Americanized they want to deny that they're Mexican. And the song is all in Spanish, except one part where the father asks his son in Spanish if he'd like to go back to Mexico, and the son answers in English, "Whatcha talkin' about Dad? I don't want to go back to Mexico. No way, Dad." ' Leticia chuckled, 'It's sad but funny to hear the song, because the kid sounds like Opie from that one show ...' Leticia trailed off as she looked for something to eat. The waitress took my order and Leticia ordered a turkey club sandwich. 'Gotta have a sense of humor,' I noted. 'Yes,' replied Leticia, 'you've always reminded me of that. For Chicanas/os, Latinas/os I believe that sense of humor has been key to our survival.'

'For oppressed peoples, I think humor has been a form of survival and also a form of resistance,' I added.

While we waited for our food, I brought us back to our discussion. 'I think I'm starting to see how this figure can help you answer the question you referred to. Have you read the work of André Gorz (1967)?' 'No,' Leticia said. 'Do you think he'd be helpful?' 'I think so, but I'm not sure how,' I responded. 'Let me think out loud and we'll see. Gorz wrote *Strategies for Labor* in 1967, wherein he outlines three types of reforms: reformist, non-reformist, and revolutionary. Basically, he says reformist reforms are those which maintain the status quo, and do not challenge the system of inequality.'[8] Leticia interjected, 'So a reformist reform might work to reform a school bureaucracy, only to make the bureaucracy marginalize Chicanas/os more efficiently?'

'You could say that,' I replied. 'According to Gorz, non-reformist reforms move to change the system, but keep the system intact.[9] The difference here is that the non-reformist reform works to change the system into something more equitable, but it works within the system to make this happen.' Again, Leticia commented, 'So the system itself doesn't get challenged?' 'Right,' I said. 'And finally, revolutionary reforms work toward a radical transformation of the present system and the creation of an entirely different, more equitable system.'[10]

'Wow,' remarked Leticia, 'I think I see where this might fit in.' 'Maybe,' I said, 'The reformist reform would be somewhere in the area of being not-so-motivated toward social justice because it's more conformist resistance.' 'Yes,' Leticia nodded her head and replied, 'and maybe non-reformist reform would be somewhere in the area of motivated toward social justice, but it's in-between conformist and transformative resistance, whereas revolutionary reform sounds like it'd be in the highly motivated toward social justice and transformative resistance area.' I agreed and said, 'But do you see what I see?' Leticia asked, 'Do we as critical educators ever really engage in transformative resistance? Are our reform efforts ever non-reformist or revolutionary?' 'That's exactly what I'm seeing,' I said. 'I think at best, we engage in non-reformist reforms with an eye toward revolutionary reforms. But more than likely, many of us may be making more reformist and conformist efforts from within our academic positions.'

Leticia added, 'I think that's where we hear the frustration in the question: how do we keep our integrity as critical educators working toward social justice from within the academy? In the end, as we try to teach a critical pedagogy, we ourselves are not feeling like we've been true to the struggle because the structures of inequality remain intact.'

'Maybe we need to go back and listen to the spoken word of Gil Scott-Heron (1974) who eloquently reminded us that "The Revolution Will Not Be Televised." As critical educators, we can't become like "Chuy," the armchair revolutionary, who sits and waits for a revolution in the satire of the stalled Chicano Movement by Chicano-Latino theater group Culture Clash (see Montoya, 1998). Maybe we should go back and read some of the goals of the Chicano Movement like *El Plan de Santa Barbara*?' I said.

'Good points,' said Leticia, 'or maybe even the Black Panther Party's Ten Point Program. Those struggles surely speak to the same concerns we continue to deal with in our communities and within our educational system. And speaking of the strengths of those historical struggles, I've been trying to utilize Latina/o Critical Race Theory—LatCrit theory to extend the critical race discussions to Chicanas/os in education—and an important part is the interdisciplinary, historical aspect which we need to bring to our research.'

'I've had this conversation with other academics, but I'm wondering about your thoughts. What's the difference between LatCrit or critical race theory and Ethnic Studies frameworks?' I asked.

Leticia flipped through her notebook, stopped at a page, and said, 'I was at the last LatCrit conference in Colorado, LatCrit V, and I adapted this working definition from their LatCrit Primer (LatCrit Primer, 2000). I tailored it for my work in education.' Leticia began to read, 'A LatCrit theory in education is a framework that can be used to theorize and examine the ways in which race and racism explicitly and implicitly impact on the educational structures, processes, and discourses that affect People of Color generally and Latinas/os specifically. Important to this critical framework is a challenge to the dominant ideology, which supports deficit notions about Students of Color, while assuming "neutrality" and "objectivity." Utilizing the experiences of Latinas/os, a LatCrit theory in education also theorizes and examines the place where racism intersects with other forms of subordination such as sexism, classism, nativism, monolingualism, and heterosexism. LatCrit theory in education is conceived as a social justice project that attempts to link theory with practice, scholarship with teaching, and the academy with the community. LatCrit acknowledges that educational institutions operate in contradictory ways, with their potential to oppress and marginalize coexisting with their potential to emancipate and empower. LatCrit theory in education is transdisciplinary and draws on many other schools of progressive scholarship.' Leticia looked up and continued, 'I think what makes it different is that it combines various frameworks together, such as Ethnic Studies, internal colonialism, Marxism, feminism and other critical theoretical models in a very unique way.'

'I'm impressed with your working definition and I agree, critical race and LatCrit utilize the strengths of various critical frameworks and have the benefit of hindsight in addressing some of the weaknesses, blind spots, or underdeveloped areas of other frameworks. So critical race and LatCrit theory are not new in and of themselves, but instead are syntheses of many critical frameworks. As critical race educators, we recognize the need to incorporate the knowledge of those who have come before us and to learn from the struggles that we engage in today. And I think that the LatCrits have pushed the envelope of the ways in which we talk about race and racism, so that we focus on the intersectionality of subordination,' I said.

'Yes,' replied Leticia, 'and I think that critical race theory as a "synthesis," as you put it, demonstrates that the dynamic nature of oppressions requires dynamic responses. I also appreciate the ways in which critical race and LatCrit scholars are clear about analyzing race as a social construct.'

'Definitely,' I agreed, 'they do not approach race without challenging its very problematic ideological basis. And they are unapologetic in their focus on racism. I think this is important because they recognize that even the language we utilize to identify ourselves is grounded in archaic notions of biological determinism and anthropological "othering." Yet, they are not naïve in their critique of how notions of "race" play themselves out in very real ways, through racism. We need to understand how we are racialized, how race has been socially constructed, and how that leads us to discussions of racism and racism's intersections with other forms of oppression.'

'Exactly,' Leticia nodded her head in agreement, 'your comments remind me of bell hooks's (1994) *Teaching to Transgress*, where she quotes from an Adrienne Rich poem, "This is the oppressor's language yet I need it to talk to you" (p. 167). We need to talk about the concept of race so that we can critique and challenge racism. Like we said earlier, racism changes forms, and our ways of thinking about and responding to racism and its many subtle and overt tendencies also is an ongoing process. I see LatCrit as a natural outgrowth of critical race theory, but I do not see them as mutually exclusive. I think LatCrit scholarship is evidence of the ongoing process of finding a framework that addresses racism and its accompanying oppressions. LatCrit draws on the strengths outlined in critical race theory, and emphasizes the intersectionality of experience with oppression, and the need to extend conversations about "race" and racism beyond the Black/ White binary. And I think that Freire pushes me to also look at the intersectionality of resistance.'

'Yes,' I replied, 'I also think our goals as LatCrits are similar to Freire's goals. Freire's problem-posing approach is used to develop and move toward a critical consciousness as a means by which to create societal change. Likewise, critical race and LatCrit theorists are working toward the end of racial oppression as part of the broader goal of ending all forms of oppression such as those based on gender, class, and sexual orientation. Both Freirean pedagogy and critical race theory challenge the traditional claims of the educational and legal systems to neutrality, objectivity, and color-blindness. They see these concepts as a camouflage for the self-interest, power, and privilege of dominant groups in U.S. society.'

Leticia followed, 'As I mentioned in my working definition earlier, LatCrit and Freire would also acknowledge that educational institutions operate in contradictory ways with their potential to oppress and marginalize coexisting with their potential to emancipate and empower.'

Leticia continued, 'Both frameworks recognize that the experiential knowledge of People of Color is critical to understanding and analyzing the fields of education and law. Actually, both traditions argue that the experiences of People of Color should be examined for their ability to contribute to the establishment of a society where people participate and contribute as equals in a culturally democratic social environment.'

'Freirean pedagogy and critical race theory are about strengths, and strengths are what we should be looking for within Students and Communities of Color,' I responded.

What Does a Critical Race/LatCrit Freirean Pedagogy Look Like in my Classroom?

'So, as LatCrit educators, how are we participating in non-reformist reforms?' Leticia asked. I thought a moment, and replied, 'Looking at your working defini-tion, we are challenging the dominant ideology and are working toward social justice, but what that looks like in real life depends on the type of institution we work in. Doing critical pedagogy will be very different at a community college where you teach ten classes a year with no research and publishing responsibilities, compared to a four-year comprehensive teaching institution where you teach six or seven classes a year, but have additional research and publication pressures. Dif-ferent again will be a research institution where you teach three or four courses a year, but have the primary responsibility to conduct research, publish, and bring in grant monies. Each system is a unique balancing act of time and resources and doing critical pedagogy takes place within that context.'

I continued, 'Leticia, it's been twenty-four years since Daniel Solórzano (1989) wrote that article documenting his use of Freirean pedagogy with Chicana/o stu-dents in a community college classroom.' Leticia replied, 'Did you know that Sweet mentions Solórzano's article as one of only thirteen published articles in twenty-three years in the journal *Teaching Sociology* that practiced radical pedagogy?' I replied, 'Yes, I recall reading that. I also remember Solórzano's article because I was in a similar situation, trying to utilize Freire as a young community college instructor. Since those years in the California Community College system, I have taught in California's other two higher education systems: the California State University and the University of California. Throughout the years, I have continued to use different forms of critical pedagogy in the classroom with varying degrees of success.'

The waitress brought our food, and Leticia responded, 'That's true, you've taught in all three systems. How is it done?' As Leticia began to eat, I replied, 'Well, each one provided a different challenge. But, the common denominator gets back to my personal belief and commitment to critical pedagogy. I believe that my students bring their own set of strengths to the classroom and that I can share something with them that might reinforce those strengths and have an impact on their lives and the lives of others.'

I paused for a moment, took a few bites of my salad, and then continued, 'No matter the system I'm working in, my pedagogy is driven by my desire to effect change and struggle toward social justice. I begin all my courses by telling students who I am and what I stand for. I believe students have the right to know who we are and what we teach. Then, they can make decisions about whether they want to remain in my course. If they don't like what they hear, or who they're hearing it from, they can take another professor. It's really their call.'

As we continued eating, I commented that, 'Certain classes lend themselves to an easier transition to critical pedagogy. Ethnic and gender studies, race, ethnic, and gender relations, or social problems courses can accommodate critical pedagogy a little easier than research design or research methods. But even those classes can be adapted for use with critical pedagogy. There's an important article by critical race scholar Charles Lawrence (1992), titled "The Word and the River: Pedagogy as Scholarship and Struggle," where he describes the dilemmas we face as critical educators and how we struggle between the poles of "throwing up our hands in despair or adopting an attitude of self-righteous radical chic" (p. 2245). He responded to this dilemma by pedagogically including a community simulation exercise in law and public policy into his classes. His students must go outside the academy in order to contact and utilize the resources of seven very different inter-est groups in Black communities. This pedagogical exercise ultimately leads to short and long-term strategies for social change, as well as political and legal reform in the Black community (see Lawrence, 1992, pp. 2243–2248). I believe this model can be adapted for your classroom.'

After Leticia scribbled down the Lawrence citation, she looked up, smiled, and again went back to Sweet's (1998) article. 'Sweet used four criteria to define critical pedagogy. He concluded that radical teachers "do not test or grade in the traditional fashion ... surrender considerable power to students ... abandon lectures in favor of dialogue [and] couple learning with activism" (p. 4). How could you possibly incorporate each of those criteria in every class that you teach, in every quarter or semester?'

After the waitress cleared away our dinner and refilled our coffees, I continued, 'You have to decide for yourself how you define critical pedagogy. You then have to decide how you can incorporate the working definition into your scholarship and teaching. Once you make those decisions and, as you know, they are not easy decisions, and they are not set in stone, you can begin the process of developing a critical pedagogy that works for you. It has to work for you because you are the one who will struggle with various classroom challenges that arise for all educators. But you will have the added challenge of teaching from a critical perspective, being a woman, and being Chicana.' I knew what was going to come next as Leticia said, 'Professor, one of my biggest problems is students who somehow think that I have no right to be in front of that class, to be teaching them. I get challenged in areas where my White colleagues don't. It has been a painful process.'

I paused and then asked, 'Have you read any of the critical race and LatCrit literature that deals with this issue?' Leticia responded, 'What works did you have in mind?' I replied, 'There's Linda Greene (1990–1991), Derrick Bell (2002; see also Lawrence, 1991), and Reginald Robinson's (1997) experiences as Black law professors. Kevin Johnson (1999) talks about being a Mexican American law professor in his book. There is also an important article by Gloria Ladson-Billings (1996) that focuses on a Black woman professor's experience teaching White students about multiculturalism and race. These five pieces can help put your experience into a broader perspective. They describe the classroom experience you mentioned in much detail. You will see that many of us have and continue to experience these forms of racism in and out of our classrooms. I think our White sister and brother educators deal with some of these classroom problems, but when you add the dimensions of race, ethnicity, gender, language, accent, immigration status, and sexuality to the mix, it gets a bit more complex and I think that is where our experiences divert from theirs.'

Leticia responded, 'I know that I bring so much to the classroom. I bring the multiple consciousness of being a woman, a Chicana, and from working-class parents. After so many years of thinking these were a burden for me, I have come to view these characteristics as strengths that give me insight into multiple worlds (see Collins, 1986, 1998). I have to move and adjust to these worlds on a daily or even hourly basis. But this multiple consciousness isn't valued in the academy. I only get the validation when I meet with other Scholars of Color and feminist scholars at our annual meetings and of course from my family.'

As we finished our dinner and began looking at the dessert menu, Leticia threw a few more insightful questions at me, 'Is there a tipping point? Is there a number or percentage of minority students in the class, a tipping point, when they begin to have a positive or negative impact on the interactions within a class? I have found that I don't get the same degree and types of challenges to my being "the professor" when there are greater numbers of Students of Color in the class.' I had heard about the tipping point principle of Blacks in public housing projects and law faculties from the works of Derrick Bell (1986), and I replied, 'I think there is, but I've never been able to quantify it. Sometimes, when I teach a class that is predominantly White, I can see that they really need interaction with Students of Color. It is one thing to hear about racial and ethnic issues from me, and another when it comes from their peers. This interaction among students is a very delicate enterprise and gets even more delicate when issues of race, gender, class, and sexuality are thrown into the mix. But the interaction makes the discussion of theory, method, design, and practice so much more complex and so much more exciting. When I have a good mix of Students of Color and White students in class, our discussions are much more lively, challenging, and complex and we come up with much better action plans for our problems. They truly do learn from each other in some immediate and long-range ways. You plant seeds of critical analysis, and you nurture them, and then they leave. You try to keep up with them, and every now and then, one returns and reminds you of what you and others said or did—for better or worse.'

Leticia looked at me and replied, 'You've just given an argument for the value of diversity in the classroom. That it benefits both White students and Students of Color.' I paused, thinking of my older sister Jesse.[11] I shared this story with Leticia: 'My older sister, Jesse, had a way of explaining things that cut right to the core of the argument. When I was still in diapers, Jesse was identified as a bright kid but didn't receive the resources she was entitled to. She should have been in the GATE (Gifted and Talented Education) program, but my parents couldn't drive her to the gifted school, wait for an hour and a half while she took a special class, and drive her back to her neighborhood school. They both had to work. Jesse is one of the smartest people I've ever known. Her street-smart, eclectic knowledge base, common sense, and critical analysis skills weren't recognized or seen as strengths. Jesse ended up graduating from high school and going to a cosmetology college to become a hair stylist. She's earned a well-deserved reputation for telling her clients "what's really going on." Many years back, I remember Jesse told me "what's really going on" with the affirmative action struggle. She shared with me her ideas: "There's diversity and then there's *diversity*. Racial diversity means racial groups are merely present on the campus. On the other hand, real *diversity*, or I guess you could call it pluralism, would mean the different racial groups are not only present on the college campus, but are considered equals. This means they affirm each other's *dignidad humana* (human dignity) and are ready to benefit from each other's experience. And also it means they acknowledge each other's contributions to society in general and to the common welfare of students and faculty on the campus. Other than that, they're just taking you for a long walk off a short pier, thinking you have diversity when what's really going on is that you have a handful of people with darker skin color allowed to just sit near White people, learn about the great achievements of White people, and be reminded that they are not as 'qualified' as White people." Leticia, I've always wondered, if given the opportunities I had, what kind of scholar Jesse would have been. In many ways, my work is an acknowledgment of her influence on me. And truth be told, she influences a lot of people from that stylist chair. As you can see, my ideas come from many different sources.' I made a mental note to get my hair cut next week.

Leticia looked at me and said, 'You're right Professor, racial diversity benefits both People of Color and Whites, yet we need to push beyond the idea of diversity. In the college context, racial diversity is simply the presence of underrepresented students and faculty in colleges. On the other hand, we need to consider Jesse's words that we must go beyond diversity, toward racial pluralism. That means we must include these underrepresented groups in the college and also integrate their culture and experiences into the mission, curriculum, and pedagogy of the college. The problem is that most educators know this, but the courts, in deciding affirmative action cases, want to see it in quantifiable form and don't react favorably to stories that challenge the majoritarian mindset—the belief that decisions on admissions should be based on a "color-blind" or "meritocratic" basis (see note 3). If the stories we told reinforced those notions, we would probably see more stories. But counterstories challenge majoritarian beliefs, and it is to the benefit of those vested in the system to ignore or silence the voices and stories "at the bottom." ' I shot back, 'Then we must tell the stories, the counterstories.'

Leticia continued with a nuts and bolts question, 'What other ways can I begin this process of incorporating critical pedagogy into my courses?' I responded, 'You can begin by teaching an independent study or specialized course and work it into that format. You can also incorporate it into an existing course as an optional case study or an individual or group project. You can always incorporate it into the totality of a course and make it become the centerpiece. You have to experiment first and see what works best for you.' Leticia jumped in again, 'Time also seems to be a problem. If you are having students get involved in action projects, you probably have to work longer than one quarter or semester.' I responded, 'Ideally, it would be nice to work with a group of students for at least three quarters, two semesters, or one academic year. That is ideal but improbable.'

Leticia looked at her watch and said, 'It's already 9.30; I have to make final preparations for my symposium tomorrow. But if you don't mind, I have a last comment to make.' I shook my head no, and Leticia continued, 'Professor, I am in a constant struggle my first year. I realize that I'm the first Chicana teacher that many of my students have ever taken. I am seen as a role model by some and an interloper by others, but regardless, I feel this pressure to be there for them.' I thought about this important comment and replied, 'Leticia, you're going to make mistakes and hopefully you can learn from them. I wish we veteran teachers would honestly tell the new teachers about all the mistakes we made along the way. Knowing that you are not alone can make a lot of difference at anytime, but is probably more critical in these first years of teaching and research.' Leticia eyed her watch again, stood up, and said, 'We probably should save this topic for our next discussion. It gives us a place to begin the next time we meet. As always, I have a list of readings and a lot to think about. I have to go now. Maybe I'll see you at the symposium tomorrow? It always helps to see a smiling face or a head nodding in encouragement. I know I should be used to this, but I still get nerv-ous—kinda like the nerves I get the first day of each semester with new classes.'

'Hey,' I reminded her, 'I still get nervous. I think it's the passion for the work, the excitement of sharing your dreams of social justice and facilitating others' goals to effect social change. After all these years, I think the nervousness is a good thing. I think that when I'm no longer nervous, I need to get out of the business.'

'Thanks Professor. Lucky for me you still get nervous because that means you're still around to guide and encourage. I'll buy dinner at the NACCS (National Association for Chicana and Chicano Studies) Conference in the spring. But hope-fully I'll see you soon.'

I sat there for a minute and reflected on my own first year of teaching. I'm glad that an unanswered question in a panel brought Leticia and me together to discuss these issues related to critical pedagogy. I rarely get that opportunity. I too had struggled and I continue to struggle with many of the same issues that Leticia shared. I remember Paulo Freire (1970b) came into my life at a time when I needed some guidance. His book, *Pedagogy of the Oppressed* and old mimeograph sheets from his Harvard University seminars came in just the nick of time for a struggling high school teacher. With other young teachers, I read, discussed, analyzed, critiqued, reflected, and utilized this very important work. While difficult to read, its beauty for me was in its simplicity. It made things so clear for me. To this day, Freire's problem-posing method has a parsimony, pragmatism,[12] and poetry that makes for good teaching (see Freire, 1970a, 1973). Leticia is going to do fine. She has the heart, determination, and vision to be a good social justice educator. She would make Paulo Freire proud.[13]

Notes

This essay is a response to a question posed by a participant at the opening plenary session of LatCrit V in Breckenridge, Colorado, 4–7 May 2000.

1. For three comprehensive annotated bibliographies on critical race and LatCrit theory, see Richard Delgado and Jean Stefancic (1993, 1994) and Jean Stefancic (1998).
2. For this study, the terms People, Faculty, Scholars and Students of Color are defined as those persons or scholars of African American, Latina/o, Asian American, and Native American ancestry. Chicanas and Chicanos are defined as female and male persons of Mexican ancestry living in the United States. These terms contain a political dimension that this paper does not discuss.
3. Richard Delgado and Jean Stefancic (1993) have defined the majoritarian mindset as 'the bundle of presuppositions, perceived wisdoms, and shared cultural understandings persons in the dominant group bring to discussions of race' (p. 462).
4. Professor Leticia Garcia and Professor Sanchez are composite characters based on information from numerous interviews, focus groups, biographical, humanities, and social science literature, and personal experiences of the authors. These characters are influenced by Geneva Crenshaw and Rodrigo Crenshaw, the primary characters in the works of Derrick Bell (1987, 1992, 1996, 1998) and Richard Delgado (1995a, 1996, 1999, 2003).
5. Adapted from D. Delgado Bernal (1997); H. Giroux (1983); P. Freire (1973); D. Solórzano & D. Delgado Bernal (2001).
6. See Youth Organizing Communities at http://www.schoolsnotjails.com
7. Los Tigres del Norte, *Jaula de Noro*, on Los Tigres del Norte 16 Super Exitos (Profono, Inc., 1988).
8. A *reformist reform* 'subordinates its objectives to the criteria of rationality and practicability of a given system and policy. Reformism rejects those objectives and demands—however deep the need for them—which are incompatible with the preservation of the system' (Gorz, 1967, p. 7).
9. A *non-reformist reform* 'does not base its validity and its right to exist on capitalist needs, criteria, and rationales. A non-reformist reform is determined not in terms of what can be, but what should be' (Gorz, 1967, pp. 7–8).
10. A *revolutionary reform* makes an 'advance toward a radical transformation of society' (Gorz, 1967, p. 6).
11. Jesse is a composite character whose name is inspired by the Jesse B. Simple character from Langston Hughes's work. Hughes first introduced this character in the *Chicago Defender* newspaper in 1943 (see Harper, 1994). Derrick Bell reintroduced him as Jesse B. Semple in *Faces at the Bottom of the Well: The permanence of racism* (1992).
12. Charles Lawrence (1992) argues that 'pragmatism helps the scholar avoid elitism by forcing it always to judge the efficacy of theory by its usefulness in righting the everyday wrongs committed against those who are most oppressed' (p. 2260).
13. Paulo Freire died in 1997 but his work lives on.

References

Barnes, L., Christensen, C. & Hansen, A. (1994) *Teaching and the Case Method: Test, cases, and readings*, 3rd edn (Boston, Harvard Business School Press).
Barnes, R. (1990). Race Consciousness: The thematic content of racial distinctiveness in critical race scholarship, *Harvard Law Review*, 103, pp. 1864–1871.
Bell, D. (1986) Application of the 'Tipping Point' Principle to Law Faculty Hiring Policies, *Nova Law Journal*, 10, pp. 319–327.
Bell, D. (1987) *And We Will Not Be Saved: The elusive quest for racial justice* (New York, Basic Books).

Bell, D. (1992) *Faces at the Bottom of the Well: The permanence of racism* (New York, Basic Books).

Bell, D. (1995) Brown v. Board of Education and the Interest Convergence Dilemma, in: K. Crenshaw, N. Gotanda, G. Peller & K. Thomas (eds), *Critical Race Theory: The key writings that formed the movement* (New York, New Press), pp. 20–29.

Bell, D. (1996) *Gospel Choirs: Psalms of survival for an alien land called home* (New York, Basic Books).

Bell, D. (1998) *Afrolantica Legacies* (Chicago, Third World Press).

Bell, D. (2002) *Ethical Ambition: Living a life of meaning and worth* (New York: Bloomsbury).

Berkeley Art Center (1982) *Ethnic Notions: Black images in the white mind* (Berkeley, CA, Author) (there is also an accompanying film/video of the same name).

Bowles, S. & Gintis, H. (1976) *Schooling in Capitalist America: Educational reform and the contradiction of economic life* (New York, Basic Books).

Calmore, J. (1992) Critical Race Theory, Archie Shepp, and Fire Music: Securing an authentic intellectual life in a multicultural world, *Southern California Law Review*, 65, pp. 2129–2231.

Calmore, J. (1997) Exploring Michael Omi's 'Messy' Real World of Race: An essay for 'naked people longing to swim free', *Law and Inequality*, 15, pp. 25–82.

Carrasco, E. (1996) Collective Recognition as a Communitarian Device: Or, of course we want to be role models!, *La Raza Law Journal*, 9, pp. 81–101.

Collins, P. H. (1986) Learning from the Outsider Within: The sociological significance of Black feminist thought, *Social Problems*, 33, S14–S32.

Collins, P. H. (1998) *Fighting Words: Black women & the search for justice* (Minneapolis, University of Minnesota Press).

Cook, A. (1992) The Spiritual Movement towards Justice, *University of Illinois Law Review*, pp. 1007–1020.

Crenshaw, K. (1989) Demarginalizing the Intersection of Race and Sex: A Black feminist critique of antidiscrimination doctrine, feminist theory and antiracist politics, *University of Chicago Legal Forum*, pp. 139–167.

Crenshaw, K. (1993) Mapping the Margins: Intersectionality, identity politics, and the violence against Women of Color, *Stanford Law Review*, 43, pp. 1241–1299.

Crenshaw, K., Gotanda, N., Peller, G. & Thomas, K. (eds) (1995) *Critical Race Theory: The key writings that formed the movement* (New York, New Press).

Delgado, R. (1984) The Imperial Scholar: Reflections on a review of civil rights literature, *University of Pennsylvania Law Review*, 132, pp. 561–578.

Delgado, R. (1989) Storytelling for Oppositionists and Others: A plea for narrative, *Michigan Law Review*, 87, pp. 2411–2441.

Delgado, R. (1992) The Imperial Scholar Revisited: How to marginalize outsider writing, ten years later, *University of Pennsylvania Law Review*, 140, pp. 1349–1372.

Delgado, R. (1993) On Telling Stories in School: A reply to Farber and Sherry, *Vanderbilt Law Review*, 46, pp. 665–676.

Delgado, R. (1995a) *The Rodrigo Chronicles: Conversations about America and race* (New York, New York University Press).

Delgado, R. (ed.) (1995b) *Critical Race Theory: The cutting edge* (Philadelphia, Temple University Press).

Delgado, R. (1996) *The Coming Race War?: And other apocalyptic tales of America after affirmative action and welfare* (New York, New York University Press).

Delgado, R. (1999) When Equality Ends: Stories about race and resistance (Boulder, Westview Press).

Delgado, R. (2003) *Justice at War: Civil liberties and civil rights during times of crisis* (New York, New York University Press).

Delgado, R. & Stefancic, J. (1993) Critical Race Theory: An annotated bibliography *Virginia Law Review*, 79, pp. 461–516.

Delgado, R. & Stefancic, J. (1994) Critical Race Theory: An annotated bibliography 1993, a year of transition, *University of Colorado Law Review*, 66, pp. 159–193.

Delgado Bernal, D. (1997) *Chicana School Resistance and Grassroots Leadership: Providing an alternative history of the 1968 East Los Angeles blowouts* (unpublished doctoral dissertation, University of California, Los Angeles).

Deloria, V. (1969) *Custer Died for Your Sins: An Indian manifesto* (New York, Avon).

Fay, B. (1987) *Critical Social Science: Liberation and its limits* (Ithaca, Cornell University Press).

Freire, P. (1970a) *Cultural Action for Freedom* (Cambridge, Harvard Educational Review Monograph).

Freire, P. (1970b) *Pedagogy of the Oppressed* (New York, Continuum Publishing Company).

Freire, P. (1973) *Education for a Critical Consciousness* (New York, Seabury Press).

Garcia, R. (1995) Critical Race Theory and Proposition 187: The racial politics of immigration law, *Chicano-Latino Law Review*, 17, pp. 118–148.

Giroux, H. (1983) Theories of Reproduction and Resistance in the New Sociology of Education: A critical analysis, *Harvard Educational Review*, 55, pp. 257–293.

Gorz, A. (1967) *Strategies for Labor: A radical proposal* (New York, Beacon Press).

Greene, L. (1990/1991) Tokens, Role Models, and Pedagogical Politics: Lamentations of an African American female law professor, *Berkeley Women's Law Journal*, 6, pp. 81–92.

Harper, A. (1994) *Langston Hughes: The return of simple* (New York, Hill and Wang).

Harris, A. (1994) Forward: The jurisprudence of reconstruction, *California Law Review*, 82, pp. 741–785.

hooks, b. (1989) *Talking Back: Thinking feminist, thinking black* (Boston, South End Press).

hooks, b. (1994) *Teaching to Transgress: Education as the practice of freedom* (New York, Routledge).

Johnson, K. (1999) *How Did You Get to Be Mexican? A White/Brown man's search for identity* (Philadelphia, Temple University Press).

Ladson-Billings, G. (1996) Silences as Weapons: Challenges of a Black professor teaching White students, *Theory Into Practice*, 35, pp. 79–85.

LatCrit Primer (2000) Fact Sheet: LatCrit. Presented to the 5th Annual LatCrit Conference, 'Class in LatCrit: Theory and praxis in the world of economic inequality', The Village at Breckenridge Resort, Breckenridge, CO, 4–7 May 2000.

Lawrence, C. (1991) Doing the 'James Brown' at Harvard: Professor Derrick Bell as liberationist teacher, *Harvard BlackLetter Journal*, 8, pp. 263–273.

Lawrence, C. (1992) The Word and the River: Pedagogy as scholarship as struggle, *Southern California Law Review*, 65, pp. 2231–2298.

Lawson, R. (1995) Critical Race Theory as Praxis: A view from outside to the outside, *Howard Law Journal*, 38, pp. 353–370.

Marable, M. (1992) *Black America* (Westfield, Open Media).

Matsuda, M. (1987) Looking to the Bottom: Critical legal studies and reparations, *Harvard Civil Rights–Civil Liberties Law Review*, 22, pp. 323–399.

Matsuda, M. (1991) Voices of America: Accent, antidiscrimination law, and a jurisprudence for the last reconstruction, *Yale Law Journal*, 100, pp. 1329–1407.

Matsuda, M., Lawrence, C., Delgado, R. & Crenshaw, K. (1993) *Words that Wound: Critical race theory, assaultive speech, and the First Amendment* (Boulder, Westview Press).

Montoya, R. (1998) *Culture Clash: Life, death, and revolutionary comedy* (New York, Theatre Communications Group).

Olivas, M. (1990) The Chronicles, My Grandfather's Stories, and Immigration Law: The slave traders chronicle as racial history, *Saint Louis University Law Journal*, 34, pp. 425–441.

Paredes, A. (1977) On Ethnographic Work among Minority Groups: A folklorist's perspective, *New Scholar*, 6, pp. 1–32.

Robinson, R. (1997) Teaching from the Margins: Race as a pedagogical sub-text, *Western New England Law Review*, 19, pp. 151–181.

Russell, M. (1992) Entering Great America: Reflections on race and the convergence of progressive legal theory and practice, *Hastings Law Journal*, 43, pp. 749–767.

Scott-Heron, G. (1974) The Revolution Will Not Be Televised, on: *The Revolution Will Not Be Televised* (album) (New York, Flying Dutchman Productions).

Solórzano, D. (1989) Teaching and Social Change: Reflections on a Freirean approach in a college classroom, *Teaching Sociology*, 17, pp. 218–225.

Solórzano, D. (1997) Images and Words that Wound: Critical race theory, racial stereotyping, and teacher education, *Teacher Education Quarterly*, 24, pp. 5–19.

Solórzano, D. (1998) Critical Race Theory, Racial and Gender Microaggressions, and the Experiences of Chicana and Chicano Scholars, *International Journal of Qualitative Studies in Education*, 11, pp. 121–136.

Solórzano, D. & Delgado Bernal, D. (2001) Critical Race Theory, Transformational Resistance, and Social Justice: Chicana and Chicano students in an urban context, *Urban Education*, 36, pp. 308–342.

Solórzano, D. & Solórzano, R. (1995) The Chicano Educational Experience: A proposed framework for effective schools in Chicano communities, *Educational Policy*, 9, pp. 293–314.

Solórzano, D. & Villalpando, O. (1998) Critical Race Theory, Marginality, and the Experience of Minority Students in Higher Education, in: C. Torres & T. Mitchell (eds), *Emerging Issues in the Sociology of Education: Comparative perspectives* (New York, SUNY Press), pp. 211–224.

Solórzano, D. & Yosso, T. (2000) Toward a Critical Race Theory of Chicana and Chicano Education, in: C. Tejeda, C. Martinez & Z. Leonardo (eds), *Charting New Terrains of Chicana(o)/Latina(o) Education* (Cresskill, Hampton Press), pp. 35–65.

Solórzano, D. & Yosso, T. (2001) Critical Race and LatCrit Theory and Method: Counter-storytelling Chicana and Chicano graduate school experiences, *International Journal of Qualitative Studies in Education*, 14:4, pp. 471–495.

Stefancic, J. (1998) Latino and Latina Critical Theory: An annotated bibliography, *La Raza Law Journal*, 10, pp. 423–498.

Sweet, S. (1998) Radical Curriculum and Radical Pedagogy: Balancing political sympathies with institutional constraints, *Teaching Sociology*, 26, pp. 100–111.

Tierney, W. (1993) *Building Communities of Difference: Higher education in the twenty-first century* (Westport, Bergin and Garvey).

Williams, R. (1997) Vampires Anonymous and Critical Race Practice, *Michigan Law Review*, 95, pp. 741–765.

4

The Social Construction of Difference and the Quest for Educational Equality

JAMES A. BANKS

University of Washington, Seattle

Je est un autre (I am an other).

—Rimbaud, in Todorov, 1987, p. 3

Historical, political, and social developments within the last half century were a watershed in the quest for educational equality in the United States. Racial segregation within the nation's educational institutions and within the larger society received a major blow when the Supreme Court, in *Brown v. the Board of Education of Topeka* (1954), declared separate but equal schools unconstitutional. The Brown decision paved the way for the Civil Rights Movement of the 1960s and 1970s.

In education, developments aimed at increasing educational equality emerged, including school desegregation, affirmative action, bilingual education, and multicultural education. Each has been contested and has stimulated acid debates, and each has changed the nation and its educational institutions in ways that will have profound consequences in the new century. Equality will be an essential component of educational discourse in the twenty-first century.

School desegregation, affirmative action, bilingual education, and multicultural education have brought the nation closer to the democratic values of its founding documents—the Declaration of Independence, the Constitution, and the Bill of Rights. Progress toward democratic ideals during the last half century, however, has been cyclic and uneven rather than linear and straightforward. Progress during the new century will continue, but will also be cyclic and uneven. Periods of progress will be followed by periods of retrogression. But during retrogressive periods, some progress attained in previous periods will be maintained. Regression and progress will often occur at the same time. Today, for example, some communities are strongly contesting bilingual education, while throughout the nation, multicultural content is becoming institutionalized in school textbooks and in college and university courses.

During the last thirty years, such educational developments have revealed the inconsistency between America's democratic ideals and its educational practices, a gap that has been called the 'American dilemma' (Myrdal, 1944). Uncovering this dilemma is an essential step in the march toward educational equality. Positive steps have included identifying the issues related to educational equality, discussing them in public forums, and implementing programs and practices that create greater educational equality for groups on society's margins.

The quest for educational equality resulted in the participation of more women, people of color, language minority groups, and people with disabilities in shaping educational research, policy, and practice. Their efforts uncovered—as well as contested—established paradigms, canons, categories, and concepts that they believed justified their marginalized status, defined them as the 'other,' and played a role in denying them equal educational opportunities.

The most powerful groups in a society largely determine what knowledge is produced and becomes institutionalized in schools, colleges, and universities. The battle over whose knowledge should be institutionalized was an important consequence of the pursuit for educational equality in the closing decades of the twentieth century (Schlesinger, 1991; Sleeter, 1995); that battle will continue until marginalized groups become equal-status participants in mainstream U.S. society.

Grounded in the sociology of knowledge (Mannheim, 1985/1936; Berger & Luckmann, 1966), this chapter examines how race, mental retardation, and giftedness are socially constructed categories that have been used to reinforce the privileged positions of powerful groups, established practices, and institutions. It also discusses how marginalized groups contested these concepts and created oppositional knowledge aimed at increasing their educational opportunities and possibilities. Emerging issues related to these concepts will continue to manifest themselves in the new century.

In my examination, I do not intend to obscure the concepts' distinct histories, purpose and aims. I realize that most special and gifted educators believe that their work helps actualize educational equality by providing essential resources and support for targeted groups of students. Some educational programs with humanitarian goals, however, have latent functions that contradict those goals and promote inequality (Tomlinson, 1982). For example, classes for mentally retarded students—whose public aim is to provide special instruction for students who need it—are overpopulated by males, low-income students, and students of color. My sociological analysis focuses on the latent rather than the manifest function of knowledge and the institutions it supports (Merton, 1968).

Any body of knowledge can be socially established as reality (Berger & Luckmann, 1966). Varenne and McDermott (1998) call socially constructed knowledge 'cultural facts.' The cultural facts about race, mental retardation, and giftedness have often been used to justify and legitimize educational practices limiting the academic achievement of students of color, language minority students, students with disabilities, and students from lower socioeconomic groups.

I encourage readers to consider these questions as they read this chapter:

- Who has the power to define groups and institutionalize their concepts within schools, colleges, and universities?
- What is the relationship between knowledge and power?
- Who benefits from how race, mental retardation, and giftedness are defined and conceptualized in the larger society and within educational institutions? Who loses?
- How can race, mental retardation, and giftedness be reconstructed so that they can empower marginalized groups and create greater educational equality?

To provide a historical context for discussing the construction of categories and the quest for educational equality, I begin by describing the state of race relations as we enter the new century.

Race Relations at the Dawn of a New Century

Race relations and racial equality in the United States are at a turning point. The nation made notable progress toward eliminating racial, ethnic, and gender discrimination from the 1960s to the early 1980s. Significant advances in racial equality continued from the Brown decision (1954) to the Reagan presidential years (1981–1989), when progress was slowed. Even during the Reagan and Bush years, however, people of color and women made substantial progress toward educational equality and inroads toward full inclusion into mainstream society. Because they were already a part of mainstream society and had substantial educational, financial, and cultural capital, middle- and upper-class White women progressed further than ethnic groups of color within the last twenty-five years. Even so, however, they still face intractable glass ceilings in some of the most coveted jobs and in the world of business and finance.

Although racial and ethnic groups and women made considerable progress in the decades between 1960 and 1980, the gap between the rich and the poor widened considerably within the last several decades (Wilson, 1996). After declining for forty years, the share of the nation's wealth held by the wealthiest households (0.5 percent) rose sharply in the 1980s. In 1976, this segment of the population held 14 percent of the nation's wealth. In 1983, it held 26.9 percent (Phillips, 1990). In 1992, the top 20 percent of American households received eleven times as much income as the bottom 2 percent. In 1997, 35.6 percent of Americans were living in poverty, which included a high concentration of African Americans and Hispanics (U.S. Bureau of the Census, 1998a). In 1997, the poverty rate for non-Hispanic Whites was 8.6 percent, compared to 25.5 percent and 27.1 percent for African Americans and Hispanics, respectively.

Although groups of color such as African Americans, Puerto Ricans in the United States, and Mexican Americans have disproportionately high poverty rates, many individuals of color joined the middle class. Class divisions increased within both ethnic minority and majority groups during the last three decades. The nation's student population reflects the widening social class gap. In 1990, about one in five students lived below the official government poverty line (U.S. Bureau of the Census, 1998a). The class divide between teachers and students, and between middle-class and low-income students, will be a major influence on the quest for educational equality in the twenty-first century.

The nation seems exhausted in its struggle for racial equality. Some conservative leaders and scholars argue that the playing field is now even and that people of color must join the race for progress without governmental intervention or help (Thernstrom & Thernstrom, 1997; Steele, 1998). These individuals appear to ignore the long history of institutionalized discrimination in the United States and have not acknowledged that we cannot correct problems in several decades that have been in the making for nearly four centuries (Franklin, 1993; Lawrence & Matsuda, 1997).

We begin the new century with the problems of institutional discrimination still with us and with a nationally organized and effective conservative backlash. The backlash is not only stemming governmental intervention to create a more just society but is also eroding gains that ethnic minorities have made within the last three decades. The actions of conservative groups and institutions, which include federal court actions, have been both ominous and effective. For example, the decision in the *Hopwood v. State of Texas* case ended affirmative action at the University of Texas Law School; Initiative 209 in California and Initiative 200 in Washington State prohibit affirmative action in government employment and university admissions (Orfield & Miller, 1998).

That affirmative action is being dismantled at the same time that the first data-based study reveals its success is ironic: it has enabled more African Americans to gain admission to college and graduate school, enter mainstream society, and contribute substantially to their communities and society (Bowen & Bok, 1998). Institutions of higher education in California and in Washington State are faced with finding new ways to achieve student and faculty diversity now that established practices are illegal. Success in California and Washington will most likely encourage affirmative action opponents to take their campaign to other states. Affirmative action policies within several schools have also been challenged, a trend that is likely to continue into the foreseeable future.

An anti-bilingual movement has emerged in response to the significant increase in the percentage of students who speak a first language other than English. U.S. English, formed in the 1980s, is a group that lobbies to make English the nation's official language and the only language used in public places. By 1998, twenty-five states had made English their official language, either by amending their state constitutions or by enacting new legislation (U.S. English, 1999). Arizona's law, enacted in 1988, was declared unconstitutional by the Arizona Supreme Court in 1998.

Another indication of anti-bilingual sentiment is the large number of California residents who voted for Proposition 227 (also known as the Unz Amendment, after the millionaire Ron Unz, who led the campaign for it). Proposition 227, which essentially eliminates bilingual education, was approved overwhelmingly at the polls. This vote is ironic because research indicates that the best way for students to learn a second language, such as English, is to strengthen—not eradicate—their first language (August & Hakuta, 1997).

The Challenge of Fostering Diversity and Equity

Two somewhat contradictory developments make it imperative for U.S. educators to set a high priority on diversity and equity. One is the challenge from individuals and groups opposed to affirmative action and other diversity initiatives. The other is the growth of ethnic, cultural, and language diversity in the nation. Educators need to be a counterforce and help students acquire a strong commitment to democratic values and become reflective citizens. Students should also be helped to understand that a gap between ideals and realities always exists in a democratic society and that their role as citizens is to take actions to help close that gap (Banks, 1997a).

I call the significant changes in the racial, ethnic, and language groups that make up the nation's population the 'demographic imperative' (Banks, 1997a). The United States is experiencing its largest influx of immigrants since the beginning of the twentieth century. Between 1980 and 1990, 80 percent of the documented immigrants came from nations in Latin America and Asia (U.S. Bureau of the Census, 1994). In contrast, only 9 percent came from Europe. The U.S. Bureau of the Census projects that people of color will make up 47.5 percent of the nation's population by 2050.

Increases in racial, ethnic, and linguistic diversity in the general population are reflected in the student population. It is projected that students of color will make up about 48 percent of school-age youths by 2020 (Pallas *et al.*, 1989). In 1990, 14 percent of school-age youths spoke a first language at home other than English (U.S. Bureau of the Census, 1994). A document from the Teachers of English to Speakers of Other Languages (1997) states, 'Current projections estimate that by the year 2000, the majority of the school-age population in 50 or more major U.S. cities will be from language minority backgrounds' (p. 1). A research synthesis published by the National Research Council highlights the nation's growing language minority population and describes its instructional needs as an important priority for its schools (August & Hakuta, 1997).

Increased diversification in the school population has produced serious academic and social problems needing urgent and thoughtful attention. Despite gains within the last decade, African American and Latino youths are still substantially behind Anglo mainstream youths on many indexes of academic achievement. They also have lower high-school graduation rates and higher retention, suspension, and dropout rates (Gay, 1997).

School-based reforms are needed to help students learn how to live together in civic, moral, and just communities that respect and value all students' rights and cultural characteristics. Such efforts are made more difficult because an increasing percentage of students of color attend racially segregated schools (Orfield *et al.*, 1996), and because segregation often exists within racially and ethnically mixed schools using tracking and special programs.

A Focus on Difference

Increasing diversity, the widening gap between the rich and the poor, and renewed efforts by marginalized groups to gain recognition and legitimacy have focused attention on issues related to difference within the last three decades. Because such issues are unresolved—for example, backlashes against affirmative action and bilingual education—this focus is likely to increase and intensify in the new century.

A major problem facing the nation-state is how to recognize and legitimize difference and yet construct an overarching national identity that incorporates the voices, experiences, and hopes of the diverse groups that compose it. What groups will participate in constructing a new national identity, and what factors will be used to motivate powerful groups to share power with marginalized groups, are also issues that have to be addressed. Power sharing is an essential characteristic of a nation-state that reflects the cultures of its diverse population.

New Conceptions of Difference

Traditional categories used to differentiate and define human population groups will become more contested as marginalized racial, ethnic, cultural, and language groups grow in size, power, and legitimacy. Uncovering and deconstructing these institutionalized conceptions that deny human population groups equal educational opportunities, and replacing them with liberatory concepts, paradigms, and theories, are important agenda items for the new century. These new conceptions should view human potential as unlimited and describe ways in which group boundaries are flexible and interactive, rather than limited and distinct. Schools, colleges, and universities should integrate these ideas into programs to educate teachers and educational leaders.

The Social Construction of Race

Race is one of the main categories used to construct differences in the United States and in other societies (Montagu, 1997). Racialization is a characteristic of both past and present societies (Hannaford, 1996). Groups holding political and economic power construct racial categories to privilege members of their groups and marginalize outside groups. Jacobson (1998) calls races 'invented categories' (p. 4). Omi and Winant (1994) state that the 'determination of racial categories is an intensely political process' (p. 3). Their theory of racial formation 'emphasizes the social nature of race, the absence of any essential racial characteristics, the historical flexibility of racial meanings and categories ... and the irreducible political aspect of racial dynamics' (p. 4).

Racial categories have shifted over time, established racial categories have been deconstructed, and new ones have been formed. The large influx of immigrants from Ireland in the 1840s and from eastern, southern, and central Europe in the late 1800s challenged the category of whiteness. White ethnic groups who were already established in the United States and who had social, economic, and political power defined the 'huddled masses' of new immigrants as peoples from different races. Writes Jacobson (1998), 'Upon the arrival of the massive waves of Irish immigrants in the 1840s, whiteness itself would become newly problematic, and in some quarters, would begin to lose its monolithic character' (pp. 37–38).

Jacobson describes these developments as 'the fracturing of whiteness' (p. 38). Various groups of Whites became distinct races that were ranked, such as the Celtic, Slav, Hebrew, Iberic, Mediterranean, and Anglo-Saxon. Anglo-Saxon was classified as the superior race. One writer stated that because of their 'Celtic blood,' the Irish threatened the American republic (Jacobson, 1998, p. 49). A newspaper described the Irish as a 'savage mob,' 'a pack of savages,' and 'incarnate devils'

(Jacobson, 1998, p. 55). The Irish became defined as the other and consequently were denied opportunities that the Anglo-Saxons enjoyed.

Italians and Jews were also defined as the other near the turn of the century and experienced racial discrimination and hostility. Italians were often called by disparaging terms, such as 'dagos' and 'white niggers.' In some parts of the South, Italians were forced to attend all-Black schools (Waters, 1990). In 1891, during the height of American nativism, eleven Italians were lynched after being accused of murdering the police chief of New Orleans.

Leo Frank, a Jewish northerner, became a victim of anti-Semitism and racial hostility when he was accused of murdering a White girl who worked in a pencil factory he co-owned. In 1915, he was found guilty in an unfair trial. When the governor of Georgia commuted his sentence, a White mob forcibly removed him from jail and lynched him.

Multiple categories that had described the races among White ethnic groups in the mid-nineteenth century became one racial category in the twentieth century (Alba, 1990; Ignatiev, 1995; Jacobson, 1998). A single White racial category formed when the various White ethnic groups assimilated culturally, racially identified as one group, and defined themselves in opposition to African Americans (Morrison, 1992).

Lessons from the Past

The past has taught us that racial categories and their meanings will keep changing, that groups with power will construct race to benefit themselves and disadvantage powerless groups, and that race is a powerful variable in the American conscience and society. Politicians are keenly aware of race's power. This savviness became evident when George Bush, who was lagging in the presidential polls in 1988, used a commercial that featured a Black escaped criminal (Willie Horton) to solicit support from White voters.

History has also taught us that once groups attain sufficient power, they will challenge existing conceptions of race if necessary and push for redefining the meaning of racial categories. Such opposition will most likely come from biracial individuals and from Latino groups who are expected to outnumber African Americans by 2020 if their current birthrates and immigration rates continue.

In 1990, biracial individuals challenged the racial categories that the Census Bureau used. After reviewing the results of tests and hearings, the Office of Management and Budget changed a 2000 Census question so that an individual may check one or more racial categories. The Bureau expects this change to affect its results only slightly because 'fewer than 2 percent of respondents in recent tests used this option' (U.S. Bureau of the Census, 1998b).

Many biracial individuals who have one African American and one White parent believe that they should not be forced to belong to one racial category, but rather should be able to indicate that they are both African American and White. Ironically, the push by biracial individuals to create new racial categories reifies the concept of race itself, which many scholars think is a bogus and unscientific concept (Montagu, 1997).

Biracial marriages and births in the United States have increased significantly within the last several decades and are likely to continue increasing in the twenty-first century. Between 1970 and 1992, the number of African American–White couples quadrupled, to 246,000 (Kalish, 1995). Interracial births more than doubled between 1978 and 1992, while total births increased 22 percent (Kalish, 1995). Interracial marriages are also increasing.

The biracial and multiracial student population is increasing, creating a greater need for educators to help students realize that interracial relationships and biracial children from these unions have a long history in the United States. That history is evidenced by the relationship between Sally Hemings and Thomas Jefferson (Gordon-Reed, 1997; Murray & Duffy, 1998), the often silenced and denied Black heritages within White families (Ball, 1998), and the mixed racial heritage of many eminent African Americans. Both Booker T. Washington and Frederick Douglass had White fathers and enslaved mothers.

Whites and African Americans, Native Americans and Whites, and Native Americans and African Americans have produced offspring with mixed heritages since these groups first interacted in the Americas (Nash, 1982). The dominant racial and ethnic group in Mexico and throughout most of Latin America is racially mixed. The Mexican people were created when the Spaniards colonized Mexico and produced offspring (known as *mestizos*) with Native American women. The Africans who were brought to Mexico added to its ethnic mix. Legitimizing interracial mixtures in the United States is a recent phenomenon, although interracial mixture itself is historic. This is an important distinction that teachers and students need to understand.

Existing racial categories are also challenged by how some students perceive their racial and ethnic identification. Research in inner-city communities found that many youths of color refused to identify with a particular ethnic group (Heath & McLaughlin, 1993). They said that they were simply 'ethnic.' According to Heath (1995), 'Contrary to general perceptions, within the daily lives of young people in many (not all) inner cities, racial or ethnic identities are always situated and multiple' (p. 48).

Ethnic identities are not fixed but are constantly changing, in part because of group interactions within a society characterized by racial, ethnic, language, and religious diversity (Nieto, 1998). Both mainstream White students and students of color are changed in these interactions.

The complex and changing nature of ethnic groups within U.S. society challenges the idea that educators can accurately identify a student's racial or ethnic group membership by physical characteristics or behaviors. The significant number of African American and Latino students entering the middle and upper classes also defies static classification.

The Continuing Significance of Race

In a nation such as the United States, where racism is embedded within the societal structure, how individuals identify themselves racially can be at odds with how outside groups and institutions view and respond to them. For example, schools may treat biracial students who have an African American parent as African

American, even though the students identify with two races. The difference in classification indicates that self-identification of race is insufficient to establish one's racial identification within a racially stratified society.

The Continuing Significance of Culture

Cultural issues will likely continue to be important in educating students from diverse groups because culture and social class interact in complex ways. Many students of color are socialized in low-income, predominantly minority communities, where they learn cultural behaviors, communication styles, and values that do not always integrate smoothly into the mainstream culture of schools (Anyon, 1997; Wilson, 1996).

A number of researchers have described the cultures of various ethnic groups, argued that cultural conflicts exist between the schools and the cultures of ethnic minority students, and explained ways that teachers can adapt their teaching to make it culturally congruent. Among the most significant are Philips's (1983) study of the participation structures that Native American students use; Au's (1980) study of participation structures that native Hawaiian students use; Heath's (1983) study of language socialization patterns in an African American and a White community; and Lee's (1993) study of African American language usage. Another influential and informative study profiles eight teachers who implemented culturally congruent teaching in their classroom (Ladson-Billings, 1994).

It is important to remember that work on the cultural differences of students is not static; practitioners should view it within the context of students' changing ethnic identities and cultural characteristics.

Expansions of Educational Equality for Students with Disabilities

Before the Civil Rights Movement, many students with disabilities were isolated in special schools and classes, stigmatized, viewed as the other, and sometimes denied the opportunity to attend their local public schools. The Supreme Court decision in the Brown case in 1954 established the principle that segregated schooling on the basis of race was inherently unequal and denied students equal educational opportunities. Advocates for students with disabilities reasoned that if segregating students on the basis of race was unconstitutional, segregating students with disabilities could also be challenged. Encouraged by the opportunities that African Americans attained as a result of their leadership and work in the Civil Rights Movement, they contested the segregation of students with disabilities within schools and classrooms. The enactment of Public Law 94-142 in 1975, the Education for All Handicapped Children Act, was a major victory.

Intellectual Hierarchies

Psychology's historic and strong influence on educational theory, research, and practice has entrenched the bell curve and its implications in schools. The bell curve assumes that only small percentages of the population will have high or low levels of intellectual ability. It does not focus on ways to create and nurture intellectual ability. This institutionalized hierarchical notion of mental ability is reflected in practices such as academic tracking—students are given differential access to high-status knowledge and skills (Oakes, 1985; Darling-Hammond, 1995)—and in programs for mentally retarded students and for gifted students.

Hierarchical conceptions of intellectual ability have also led to a focus on the individual characteristics of students rather than on ways that social systems structure academic norms and expectations (Brookover *et al.*, 1979). Schools have done little to change norms and expectations to create intellectual ability (Levine & Lezotte, 1995).

Disability and Race

One of the most contested aspects of special education programs is the disproportionate percentage of African American and Latino students who are categorized as mildly mentally retarded and as having emotional/behavior disorders (Artiles & Trent, 1994). Special education programs for students with speech and language problems tend to have a disproportionate percentage of Latino students (Artiles & Trent, 1994).

Parents and other student advocates have legally challenged the disproportionate percentage of students of color in special education programs. Several courts have ruled in favor of the plaintiffs, including verdicts in *Diana v. California State Board of Education* (1970) and *Larry P. v. Wilson Riles* (1986). In the *Diana* case, the plaintiffs alleged that the California State Board of Education used biased tests in the procedures that assigned Mexican American and Chinese American students to special education classes. The state of California agreed to develop tests that reflect its diverse cultures. In the *Larry P.* case, the U.S. District Court for the Northern District of California prohibited the use of IQ tests to place African Americans in special education programs (Mercer, 1989).

The Social Construction of Mental Retardation

In her pioneering work, Mercer (1973) proposes that mental retardation is a social construction and describes it from both a clinical and a social system perspective. From a clinical perspective, mental retardation is viewed as a handicapping condition because individuals' attributes prevent them from functioning effectively within the mainstream society. This individual condition 'can be diagnosed by clinically trained professionals using properly standardized assessment techniques' (Mercer, 1973, p. 2). Mercer states that the clinical perspective uses a pathological or medical model that classifies individuals as mentally retarded when they deviate from the mean or norm of the mainstream population.

Mercer (1973) describes how the clinical perspective is problematic in a society where many individuals are socialized within socioeconomic and ethnic cultures that differ substantially from the mainstream culture. Their behaviors and cultural characteristics are functional and sanctioned within their ethnic and socioeconomic subsocieties but are considered deviant and are devalued within the mainstream society. Consequently, students who are judged competent in their ethnic subsocieties may be labeled mentally retarded in the mainstream society and thus in schools. Mercer states that the core mainstream society consists primarily of cultural patterns of middle- and upper-class Anglo-Protestant Americans.

From a social system perspective, normal behavior is determined by examining how an individual functions within that individual's specific cultural community (Mercer, 1973). Behavior is judged deviant when it varies greatly from behavior expected by the ethnic group or community. The point of reference is the cultural or ethnic community, not the mainstream society.

When a social system perspective is used to determine mental retardation, individuals who are considered normal in their families or neighborhoods might be considered mentally retarded in a school setting. Mercer found that Mexican American youths who were considered normal in their families and communities and who functioned effectively in those settings were labeled mentally retarded in school. She writes, 'Mental retardation is not a characteristic of individuals, nor a meaning inherent in behavior, but a socially determined status, which he [she] may occupy in some social systems and not in others, depending on their norms' (Mercer, 1973, p. 31; emphasis added).

The Social Construction of Giftedness

The socioeconomic groups and groups of color that are overrepresented in programs and classes for mentally retarded students and for students with emotional/behavior disorders are underrepresented in classes and programs for gifted and talented students. In 1984, Whites made up 71 percent of the general student population and 81.4 percent of the students enrolled in programs for gifted and talented students (Fisher, 1998). In contrast, Latinos and African Americans made up 9.1 percent and 16.2 percent of the general student population and 4.7 percent and 8.4 percent, respectively, of the students enrolled in programs for gifted and talented students.

Sapon-Shevin (1994) describes giftedness 'as a social construct, a way of thinking and describing that exists in the eyes of the definers' (p. 16). Individuals and groups who are defined as gifted vary with the times, state and school district guidelines and procedures, assessment measures used to identify gifted students, and opportunities to learn that have been available to the students being considered for gifted programs. Giftedness is contextual and situational: 'The particular criteria are constantly changing and vary from place to place. What all programs share is their attempt to identify children they think are especially deserving of extra opportunities' (Oakes & Lipton, 1994, p. xi).

Political factors also influence which students become categorized as gifted. A number of school districts in large cities have lost many middle-class White students to suburban school districts and to private schools within the last two decades. Special programs, magnet schools, and gifted programs are sometimes used in these districts—which have declining enrollments and an eroding tax base—to lure White middle-class parents back to city schools.

Middle-class White parents also have more political and cultural capital than most lower socioeconomic parents and parents of color; they use their cultural know-how and political clout to pressure school districts to admit their children to programs for gifted and talented students. Parents compete to get their children admitted to programs for gifted and talented students because they view the benefits of these programs as a limited resource.

Programs for gifted and talented students tend to have better-qualified teachers, lower teacher–pupil ratios, and more intellectually engaging teaching than classes for lower-track students (Oakes, 1985). Classes for lower-track students tend to be characterized by low-level instruction, drill exercises, and a lack of higher-level content. Schools that are racially desegregated often have gifted, special education, and bilingual programs and classes—a type of segregation.

The factors that result in higher enrollment levels of African Americans and Latinos in classes for mentally retarded students are probably the same ones that account for their low enrollment in classes for gifted and talented students. These factors include their lower scores on standardized tests often used to determine placement in both types of classes; fewer opportunities to learn the content and skills that the standardized tests measure; and cultural and language characteristics that are inconsistent with those valued by the schools and test-makers.

Using Power to Define Categories

People and groups who have power exercise authority over others and influence their perceptions, beliefs, and behaviors. Shafritz (1988) states that expert power 'is based on the perception that the leader possesses some special knowledge or expertise.' Leaders exercise legitimate power when followers believe that the leaders have 'the legitimate right or authority to exercise influence' (p. 427). Bourdieu (in Swartz, 1997) argues that power cannot be exercised unless it is legitimate.

One way that powerful groups legitimize their power is through the construction of knowledge, which includes concepts and propositions that justify their privileged position and explain why marginalized groups deserve a low status in society. When Columbus arrived in the Caribbean, he knew that the Indians called the islands Guanahani, yet he renamed them when he claimed ownership. Writes Todorov (1987), 'Columbus knows perfectly well that these islands already have names ... however, he seeks to rename places in terms of the rank they occupy in his discovery, to give them the right names; moreover nomination is equivalent to taking possession' (p. 27).

When establishing categories for race, mental retardation, and giftedness, individuals and groups with power construct categories and characteristics and distribute rewards and privileges that benefit the existing hierarchies (Sleeter, 1986; Sapon-Shevin, 1994). Ford (1996) describes the problems and limitations of such categories:

No group has a monopoly on gifted. It is illogical and statistically impossible for giftedness to be the prerogative of one racial, gender, or socioeconomic group. Nonetheless, gifted programs represent the most segregated programs in public schools; they are disproportionately white and middle class. (pp. ix–x)

Just as groups with power and hegemony construct knowledge and categories that benefit entrenched institutions, marginalized individuals and groups create oppositional knowledge that challenges established knowledge, ideologies, practices, behaviors, and institutions (Banks, 1996). These groups also demand that hegemonic knowledge structures be dismantled and that more democratic forms of knowledge be created and implemented in institutions, including schools, colleges, and universities. In another publication (Banks, 1998), I describe case studies of researchers' lives and the ways in which their community cultures, biographical journeys, and status within the social structure influence the knowledge they construct. I also explain how mainstream researchers construct concepts and paradigms that reinforce their privilege positions, and how researchers on the margins of society contest knowledge systems and canons that privilege established groups and contribute to the victimization of marginalized groups.

To create democratic schools, colleges, and universities, the established concepts and knowledge systems must not privilege any particular racial, ethnic, social class, or gender group, but rather reflect the experiences of all groups that make up the nation-state. Consequently, educators must reform the cultures of the nation's schools, as well as the curriculum, to institutionalize and legitimize the knowledge systems, perspectives, ideologies, and behaviors of diverse ethnic, racial, cultural, social class, and language groups. This reform requires that more liberatory and multicultural paradigms and canons be constructed and institutionalized. In the last two decades, work in ethnic studies (Banks, 1997b), women's studies (Schmitz *et al.*, 1995), and multicultural education (Banks & Banks, 1995) has provided an important foundation for such efforts. Much of this work is reviewed and discussed in the *Handbook of Research on Multicultural Education* (Banks & Banks, 2004).

Reforming Schools

In the twenty-first century, schools, colleges, and universities can help teachers and students uncover old conceptions of difference and construct and institutionalize new conceptions of marginalized groups. Teachers and students need to rethink, re-imagine, and reconstruct their images and representations of groups of color and of American exceptionalism as presented in textbooks and in the popular culture (Appleby, 1992; Banks, 1996).

Students bring to the school community a set of values, commitments, ideologies, assumptions, and knowledge that influences their interactions with teachers, other students, and the school curriculum. These kinds of knowledge are becoming increasingly varied with the increase in student diversity, which will continue in the new century. Teachers should help students critically examine their cultural and community knowledge, understand how it relates to institutionalized knowledge systems, and construct new paradigms and conceptions about human diversity.

Teacher education needs to be reformed so that teachers can examine their own personal knowledge and values. They also need to uncover and examine the knowledge and values that underlie, justify, and legitimize practices in schools—such as the classification of racial and ethnic groups, special education programs, and programs for gifted and talented students—and the knowledge related to institutionalized beliefs—such as knowledge about skill grouping (Mosteller *et al.*, 1996), characteristics of Black English or Ebonics (Baugh, 1983), and the effects of loss of first language on learning English as a second language (August & Hakuta, 1997).

Concepts such as race, mental retardation, and giftedness are undergirded by strong normative claims and assumptions. Race assumes that human groups can be divided on the basis of their biological and physical characteristics, a highly contested claim (Omi & Winant, 1994; Montagu, 1997). Mental retardation focuses on the characteristics of individuals rather than on the social systems in which they are required to function (Mercer, 1973; Tomlinson, 1982; Mehan *et al.*, 1986; Varenne & McDermott, 1998). Giftedness is rarely defined in a way that indicates that all individuals have gifts as well as disabilities (Sapon-Shevin, 1994).

Other concepts in the school curriculum and teacher education that are often used without deep reflection to uncover their implicit meanings carry strong value claims and assumptions, such as the westward movement, at-risk students, and busing. In U.S. history, the term westward movement implies that a group foreign to a land can name as well as claim it. The term also suggests that the West was a wilderness before it was settled by European pioneers, another value-loaded concept. At-risk students suggests that some groups of students are at risk, and others are not, and that at-risk students can be identified (Cuban, 1989). Missing from this concept is the idea that every student and individual, including every educator, is at risk on some variable. Busing is not used to describe transporting students from their homes in predominantly White neighborhoods to predominantly White schools. Rather, busing is a term that contains specific value judgements about race and racial mixing in schools.

The Road Ahead

The new century poses challenges but also offers opportunities in the continuing quest for educational equality. Challenges include the widening gap between the rich and the poor; the growing isolation of low-income, inner-city students within the nation's aging cities; and the conservative backlashes against affirmative action and bilingual education.

The growing percentage of racial, ethnic, and language groups poses challenges to established institutions but is a potential source of hope and renewal. As Okihiro (1994) points out in his thoughtful and empowering book *Margins and Mainstreams*, groups on the margins of American society have forced it to live up to its democratic ideals. A salient example is the Civil Rights Movement, which forced the United States to eradicate apartheid. As groups who are victimized by established concepts and practices challenge and reconstruct them—and therefore acquire more freedom and liberation—all of us will become more humanized and free, because all Americans are 'caught in an inescapable network of mutuality' and 'tied in a single garment of destiny' (King, 1994, p. 3). We are the other, and the other is us.

Acknowledgements

I am grateful to the following colleagues for their perceptive and helpful comments on an earlier draft of this chapter: Cherry A. McGee Banks, Ron Brandt, Eugene B. Edgar, Sonia Nieto, and Christine E. Sleeter.

References

Alba, R. D. (1990) *Ethnic Identity: The transformation of white America* (New Haven, CT, Yale University Press).

Anyon, J. (1997) *Ghetto Schooling: A political economy of urban educational reform* (New York, Teachers College Press).

Appleby, J. (1992) Recovering America's Historic Diversity: Beyond exceptionalism, *Journal of American History*, 79, pp. 413–431.

Artiles, A. J. & Trent, S. C. (1994) Overrepresentation of Minority Students in Special Education: A continuing debate, *Journal of Special Education*, 27, pp. 410–437.

Au, K. (1980) Participation Structures in a Reading Lesson with Hawaiian Children, *Anthropology and Education Quarterly*, 11:2, pp. 91–115.

August, D. & Hakuta, K. (1997) *Improving Schooling for Language-Minority Children: A research agenda* (Washington, DC, National Academy Press).

Ball, E. (1998) *Slaves in the Family* (New York, Farrar, Straus, and Giroux).

Banks, J. A. (ed.) (1996) *Multicultural Education, Transformative Knowledge, and Action: Historical and contemporary perspectives* (New York, Teachers College Press).

Banks, J. A. (1997a) *Educating Citizens in a Multicultural Society* (New York, Teachers College Press).

Banks, J. A. (1997b) *Teaching Strategies for Ethnic Studies*, 6th edn (Boston, Allyn and Bacon).

Banks, J. A. (1998) The Lives and Values of Researchers: Implications for educating citizens in a multicultural society, *Educational Researcher*, 29, pp. 4–17.

Banks, J. A. & Banks, C. A. M. (eds) (2004) *Handbook of Research on Multicultural Education*, 2nd edn (San Francisco, Jossey-Bass).

Baugh, J. (1983) *Black Street Speech: Its history, structure, and survival* (Austin, TX, University of Texas Press).

Berger, P. L. & Luckmann, T. (1966). *The Social Construction of Reality: A treatise in the sociology of knowledge* (New York, Anchor).

Bowen, W. G. & Bok, D. (1998) *The Shape of the River: Long-term consequences of considering race in college and university admissions* (Princeton, NJ, Princeton University Press).

Brookover, W. B., Beady, C., Flood, P., Schweitzer, J. & Wisenbaker, J. (1979) *School Social Systems and Student Achievement: Schools can make a difference* (New York, Praeger).

Cuban, L. (1989) The 'At Risk' Label and the Problem of Urban School Reform, *Phi Delta Kappan*, 70, pp. 780–801.

Darling-Hammond, L. (1995) Inequality and Access to Knowledge, in: J. A. Banks & C. A. M. Banks (eds), *Handbook of Research on Multicultural Education* (New York, Macmillan), pp. 465–497.

Fisher, M. (with Perez, S. M., Gonzalez, B., Njus, J. & Kamasaki, C. (1998) *Latino Education: Status and prospects: State of Hispanic America 1998* (Washington, DC, National Council of La Raza).

Ford, D. Y. (1996) *Reversing Underachievement among Gifted Black Students: Promising practices and programs* (New York, Teachers College Press).

Franklin, J. H. (1993) *The Color Line: Legacy for the twenty-first century* (Columbia, MO, University of Missouri Press).

Gay, G. (1997) Educational Equality for Students of Color, in: J. A. Banks & C. A. M. Banks (eds), *Multicultural Education: Issues and perspectives*, 3rd edn (Boston, Allyn and Bacon), pp. 195–228.

Gordon-Reed, A. (1997) *Thomas Jefferson and Sally Hemings: An American controversy* (Charlottesville, VA, University Press of Virginia).

Hannaford, I. (1996) *Race: The history of an idea in the West* (Baltimore: Johns Hopkins University Press).

Heath, S. B. (1983) *Ways with Words: Language, life, and work in communities and classrooms* (New York, Cambridge University Press).

Heath, S. B. (1995) Race, Ethnicity, and the Defiance of Categories, in: W. D. Hawley & A. W. Jackson (eds), *Toward a Common Destiny: Improving race and ethnic relations in America* (San Francisco, Jossey-Bass), pp. 39–70.

Heath, S. B. & McLaughlin, M. W. (eds) (1993) *Identity and Inner-city Youth: Beyond ethnicity and gender* (New York, Teachers College Press).

Ignatiev, N. (1995). *How the Irish became White* (New York, Routledge and Kegan Paul).

Jacobson, M. F. (1998) *Whiteness of a Different Color: European immigrants and the alchemy of race* (Cambridge, MA, Harvard University Press).

Kalish, S. (1995) Multiracial Birth Increases as U.S. Ponders Racial Definitions, *Population Today*, 23:4, pp. 1–2.

King, M. L. (1994) *Letter from the Birmingham Jail* (New York, HarperCollins).

Ladson-Billings, C. (1994) *The Dreamkeepers: Successful teachers of African American children* (San Francisco, Jossey-Bass).

Lawrence, C. R., III & Matsuda, M. J. (1997) *We Won't Go Back: Making the case for affirmative action* (Boston, Houghton Mifflin).

Lee, C. F. (1993) *Signifying as a Scaffold for Literary Interpretation: The pedagogical implications of an African American discourse* (Urbana, IL, National Council of Teachers of English).

Levine, D. U. & Lezotte, L. W. (1995) Effective Schools Research, in: J. A. Banks & C. A. M. Banks (eds), *Handbook of Research on Multicultural Education* (New York, Macmillan), pp. 525–547.

Mannheim, K. (1985/1936) *Ideology and Utopia: An introduction to the sociology of knowledge* (San Diego, CA, Harcourt Brace Jovanovich). (Original work published 1936.)

Mehan, H., Hertweck, A. & Meihis, J. L. (1986) *Handicapping the Handicapped: Decision making in students' educational careers* (Stanford, CA, Stanford University Press).

Mercer, J. R. (1973) *Labeling the Mentally Retarded* (Berkeley, CA, University of California Press).

Mercer, J. R. (1989) Alternative Paradigms for Assessment in a Pluralistic Society, in: J. A. Banks & C. A. M. Banks (eds), *Multicultural Education: Issues and perspectives*, 1st edn (Boston, Allyn and Bacon), pp. 289–304.

Merton, R. K. (1968) Manifest and Latent Functions, in: R. K. Merton, *Social Theory and Social Structure*, enlarged edn (New York, Free Press), pp. 73–138.

Montagu, A. (1997) *Man's Most Dangerous Myth: The fallacy of race*, 6th edn (Walnut Creek, CA, AltaMira Press).

Morrison, T. (1992) *Playing in the Dark: Whiteness and the literary imagination* (Cambridge, MA, Harvard University Press).

Mosteller, F., Light, R. J. & Sachs, J. A. (1996) Sustained Inquiry in Education: Lessons from skill grouping and class size, *Harvard Educational Review*, 66, pp. 797–828.

Murray, B. & Duffy, B. (1998) Did the Author of the Declaration of Independence Take a Slave for his Mistress? DNA tests say yes, *U.S. News and World Report*, 125 (9 November), pp. 59–63.

Myrdal, G. (with Sterner, R. & Rose, A.) (1944) *An American Dilemma: The Negro problem and modern democracy* (New York, Harper).

Nash, C. 13. (1982). *Red, White, and Black: The peoples of early America*, 2nd edn (Englewood, Cliffs, NJ, Prentice-Hall).

Nieto, S. (1998) On Becoming American: An exploratory essay, in: W. Ayers & J. L. Miller (eds), *A Light in Dark Times: Maxine Greene and the unfinished conversation* (New York, Teachers College Press), pp. 45–57.

Oakes, J. (1985) *Keeping Track: How schools structure inequality* (New Haven, CT, Yale University Press).

Oakes, J. & Lipton, M. (1994) Foreword, in: M. Sapon-Shevin, *Playing Favorites: Gifted education and the disruption of community* (Albany, State University of New York Press), pp. ix–xvi.

Okihiro, G. Y. (1994) *Margins and Mainstreams: Asians in American history and culture* (Seattle, WA, University of Washington Press).

Omi, M. & Winant, H. (1994) *Racial Formation in the United States: From the 1960s to the 1990s*, 2nd edn (New York, Routledge and Kegan Paul).

Orfield, G., Eaton, S. E. & The Harvard Project on School Desegregation (1996) *Dismantling Desegregation: The quiet reversal of Brown v. Board of Education* (New York, New Press).

Orfield, G. & Miller, E. (1998) *Chilling Admissions: The affirmative action crisis and the search for alternatives* (Cambridge, MA, Harvard Education Publishing Group).

Pallas, A. M., Natriello, C. & McDill, E. L. (1989) The Changing Nature of the Disadvantaged Population: Current dimensions and future trends, *Educational Researcher*, 78:5, pp. 16–22.

Philips, S. (1983). *The Invisible Culture: Communication in classroom and community on the Warm Springs Indian Reservation* (New York, Longman).

Phillips, K. (1990) *The Politics of Rich and Poor: Wealth and the American electorate in the Reagan aftermath* (New York, Random House).

Sapon-Shevin, M. (1994) *Playing Favorites: Gifted education and the disruption of community*. (Albany, State University of New York Press).

Schlesinger, A. M. (1991). *The Disuniting of America: Reflections on a multicultural society* (Knoxville, TN, Whittle Direct Books).

Schmitz, B., Butler, J. E., Rosenfelt, D. & Guv-Sheftall, B. (1995) Women's Studies and Curriculum Transformation, in: J. A. Banks & C. A. M. Banks (eds), *Handbook of Research on Multicultural education* (New York, Macmillan), pp. 708–728.

Shafritz, J. M. (1988) *The Dorsey Dictionary of American Government and Politics* (Chicago, Dorsey Press).

Sleeter, C. E. (1986) Learning Disabilities: The social construction of a special education category, *Exceptional Children*, 53:1, pp. 46–54.

Sleeter, C. E. (1995) An Analysis of the Critiques of Multicultural Education, in: J. A. Banks & C. A. M. Banks (eds), *Handbook of Research on Multicultural Education* (New York, Macmillan), pp. 81–96.

Steele, S. (1998) *A Dream Deferred: The second betrayal of black freedom in America* (New York, HarperCollins), pp. 81–96.

Swartz, D. (1997) *Culture and Power: The sociology of Pierre Bourdieu* (Chicago, University of Chicago Press).

Teachers of English to Speakers of Other Languages (1997) *ESL Standards for Pre-K-12 Students* (Alexandria, VA, Author).

Thernstrom, S. & Thernstrom, A. (1997) *America in Black and White: One nation, indivisible* (New York, Simon and Schuster).

Todorov, T. (1987) *The Conquest of America: The question of the other* (New York, HarperCollins).

Tomlinson, S. (1982) *A Sociology of Special Education* (London, Routledge and Kegan Paul).

U.S. Bureau of the Census (1994) *Statistical Abstract of the United States*, 114th edn (Washington, DC, U.S. Government Printing Office).

U.S. Bureau of the Census (1998a) *Statistical Abstract of the United States*, 118th edn (Washington, DC, U.S. Government Printing Office).

U.S. Bureau of the Census (1998b) Questions and Answers about Census 2000; available: http://www.census.gov/dmd/www/advisory.html

U.S. English (1999) States with Official English Laws; available: http://usenglish.org (10 June).

Varenne, H. & McDermott, R. (1998) *Successful Failure: The school America builds* (Boulder: Westview Press).

Waters, M. C. (1990) *Ethnic Options: Choosing identities in America* (Berkeley, CA, University of California Press).

Wilson, W. J. (1996) *When Work Disappears: The world of the new urban poor* (New York, Alfred A. Knopf).

5

Anti-racism: From policy to praxis

DAVID GILLBORN
University of London

> As a black woman educator, border pedagogy means more to me than just creating certain conditions of learning. It is also about investigating the ways in which certain conditions of learning make possible the tension between embracing one's borderland and moving to another ... Border pedagogy is about acknowledging that what I do in the classroom is more than an intellectual exercise, a tossing around of ideas for debate. Rather, my teaching is about challenging belief systems that are part of everyday living.
>
> —Dlamini, 2002, p. 64

In a deeply personal and politically challenging essay, S. Nombuso Dlamini reflects on the experience of critical pedagogy from both sides of the desk; as both student and teacher. Dlamini's conclusions point to the central importance of power in education. She describes how, as a student, she felt marginalised and oppressed even in a class taught by a renowned critical pedagogue. Subsequently, she describes how, when on 'the Other side of the desk', the racist structures of society mean that, despite being a professor, she continues to be subject to the assertions and assumptions of white students:

> Some students outwardly challenge my choice of material, pointing out lenience towards material that is 'biased against white students'. Other students outwardly challenge my authority, questioning not only decisions I make about classroom discourse but about course content. They question the appropriateness of certain materials, wondering if I 'read the book'. Some will ask me to do the impossible: 'prove' that a narrative was indeed motivated by racism. (Dlamini, 2002, p. 63)

Racist power structures saturate the classroom. Attempts to challenge the taken-for-granted assumptions of white supremacy highlight the deep-rooted nature of the processes that sustain and extend the racial structuring of opportunity in society. Such attempts can be highly controversial; they are often uncertain; and almost always resisted. At a time when the World's last remaining superpower (and its partner in war-crimes, the UK) feels itself to be at once at its strongest and its most vulnerable, the education system is no less a battlefield than the ruins of the Middle East war zones.

In many nation states 'education' is increasingly being reduced to a system akin to a batch processing model of production (Elmore, 1987) where students are sorted into separate groups and processed via mandated curricula that are assessed through fixed and crude tests. In the name of 'standards' and 'accountability', teachers' scope for professional reflection and innovation is being systematically attacked. The 'No Child Left Behind' legislation in the USA, just like earlier education reforms in the UK, asserts a simple, authoritarian approach to knowledge, learning and teaching. In this scheme teachers are rendered little more than trained deliverers of pre-packaged ideas and conclusions (all officially verified and approved). The scope for any kind of critical, reflexive pedagogy is fast being eroded before our eyes. Our attempts to retain and extend critical pedagogy are more than a technical concern for scholars in the classroom, they are matters of power and struggle for those who seek change:

> critical pedagogy and anti-racism education are not just about elements in a curriculum that are intended to make students aware of racism and to work toward the elimination of racist attitudes and behaviour in students. Both critical pedagogy and anti-racism education embrace the notion of raising consciousness. (Dlamini, 2002, p. 54)

This chapter reflects on the recent history of 'anti-racism' in education policy and practice. In particular, I focus on the ways in which anti-racism has developed as an overtly radical and oppositional approach that stands apart from self-consciously liberal and consensual 'multicultural' schools of thought. This approach to anti-racism has been especially prominent among radical scholars in the UK, Canada, Australasia and South Africa (see, for example, Dei *et al.*, 2004). Elements of this same critique are present in some versions of 'critical' multiculturalism and, increasingly, within race critical scholarship informed by cross-disciplinary and poststructuralist perspectives (Essed & Goldberg, 2002; Ladson-Billings, 2004; Parker *et al.*, 1999). Regardless of our chosen nomenclature, however, a key lesson concerns the importance of *praxis*: the combination of theory, practice and experience which—at its best—demands a serious engagement with the complex and changing contours of racism. There is no fixed and finished rule book for anti-racism, critical race theory, or critical pedagogy. If we take seriously the word 'critical', then we must not only critique the workings of late capitalism and the new globalised forms of colonialism, which simultaneously discipline and subjugate US inner cities just as they seek to control nation states abroad. In order to forge a critical pedagogy that is sufficiently anti-racist, educators must also remain self-critical and reflexive about the current racial formation.

Anti-racism

Anti-racism is an ill-defined and changing concept. For some the term denotes any opposition to racism, ranging from organised protest to individual acts of resistance through a refusal to adopt white supremacist assumptions (Aptheker, 1993). For others anti-racism describes a more systematic perspective that both provides a theoretical understanding of the nature of racism and offers general guidance for its opposition through emancipatory practice (Mullard, 1984). The former, broad conception of anti-racism is among the most common understandings internationally, while in Britain the latter more specific usage is dominant. Anti-racism has achieved a degree of public recognition in Britain beyond that attained in most other countries. For this reason I will begin by using the British case as a vehicle for describing anti-racism in education, especially in relation to the sometimes complementary, sometimes conflicting understandings of *multiculturalism*. I will broaden the focus later in the piece, particularly with reference to newly emerging discourses of critical anti-racism and praxis.

In Britain, anti-racism was most prominent in social policy debates during the 1980s. Although this period saw a Conservative government re-elected to power at a national level throughout the decade, it was at the local level, especially through the work of local authorities, that anti-racism enjoyed its most influential period. Anti-racism in the 1980s came to denote a wide variety of practices, especially those associated with radical left authorities (such as those in London, Sheffield and Manchester), trade unions and organisations (such as the Anti-Nazi League) which attempted to mobilise young people in opposition to racist organisations like the National Front and later the British National Party (Solomos & Back, 1996). Education emerged as a particularly important arena for anti-racist debate. Although anti-racist policies were adopted in many spheres, it was in education that local policy-makers and practitioners (including teachers' trade unions) achieved some notable changes in policy and practice, although progress was by no means universal or unproblematic.

Attempts to challenge racism in British education have a long and troubled ancestry. Historically, schools and local authorities have been able to take advantage of a system that allowed for an unusually high degree of autonomy, freeing educationists to be among the most consistently active professional groups in the struggle against racism. In the 1980s and 1990s, however, these activities came under severe threat. Education emerged as a key ideological battleground; an arena where each new government initiative was assumed to have a natural consequence requiring further reform of an already shell-shocked system. A succession of reforms, for example, institutionalised a national system of testing linked to a compulsory (and overwhelmingly Eurocentric) curriculum. This added to the divisive effects of an education system that already operated in racialized ways and disadvantaged many minority pupils (Gillborn & Gipps, 1996; Gillborn & Youdell, 2000). In addition to its symbolic importance as a crucial field of social policy, therefore, education is especially significant because it provides a testing ground for many new initiatives and strategies. It highlights both the damage that can be done, and the progress that is possible.

Always a target for right-wing critics, during the 1990s anti-racism increasingly came under attack from *left* academics who questioned the notions of identity and politics that underlay certain versions of anti-racist practice. Additionally, attempts to marketise the education system (e.g. by introducing direct competition between schools) and the adoption of a colour-blind rhetoric of 'standards' (that privileged average attainments and ignored race-specific inequalities) further diverted attention away from equal opportunities issues. Despite this hostile environment, anti-racism continues to feature prominently in research and policy-debates, particularly at the level of the local state and in community activism. Always a highly controversial aspect of policy and practice, the search for distinctively anti-racist pedagogy and philosophy continues.

Anti-racism and Multiculturalism

For the conservative critics, it (multicultural education) represents an attempt to politicise education in order to pander to minority demands, whereas for some radicals it is the familiar ideological device of perpetuating the reality of racist exploitation of ethnic minorities by pampering their cultural sensitivities (Bhikhu Parekh, quoted in Modgil *et al.*, 1986, p. 5).

Right-wing critics have attacked even the most limited attempts to introduce multicultural elements into the formal curricula of British schools. John Marks (a member of several influential pressure groups and an official adviser to successive Conservative governments) contributed to a volume entitled *Anti-Racism—An Assault on Education and Value*, arguing that attacks on racism in education (regardless of their 'multicultural' or 'anti-racist' label) shared a common goal of 'the destruction and revolutionary transformation of all the institutions of our democratic society' (Marks, 1986, p. 37). At the other end of the political spectrum, during the 1980s many left-wing education critics devoted their time to a deconstruction of multicultural education, presenting it as a tokenist gesture meant to placate minority students and their communities while preserving intact the traditional curricular core of high status ('official') knowledge (Figueroa, 1995). Barry Troyna, for example, used the phrase *'the three S's'* (saris, samosas and steel bands) to characterise the superficial multiculturalism that paraded exotic images of minority peoples and their 'cultures' while doing nothing to address the realities of racism and unequal power relations in the 'host' society (Troyna, 1984). Godfrey Brandt's (1986) study *The Realization of Anti-racist Teaching* made a significant contribution to the development of the field at that point, summarising the anti-racist critique of multiculturalism and offering strategies for the development of an anti-racist pedagogy.

In many ways, Brandt's work typified the dominant characteristics of 1980s anti-racist education in Britain, including a strident attack on multiculturalism and an emphasis on oppositional forms. Drawing heavily on the work of Chris Mullard (1982, 1984), Brandt argued that 'multicultural education can be seen as the Trojan horse of institutional racism. Within it resides an attempt to renew the structure and processes of racism in education' (Brandt, 1986, p. 117). He argued that, whereas multiculturalists typically sought to *respond* to ethnic minorities' experiences, anti-racist teaching should accord minorities an active and central role: 'anti-racism must be dynamic and led by the experience and articulations of the Black community as the ongoing victims of rapidly changing ideology and practice of racism' (Brandt, 1986, p. 119). Throughout his analysis Brandt was keen to foreground the oppositional nature of anti-racism: 'The aims of anti-racist education must be, by definition, oppositional' (Brandt, 1986, p. 125). This strand was exemplified in the language that Brandt used, for example, by carefully contrasting the language of multiculturalism and anti-racism. According to Brandt, multiculturalism focused on key terms that shared a rather distant and liberal character, such as monoculturalism/ethnicism, culture, equality, prejudice, misunderstanding, and ignorance; its process was characterised as providing information and increasing 'awareness'. In contrast, Brandt presented anti-racism in terms of a hard-edged, more immediate lexicon as concerned with conflict, oppression, exploitation, racism, power, structure and struggle: its process was described as '*dismantle, deconstruct, reconstruct*' (Brandt, 1986, p. 121; original emphasis). These differences in language are not superficial, they indicate a conscious stance that distances itself from previous multicultural concerns and adopts an openly political position that emphasises the need actively to identify and resist racism.

The oppositional language of anti-racism has been both a strength and a weakness. On one hand, it has highlighted the dynamic and active role that schools and teachers can play in confronting racism; on the other hand, it has also provided ammunition for those cultural restorationists who would characterise any left-liberatory reforms as necessarily lowering academic standards, threatening the majority culture and destabilising society (see Apple, 1996; Ball, 1990). Additionally, the issue of language points to one of the most important weaknesses in much 1980s anti-racism: the dominance of rhetoric over practical applications.

In both the United States and Britain, under Reagan and Thatcher respectively, the 1980s witnessed increased centralisation of power, the dominance of market economics and attacks on state intervention in social policy areas such as public health, welfare and education. In Britain it was local authorities, usually controlled by the Labour Party (then in opposition nationally), who defended the need for state intervention and, in some cases, funded high-profile anti-racist campaigns. The Greater London Council (GLC) and the Inner London Education Authority (ILEA) were especially active—both bodies were eventually abolished by a Thatcher government. Despite the hostile national government, therefore, for most of the 1980s anti-racism retained a strong presence in some areas: many education authorities, for example, adopted multicultural and/or anti-racist policy statements. However, the impact of such policies was often negligible. Troyna argued that such policies continued to present 'race' and racism as 'superficial features of society; aberrations, rather than integral to our understanding of the way society functions' (Troyna, 1993, pp. 41–42). In this way, the policies deployed key terms, such as 'pluralism', 'justice' and 'equality', as 'condensation symbols' (after Edelman, 1964). That is, they functioned as textual devices that could generate widespread support (and reassure diverse groups that their interests were taken into account) when in fact their meaning was shifting and imprecise, so that power-holders were not constrained by any meaningful directives with clear practical consequences.

In Britain, therefore, the 1980s marked anti-racism's most prominent policy phase but produced uncertain achievements; although many local education authorities committed themselves to anti-racist positions, this was a field where rhetoric far outweighed practical action. As the decade came to an end, anti-racism was dealt what many commentators (mistakenly) interpreted as a wholesale critique from within; at the same time, left-wing academics and cultural critics became increasingly vocal in their attacks on anti-racism. It is to these developments that I turn next.

Left Critiques of Municipal Anti-racism

Most left critiques of anti-racism in Britain take as their focus a brand of high-profile 'municipal' anti-racism (Gilroy, 1987) practised by certain Labour-controlled local authorities, most notably the GLC. Tariq Modood has been particularly critical of the emphasis on 'colour racism', arguing that this excludes minority groups whose most deeply felt identity concerns culture, not colour (Modood, 1996). Modood has argued against *racial dualism*, a view that splits society into two groups: white and black. Not only does this ignore significant social, economic, religious and political differences (between and within different ethnic groups), it also leads to a narrow definition of what counts as legitimate anti-racist politics:

> Media interest, reflecting the social policy paradigm of the 1980s, has been narrowly circumscribed by racism and anti-racism: ethnic minorities are of interest if and only if they can be portrayed as victims of or threats to white society. (Modood, 1989, p. 281)

Modood argued that this 'radicals and criminals' perspective played an important role in stifling peaceful protest against *The Satanic Verses* (Rushdie, 1988), thereby fuelling Muslim anger and encouraging 'the unfortunate but true conclusion that they would remain unheeded till something shocking and threatening was done' (Modood, 1989, p. 282). In a succession of critical pieces Modood argued that anti-racists should recognise that 'culture' is not a surface factor that can be dismissed as unimportant—as if minorities who do not see themselves in terms of colour are somehow deluded about where their true interests lie. Municipal anti-racism's constant privileging of 'colour', he argued, meant that it was bound to fail to connect with many minority populations:

> in terms of their own being, Muslims feel most acutely those problems that the anti-racists are blind to; and respond weakly to those challenges that the anti-racists want to meet with most force ... We need concepts of race and racism that can critique socio-cultural environments which devalue people because of their physical differences but also because of their membership of a cultural minority and, critically, where the two overlap and create a double disadvantage. (Modood, 1990, p. 157)

Modood's critique identified several weaknesses in the kinds of emphasis characteristic of the local state's attempt to challenge racism. In particular, the failure to acknowledge ethnic *culture*, as a genuine and vital part of shifting and complex ethnic identities, was revealed as a serious mistake in attempts to encourage wider political mobilisation around anti-racist concerns.

The absence of culture from many anti-racist agendas reflected the bitter disputes between multiculturalists and anti-racists in the late 1970s and 1980s.

Modood's critique highlighted one of many negative consequences that arose because of the way the debate became polarised. However, we should not forget the historical reasons for anti-racists' unease about the political and epistemological status of culture. Paul Gilroy, for example, has attacked some anti-racists for accepting too readily 'the absolutist imagery of ethnic categories beloved of the New Right' (Cross, 1990, p. 3). Gilroy (like Modood) has attacked the simplistic assumptions that exposed much 'municipal anti-racism' to ridicule while failing to connect with the lived experiences and struggles of minority groups. At the same time, however, he took a rather different position on the politics of culture within anti-racism; a position that highlights the complexity of identity, 'race' and culture in contemporary society.

Paul Gilroy has been especially critical of the conceptions of 'race' and racism that underlie municipal anti-racism. He attacked the 'coat-of-paint theory of racism' that viewed racism as a blemish 'on the surface of other things' and never called into doubt 'the basic structures and relations of [the] British economy and society' (Gilroy, 1990, p. 74). He argued that such an approach effectively placed racism outside key debates, characterising it as a complicating factor of marginal importance rather than a central defining concern. In contrast, he sought to position racism 'in the mainstream' as 'a volatile presence at the very centre of British politics actively shaping and determining the history not simply of blacks, but of this country as a whole at a crucial stage in its development' (Gilroy, 1990, p. 73). He argued for a wider and more dynamic understanding of 'race' and racism, one that foregrounds the socially constructed nature of 'racial' categories and draws attention to their historically constituted and specific nature—an analysis that strongly echoed some of the most influential and insightful work by prominent cultural theorists in the US (see, for example, Omi & Winant, 1986). By accepting a fixed and simple notion of culture, therefore, municipal anti-racism had itself come to accept a spurious ideology of 'culturalism and cultural absolutism' (Gilroy, 1990, p. 82) that paralleled the position of the New Right. This development reflected several factors, not least a concern to support campaigns by minority groups and to highlight distinctive cultural identities and activities as a corrective to the deficit pathological models proposed by right-wing politicians and commentators (Apple & Zenck, 1996). By simply *inverting* the right's pathological view of minority culture, however, municipal anti-racism unwittingly repeated and sustained the basic culturalist analyses that presented 'culture' as if it were a fixed ahistorical 'thing' rather than a constructed, contested and continually changing discourse. For example:

> 'Same-race' adoption and fostering for 'minority ethnics' is presented as an unchallenged and seemingly unchallengeable benefit for all concerned. It is hotly defended with the same fervour that denounces white demands for 'same race' schooling as a repellent manifestation of racism. (Gilroy, 1990, p. 81)

Paul Gilroy's attack on such policies highlighted their *essentialist* and *reductionist* character: although born of anti-oppressive aims, they actually committed the same errors that typified the racist thinking they sought to oppose. That is, such policies came to argue that there is some innate quality that characterises the true/authentic *essence* of a particular 'racial'/cultural group. This 'sad inability to see beyond the conservation of racial identities to [the] possibility of their transcendence' reinforced assumptions about inherent difference between cultural groups and trivialised 'the rich complexity of black life by reducing it to nothing more than a response to racism' (Gilroy, 1990, pp. 81, 83). Gilroy argued that, just as they must adopt a more sophisticated understanding of 'race', so anti-racists had to break with limiting notions of 'culture' as in any way natural, homogeneous or fixed:

> Culture, even the culture which defines the groups we know as races, is never fixed, finished or final. It is fluid, it is actively and continually made and re-made. In our multi-cultural schools the sound of steel pan may evoke Caribbean ethnicity, tradition and authenticity yet they originate in the oil drums of the Standard Oil Company rather than the mysterious knowledge of ancient African griots. (Gilroy, 1990, p. 80)

Gilroy argued, therefore, for a conception of culture and 'race' politics that recognised the fluid, dynamic and highly complex character of the new cultural politics of difference (see also Goldberg, 1993, 1997; Hall, 1992; West, 1990). These arguments reflect a shift in social theory often associated with postmodern or poststructuralist approaches (see, for example, Aronowitz & Giroux, 1991; Thompson, 1992). At times such approaches can seem overly complex and removed from the lived reality of schools, teachers and students (Skeggs, 1991). However, many of the same points have been raised (in a more immediate and school-focused way) in relation to a racist murder, and the conditions that surrounded it, in a Manchester secondary school, *Burnage High*. The episode, and the subsequent inquiry, represents a fault line in British anti-racist politics.

The Failure of Symbolic Anti-racism: Learning from Burnage

On Wednesday 17 September 1986, Ahmed Iqbal Ullah (a 13-year-old Bangladeshi student) was murdered in the playground of Burnage High School, Manchester (England). His killer was a white peer at the same school. A subsequent inquiry, led by Ian Macdonald QC, investigated the background to the murder and presented a full report to Manchester City Council. Afraid of possible legal action by people mentioned in the report, the council refused to publish the inquiry's findings. Following widespread 'leaks' and misreporting in the popular press, the inquiry team itself decided to publish their findings (Macdonald *et al.*, 1989).

> The committee of inquiry, composed of individuals with impressive antiracist credentials—Ian Macdonald, Gus John, Reena Bhavnani, Lily Khan—delivered a strong and, for some, an astonishing condemnation of the antiracist policies apparently vigorously pursued at the school, castigating them as doctrinaire, divisive, ineffectual and counterproductive. (Rattansi, 1992, p. 13)

The inquiry team were highly critical of the particular form of anti-racism that had been practised in Burnage; what they called *'symbolic, moral and doctrinaire' anti-racism*. It is a form of anti-racism that is essentialist and reductionist in the extreme. Within such a perspective 'race' and racism are assumed always to be dominant factors in the experiences of 'black' and white students, with the former cast as victims, the latter as aggressors. According to symbolic anti-racism:

> since black students are the victims of the immoral and prejudiced behaviour of white students, white students are all to be seen as 'racist', whether they are ferret-eyed fascists or committed anti-racists. Racism is thus placed in some kind of moral vacuum and is totally divorced from the more complex reality of human relations in the classroom, playground or community. In this model of anti-racism there is no room for issues of class, sex, age or size. (Macdonald *et al.*, 1989, p. 402)

The inquiry report documented the way this approach combined with several other factors (including the style of management and 'macho' disciplinary atmosphere in the school) to increase tension and damage relationships (between school and community; staff and students; students and their peers; teachers and their colleagues). While the report was damning in its criticism of Burnage's 'symbolic' anti-racism, it was absolutely clear about the reality of racism and the need for more sensitive and sophisticated approaches to anti-racism. Although this point was reflected in the first press coverage (in a local paper in Manchester), the national press took a rather different line, representing the report as 'proof' that anti-racism is a damaging extremist political creed. One national paper presented Ahmed as a victim, not of a white racist, but of anti-racism: 'Anti-racist policy led to killing' (*Daily Telegraph*, quoted in Macdonald *et al.*, 1989, p. xx). The distorted press coverage had a significant effect: in education and academia, the 'Burnage report'—though rarely read in detail—was frequently understood as an attack on anti-racism *per se* (see, for example, Rattansi, 1992). Such an interpretation does the report a major disservice. The inquiry team were careful to reject the press interpretation of events at Burnage and emphasised their continuing support for anti-racist education policies:

> It is because we consider the task of combating racism to be such a critical part of the function of schooling and education that we condemn symbolic, moral and doctrinaire anti-racism. We urge care, rigour and caution in the formulating and implementing of such policies because we consider the struggle against racism and racial injustice to be an essential element in the struggle for social justice which we see as the ultimate goal of education ... We repudiate totally any suggestion that the anti-racist education policy of Burnage High School led ... to the death of Ahmed Ullah ... [W]e state emphatically that the work of all schools should be informed by a policy that recognises the pernicious and all-pervasive nature of racism in the lives of students, teachers and parents, black and white, and the need to confront it. (Macdonald *et al.*, 1989, pp. xxiii–xxiv)

In its attack on essentialist and reductionist analyses of 'race' and racism, the Burnage report shared several key features with other left critiques of anti-racist theory and practice. Although the critiques have been generated by a range of writers, with diverse agendas, several important lessons can be learnt.

The Critical Revision of Anti-racism

The critical thrust of left academics like Gilroy and Modood in Britain has been echoed internationally by authors who emphasise the complexity and fluidity of 'racial' and ethnic categories (Carrim, 1995a, 1995b; McCarthy, 1990; Rizvi, 1993; Walcott, 1994). In the light of such theoretical advances, it is argued, anti-racism must grow into a more sophisticated and flexible strategy that moves away from the racial dualism of its past—what Bonnett and Carrington (1996) characterise as a model of 'White racism versus Black resistance'. However, much anti-racism continues to be characterised by a preference for rhetoric over practical application. Writing with reference to the Australian case, for example, Rod Allen and Bob Hill have recently commented on the 'lamentable absence of studies evaluating school-based programs to combat racism' (Allen & Hill, 1995, pp. 772–773). There may be several reasons for this. First, academics have a history of critique that enables them to perceive many shortcomings in practical strategies but does not dispose them well to identifying things that work. This is particularly the case with sociologists, who have been especially active in developing theoretical approaches to anti-racism. Their disciplinary roots teach sociologists to be aware of the many constraints that shape, limit and frustrate attempts to reform the educational systems of advanced capitalist economies. Given their acute awareness of such limits, it can be difficult for them to move from a 'language of critique' to a 'language of possibility' (McCarthy & Apple, 1988, p. 31). More practically, research on anti-racism at the school level is likely to require careful and lengthy qualitative research that can prove expensive in terms of time and resources. Despite these problems, there is now a small, but growing, range of studies that attempt to identify, describe and (constructively) critique the development of anti-racist practice at the school level—including work from pre-school through to post-compulsory education. In Britain, for example, there are now studies of anti-racist practice in early years education (Siraj-Blatchford, 1994), primary schools (Connolly, 1994; Epstein, 1993), secondary schools (Gillborn, 1995; Troyna, 1988) and beyond (Troyna & Selman, 1991; Neal, 1998). The studies reveal the complex, politically explosive and often painful nature of anti-racist change. They demonstrate the futility of attempts to create an anti-racist 'blueprint' for school change, but point to the micro-political nature of change (Ball, 1987), where conflict may be more or less hidden, but consensus is always fragile and prone to destabilisation by events locally (such as a racist incident in the vicinity of the school), nationally (e.g. a scare story about 'political correctness' in the media) and globally (the Gulf War and Salman Rushdie affair, for example, galvanised Muslim communities in Britain and forced many schools to reappraise previous perspectives and practices: Gillborn, 1995; Parker-Jenkins & Haw, 1998).

Studies of anti-racist school practice show that advances are easier where there is wider institutional support for anti-oppression politics (at a local and/or national government level); nevertheless, even where the national government has never accepted anti-racism as a legitimate policy direction, considerable headway can be made at the school level (see Carrim & Gillborn, 1996). Meaningful school change requires the support of the headteacher/principal and cannot be won without the involvement of wider sections of the school staff, its pupils and feeder communities. Anti-racist changes threaten many deeply held assumptions and, in larger schools, it seems that small 'core' groups of staff may be needed to act as the vanguard for anti-racist developments: researching initiatives elsewhere, organising events, and pushing forward school policy. Making genuine links with local communities is a vital part of successful anti-racist change: such developments can be extremely difficult to engineer but, once established, offer schools an immense resource of support and continually argue the need for schools to deal with the complexities of racialised identities by challenging received stereotypes. Finally, students themselves can play a crucial role in pushing forward school-based anti-racist change. The democratic participation of *all* students (including whites) strengthens anti-racist change where teachers come to realise the need to see beyond simple 'race' labels, to engage with the cross-cutting realities of gendered, sexualised and class-based inequalities that also act on and through the lives of young people.

Studies of anti-racist developments in school show that a concern with theory and practice need not be mutually exclusive. Although anti-racists' historical preference for rhetoric over practice has not always encouraged school-based developments, it is possible to reflect critically on some of the theoretical assumptions that have informed earlier approaches by focusing on the experiences, failures and advances of anti-racist practitioners. To take a single example, it has often been argued that anti-racism should adopt a theoretical position that defines racism as a whites-only activity, in order to 'acknowledge the asymmetrical power relations between black and white citizens' (Troyna & Hatcher, 1992, p. 16). A frequent observation among poststructuralist critics has been that such a view is essentialist and, paradoxically, refuses to allow minorities the same diversity and complexity of perspective recognised in whites. At a practical level such a position can be difficult to justify to white students without falling into the doctrinaire and morally condemnatory tone of symbolic anti-racism: put simply, white working-class young people rarely feel very powerful; to argue that their skin colour alone identifies them as beneficiaries of centuries of exploitation can destroy the credibility of anti-racism in their eyes. In contrast, it has been noted that some schools have, for reasons of pragmatism, adopted a standpoint that echoes the revisionist critics' point that '*racism and ethnocentrism are not necessarily confined to white groups*' (Rattansi, 1992, p, 36; original emphasis). This is not to say, of course, that racism is equally a problem for all groups: in 'the West' the dominant racist ideologies and the most frequent racists are white. Nevertheless, to deny that white students *can ever* be victims of racist violence is to devalue anti-racism. In schools that have adopted a wider understanding of racism, for example, it is still the case that the vast majority of students using racist harassment procedures are black; however, the acknowledgement that all students can, in principle, use the procedures has served to strengthen wider commitment to the developments and helped support the involvement of all student groups (Dei, 1996b; Gillborn, 1995). Pragmatism is no panacea – it has too often served as an excuse for doing nothing to challenge racism: the point here is that anti-racism (as both theory and practice) can learn from the complex and changing realities faced by students, teachers, parents and other community members. Anti-racism is not a *gift* bestowed by intellectuals and liberals, it is a vital, developing and changing combination of activism and opposition that must continually involve diverse groups and be sensitive to its own limitations in vision and action. The best anti-racism seems likely to reflect a dynamic mix of experience and critical reflection—*praxis*. The need to focus on developments at the school level does not militate against further theoretical developments in this field.

Opposing Racism and Staying *Critical*

The adjective 'critical' is seemingly one of the most frequently used terms in contemporary social science, running a close second to 'the almost ritualistic ubiquity of "post" words in current culture' (McClintock, 1995, p. 10). In many cases, 'critical' is invoked as a descriptor to signal a break with previous assumptions about an issue or approach while maintaining a sense of uncertainty, avoiding closure about the necessary form of future analyses and/or actions. Critical social research, for example, 'tries to dig beneath the surface ... It asks how social systems really work, how ideology or history conceals the processes which oppress and control people' (Harvey, 1990, p. 6). Critical social research may take many forms but is not bound by the limits of conventional positivist assumptions about what counts as 'scientific' rigour, since such assumptions may themselves be implicated in the very processes of oppression that are at issue (Troyna, 1995). Similarly, 'critical multiculturalism' has been proposed—though adherents differ about the precise meaning of the term (cf. Berlant & Warner, 1994; Chicago Cultural Studies Group, 1994; May, 1994, 1999; McLaren, 1994, 1995; Nieto, 1999). It has also been argued that a *critical anti-racism* should learn from past errors (such as the Burnage tragedy) to position a more complex and contextualised understanding of racialised difference at the centre of attempts to oppose racism in the policy and practice of education (Carrim & Soudien, 1999; Carrim & Gillborn, 1996; Dei, 1996a; Gillborn, 1995). The emerging approaches within 'critical race theory' similarly display a wide variety of perspectives, pedagogy and praxis, but often share a determination to identify, name and oppose racism in its many diverse forms: recognising that racism is a deeply ingrained feature of capitalist societies; challenging claims to legal, academic and political neutrality; and pursuing a complex and contextually sensitive understanding of the construction of knowledge/ identity boundaries (see Matsuda *et al.*, 1993; Tate, 1997). Whatever nomenclature is adopted, the processes are frequently difficult, always opposed and sometimes pursued at considerable personal cost (see Banks, 1998; Grant, 1999).

To some readers such debates about terminology might seem trivial or obsessive. It has been argued, for example, that the 'unhelpful dichotomization of multicultural and antiracist education' in Britain (May, 1999, p. vii) diffused anti-oppressive efforts during the height of Thatcherism and still detracts from shared agendas. But as Nazir Carrim and Crain Soudien (1999) have argued, in relation to education in South Africa, there is frequently a qualitative and historically significant difference between interventions informed by multiculturalism and anti-racism. In the UK, South Africa, Canada and Australia, for example (where multiculturalism versus anti-racism debates have attained prominence), the former have frequently been associated with exoticised, superficial approaches more concerned with life styles than life chances (Troyna, 1993). To argue that multiculturalism *can* conceivably be as critical, oppositional and dynamic as anti-racism may be to underestimate the historical and practical dangers in concepts, such as 'culture' and 'multiculturalism', that have too often been framed in uni-dimensional and fixed ways that are irreconcilable with the decentred and anti-essentialised view of identity, knowledge and power at the heart of critical anti-racist praxis (Dei, 1996b). As Carrim and Soudien have noted:

> A critical antiracism, which incorporates a notion of 'difference' would, therefore, work with complex, non-stereotypical and dynamic senses of identity, and would 'talk to' the actual ways in which people experience their lives, worlds, and identities. ... the use of culturalist language in the schools we report on tends to be assimilationist ... These 'bad' multiculturalist practices essentialize cultures, homogenize and stereotype people's identities and do not address the power dimensions of racism. ... [The] possibility of 'good', critical multicultural practices is indeed conceivable ... but we do not have evidence of this existing in any of the South African experiences, either historically or in the contemporary situation. (Carrim & Soudien, 1999, pp. 154–155, 169)

What is perhaps of central importance in these debates is the requirement to remain critical, not only of others, but of our own attempts to understand and oppose racism. An examination of anti-racist policy and practice demonstrates clearly that there is no blueprint for successful anti-racism—no one 'correct' way. What succeeds at one time, or in one context, may not be appropriate at a later date or in another context. Racism changes: it works differently through different processes, informs and is modified by diverse contemporary modes of representation, and changes with particular institutional contexts. Anti-racism must recognise and adapt to this complexity. In practice this means facing up to the complexities of racism: identifying and combating racism will always be difficult. Racism is often entrenched in commonsense understandings about 'ability', 'aptitude', 'the right attitude' etc. Race is a constant presence in policy and pedagogy—even when it appears absent (Apple, 1999). When legislation adopts a deracialised discourse, for example by espousing a desire to help 'all' children regardless of ethnic origin, the consequences of reform have almost invariably been to remake differences that further entrench and extend all too familiar patterns of exclusion and oppression

(Gillborn & Youdell, 2000). Although anti-racism has enjoyed more prominent periods, therefore, the need for anti-racist research, analysis and practice is as great as ever. It is to be hoped that anti-racism can win wider acceptance and affect more meaningful change in the future than has been achieved generally in the past.

References

Allen, R. & Hill, B. (1995) Multicultural Education in Australia: Historical development and current status, in: J. A. Banks & Cherry A. McGee Banks (eds), *Handbook of Research on Multicultural Education* (New York, Macmillan), pp. 763–777.

Apple, M. W. (1996) *Cultural Politics & Education* (Buckingham, Open University Press).

Apple, M. W. (1999) The Absent Presence of Race in Educational Reform, *Race Ethnicity and Education*, 2:1.

Apple, M. W. & Zenck, C. (1996) American Realities: Poverty, economy, and education, in: M. W. Apple, *Cultural Politics & Education* (Buckingham, Open University Press).

Aptheker, Herbert (1993) *Anti-racism in US History: The first two hundred years* (Westport, CT, Praeger).

Aronowitz, S. & Giroux, H. A. (1991) *Postmodern Education: Politics, culture & social criticism* (Oxford, University of Minnesota Press).

Ball, S. J. (1987) *The Micro-Politics of the School: Towards a theory of school organization* (London, Methuen).

Ball, S. J. (1990) *Politics and Policy Making in Education: Explorations in policy sociology* (London, Routledge).

Banks, J. A. (1998) The Lives and Values of Researchers: Implications for educating citizens in a multicultural society, *Educational Researcher*, 27:7, pp. 4–17.

Berlant, L. & Warner, M. (1994) Introduction to 'Critical Multiculturalism', in: D. T. Goldberg (ed.), *Multiculturalism: A critical reader* (Oxford, Blackwell).

Bonnett, A. & Carrington, B. (1996) Constructions of Anti-racist Education in Britain and Canada, *Comparative Education*, 32:3.

Brandt, G. L. (1986) *The Realization of Anti-Racist Teaching* (Lewes, Falmer).

Carrim, N. (1995a) From 'Race' to Ethnicity: Shifts in the educational discourses of South Africa and Britain in the 1990s, *Compare*, 251, pp. 17–33.

Carrim, N. (1995b) 'Working With and Through Difference in Antiracist Pedagogies, *International Studies in Sociology of Education*, 5:1, pp. 25–39.

Carrim, N. & Gillborn, D. (1996) Racialized Educational Disadvantage, Antiracism and Difference: Countering racism at the school level in South Africa and England, paper presented at the annual meeting of the American Educational Research Association, New York (April).

Carrim, N. & Soudien, C. (1999) Critical Antiracism in South Africa, in: S. May (ed.), *Critical Multiculturalism: Rethinking multicultural and antiracist education* (London, Falmer).

Chicago Cultural Studies Group (1994) Critical Multiculturalism, in: D. T. Goldberg (ed.), *Multiculturalism: A critical reader* (Oxford, Blackwell).

Connolly, P. (1994) 'All Lads Together?: Racism, masculinity and multicultural/anti-racist strategies in a primary school, *International Studies in Sociology of Education*, 4:2, pp. 191–211.

Cross, M. (1990) Editorial, *New Community*, 17:1, pp. 1–4.

Dei, G. J. S. (1996a) *Anti-Racism Education in Theory and Practice* (Halifax, Fernwood).

Dei, G. J. S. (1996b) Critical Perspectives in Antiracism: An introduction, *Canadian Review of Sociology and Anthropology*, 33:3, pp. 247–267.

Dei, G. J. S., Karumanchery, L. L. & Karumanchery-Luik, N. (2004) *Playing the Race Card: Exposing white power and privilege* (New York, Peter Lang).

Dlamini, S. N. (2002) From the Other Side of the Desk: Notes on teaching about race when racialised, *Race Ethnicity & Education*, 5:1, pp. 51–66.

Edelman, M. (1964) *The Symbolic Uses of Politics* (Urbana, University of Illinois Press).

Elmore, R. F. (1987) Reform and the Culture of Authority in Schools, *Educational Administration Quarterly*, 23:4, pp. 60–78.

Epstein, D. (1993) *Changing Classroom Cultures: Anti-racism, politics and schools* (Stoke-on-Trent, Trentham).

Essed, P. & Goldberg, D. T. (eds) (2002) *Race Critical Theories* (Oxford, Blackwell).

Figueroa, P. (1995) Multicultural Education in the United Kingdom: Historical development and current status, in: J. A. Banks & C. A. M. Banks (eds), *Handbook of Research on Multicultural Education* (New York, Macmillan).

Gillborn, D. (1995) *Racism and Antiracism in Real Schools: Theory. Policy. Practice* (Buckingham, Open University Press).

Gillborn, D. & Gipps, C. (1996) *Recent Research on the Achievements of Ethnic Minority Pupils* (London, HMSO).

Gillborn, D. & Youdell, D. (2000) *Rationing Education* (Buckingham, Open University Press).

Gilroy, P. (1987) *There Ain't No Black in the Union Jack* (London, Hutchinson).

Gilroy, P. (1990) The End of Anti-racism, *New Community*, 17:1, pp. 71–83.

Goldberg, D. T. (1993) *Racist Culture: Philosophy and the politics of meaning* (Oxford, Blackwell).

Goldberg, D. T. (1997) *Racial Subjects: Writing on race and America* (London, Routledge).

Grant, C. A. (ed.) (1999) *Multicultural Research: A reflective engagement with race, class, gender and sexual orientation* (London, Falmer).

Hall, S. (1992) New Ethnicities, in: J. Donald & A. Rattansi (eds), *'Race', Culture & Difference* (London, Sage).

Harvey, L. (1990) *Critical Social Research* (London, Allen and Unwin).

Ladson-Billings, G. (2004) Just What Is Critical Race Theory and What's It Doing in a *Nice* Field like Education?, in: G. Ladson-Billings & D. Gillborn (eds), *The RoutledgeFalmer Reader in Multicultural Education* (New York: RoutledgeFalmer), pp. 49–67.

Macdonald, I., Bhavnani, R., Khan, L. and John, G. (1989) *Murder in the Playground: The report of the Macdonald inquiry into racism and racial violence in Manchester schools* (London, Longsight).

Marks, J. (1986) 'Anti-racism'—Revolution Not Education, in: F. Palmer (ed.), *Anti-Racism— An Assault on Education and Value* (London, Sherwood Press).

Matsuda, M. J., Lawrence, C. R., Delgado, R. & Crenshaw, K. W. (eds) (1993) *Words that Wound: Critical race theory, assaultive speech, and the First Amendment* (Boulder, CO, Westview).

May, S. (1994) *Making Multicultural Education Work* (Clevedon, Multilingual Matters).

May, S. (ed.) (1999) *Critical Multiculturalism: Rethinking multicultural and antiracist education* (London, Falmer).

McCarthy, C. (1990) *Race and Curriculum: Social inequality and the theories and politics of difference in contemporary research on schooling* (Lewes, Falmer).

McCarthy, C. & Apple, M. W. (1988) Race, Class and Gender in American Educational Research: Towards a nonsynchronous parallelist position, in: L. Weis (ed.), *Class, Race & Gender in American Education* (Albany, State University of New York Press).

McClintock, A. (1995) *Imperial Leather: Race, gender and sexuality in the colonial contest* (New York, Routledge).

McLaren, P. (1994) White Terror and Oppositional Agency: Towards a critical multiculturalism, in: D. T. Goldberg (ed.), *Multiculturalism: A critical reader* (Oxford, Blackwell).

McLaren, P. (1995) *Critical Pedagogy and Predatory Culture* (London, Routledge).

Modgil, S., Verma, G. K., Mallick, K. and Modgil, C. (eds) (1986) *Multicultural Education: The interminable debate* (Lewes, Falmer).

Modood, T. (1989) Religious Anger and Minority Rights, *Political Quarterly*, July, pp. 280–284.

Modood, T. (1990) British Asian Muslims and the Rushdie Affair, *Political Quarterly*, April, pp. 143–160.

Modood, T. (1996) The Changing Context of 'Race' in Britain, *Patterns of Prejudice*, 30:1, pp. 3–13.

Mullard, C. (1982) Multiracial Education in Britain: From assimilation to cultural pluralism, in: J. Tierney (ed.), *Race, Migration and Schooling* (London, Holt, Rinehart & Winston).

Mullard, C. (1984) *Anti-racist Education: The three O's* (Cardiff, National Antiracist Movement in Education).

Neal, S. (1998) *The Making of Equal Opportunities Policies in Universities* (Buckingham, Open University Press).

Nieto, S. (1999) Critical Multicultural Education and Students' Perspectives, in: S. May (ed.), *Critical Multiculturalism: Rethinking multicultural and antiracist education* (London, Falmer).

Omi, M. & Winant, H. (1986) *Racial Formation in the United States: From the 1960s to the 1980s* (New York, Routledge).

Parker-Jenkins, M. & Haw, K. F. (1998) Educational Needs of Muslim Children in Britain: Accommodation or neglect?, in: S. Vertovec & A. Rogers (eds), *Muslim European Youth: Reproducing ethnicity, religion, culture* (Aldershot, Ashgate).

Parker, L., Deyhle, D. & Villenas, S. A. (eds) (1999) *Race Is ... Race Isn't: Critical race theory and qualitative studies in education* (Boulder, Westview Press).

Rattansi, A. (1992) Changing the Subject? Racism, culture and education, in: J. Donald & A. Rattansi (eds), *'Race', Culture & Difference* (London, Sage).

Rizvi, F. (1993) Race, Gender and the Cultural Assumptions of Schooling, in: C. Marshall (ed.), *The New Politics of Race and Gender* (London, Falmer).

Rushdie, S. (1988) *The Satanic Verses* (London, Viking).

Siraj-Blatchford, I. (1994) *The Early Years: Laying the foundations for racial equality* (Stoke-on-Trent, Trentham).

Skeggs, B. (1991) Postmodernism: What is all the fuss about?, *British Journal of Sociology of Education*, 12:2, pp. 255–267.

Solomos, J. & Back, L. (1996) *Racism and Society* (Basingstoke, Macmillan in association with the British Sociological Association).

Tate, W. F. (1997) Critical Race Theory and Education: History, theory, and implications, in: M. W. Apple (ed.), *Review of Research in Education*, vol. 22 (Washington, DC, American Educational Research Association).

Thompson, K. (1992) Social Pluralism and Post-modernity, in: S. Hall, D. Held & T. McGrew (eds), *Modernity and its Futures* (Cambridge, Polity).

Troyna, B. (1984) Multicultural Education: Emancipation or containment?, in: L. Barton & S. Walker (eds), *Social Crisis and Educational Research* (Beckenham, Croom Helm), pp. 75–92.

Troyna, B. (1988) The Career of an Antiracist Education School Policy: Some observations on the mismanagement of change, in: A. G. Green & S. J. Ball (eds), *Progress and Inequality in Comprehensive Education* (London, Routledge), pp. 158–78.

Troyna, B. (1993) *Racism and Education: Research perspectives* (Buckingham, Open University Press).

Troyna, B. (1995) Beyond Reasonable Doubt? Researching 'race' in educational settings, *Oxford Review of Education*, 21:4, pp. 395–408.

Troyna, B. & Hatcher, R. (1992) *Racism in Children's Lives: A study of mainly white primary schools* (London, Routledge).

Troyna, B. & Selman, L. (1991) *Implementing Multicultural and Anti-Racist Education in Mainly White Colleges* (London, Further Education Unit).

Walcott, R. (1994) The Need for a Politics of Difference, *Orbit*, 21:2, pp. 4–6.

West, C. (1990) The New Cultural Politics of Difference, reprinted in: S. During (ed.), *The Cultural Studies Reader* (London, Routledge).

6

Critical Race Theory, Afrocentricity, and their Relationship to Critical Pedagogy

MARVIN LYNN
University of Maryland, College Park

Introduction

> *Enye sika nko ne ohia.* (Lack of money is not the only kind of poverty.)
> —Kofi Asare Opoku, *Hearing and Keeping: Akan Proverbs*, 1997

There has been some debate about whether 'critical pedagogy,' as a field of study, adequately incorporates issues of race and racism into its analysis of schooling and society (Gordon, 1995). Among other things, researchers have suggested that critical pedagogy, with its foundation in Marxist critiques of schooling and society, has privileged issues of social class over race or gender (Ellsworth, 1989; Gordon, 1995; McCarthy, 1988; Lynn, 1999). While critical pedagogy's racial blindspots have been illuminated by a number researchers, there have been very few efforts to examine the ways in which theories of race can and should be linked to teaching and learning in urban schools. In this essay, I will extend previous work that aligns theories of race with notions of liberatory pedagogy and practice (Ladson-Billings, 1995; Lynn, 1999).

In the past decade, scholarship that examines the links between race, culture and schooling has proliferated (Irvine, 1990; Scheurich & Young, 1997). While some work in this area attempts to align the views and perceptions of African American teachers with race-based theory (Beauboeuf-Lafontant, 1999; Irvine, 1988; King, 1991), other work has explicitly drawn links between the pedagogical beliefs and practices of African American social justice teachers and critical race theory (Lynn, 1999; Morris, 2001) or African-centered thought and practice (Ladson-Billings, 1994, 1995). In doing so, scholars with interests in race and culture have literally begun to put the 'race' back into critical pedagogy by developing new ways of looking at the links between race, culture and pedagogy. For example, Ladson-Billings's (1994, 1995) groundbreaking work in developing a notion she refers to as 'culturally relevant teaching'—conjoining fundamental aspects of critical pedagogy with important elements of culture-centered teaching—has revolutionized the ways in which liberatory teaching is conceptualized and practiced. Extending Ladson-Billings's work (Ladson-Billings & Tate, 1995) and drawing from the work of critical pedagogists such as Kanpol (1988, 1992), Darder (1991, 1993), Freire (1973, 1993), and the scholarship on Black teachers (Foster, 1997; Henry, 1998; Irvine, 1988), Lynn (1999) has developed a notion referred to as 'critical race pedagogy' which explicitly connects African American teachers' liberatory practice with theories of race and racism in the law.

'Critical race pedagogy' could be defined as an analysis of racial, ethnic and gender subordination in education that relies mostly upon the perceptions, experiences and counter-hegemonic practices of educators of color. This approach necessarily leads to an articulation and broad interpretation of emancipatory pedagogical strategies and techniques proven to be successful with racially and culturally subordinated students. A critical race pedagogy is constructed via the reflections of African American practitioners/intellectuals who were strongly committed to the ideals and principles found in 'critical race theory' and/or Afrocentricity. For example, in conversations with Black social justice educators about their views on society and the nature of schooling, it was argued that critical race pedagogues seemed to be concerned with the following general issues: the persistence of racial discrimination in schools and in the wider society; the struggle to maintain and develop their own cultural identities, and the ways in which class interacts with race to make the lives of the Black poor even more miserable. They were also committed to understanding how to *practice a liberatory pedagogy* that involves: (1) teaching children about the importance of African culture; (2) dialogical engagement in the classroom; (3) engaging in daily acts of self-affirmation; and (4) resisting and challenging hegemonic administrators (Lynn, 1999). As such, the research did indicate that Black social justice teachers were committed to principles that could be found in more than one theoretical framework—namely critical race theory and Afrocentricity.

While it is important to have conversations about what a liberatory pedagogy looks like and how it is practiced by educators committed to the wholeness and wellness of racially subordinated youth in urban schools, it is also important to have deeper conversations about theory. Theories of race (Crenshaw *et al.*, 1995; Omi & Winant, 1994; West, 1993) and culture (Asante, 1987, 1988, 1991) are borne out by people's lived experiences with racial and cultural domination (Collins, 1991). To that end, a discussion about how critical race theory—as a field of study—came to life is, in many ways, a discussion about the development of a complex theory that both frames and contextualizes the historically situated narratives of racially subjugated peoples. In the same vein, an unveiling of the historicity of Afrocentricity as a cultural framework provides a telescopic lens through which we are able to view more fully the entire constellation of historical wrongs experienced by peoples uprooted from their homelands and forced to endure hundreds of years of cultural domination (Ani, 1994). In the next sections, I will explore both theories and then articulate their points of coherence and disjuncture. Then I will argue why they are both important for use in the continued development and articulation of a critical race pedagogy that re-articulates and re-centers race in the debates over schooling and liberatory praxis in urban schools.

Defining the Key Elements of Critical Race Theory

Critical race theory (CRT) has been defined by a number of scholars as a legal counter-discourse generated by legal scholars of color concerned about issues of racial oppression in the law and society. While this scholarship initially developed as a critique of critical legal studies—a Marxist analysis of the US legal system— critical race theorists are also concerned about creating and sustaining a politicized discourse that was by and about people of color. Critical race scholars argue that CRT, as an analytic framework for addressing issues of social inequity, can be utilized as a way in which to uncover the racism embedded within American social structures and practices. More importantly, critical race theorists seek to reveal the hidden curriculum of racial domination and talk about the ways in which it is central to the maintenance of white supremacy.

A number of CRT scholars argue that there are at least five tenets that guide their work. First, they believe that the legal system in the US is inherently unfair with regard to people of color and that it must be incessantly and systematically critiqued for its failure to address racism in the law. This criticism is most evident in the works of Derrick Bell (1992, 1995), who argued that the prevailing civil rights discourse in the law did little to acknowledge the extent of the problems faced by African Americans who continued to be subjected to unfair legal practices. To this extent, the work of critical race theorists is also meta-critical in the way that it offers a critique of existing critiques of the law—namely the Marxist and liberal critiques of the law which fail to account for, name, and critique the racial and/or racist dimensions of the law. For example, they suggest that CRT 'uncovers the ongoing dynamics of racialized power, and its embeddedness in practices and values which have been shorn of any explicit, formal manifestations of racism' (Crenshaw *et al.*, 1995, p. xxix).

Secondly, they recognize the centrality of race and intransigence of racism in contemporary American society. Derrick Bell (1995) has reiterated this argument most vociferously in his 'Racial Realism' thesis. He argues fervently that because racism is endemic to American culture and society, cultural workers and others attempting to liberate the oppressed must accept the permanence of racism and work toward improving conditions for such groups. Recognizing that race and racism are deeply rooted in American cultural and social practices, Crenshaw *et al.* (1995) suggest that 'Critical Race Theory aims to reexamine the terms by which race and racism have been negotiated in American consciousness, and to recover and revitalize the radical tradition of race consciousness among African Americans' (p. xiv). While critical race theorists agree that race is a socially constructed notion, they do not believe that limiting one's use of the term will increase the likelihood that racism will be eliminated as a social problem. Instead, they advocate a vigorous dialogical and pedagogical engagement with the term and the resultant privileging of certain racial groups over others.

Thirdly, critical race theorists reject West-European/Modernist claims of neutrality, objectivity, rationality, and universality. Charles Lawrence (1991) and Kendall Thomas (1995) argue that scholars of color should concern themselves with the way that the positivist paradigm in social science and the law has not only failed to address the subjective but has attempted to obliterate it completely from discussions of the law and history. These authors begin to call into question the notion that there exists an objective truth that remains unaffected and unsullied by the subjective nature of the human experience. In fact, they argue that emphasis must be placed on the subjective. In other words, those subjective components of experience should be relied upon heavily as a way in which to reconstruct the past and critique the law. This is also consistent with CRT's fourth principle, which is that it historicizes its critiques of the law by relying heavily upon the experiential, situated and 'subjugated' knowledge of people of color. This principle has implications for the ways in which theories of liberation that are grounded in the experiences of the oppressed can be constructed. Patricia Hill Collins, for example, has constructed a theory of 'Black feminist thought' that is grounded in the everyday experiences of Black women. Critical race theorists seek to do the same as regards people of color.

Finally, CRT is interdisciplinary, with deep roots in postmodern, Marxist, nationalist and feminist discourses. Clearly, much of the work of critical scholars is rooted in and sometimes in opposition to sociological, anthropological and historical scholarship on race and racism in the United States. Neil Gotanda, for example, bases his work on major anthropological work on race while articulating the ways that the concept of race has changed over time in the law. While the work is interdisciplinary, it also borrows from a number of epistemological traditions such as feminism. Likewise, Kimberle Creshaw's concept of 'intersectionality' is based on the notion that socially constructed categories such as gender and race are not and should not be considered mutually exclusive. In making such a claim, the author, like many others who work inside this tradition, inserts her identity as 'Blackwoman' race theorist who is equally committed to issues of gender and race oppression. To that extent, Crenshaw borrows heavily from the feminist tradition in order to craft a critique about the ways that women of color have suffered maltreatment and neglect in a society that does not favor Blacks or women. Furthermore, Cheryl Harris in her article 'Whiteness as Property' analyzes the relationships between white entitlement and the actual ownership of material assets that confirm the privileged status of the white dominant group. This is related, of course, to the last principle, which is that they seek to eliminate racial oppression in the US by linking to it other forms of oppression such as sexism and classism/elitism.

Critical Race Theory and its Links to Education

Recently, a number of scholars in the field of education have applied critical race analyses to educational issues (Ladson-Billings, 1995, 1998; Solórzano, 1997, 1998, Solórzano & Villalpando, 1998; Solórzano & Yosso, 2000, Tate, 1997). Ladson-Billings (1998) argues that a critical race analysis in education would necessarily focus on 'curriculum, instruction, assessment, school funding, and desegregation as exemplars of the relationship that can exist between CRT and education' (p. 18), schools and the larger society. A major concern of a critical race analysis of education would be to look analytically at the failure of the educational system in the US to properly educate the majority of culturally and racially subordinated students. Even more importantly, a critical race analysis of education might begin to examine the ways that schools participate in explicit forms of racial sorting whereby students of color are not only tracked into lower academic tracks, but are over-represented in special education programs, and 'pushed out' of public urban schools. Considering that many of these students are then tracked into lower-paying jobs requiring few skills, or shipped off to jails in order to meet the growing demand for free prison labor, adds yet another analytical dimension. Moreover, the glaring absence of teachers of color from schools where the majority of students are Black or Latino speaks to yet another dimension of a critical race analysis of schooling (Darder, 1993; Irvine, 1988). In this case, the racial homogeneity of the teaching force is not viewed as a simple accident of history. It is viewed as a result of the systematic annihilation of Black and Brown students at every step of the educational pipeline from kindergarten to graduate school. While these issues and others that affect the ability of racially subordinated peoples to participate fully in democratic life are often framed primarily in terms of social class differences, it has also been suggested for some time there are very clear racial dimensions. The development of a critical race project in education can help to move us closer toward developing an understanding that considers strongly the race-effects of schools and schooling process. However, before we can begin this process, we must articulate clearly the nature of the paradigm we propose to employ.

According to Daniel Solórzano and Tara Yosso (2000) critical race theory in education is 'a framework or set of basic perspectives, methods, and pedagogy that seeks to identify, analyze, and transform those structural, cultural, and inter-personal aspects of education that maintain the subordination of Students of Color' (p. 42). In addition, they state that CRT in education 'asks such questions as: what roles do schools themselves, school processes, and school structures play in helping to maintain racial, ethnic and gender subordination?' (p. 40). They also argue that CRT can be utilized as a point from which to begin the dialogue about the possibilities for schools to engage in the transformation of society by putting forth the question: 'Can schools help *end* [my emphasis] racial, gender, and ethnic subordination?' Solórzano has created a theoretical starting point from which to begin to think directly on the possibilities which lie in connecting CRT to a broader discourse on pedagogy, particularly the emancipatory teaching practices of people of color attempting to utilize such liberatory strategies as a vehicle for counteracting the devaluation of racially oppressed students.

Afrocentricity

Afrocentricity is an African-centered critique of Eurocentrism that offers a detailed critique of European cultural and ideological domination. According to Molefi Asante (1988), 'Afrocentricity is the belief in the centrality of Africans in post modern history' (p. 6). In other words, it is a call to reclaim African and African

American history, philosophy and science and to begin the conversation about the ways in which these new discourses can be used for liberatory means. Afrocentricity is a way of seeing the world; a way of thinking that serves to affirm African people and delegitimize the myths of African inferiority. This body of knowledge operates in some ways as a counter-narrative to the ideology of white supremacy that constructs Blacks as inferior beings without an historical legacy to which they can lay claim. Afrocentricity could also be referred to as a movement toward Pan-African unity and collective consciousness building. To that extent, a major task of Afrocentrists is to talk specifically about the ways in which Africans around the globe share cultural, linguistic, and social links that have not been severed by the reign of European world domination.

According to Asante (1988), Afrocentricity traces its lineage back to the work of African American men such as: (a) W. E. B. Du Bois for its intellectual rigor and incessant demand that scholarship be done with activist intentions; (b) Marcus Garvey for its attention to the African condition and promotion of racial separation as solution to the problem of Black oppression in the United States; (c) Booker T. Washington for its arguing for the need for African American economic independence. The work of cultural nationalist Maulana Karenga is also used in many ways to ground this work philosophically. For example, Kawaida, an African American 'religion and ideology founded by Maulana Karenga in the 1960's' is also utilized as a foundation from which Asante builds a more unified theory of Afrocentricity.

Another important task is the re-Africanization of Africans who, many claim, have, for example, negated their own spiritual centers. For this reason, there is a focus on the relearning and reteaching of traditional African traditions, customs and ways of thinking. In this regard, Asante outlines what he calls 'levels of Afrocentric awareness'. According to Asante (1988):

> The first level is called skin recognition ... The second level is environmental recognition ... [where] a person sees the environment as indicating his or her blackness through discrimination and abuse. The third level is personality awareness ... [where] a person ... talks black, acts black, dances black, and eats black, but does not think black ... The fourth level is interest-concern ... [where one] tries to deal intelligently with the issues of African people ... Afrocentric awareness ... is when the person becomes committed to a conscious level of involvement in the struggle for his or her own mind liberation ... [and is committed to struggling for] African liberation ... [or making a] constant determined effort to repair any psychic, economic, physical, or cultural damage done to Africans. (p. 8)

There are elements of Afrocentric theory that could be characterized as psychosocial because there is an explicit focus on the ways in which the thinking and behavior of Africans either affirms or negates their African identity. Psychologists, not all of them Afrocentric, have developed instruments for measuring levels of Afrocentric awareness and racial identity development.

Because Afrocentric theorists believe that their work should be accessible to the majority of African people (most of whom are working-class and have not attended a four-year collegiate institution), a great deal of the work published in the United States is written for non-academic audiences. While this has caused the work to have a greater sphere of influence on Black popular culture, it has also provided non-Afrocentric scholars with reasons to claim that the work is not rigorous, in an academic sense, and is therefore lacking in analytic utility and application. I will revisit this and other critiques later. The work of anthropologist, Marimba Ani, however, is a strong counter-example.

In her widely read book entitled *Yurugu: An African-Centered Critique of European Cultural Thought and Behavior,* Ani (1994) develops an extensive critique and analysis of the ways in which Eurocentric ideological formations have impacted the very foundations of their culture and ways of seeing the world. Situating her work within the tradition of Wade Nobles' theory of culture, which emphasizes the ideological dimensions of culture, she develops a theory of the 'cultural structuring of thought' which involves an in-depth anthropological investigation of European customs and traditions—particularly as they regard epistemology, axiology and ontology. In general, this work serves as a way to deconstruct and decenter traditional western scholarship, especially in terms of the way in which it constructs Blacks. After a brief review of some of the key works in the field, I would suggest that there are three domains within which the majority of literature considered to be Afrocentric is written. For the purposes of this paper, I refer to them as (1) Historical Reconstructionist, (2) Cultural Analyst, and (3) Cultural Archeologist. Historical reconstructionists such as Cheik Anta Diop seek to retell African History from the African perspective (Karenga, 1993). Cultural analysts such as Marimba Ani (1994) engage in an extensive critique of European cultural practices and traditions, while cultural archeologists like Maulana Karenga have attempted, as others have, to engage in actual historical research as a way in which to recover lost elements of African culture, particularly Ancient Egyptian or Kemetic culture. Other more popular Afrocentric literature operates within and outside of many of these frames simultaneously, though they might more closely be associated with what I call the cultural analyst paradigm which has a tendency to argue that there exists a biological basis for European cultural practices that have disenfranchised others.

Afrocentric Education

Afrocentric or culture-centered educational theory existed long before the postmodern concept of Afrocentricity came into being. In fact, in the early twentieth century, noted author and scholar Carter G. Woodson (1998) vociferously addressed the cultural miseducation of African peoples in public schools. Others have suggested that schools for Africans, as they were conceptualized by white abolitionists, were not created with the intent of being spiritually, emotionally and intellectually emancipating. Rather they served as a way for whites to maintain control over the minds of newly freed slaves (Butchart, 1976; Woodson, 1998).

Other African American scholars (Kunjufu, 1985; Lee, 1992; Shujaa, 1994) have continued the tradition of building sound arguments about the failure of schools to properly educate the vast majority of African Americans.

While Afrocentric scholars have consistently critiqued the US educational system for alienating African Americans from their cultural roots, a number of them have also worked to define the 'Afrocentric Idea in Education' (Asante, 1991). Carol D. Lee (1992), Mwalimu Shujaa (1994) and others have defined Afrocentric education in very specific ways. According to Lee,

> An effective African-centered pedagogy: legitimizes African stores of knowledge; positively exploits and scaffolds productive community and cultural practices; extends and builds upon the indigenous language; reinforces community ties and idealizes service to one's family, community, nation, race and world; promotes positive social relationships; imparts a world view that idealizes a positive, self-sufficient future for one's people without denying the self-worth and right to self-determination of others; and supports cultural continuity while promoting critical consciousness. (pp. 164 and 165)

In other words, a practice of teaching that is Afrocentric centralizes and normalizes the narratives of people of African descent within the context of community— taking into account historically rooted ways of being and knowing. More important, Afrocentric education—with its emphasis on the teaching of the history of African and African American peoples—helps students develop a commitment to community (Lee, 1992). As mentioned previously, 'culturally relevant' pedagogy (Ladson-Billings, 1995), 'culturally responsive' teaching (Gay, 2000; Irvine, 2000), and other culture-centered frameworks in education (King, 1995) are rooted in Afrocentric educational theory and practice with links to critical theory and pedagogy. With that in mind, it seems important to talk about the ways in which Afrocentricity as a body of knowledge is similar to or different from critical race theory as an emerging critical discourse on the law.

Critical Comparative Analysis of CRT and Afrocentricity

There is some suggestion, within the pages of the introduction to widely read compendia of leading articles on race and the law, that critical race theory has taken the position that racial essentialism (in my mind, a code word for Afrocentricity and/or cultural nationalism) is not consistent with what they imagine to be emancipatory or liberatory praxis (Crenshaw et al., 1995). They suggest that these discourses operate as totalizing metanarratives that are largely based on the experiences of Black men who rarely concern themselves with the ways that gender and class oppression interact with race oppression (Crenshaw, 1988). Crenshaw further elaborates on this notion in her discussion of intersectionality or the relationships between race and gender oppression. She cites specific examples of 'Afrocentric' literature that argue for the containment and control of the Black woman through physical abuse. She argues that work of this nature not only undermines the quest for social justice but also further delimits the agency of Black women. To that extent, critical race theorists, Crenshaw being chief among them, raise serious questions about the degree to which a politics of cultural consciousness can lead us toward a greater degree of freedom. Besides the critique of Afrocentric thought as gender-blind, some also see it as racial essentialism: the ascribing of specific qualities, albeit good ones, to any one race. Furthermore, while critical race theorists argue for the use of race in discussions of social inequality, they also contend that there are various forms of race. Gotanda (1995), for example, argues that there are biological, social, political, and cultural ways of understanding race that are appropriate given the particular context in which they are being utilized. To that extent, critical race theorists also argue that there are no fixed notions of race or racial/cultural identity and that racial and cultural identity, though they are important in helping one to develop a sense of consciousness about social inequality, are not to be judged, valued, or measured. To that end, most critical race theorists lean more heavily toward a constructionist view of race, arguing that race is primarily a construct which is made and remade for different purposes and for different uses (Lee, 1995).

There has been some discussion regarding the ways in which critical race theory, as a discourse on race in the law and education, fails to address issues of culture and language (Perea, 1997; Revilla & Asato, 2002). Critiques have asked questions like, 'Why aren't critical race theorists taking up the question of cultural domination as an integral part of racial subordination in a white supremacist context?' Morover, as I suggested previously, one could seriously question CRT's silence on the question of culture and language (Perea, 1997). For example, while critical race theorists talk about the importance of experiential knowledge and the use of narratives as a way in which to more accurately tell the stories of oppressed people of color, there is no discussion regarding the source (other than experiences with oppression) of the experiential knowledge of the people of color. What does it mean to utilize the knowledge of the oppressed as grounding for theoretical construct-building when the oppressed are only defined in relation to their oppressors? What is it that makes the story of the oppressed valid anyways? Does it not have something to do with their pasts? Furthermore, while critical race theorists reject claims of objectivity and neutrality, they are not clear about which claims they do, in fact, embrace. The Afrocentric would ask, for example, do they embrace Kemetic onto-logical, epistemological or axiological claims? This also leads us to ask: Is it enough to simply reject prevailing modes of thought or does one have a responsibility to be explicit about one's epistemological underpinnings?

Afrocentric theorists might also argue that CRT's commitment to racial equality is little more than a pipe dream, given the fact that white power in the United States has become so entrenched. While Derrick Bell does argue that racial equality is an unrealistic goal for African Americans, his suggestions for improved conditions do not argue for complete social transformation or separation of the races, as many Afrocentrists might advocate. For many Afrocentrists, the only solution is to divest totally from mainstream American culture and begin the process of nation building (Akoto, 1992). While some critical race theorists might see this as a worthy goal, others would frown upon the Afrocentrists' tendency toward a separatist politics, which, they would argue, remains somewhat blind to the fact that there must be action behind our words; that we must strongly resist racism in all its variegated manifestations. So, while Afrocentric theorists might critique CRT for not addressing the culture question, and presuming that racial equality in a white society is possible, critical race theorists have argued, on some level, that the Afrocentrists practice an essentialist politics that gives women little or no voice. However, as I will show in the next section, the points of agreement between these paradigms is far greater than the sum of their differences.

Conclusion: Exploring the Connections

In an article about the deep-rooted racist nature of social science research method-ology, Sheurich and Young (1997) refer to both Afrocentricity and critical race theory as 'race-based epistemologies' (p. 10) that offer important alternatives to Eurocentric ways of knowing and theorizing about the world. While this categor-ization of these and other transformative epistemologies can be viewed as a form of ghettoization of research and theory that addresses the needs of racially subordin-ated peoples, I find it useful for the purposes of helping me to better understand the points of connection between two paradigms that have similar aims. For example, while many Afrocentric theorists would not refer to their work as race-based, they would probably agree with critical race theorists who argue that race and its progeny, racism, must be utilized as tools through which we can theorize about the ways in which people of color are oppressed. To that extent, they both level rather harsh critiques at Marxist, liberal and conservative demagogues who attempt to assert that race-consciousness is but a mere game of identity politics (Asante, 1987, 1988; Ani, 1994; Crenshaw *et al.*, 1995; Gordon, 1995).

What do CRT and Afrocentricity have in common? Both offer new discourses about the ways that people of color have been historically marginalized and oppressed in a race-obsessed society that privileges white over Black. In this sense, it could be argued that both theoretical paradigms have eventuated in an epistemo-logical revolution or, to use Khunian terms, a major paradigm shift. To that extent, both could be referred to as *epistemologies of transformation and liberation*. CRT and Afrocentricity also attempt to operate from the vantage point of oppressed people or people of color. In doing so, Mari Matsuda (1987) and Molefi Asante (1988) both argue, in slightly different ways, that people of color can and should be placed at the center of the analysis and not at the margins. Both epistemologies offer implications for the way that research can and should be conducted in communities of color. In other words, they offer valuable ideas about the way that *culturally sensitive and attuned research* can be done.

Finally, both areas of study offer extensive critiques of the ways that Blacks have been constructed by whites in this context of white supremacy. This is exemplified through a comparison of the work of Kimberlé Crenshaw and Marimba Ani. In an article which explores the ways that Blacks are constructed in a white supremacist context, Crenshaw argues that the ideology of racism has constructed Blacks as 'lazy, unintelligent, immoral, ignorant ... criminal, shiftless, [and] lascivious' (p. 113). She further argues that as races were constructed, specific characteristics were tied to certain races. Marimba Ani (1994) has written extensively about how Blacks have been otherized in western societies. In her chapter on Europeans' 'image of others,' she argues that while Europeans tend to view 'others' as 'irrational, noncritical, illogical, uncivilized, primitive, unlawful, unruly, lazy, passive, apathetic' they tend to view themselves as the direct antithesis of this (p. 307). These analyses of the ways that Blacks are constructed provide a well-developed *critique of white supremacy*. This analysis critiques the ways that racism as an ideological formation dictates that whites and even Blacks learn to believe a certain kind of story about Black people, what it means to be Black and what it means to not be Black.

In sum, both frameworks could be referred to as: (1) epistemologies of transformation and liberation; (2) theoretical constructs that help us to do empirical research that is culturally sensitive; and (3) race-based critiques of white racial and cultural supremacy in the United States and in the world. These three commonalities, of course, cannot begin to account for the complexity of both theories. However, this new framing of the issue does suggest the importance of 'digging out' what's good and utilizing it for liberatory means. In that sense, I do not find it a useful exercise to write excessively about the deficiencies of these two theories. Instead, I have tried to take from them what I find to be useful in helping me to frame the nature of Black teachers' emancipatory practice. It is my hope that other critical pedagogists, with perhaps less of a vested interest in these issues, will begin the work of excavating the literature and looking at the ways that it can enhance their own work as we continue to explore the role of theory in the development of pedagogy and praxis that helps make the world whole.

References

Akato, K. A. (1992) *Nationbuilding: Theory & Practice in Afrikan Centered Education* (Washington, DC, Pan Afrikan World Institute).

Ani, M. (1994) *Yurugu: An African-centered critique of European cultural thought and behavior* (Trenton, Africa World Press, Inc.).

Asante, M. K. (1987) *The Afrocentric Idea* (Philadelphia, Temple University Press).

Asante, M. K. (1988) *Afrocentricity* (Trenton, NJ, Africa World Press).

Asante, M. K. (1991) The Afrocentric Idea in Education, *Journal of Negro Education*, 60:2, pp. 170–180.

Beauboeuf-Lafontant, T. (1999) A Movement Against and Beyond Boundaries: 'Politically relevant teaching' among African American teachers, *Teachers College Record*, 100:4, pp. 702–723.

Bell, D. (1992) *Faces at the Bottom of the Well: The permanence of racism* (New York, Basic Books).

Bell, D. (1995) The Racism Is Permanent Thesis: Courageous revelations or unconscious denial of racial genocide, *Capital University Law Review*, 22, pp. 571–578.

Butchart, R. E. (1976) *Educating for Freedom: Northern whites and the origins of black education in the South, 1862–1875* (unpublished doctoral diss., State University of New York, Binghamton).

Collins, P. H. (1991) *Black Feminist Thought: Knowledge, consciousness, and the politics of empowerment* (New York, Routledge).

Crenshaw, K. W. (1988) Race, Reform, and Retrenchment: Transformation and legitimation in antidiscrimination law, *Harvard Law Review*, 101, pp. 1331–1387.

Crenshaw, K., Gotanda, N., Peller, G. & Thomas, K. (eds) (1995) *Critical Race Theory: Key writings that formed the movement* (New York, New Press).

Darder, A. (1991) *Culture and Power in the Classroom: A critical foundation for bicultural education* (Westport, CT, Bergin & Garvey).

Darder, A. (1993) How Does the Culture of the Teacher Shape the Classroom Experience of Latino Students?: The unexamined question in critical pedagogy, in: S. Rothstein (ed.), *Handbook of Schooling in Urban America* (Westport, CT, Greenwood Press).

Ellsworth, E. (1989) Why Doesn't This Feel Empowering? Working through the repressive myths of critical pedagogy, *Harvard Educational Review*, 59:3, pp. 297–324.

Foster, M. (1997) *Black Teachers on Teaching* (New York, New Press).

Freire, P. (1973) *Education for Critical Consciousness* (New York, Seabury Press).

Freire, P. (1993) *Pedagogy of the Oppressed*, 20th-anniversary edition (New York, Continuum).

Gay, G. (2000) *Culturally Responsive Teaching: Theory, research and practice* (New York, Teachers College Press).

Gordon, B. M. (1995) Knowledge Construction, Competing Critical Theories, and Education, in: J. A. Banks & C. A. McGee Banks (eds), *Handbook of Research on Multicultural Education* (New York, Macmillan).

Gotanda, N. (1995) A Critique of 'Our Constitution is Color-Blind', in: K. Crenshaw, N. Gotanda, G. Peller & K. Thomas (eds), *Critical Race Theory: Key writings that formed the movement* (New York, New Press).

Henry, A. (1998) *Taking Back Control: African Canadian women teachers' lives and practice* (Albany, NY, SUNY Press).

Irvine, J. J. (1988) An Analysis of the Problem of Disappearing Black Educators, *Elementary School Journal*, 88:5, pp. 503–513.

Irvine, J. J. (1990) *Black Students and School Failure: Policies, practices, and prescriptions* (Westport, CT, Greenwood Press).

Irvine, J. J. (2000) DeWitt Wallace–Reader's Digest Distinguished Lecture, paper presented at the Annual meeting of the American Educational Research Association, New Orleans.

Kanpol, B. (1988) Teacher Work Tasks as Forms of Resistance and Accommodation to Structural Factors of Schooling, *Urban Education*, 23:2, pp. 173–187.

Kanpol, B. (1992) *Towards a Theory and Practice of Teacher Cultural Politics: Continuing the postmodern debate* (Norwood, NJ, Ablex).

Karenga, M. (1993) *Introduction to Black Studies*, 2nd edn (Los Angeles, CA, University of Sankore Press).

King, J. E. (1991) Unfinished Business: Black student's alienation and Black teachers' pedagogy, in: M. Foster (ed.), *Readings on Equal Education: Qualitative investigations in schools and schooling* (New York, AMS Press).

King, J. E. (1995) Culture-centered Knowledge: Black studies, curriculum transformation, and social action, in: J. A. Banks & C. A. McGee Banks (eds), *Handbook of Research on Multicultural Education* (New York, Macmillan).

Kunjufu, J. (1985) *Countering the Conspiracy to Destroy Black Boys* (Chicago, African-American Images).

Ladson-Billings, G. (1994) *The Dream Keepers: Successful teachers of African-American children* (San Francisco, Jossey-Bass Publishers).

Ladson-Billings, G. (1995) Toward a Theory of Culturally Relevant Teaching, *American Educational Research Journal*, 32:3, pp. 465–491.

Ladson-Billings, G. (1998) Just What Is Critical Race Theory and What's It Doing in a *Nice* Field Like Education?, *International Journal of Qualitative Studies in Education*, 11:1, pp. 7–24.

Ladson-Billings, G. & Tate, W. F. (1995) Toward a Critical Race Theory of Education, *Teachers College Record*, 97:1, pp. 47–68.

Lawrence, C. (1991) The Word and the River: Pedagogy as scholarship and struggle, *Southern California Law Review*, 65, pp. 2231–2298.

Lee, C. D. (1992) Profile of an Independent Black Institution: African-centered education at work, *Journal of Negro Education*, 61:2, pp. 160–177.

Lee, J. (1995) Navigating the Topology of Race, in: K. Crenshaw, N. Gotanda, G. Peller & K. Thomas (eds), *Critical Race Theory: Key writings that formed the movement* (New York, New Press).

Lynn, M. (1999) Toward a Critical Race Pedagogy: A research note, *Urban Education*, 33:5, pp. 606–626.

Matsuda, M. (1987) Looking to the Bottom: Critical legal studies and reparations, *Harvard Civil Rights–Civil Liberties Law Review*, 22, pp. 323–399.

Matsuda, M., Lawrence, C., Delgardo, R. & Crenshaw, K. (eds) (1993) *Words that Wound: Critical race theory, assaultive speech, and the First Amendment* (Boulder, CO, Westview Press).

McCarthy, C. (1988) Rethinking Liberal and Radical Perspectives on Racial Inequality in Schooling: Making the case for nonsynchrony, *Harvard Educational Review*, 58:3, pp. 265–279.

Morris, J. E. (2001) Forgotten Voices of Black Educators: Critical race perspectives on the implementation of a desegregation plan, *Educational Policy*, 15:4, pp. 575–600.

Omi, M. & Winant, H. (1994) *Racial Formation in the United States: From the 1960's to the 1990's*, 2nd edn (New York, Routledge).

Opoku, K. A. (1997) *Hearing and Keeping: Akan proverbs* (Accra, Ghana, Asempa Publishers).

Perea, J. F. (1997) The Black/White Binary Paradigm of Race: The 'normal science' of American racial thought, *California Law Review*, 85, pp. 1213–1258.

Revilla, A. T. & Asato, J. (2002) The Implementation of 227 in California Schools: A critical analysis of the effect of proposition 227 on teacher beliefs and classroom practices, *Equity and Excellence in Education Journal*, 35:2.

Scheurich, J. J. & Young, M. D. (1997) Coloring Epistemologies: Are our research epistemologies racially biased?, *Educational Researcher*, 26:4, pp. 4–16.

Shujaa, M. J. (ed.) (1994) *Too Much Schooling, Too Little Education: A paradox of Black life in White societies* (Trenton, NJ, Africa World Press).

Solórzano, D. (1997) Images and Words that Wound: Critical race theory, racial stereotyping, and teacher education, *Teacher Education Quarterly*, 24, pp. 5–19.

Solórzano, D. (1998) Critical Race Theory, Racial Microaggressions, and the Experiences of Chicana and Chicano Scholars, *International Journal of Qualitative Studies in Education*, 11:1, pp. 7–24.

Solórzano, D. & Villalpando, O. (1998) Critical Race Theory, Marginality, and the Experience of Minority Students in Higher Education, in: C. Torres & T. Mitchell (eds), *Emerging Issues in the Sociology of Education: Comparative perspectives* (New York, SUNY Press).

Solórzano, D. & Yosso, T. (2000) Toward a Critical Race Theory of Chicana and Chicano Education, in: C. Tejeda, C. Martinez & Z. Leonardo (eds), *Charting New Terrains of Chicana(o)/Latina(o) Education* (Cresskill, NJ, Hampton Press).

Tate, W. F. (1997) Critical Race Theory and Education: History, theory and implications, *Review of Research in Education*, 22, pp. 195–247.

Thomas, K. (1995) Rouge et Noir Reread: A popular constitutional history of the Angelo Herndon case, in: K. Crenshaw, N. Gotanda, G. Peller & K. Thomas (eds), *Critical Race Theory: Key writings that formed the movement* (New York, New Press).

West, C. (1993) *Race Matters* (Boston, Beacon).

Woodson, C. G. (1998) *The Miseducation of the Negro*, 10th edn (Trenton, Africa World Press).

7

Class Dismissed? Historical materialism and the politics of 'difference'

VALERIE SCATAMBURLO-D'ANNIBALE & PETER MCLAREN
University of Windsor, Ontario; University of California, Los Angeles

Introduction

Perhaps one of the most taken-for-granted features of contemporary social theory is the ritual and increasingly generic critique of Marxism in terms of its alleged failure to address forms of oppression other than that of 'class.' Marxism is considered to be theoretically bankrupt and intellectually passé, and class analysis is often savagely lampooned as a rusty weapon wielded clumsily by those mind-locked in the jejune factories of the nineteenth and twentieth centuries. When Marxist class analysis has not been distorted or equated with some crude version of 'economic determinism,' it has been attacked for diverting attention away from the categories of 'difference'—including 'race' (Gimenez, 2001). To overcome the presumed inadequacies of Marxism, an entire discursive apparatus, sometimes called 'post-Marxism', has arisen to fill the void.

Serving as academic pallbearers at the funeral of the old bearded devil, post-Marxists (who often go by other names such as postmodernists, radical multiculturalists, etc.) have tried to entomb Marx's legacy while simultaneously benefiting from it. Yet, the crypt designed for Marx, reverential in its grand austerity, has never quite been able to contain his impact on history. For someone presumably dead, Marx has a way of escaping from his final resting place and reappearing with an uncanny regularity in the world of ideas. His ghost, as Greider (1998) notes, 'hovers over the global landscape' as he continues to shape our understandings of the current crises of capitalism that haunt the living present. Regardless of Marx's enduring relevance and even though much of post-Marxism is actually an outlandish 'caricature' of Marx and the entire Marxist tradition, it has eaten through the Left 'like a cancer' and has 'established itself as the new common sense' (Johnson, 2002, p. 129). What has been produced is a discourse eminently more digestible to the academic 'Left' whose steady embourgeoisement appears to be altering the political palate of career social theorists.

Eager to take a wide detour around political economy, post-Marxists tend to assume that the principal political points of departure in the current 'postmodern' world must necessarily be 'cultural.' As such, most, *but not all* post-Marxists have gravitated towards a politics of 'difference' which is largely premised on uncovering relations of power that reside in the arrangement and deployment of subjectivity in cultural and ideological practices (cf. Jordan & Weedon, 1995). Advocates of 'difference' politics therefore posit their ideas as bold steps forward in advancing the interests of those historically marginalized by 'dominant' social and cultural narratives.

There is no doubt that post-Marxism has advanced our knowledge of the hidden trajectories of power within the processes of representation and that it remains useful in adumbrating the formation of subjectivity and its expressive dimensions as well as complementing our understandings of the relationships between 'difference,' language, and cultural configurations. However, post-Marxists have been woefully remiss in addressing the constitution of class formations and the machinations of capitalist social organization. In some instances, capitalism and class relations have been thoroughly 'otherized;' in others, class is summoned only as part of the triumvirate of 'race, class, and gender' in which class is reduced to merely another form of 'difference.' Enamored with the 'cultural' and seemingly blind to the 'economic,' the rhetorical excesses of post-Marxists have also prevented them from considering the stark reality of contemporary class conditions under global capitalism. As we hope to show, the radical displacement of class analysis in contemporary theoretical narratives and the concomitant decentering of capitalism, the anointing of 'difference' as a primary explanatory construct, and the 'culturalization' of politics, have had detrimental effects on 'left' theory and practice.

Reconceptualizing 'Difference'

The manner in which 'difference' has been taken up within 'post-al' frameworks has tended to stress its cultural dimensions while marginalizing and, in some cases, completely ignoring the *economic* and *material dimensions* of difference. This posturing has been quite evident in many 'post-al' theories of 'race' and in the realm of 'ludic'[1] cultural studies that have valorized an account of difference—particularly 'racial difference'—in almost exclusively 'superstructuralist' terms (Sahay, 1998). But this treatment of 'difference' and claims about 'the "relative autonomy" of "race"' have been 'enabled by a reduction and distortion of Marxian class analysis' which 'involves equating class analysis with some version of economic determinism.' The key move in this distorting gesture depends on the 'view that the economic is the base, the cultural/political/ideological the superstructure.' It is then 'relatively easy to show that the (presumably non-political) economic base does not cause the political/cultural/ideological superstructure, that the latter is/are not epiphenomenal but relatively autonomous or autonomous causal categories' (Meyerson, 2000, p. 2). In such formulations the 'cultural' is treated as a separate and autonomous sphere, severed from its embeddedness within sociopolitical and economic arrangements. As a result, many of these 'culturalist' narratives have produced autonomist and reified conceptualizations of difference which 'far from enabling those subjects most marginalized by racial difference' have, in effect, reduced 'difference to a question of knowledge/power relations' that can presumably be 'dealt with (negotiated) on a discursive level without a fundamental change in the relations of production' (Sahay, 1998).

At this juncture, it is necessary to point out that arguing that 'culture' is generally conditioned/shaped by material forces does not reinscribe the simplistic and presumably 'deterministic' base/superstructure metaphor which has plagued some strands of Marxist theory. Rather, we invoke Marx's own writings from both the *Grundrisse* and *Capital* in which he contends that there is a consolidating logic in the relations of production that permeates society in the complex variety of its 'empirical' reality. This emphasizes Marx's understanding of capitalism and capital as a 'social' relation—one which stresses the interpenetration of these categories, the realities which they reflect, and one which therefore offers a unified and dialectical analysis of history, ideology, culture, politics, economics and society (see also Marx, 1972, 1976, 1977).[2]

Foregrounding the limitations of 'difference' and 'representational' politics does not suggest a disavowal of the importance of cultural and/or discursive arena(s) as sites of contestation and struggle. We readily acknowledge the significance of contemporary theorizations that have sought to valorize precisely those forms of 'difference' that have historically been denigrated. This has undoubtedly been an important development since they have enabled subordinated groups to reconstruct their own histories and give voice to their individual and collective identities. However, they have also tended to redefine politics as a signifying activity generally confined to the realm of 'representation' while displacing a politics grounded in the mobilization of forces against the material sources of political and economic marginalization. In their rush to avoid the 'capital' sin of 'economism,' many post-Marxists (who often ignore their own class privilege) have fallen prey to an ahistorical form of culturalism which holds, among other things, that cultural struggles external to class organizing provide the cutting edge of emancipatory politics.[3] In many respects, this posturing, has yielded an 'intellectual pseudopolitics' that has served to empower 'the theorist while explicitly disempowering' real citizens (Turner, 1994, p. 410). We do not discount concerns over representation; rather our point is that progressive educators and theorists should not be straightjacketed by struggles that fail to move beyond the politics of difference and representation in the cultural realm. While space limitations prevent us from elaborating this point, we contend that culturalist arguments are deeply problematic both in terms of their penchant for de-emphasizing the totalizing (yes totalizing!) power and function of capital and for their attempts to employ culture as a construct that would diminish the centrality of class. In a proper historical materialist account, 'culture' is not the 'other' of class but, rather, constitutes part of a more comprehensive theorization of class rule in different contexts.[4]

'Post-al' theorizations of 'difference' circumvent and undermine any systematic knowledge of the material dimensions of difference and tend to segregate questions of 'difference' from class formation and capitalist social relations. We therefore believe that it is necessary to (re)conceptualize 'difference' by drawing upon Marx's materialist and historical formulations. 'Difference' needs to be understood as the product of social contradictions and in relation to political and economic organization. We need to acknowledge that 'otherness' and/or difference is not something that passively happens, but, rather, is actively produced. In other words, since systems of differences almost always involve relations of domination and oppression, we must concern ourselves with the economies of relations of difference that exist in specific contexts. Drawing upon the Marxist concept of *mediation* enables us to unsettle our categorical approaches to both class and difference, for it was Marx himself who warned against creating false dichotomies in the situation of our politics—that it was absurd to 'choose between consciousness and the world, subjectivity and social organization, personal or collective will and historical or structural determination.' In a similar vein, it is equally absurd to see 'difference as a historical form of consciousness unconnected to class formation, development of capital and class politics' (Bannerji, 1995, p. 30). Bannerji points to the need to historicize 'difference' in relation to the history and social organization of capital and class (inclusive of imperialist and colonialist legacies). Apprehending the meaning and function of difference in this manner necessarily highlights the import-ance of exploring (1) the institutional and structural aspects of difference; (2) the meanings that get attached to categories of difference; and (3) how differences are produced out of, and lived within specific historical formations.[5]

Moreover, it presents a challenge to those theorizations that work to consolidate 'identitarian' understandings of difference based exclusively on questions of cultural or racial hegemony. In such approaches, the answer to oppression often amounts to creating greater cultural space for the formerly excluded to have their voices heard (represented). In this regard, much of what is called the 'politics of difference' is little more than a demand for inclusion into the club of representation —a posture which reinscribes a neo-liberal pluralist stance rooted in the ideology of free-market capitalism. In short, the political sphere is modeled on the marketplace and freedom amounts to the liberty of all vendors to display their 'different' cultural goods. What advocates of this approach fail to address is that the forces of diversity and difference are allowed to flourish provided that they remain within the prevailing forms of capitalist social arrangements. The neo-pluralism of difference politics (including those based on 'race') cannot adequately pose a substantive challenge to the productive system of capitalism that is able to accommodate a vast pluralism of ideas and cultural practices, and cannot capture the ways in which various manifestations of oppression are intimately connected to the central dynamics of capitalist exploitation.

An historical materialist approach understands that categories of 'difference' are social/political constructs that are often encoded in dominant ideological forma-tions and that they often play a role in 'moral' and 'legal' state-mediated forms of ruling. It also acknowledges the 'material' force of ideologies—particularly racist ideologies—that assign separate cultural and/or biological essences to different segments of the population which, in turn, serve to reinforce and rationalize existing relations of power. But more than this, an historical materialist understanding foregrounds the manner in which 'difference' is central to the exploitative production/ reproduction dialectic of capital, its labor organization and processes, and in the way labor is valued and renumerated.

The real problem is the internal or dialectical relation that exists between capital and labor within the capitalist production process itself—a social relation in which capitalism is intransigently rooted. This social relation—essential to the production of abstract labor—deals with how already existing value is preserved and new value (surplus value) is created (Allman, 2001). If, for example, the process of actual exploitation and the accumulation of surplus value is to be seen as a state of constant manipulation and as a realization process of concrete labor in actual labor time—within a given cost-production system and a labor market—we cannot underestimate the ways in which 'difference' (racial as well as gender difference) is encapsulated in the production/reproduction dialectic of capital. It is this relationship that is mainly responsible for the inequitable and unjust distribution of resources. A deepened understanding of this phenomenon is essential for understanding the emergence of an acutely polarized labor market and the fact that disproportionately high percentages of 'people of color' are trapped in the lower rungs of domestic and global labor markets (McLaren & Farahmandpur, 1999). 'Difference' in the era of global capitalism is crucial to the workings, movements and profit levels of multinational corporations but those types of complex relations cannot be mapped out by using truncated post-Marxist, culturalist conceptualizations of 'difference.' To sever issues of 'difference' from class conveniently draws attention away from the crucially important ways in which 'people of color' (and, more specifically, 'women of color') provide capital with its superexploited labor pools—a phenomenon that is on the rise all over the world. Most social relations constitutive of racialized differences are considerably shaped by the relations of production and there is undoubtedly a racialized and gendered division of labor whose severity and function vary depending on where one is situated in the capitalist global economy (Meyerson, 2000).[6]

In stating this, we need to include an important caveat that differentiates our approach from those invoking the well-worn race/class/gender triplet which can sound, to the uninitiated, both radical and vaguely Marxian. It is not. Race, class and gender, while they invariably intersect and interact, are not co-primary. This 'triplet' approximates what the 'philosophers might call a category mistake.' On the surface the triplet may be convincing—some people are oppressed because of their race, others as a result of their gender, yet others because of their class—but this 'is grossly misleading' for it is not that 'some individuals manifest certain characteristics known as "class" which then results in their oppression; on the contrary, to be a member of a social class just *is* to be oppressed' and in this regard class is 'a wholly social category' (Eagleton, 1998, p. 289). Furthermore, even though 'class' is usually invoked as part of the aforementioned and much vaunted triptych, it is usually gutted of its practical, social dimension or treated solely as a cultural phenomenon—as just another form of 'difference.' In these instances, class is transformed from an economic and, indeed, social category to an exclusively cultural or discursive one or one in which class merely signifies a 'subject position.' Class is therefore cut off from the political economy of capitalism and class power severed from exploitation and a power structure 'in which those who control collectively produced resources only do so because of the value generated by those who do not' (Hennessy & Ingraham, 1997, p. 2).

Such theorizing has had the effect of replacing an *historical materialist class analysis with a cultural analysis of class*. As a result, many post-Marxists have also stripped the idea of class of precisely that element which, for Marx, made it radical—namely its status as a universal form of exploitation whose abolition required (and was also central to) the abolition of all manifestations of oppression (Marx, 1978, p. 60). With regard to this issue, Kovel (2002) is particularly insightful, for he explicitly addresses an issue which continues to vex the Left—namely the priority given to different categories of what he calls 'dominative splitting'—those categories of 'gender, class, race, ethnic and national exclusion,' etc. Kovel argues that we need to ask the question of *priority* with respect to what? He notes that if we mean priority with respect to *time*, then the category of gender would have priority since there are traces of gender oppression in all other forms of oppression. If we were to prioritize in terms of *existential significance*, Kovel suggests that we would have to depend upon the immediate historical forces that bear down on distinct groups of people—he offers examples of Jews in 1930s Germany who suffered from brutal forms of anti-Semitism and Palestinians today who experience anti-Arab racism under Israeli domination. The question of what has *political priority*, however, would depend upon which transformation of relations of oppression are practically more urgent and, while this would certainly depend upon the preceding categories, it would also depend upon the fashion in which all the forces acting in a concrete situation are deployed. As to the question of which split sets into motion all of the others, the priority would have to be given to *class* since class relations

> entail the state as an instrument of enforcement and control, and it is the state that shapes and organizes the splits that appear in human ecosystems. Thus class is both logically and historically distinct from other forms of exclusion (hence we should not talk of 'classism' to go along with 'sexism' and 'racism,' and 'species-ism'). This is, first of all, because class is an essentially man-made category, without root in even a mystified biology. We cannot imagine a human world without gender distinctions—although we can imagine a world without domination by gender. But a world without class is eminently imaginable—indeed, such was the human world for the great majority of our species' time on earth, during all of which considerable fuss was made over gender. Historically, the difference arises because 'class' signifies one side of a larger figure that includes a state apparatus whose conquests and regulations create races and shape gender relations. Thus there will be no true resolution of racism so long as class society stands, inasmuch as a racially oppressed society implies the activities of a class-defending state. Nor can gender inequality be enacted away so long as class society, with its state, demands the super-exploitation of women's labor. (Kovel, 2002, pp. 123–124)

Contrary to what many have claimed, Marxist theory does not relegate categories of 'difference' to the conceptual mausoleum; rather, it has sought to reanimate these categories by interrogating how they are refracted through material relations of power and privilege and linked to relations of production. Moreover, it has emphasized and insisted that the wider political and economic system in which they are embedded needs to be thoroughly understood in all its complexity. Indeed, Marx made clear how constructions of race and ethnicity 'are implicated in the circulation process of variable capital.' To the extent that 'gender, race, and ethnicity are all understood as social constructions rather than as essentialist categories' the effect of exploring their insertion into the 'circulation of variable capital (including positioning within the internal heterogeneity of collective labor and hence, within the division of labor and the class system)' must be interpreted as a 'powerful force reconstructing them in distinctly capitalist ways' (Harvey, 2000, p. 106). Unlike contemporary narratives which tend to focus on one or another form of oppression, the irrefragable power of historical materialism resides in its ability to reveal (1) how forms of oppression based on categories of difference do not possess relative autonomy from class relations but rather constitute the ways in which oppression is lived/experienced within a class-based system; and (2) how all forms of social oppression function within an overarching capitalist system.

This framework must be further distinguished from those that invoke the terms 'classism' and/or 'class elitism' to (ostensibly) foreground the idea that 'class matters' (cf. hooks, 2000) since we agree with Gimenez (2001, p. 24) that 'class is not simply another ideology legitimating oppression.' Rather, class denotes 'exploitative relations between people mediated by their relations to the means of production.' To marginalize such a conceptualization of class is to conflate an individual's objective location in the intersection of structures of inequality with people's subjective understandings of who they really are based on their 'experiences.'

Another caveat. In making such a claim, we are not renouncing the concept of experience. On the contrary, we believe it is imperative to retain the category of lived experience as a reference point in light of misguided post-Marxist critiques which imply that *all* forms of Marxian class analysis are dismissive of subjectivity. We are not, however, advocating the uncritical fetishization of 'experience' that tends to assume that experience somehow guarantees the authenticity of knowledge and which often treats experience as self-explanatory, transparent, and solely individual. Rather, we advance a framework that seeks to make connections between seemingly isolated situations and/or particular experiences by exploring how they are constituted in, and circumscribed by, broader historical and social circumstances. Experiential understandings, in and of themselves, are suspect because, dialectically, they constitute a unity of opposites—they are at once unique, specific, and personal, but also thoroughly partial, social, and the products of historical forces about which individuals may know little or nothing (Gimenez, 2001). In this sense, a rich description of immediate experience in terms of consciousness of a particular form of oppression (racial or otherwise) can be an appropriate and indispensable point of departure. Such an understanding, however, can easily become an isolated 'difference' prison unless it transcends the immediate perceived point of oppression, confronts the social system in which it is rooted, and expands into a complex and multifaceted analysis (of forms of social mediation) that is capable of mapping out the general organization of social relations. That, however, requires a broad class-based approach.

> Having a concept of class helps us to see the network of social relations
> constituting an overall social organization which both implicates and cuts
> through racialization/ethnicization and gender ... [a] radical political
> economy [class] perspective emphasizing exploitation, dispossession and
> survival takes the issues of ... diversity [and difference] beyond questions
> of conscious identity such as culture and ideology, or of a paradigm of
> homogeneity and heterogeneity ... or of ethical imperatives with respect
> to the 'other'. (Bannerji, 2000, pp. 7, 19)

A radical political economy framework is crucial since various 'culturalist'
perspectives seem to diminish the role of political economy and class forces in
shaping the edifice of 'the social'—including the shifting constellations and meanings
of 'difference.' Furthermore, none of the 'differences' valorized in culturalist
narratives alone, and certainly not 'race' by itself can explain the massive transformation of the structure of capitalism in recent years. We agree with Meyerson
(2000) that 'race' is not an adequate explanatory category on its own and that the
use of 'race' as a descriptive or analytical category has serious consequences for the
way in which social life is presumed to be constituted and organized. The category
of 'race'—the conceptual framework that the oppressed often employ to interpret
their experiences of inequality 'often clouds the concrete reality of class, and blurs
the actual structure of power and privilege.' In this regard, 'race' is all too often a
'barrier to understanding the central role of class in shaping personal and collective
outcomes within a capitalist society' (Marable, 1995, pp. 8, 226). In many ways,
the use of 'race' has become an analytical trap precisely when it has been employed
in antiseptic isolation from the messy terrain of historical and material relations.
This, of course, does not imply that we ignore racism and racial oppression; rather,
an analytical shift from 'race' to a plural conceptualization of 'racisms' and their
historical articulations is necessary (cf. McLaren & Torres, 1999). However, it is
important to note that 'race' doesn't explain racism and forms of racial oppression.
Those relations are best understood within the context of class rule, as Bannerji,
Kovel, Marable and Meyerson imply—but that compels us to forge a conceptual
shift in theorizing, which entails (among other things) moving beyond the ideology
of 'difference' and 'race' as the dominant prisms for understanding exploitation and
oppression. We are aware of some potential implications for white Marxist criticalists
to unwittingly support racist practices in their criticisms of 'race-first' positions
articulated in the social sciences. In those instances, white criticalists wrongly go
on 'high alert' in placing theorists of color under special surveillance for downplaying
an analysis of capitalism and class. These activities on the part of white criticalists
must be condemned, as must be efforts to stress class analysis primarily as a means
of creating a *white vanguard position* in the struggle against capitalism. Our position
is one that attempts to link practices of racial oppression to the central, totalizing
dynamics of capitalist society in order to resist white supremacist capitalist patriarchy
more fully.[7]

We have argued that it is virtually impossible to conceptualize class without
attending to the forms and contents of difference, but we insist that this does not

imply that class struggle is now outdated by the politics of difference. As Jameson (1998, p. 136) notes, we are now in the midst of returning to the 'most fundamental form of class struggle' in light of current global conditions. Today's climate suggests that class struggle is 'not yet a thing of the past' and that those who seek to undermine its centrality are not only 'morally callous' and 'seriously out of touch with reality' but also largely blind to the 'needs of the large mass of people who are barely surviving capital's newly-honed mechanisms of globalized greed' (Harvey, 1998, pp. 7–9). In our view, a more comprehensive and politically useful understanding of the contemporary historical juncture necessitates foregrounding class analysis and the primacy of the working class as the fundamental agent of change.[8]

This does not render as 'secondary' the concerns of those marginalized by race, ethnicity, etc. as is routinely charged by post-Marxists. It is often assumed that foregrounding capitalist social relations necessarily undermines the importance of attending to 'difference' and/or trivializes struggles against racism, etc., in favor of an abstractly defined class-based politics typically identified as 'white.' Yet, such formulations rest on a bizarre but generally unspoken logic that assumes that racial and ethnic 'minorities' are only conjuncturally related to the working class. This stance is patently absurd since the concept of the 'working class' is undoubtedly comprised of men and women of different races, ethnicities, etc. (Mitter, 1997). A good deal of post-Marxist critique is subtly racist (not to mention essentialist) insofar as it implies that 'people of color' could not possibly be concerned with issues beyond those related to their 'racial' or 'ethnic' 'difference.' This posits 'people of color' as single-minded, one-dimensional caricatures and assumes that their working lives are less crucial to their self-understanding (and survival) than is the case with their 'white male' counterparts.[9] It also ignores 'the fact that class is an ineradicable dimension of everybody's lives' (Gimenez, 2001, p. 2) and that social oppression is much more than tangentially linked to class background and the exploitative relations of production. On this topic, Meyerson (2000) is worth quoting at length:

> Marxism properly interpreted emphasizes the primacy of class in a number of senses. One of course is the primacy of the working class as a revolutionary agent—a primacy which does not render women and people of color 'secondary.' This view assumes that 'working class' means white—this division between a white working class and all the others, whose identity (along with a corresponding social theory to explain that identity) is thereby viewed as either primarily one of gender and race or hybrid ... [T]he primacy of class means ... that building a multiracial, multi-gendered international working-class organization or organizations should be the goal of any revolutionary movement so that the primacy of class puts the fight against racism and sexism at the center. The intelligibility of this position is rooted in the explanatory primacy of class analysis for understanding the structural determinants of race, gender, and class oppression. Oppression is multiple and intersecting but its causes are not.

The cohesiveness of this position suggests that forms of exploitation and oppression are related internally to the extent that they are located in the same totality—one which is currently defined by capitalist class rule. Capitalism *is* an overarching totality that is, unfortunately, becoming increasingly invisible in post-Marxist 'discursive' narratives that valorize 'difference' as a primary explanatory construct.

For example, E. San Juan (2003) argues that race relations and race conflict are necessarily structured by the larger totality of the political economy of a given society, as well as by modifications in the structure of the world economy. He further notes that the capitalist mode of production has articulated 'race' with class in a peculiar way. He too is worth a substantial quotation:

> While the stagnation of rural life imposed a racial or castelike rigidity to the peasantry, the rapid accumulation of wealth through the ever more intensifying exploitation of labor by capital could not so easily 'racialize' the wage-workers of a particular nation, given the alienability of labor-power—unless certain physical or cultural characteristics can be utilized to divide the workers or render one group an outcast or pariah removed from the domain of 'free labor.' In the capitalist development of U.S. society, African, Mexican, and Asian bodies—more precisely, their labor power and its reproductive efficacy—were colonized and racialized; hence the idea of 'internal colonialism' retains explanatory validity. 'Race' is thus constructed out of raw materials furnished by class relations, the history of class conflicts, and the vicissitudes of colonial/capitalist expansion and the building of imperial hegemony. It is dialectically accented and operationalized not just to differentiate the price of wage labor within and outside the territory of the metropolitan power, but also to reproduce relations of domination–subordination invested with an aura of naturality and fatality. The refunctioning of physical or cultural traits as ideological and political signifiers of class identity reifies social relations. Such 'racial' markers enter the field of the alienated labor process, concealing the artificial nature of meanings and norms, and essentializing or naturalizing historical traditions and values which are contingent on mutable circumstances.

For San Juan, racism and nationalism are modalities in which class struggles articulate themselves at strategic points in history. He argues that racism arose with the creation and expansion of the capitalist world economy. He maintains, rightly in our view, that racial or ethnic group solidarity is given 'meaning and value in terms of their place within the social organization of production and reproduction of the ideological-political order; ideologies of racism as collective social evaluation of solidarities arise to reinforce structural constraints which preserve the exploited and oppressed position of these "racial" solidarities'.

It is remarkable, in our opinion, that so much of contemporary social theory has largely abandoned the problems of labor, capitalist exploitation, and class analysis at a time when capitalism is becoming more universal, more ruthless and more deadly. The metaphor of a contemporary 'tower of Babel' seems appropriate here—academics striking radical poses in the seminar rooms while remaining oblivious to the possibility that their seemingly radical discursive maneuvers do nothing to further the struggles 'against oppression and exploitation which continue to be real, material, and not merely "discursive" problems of the contemporary world' (Dirlik, 1997, p. 176). Harvey (1998, pp. 29–31) indicts the new academic entrepreneurs, the 'masters of theory-in-and-for-itself' whose 'discourse radicalism' has deftly side-stepped 'the enduring conundrums of class struggle' and who have, against a 'sobering background of cheapened discourse and opportunistic politics,' been 'stripped of their self-advertised radicalism.' For years, they 'contested socialism,' ridiculed Marxists, and promoted 'their own alternative theories of liberatory politics' but now they have largely been 'reduced to the role of supplicants in the most degraded form of pluralist politics imaginable.' As they pursue the politics of difference, the 'class war rages unabated' and they seem 'either unwilling or unable to focus on the unprecedented economic carnage occurring around the globe.'

Harvey's searing criticism suggests that post-Marxists have been busy fiddling while Rome burns and his comments echo those made by Marx (1978, p. 149) in his critique of the Young Hegelians who were, 'in spite of their allegedly "world-shattering" statements, the staunchest conservatives.' Marx lamented that the Young Hegelians were simply fighting 'phrases' and that they failed to acknowledge that in offering only counter-phrases, they were in no way 'combating the real existing world' but merely combating the phrases of the world. Taking a cue from Marx and substituting 'phrases' with 'discourses' or 'resignifications' we would contend that the practitioners of difference politics who operate within exaggerated culturalist frameworks that privilege the realm of representation as the primary arena of political struggle question some discourses of power while legitimating others. Moreover, because they lack a class perspective, their gestures of radicalism are belied by their own class positions.[10] As Ahmad (1997a, p. 104) notes:

> One may speak of any number of disorientations and even oppressions, but one cultivates all kinds of politeness and indirection about the structure of capitalist class relations in which those oppressions are embedded. To speak of any of that directly and simply is to be 'vulgar.' In this climate of Aesopian languages it is absolutely essential to reiterate that most things *are* a matter of class. That kind of statement is ... surprising only in a culture like that of the North American university ... But it is precisely in that kind of culture that people need to hear such obvious truths.

Ahmad's provocative observations imply that substantive analyses of the carnage wrought by 'globalized' class exploitation have, for the most part, been marginalized by the kind of radicalism that has been instituted among the academic Left in North America. He further suggests that while various post-Marxists have invited us to join their euphoric celebrations honoring the decentering of capitalism, the abandonment of class politics, and the decline of metanarratives (particularly those of Marxism and socialism), they have failed to see that the most 'meta of all metanarratives of the past three centuries, the creeping annexation of the globe for the dominance of capital over laboring humanity has met, during those same decades, with stunning success' (Ahmad, 1997b, p. 364). As such, Ahmad invites us to ask anew, the proverbial question: What, then, must be done? To this question we offer no simple theoretical, pedagogical or political prescriptions. Yet we would argue that if social change is the aim, progressive educators and theorists must cease displacing class analysis with the politics of difference.

Conclusion

> ... we will take our stand against the evils [of capitalism, imperialism, and racism] with a solidarity derived from a proletarian internationalism born of socialist idealism.

> —National Office of the Black Panther Party, February 1970

For well over two decades we have witnessed the jubilant liberal and conservative pronouncements of the demise of socialism. Concomitantly, history's presumed failure to defang existing capitalist relations has been read by many self-identified 'radicals' as an advertisement for capitalism's inevitability. As a result, the chorus refrain 'There Is No Alternative', sung by liberals and conservatives, has been buttressed by the symphony of post-Marxist voices recommending that we give socialism a decent burial and move on. Within this context, to speak of the promise of Marx and socialism may appear anachronistic, even naïve, especially since the post-al intellectual vanguard has presumably demonstrated the folly of doing so. Yet we stubbornly believe that the chants of T.I.N.A. must be combated for they offer as a *fait accompli*, something which progressive Leftists should refuse to accept—namely the triumph of capitalism and its political bedfellow neo-liberalism, which have worked together to naturalize suffering, undermine collective struggle, and obliterate hope. We concur with Amin (1998), who claims that such chants must be defied and revealed as absurd and criminal, and who puts the challenge we face in no uncertain terms: humanity may let itself be led by capitalism's logic to a fate of collective suicide or it may pave the way for an alternative humanist project of global socialism.

The grosteque conditions that inspired Marx to pen his original critique of capitalism are present and flourishing. The inequalities of wealth and the gross imbalances of power that exist today are leading to abuses that exceed those encountered in Marx's day (Greider, 1998, p. 39). Global capitalism has paved the way for the obscene concentration of wealth in fewer and fewer hands and created a world increasingly divided between those who enjoy opulent affluence and those who languish in dehumanizing conditions and economic misery. In every corner of the globe, we are witnessing social disintegration as revealed by a rise in abject poverty and inequality. At the current historical juncture, the combined assets of the 225 richest people is roughly equal to the annual income of the poorest 47 percent of the world's population, while the combined assets of the three richest people exceed the combined GDP of the 48 poorest nations (CCPA, 2002, p. 3). Approximately 2.8 billion people—almost half of the world's population—struggle in desperation to live on less than two dollars a day (McQuaig, 2001, p. 27). As many as 250 million children are wage slaves and there are over a billion workers who are either un- or under-employed. These are the concrete realities of our time—realities that require a vigorous class analysis, an unrelenting critique of capitalism and an oppositional politics capable of confronting what Ahmad (1998, p. 2) refers to as 'capitalist universality.' They are realities that require something more than that which is offered by the prophets of 'difference' and post-Marxists who would have us relegate socialism to the scrapheap of history and mummify Marxism along with Lenin's corpse. Never before has a Marxian analysis of capitalism and class rule been so desperately needed. That is not to say that everything Marx said or anticipated has come true, for that is clearly not the case. Many critiques of Marx focus on his strategy for moving toward socialism, and with ample justification; nonetheless Marx did provide us with fundamental insights into class society that have held true to this day. Marx's enduring relevance lies in his indictment of capitalism which continues to wreak havoc in the lives of most. While capitalism's cheerleaders have attempted to hide its sordid underbelly, Marx's description of capitalism as the sorcerer's dark power is even more apt in light of contemporary historical and economic conditions. Rather than jettisoning Marx, decentering the role of capitalism, and discrediting class analysis, radical educators must continue to engage Marx's *oeuvre* and extrapolate from it that which is useful pedagogically, theoretically, and, most importantly, politically in light of the challenges that confront us.

The urgency which animates Amin's call for a collective socialist vision necessitates, as we have argued, moving beyond the particularism and liberal pluralism that informs the 'politics of difference.' It also requires challenging the questionable assumptions that have come to constitute the core of contemporary 'radical' theory, pedagogy and politics. In terms of effecting change, what is needed is a cogent understanding of the systemic nature of exploitation and oppression based on the precepts of a radical political economy approach (outlined above) and one that incorporates Marx's notion of 'unity in difference' in which people share widely common material interests. Such an understanding extends far beyond the realm of theory, for the manner in which we choose to interpret and explore the social world, the concepts and frameworks we use to express our sociopolitical under-standings, are more than just abstract categories. They imply intentions, organizational practices, and political agendas. Identifying class analysis as the basis for our understandings and class struggle as the basis for political transformation implies something quite different than constructing a sense of political agency around issues of race, ethnicity, gender, etc. Contrary to 'Shakespeare's assertion that a rose by any other name would smell as sweet,' it should be clear that this is not the case in political matters. Rather, in politics 'the essence of the flower lies in the name by which it is called' (Bannerji, 2000, p. 41).

The task for progressives today is to seize the moment and plant the seeds for a political agenda that is grounded in historical possibilities and informed by a vision committed to overcoming exploitative conditions. These seeds, we would argue, must be derived from the tree of radical political economy. For the vast majority of people today—people of all 'racial classifications or identities, all genders and sexual orientations'—the common frame of reference arcing across 'difference', the 'concerns and aspirations that are most widely shared are those that are rooted in the common experience of everyday life shaped and constrained by political economy' (Reed, 2000, p. xxvii). While post-Marxist advocates of the politics of 'difference' suggest that such a stance is outdated, we would argue that the categories which they have employed to analyze 'the social' are now losing their usefulness, particularly in light of actual contemporary 'social movements.' All over the globe, there are large anti-capitalist movements afoot. In February 2002, chants of 'Another World Is Possible' became the theme of protests in Porto Allegre. It seems that those people struggling in the streets haven't read about T.I.N.A., the end of grand narratives of emancipation, or the decentering of capitalism. It seems as though the struggle for basic survival and some semblance of human dignity in the mean streets of the dystopian metropoles doesn't permit much time or opportunity to read the heady proclamations emanating from seminar rooms. As E. P. Thompson (1978, p. 11) once remarked, sometimes 'experience walks in without knocking at the door, and announces deaths, crises of subsistence, trench warfare, unemployment, inflation, genocide.' This, of course, does not mean that socialism will inevitably come about, yet a sense of its nascent promise animates current social movements. Indeed, noted historian Howard Zinn (2000, p. 20) recently pointed out that after years of single-issue organizing (i.e. the politics of difference), the WTO and other anti-corporate capitalist protests signaled a turning point in the 'history of movements of recent decades,' for it was the issue of 'class' that more than anything 'bound everyone together.' History, to paraphrase Thompson (1978, p. 25) doesn't seem to be following Theory's script.

Our vision is informed by Marx's historical materialism and his revolutionary socialist humanism, which must not be conflated with liberal humanism. For left politics and pedagogy, a socialist humanist vision remains crucial, whose fundamental features include the creative potential of people to challenge collectively the circumstances that they inherit. This variant of humanism seeks to give expression to the pain, sorrow and degradation of the oppressed, those who labor under the ominous and ghastly cloak of 'globalized' capital. It calls for the transformation of those conditions that have prevented the bulk of humankind from fulfilling its potential. It vests its hope for change in the development of critical consciousness and social agents who make history, although not always in conditions of their choosing. The political goal of socialist humanism is, however, 'not a resting in difference' but rather 'the emancipation of difference at the level of human mutuality and reciprocity.' This would be a step forward for the 'discovery or creation of our real differences which can only in the end be explored in reciprocal ways' (Eagleton, 1996, p. 120). Above all else, the enduring relevance of a radical socialist pedagogy and politics is the centrality it accords to the interrogation of capitalism.

We can no longer afford to remain indifferent to the horror and savagery committed by capitalist's barbaric machinations. We need to recognize that capitalist democracy is unrescuably contradictory in its own self-constitution. Capitalism and democracy cannot be translated into one another without profound efforts at manufacturing empty idealism. Committed Leftists must unrelentingly cultivate a democratic socialist vision that refuses to forget the 'wretched of the earth,' the children of the damned and the victims of the culture of silence—a task which requires more than abstruse convolutions and striking ironic poses in the agnostic arena of signifying practices. Leftists must illuminate the little shops of horror that lurk beneath 'globalization's' shiny façade; they must challenge the true 'evils' that are manifest in the tentacles of global capitalism's reach. And, more than this, Leftists must search for the cracks in the edifice of globalized capitalism and shine light on those fissures that give birth to alternatives. Socialism today, undoubtedly, runs against the grain of received wisdom, but its vision of a vastly improved and freer arrangement of social relations beckons on the horizon. Its unwritten text is nascent in the present even as it exists among the fragments of history and the shards of distant memories. Its potential remains untapped and its promise needs to be redeemed.

Notes

This essay is a revised version of Valerie Scatamburlo-D'Annibale and Peter McLaren, 'The Strategic Centrality of Class in the Politics of "Race" and "Difference"' that appeared in *Cultural Studies/Critical Methodologies*, 3:2 (May 2003), 148–175.

1. See Ebert (1996) for a discussion of 'ludic' theory.
2. Hence, while the charge of determinism may be appropriately lodged against some Marxists, when such a charge is leveled at Marx, 'it is patently unjust' (Amin, 1998, p. 138).
3. There exists a marked distinction between underscoring the importance of culture and the rhetoric of culturalism, which not only reduces everything to questions of culture but also has a reductionist conception of culture.
4. See Scatamburlo-D'Annibale & Langman, 2002.
5. As Marx (1978, p. 207) noted in his discussion of wage labor, capital and slavery: '[A] Negro [*sic*] is a "man of the black race."' 'A Negro is a Negro. He only becomes a slave in certain relations.'
6. As Stabile (1997, pp. 142–143) notes: 'historical material analyses, instead of examining only one form of oppression—like sexism, racism, or homophobia—would explore the way they all function within the overarching system of class domination ... Sweatshop workers in New York City, for example, experience sexism and racism in quantitatively and qualitatively different ways than do middle-class women. The racism directed at poor African American youths occurs in a different context than that directed at African American women in the academy. This is not to claim that the latter forms of oppression do not exist or are inconsequential, but by situating both forms within the material context and historical framework in which they occur, we can highlight the variable discriminating mechanisms that are central to capitalism as a system'.
7. Our point is that work which has attempted to remove the concept of racial oppression from the organ of social control exercised by state power on behalf of white capitalist class interests is problematic. See Allen, 1998.
8. It is important to note that arguing that the working-class is the fundamental agent of change is not the same as suggesting that it is the *only* agent of change.
9. It also ignores a lengthy history of Black 'working class' struggle.
10. See also Adolph Reed's (2000) stinging critique of the 'new' Black 'public intellectuals.'

References

Ahmad, A. (1997a) Culture, Nationalism, and the Role of Intellectuals, in: E. Meiksins-Wood & J. Bellamy Foster (eds), *In Defense of History: Marxism and the Postmodern agenda* (New York, Monthly Review Press).

Ahmad, A. (1997b) Postcolonial Theory and the 'Post'-Condition, in: L. Panitch (ed.), *Ruthless Criticism of All That Exists, Socialist Register 1997* (New York, Monthly Review Press).

Ahmad, A. (1998) The Communist Manifesto and the Problem of Universality, *Monthly Review*, 50:2, pp. 12–23.

Allen, T. (1998) Summary of the Argument of the Invention of the White Race, *Cultural Logic*, 1:2 (Spring), <http://eserver.org/clogic/1-2/allen.html>.

Allman, P. (2001) *Critical Education Against Global Capitalism: Karl Marx and revolutionary critical education* (Westport, CT, Bergin & Garvey).

Amin, S. (1998) *Spectres of Capitalism: A critique of current intellectual fashion* (New York, Monthly Review Press).

Bannerji, H. (1995) *Thinking Through: Essays on feminism, Marxism, and anti-racism* (Toronto, Women's Press).

Bannerji, H. (2000) *The Dark Side of the Nation: Essays on multiculturalism, nationalism and gender* (Toronto, Canadian Scholars' Press).

CCPA (Canadian Centre for Policy Alternatives) (2002) *CCPA Monitor*, 8:7.

Dirlik, A. (1997) *The Postcolonial Aura: Third World criticism in the age of global capitalism* (Boulder, CO, Westview Press).

Eagleton, T. (1996) *The Illusions of Postmodernism* (Cambridge, MA, Blackwell).

Eagleton, T. (1998) Defending the Free World, in: S. Regan (ed.), *The Eagleton Reader* (Malden, MA, Blackwell).

Ebert, T. (1996) *Ludic Feminism and After* (Ann Arbor, MI, University of Michigan Press).

Gimenez, M. (2001) Marxism and Class, Gender and Race: Rethinking the trilogy, *Race, Gender & Class*, 8:2, pp. 23–33.

Greider, W. (1998) *One World, Ready or Not: The manic logic of global capitalism* (New York, Touchstone Books).

Harvey, D. (1998) The Practical Contradictions of Marxism, *Critical Sociology*, 24:1 & 2, pp. 1–36.

Harvey, D. (2000) *Spaces of Hope* (Berkeley and Los Angeles, University of California Press).

Hennessy, R. & Ingraham, C. (eds) (1997) *Material Feminism: A reader in class, difference, and women's lives* (New York and London, Routledge), pp. 1–14.

hooks, b. (2000) *Where We Stand: Class matters* (New York, Routledge).

Jameson, F. (1998) *The Cultural Turn* (London and New York, Verso).

Johnson, A. (2002) The Legacy of Rosa Luxemburg: A critical reply to Stephen E. Bronner, *New Politics*, 8:4, pp. 128–140.

Jordan, G. & Weedon, C. (eds) (1995) *Cultural Politics: Class, gender, race and the postmodern world* (Cambridge, MA, Blackwell).

Kovel, J. (2002) *The Enemy of Nature: The end of capitalism or the end of the world?* (London, Zed Books).

Marable, M. (1995) *Beyond Black and White* (London and New York, Verso Press).

Marx, K. (1967/1867) *Capital: A critical analysis of capitalist production*, vol. 1 (New York, International Publishers).

Marx, K. (1972/1863) *Theories of Surplus Value*, part 3 (London, Lawrence & Wishart).

Marx, K. (1973/1858) *Grundrisse: Foundations of the critique of political economy*, trans. M. Nicolaus (Harmondsworth, Penguin).

Marx, K. (1976/1867) *Capital: A critique of political economy*, vol. 1 (Harmondsworth, Penguin).

Marx, K. (1976/1866) *Results of the Immediate Process of Production, Addendum to 'Capital'* vol. 1 (Harmondsworth, Penguin).

Marx, K. (1977/1865) *Capital: A critique of political economy*, vol. 3 (London, Lawrence & Wishart).

Marx, K. (1977/1844) *Economic and Philosophical Manuscripts of 1844* (Moscow, Progress Publishers).

Marx, K. (1978) *The Marx-Engels Reader*, 2nd edn, ed. R Tucker (New York, W. W. Norton & Company).

McLaren, P. & Farahmandpur, R. (1999) Critical Pedagogy, Postmodernism, and the Retreat from Class: Towards a contraband pedagogy, in: D. Hill, P. Mclaren, M. Cole & G. Rikowski (eds), *Postmodernism in Educational Theory: Education and the politics of human resistance* (London, Tufnell Press).

McLaren, P. & Torres, R. (1999) Racism and Multicultural Education: Rethinking 'race' and 'whiteness' in late capitalism, in: S. May (ed.), *Critical Multiculturalism: Rethinking multiculturalism and antiracist education* (London, Falmer), pp. 42–76.

McQuaig, L. (2001) *All You Can Eat: Greed, lust and the new capitalism* (Toronto, Penguin Books).

Meyerson, G. (2000) Rethinking Black Marxism: Reflections on Cedric Robinson and others, *Cultural Logic*, 3:2, <http://eserver.org/clogic/3-1%262/ineyerson.html>.

Mitter, S. (1997) Women Working Worldwide, in: R. Hennessy & C. Ingraham (eds), *Materialist Feminism: A reader in class, difference, and women's lives* (New York, Routledge).

Reed, A. (2000) *Class Notes* (New York, New Press).

Sahay, A. (1998) Transforming Race Matters: Towards a critique-al cultural studies, *Cultural Logic*, 1:2, <http://eserver.org/clogic/1-2/sahay.html>.

San Juan, E. (2003) Marxism and the Race/Class Problematic: A re-articulation, *Cultural Logic*, <http://eserver.org/clogic/2003/sanjuan.html>.

Scatamburlo-D'Annibale, V. & Langman, L. (2002) Fanon Speaks to the Subaltern, in: J. Lehmann (ed.), *Bringing Capitalism Back for Critique by Social Theory* (Elsevier, Jai Press).

Stabile, C. (1997) Postmodernism, Feminism, and Marx: Notes from the abyss, in: E. Meiksins Wood & J. Bellamy Foster (eds), *In Defense of History: Marxism and the postmodern agenda* (New York, Monthly Review Press).

Thompson, E. P. (1978) *The Poverty of Theory* (New York, Monthly Review Press).

Turner, T. (1994) Anthropology and Multiculturalism: What is anthropology that multiculturalists should be mindful of it?, in: D. T. Goldberg (ed.), *Multiculturalism: A critical reader* (Cambridge, MA, Blackwell).

Zinn, H. (2000) A Flash of the Possible, *The Progressive*, 64:1, p. 20.

8

Actions Following Words: Critical race theory connects to critical pedagogy[1]

LAURENCE PARKER & DAVID O. STOVALL
University of Illinois at Urbana-Champaign; University of Illinois at Chicago

Critical Race Theory Class Narrative

On September 17, 1999, six African American students were involved in a melee at a high school football game in Decatur, IL. After that incident, the Decatur school board gave all of them two-year expulsions from school. Since these events took place, a firestorm of controversy has erupted surrounding issues related to school violence, race, social class, and the implementation of school district rules over student behavior and discipline. When this incident took place in the fall semester (1999), a number of students in my critical race theory class http://www.ed.uiuc.edu/EPS/people/Parker_490E.html discussed some type of response to this action in support of the African American residents in Decatur and the young men to protest the 'zero-tolerance' violence policy action by the Decatur school board. As we were reading the 'theory' of race, the students decided to take action in connection with this critical race theory. The disparate impact of the data related to race and African American student discipline also told a 'narrative' according to some of the students in class, as we not only read Kimberlé Crenshaw, Richard Delgado, Derrick Bell and other CRT founders, but critically asked questions from these CRT positions and their own personal experiences with racism, as to why we saw such high rates of disciplinary actions against African American youth in our own area?

For example the 1998–9 figures from the three neighboring towns near Decatur were illustrative of the problem of percentages of African Americans over-represented in school disciplinary actions. In the Champaign district white enrollment is at 63% and the white suspension is 36%, while the African American enrollment is at 31% and the comparable suspension rate of African Americans is at 62% for the same district. In the Urbana district the white enrollment is at 62% while the white suspension is 47%. The African American enrollment in Urbana is 28% but their suspension rate is 49%. For the Danville district, the white enrollment is at 61% while the suspension rate is 47%, but the comparable figures for African Americans are 33% and 49% respectively (Puch, 2000).

From the discussions of the CRT readings in the class, the data as narrative, the personal experiences of some of the students in the class with racism in schools and their own individual efforts to deal with it, the students decided to get involved in marches and protests because they saw it not as a local concern, but a broader civil rights problem that needed to be addressed within the national conservative 'colorblind' context of race relations and policy implementation that has had a disproportionate impact on African American students. These students felt that it was their responsibility to put the theory (i.e., class readings on the politics of race in education) into action by attending the marches and lending their effort and support to the protests. The students met and discussed their thoughts and feelings about the issues involved in the Decatur situation in the formal class sessions after the various marches, and the informal meetings and focus groups that they had on their own. Some of them also organized and participated in their own marches and vigils on campus and to the Urbana, IL, Federal District court where the law suit was filed claiming that the school board violated the due process rights of the six African American Decatur students. As an instructor, a piece of me will argue, 'students should come to class and be prepared to do the seminar work and assignments.' But the Decatur incident created an 'interest convergence' in the graduate level seminar, as theory was linked to protest by students by challenging racism in school discipline policy and overall equity for African Americans in the Decatur and Champaign-Urbana schools, and the students in the Decatur, IL, incident.

The purpose of this opening narrative is to illustrate the importance of critical race studies in education with respect to discussing race, racialism, racism, and its connection to the larger sociopolitical context and ideological forces of domination, and how critical theories of race can be linked to educational praxis and critical pedagogy. It has been noted that a major problem with critical race theory is that it reinforces a racialized politics of identity and representation that ignores the imperatives of capitalist accumulation in a globalized economy and class divisions within racialized communities (McLaren, 1998). The post-Marxist critics of CRT in particular have forcefully argued that it fails to provide a systemic analysis of global capitalism and its effect on communities. This strand of critical pedagogy argues that emphasis on race-based identity politics ignores the overwhelming tendency of capitalism to homogenize rather than diversify the human experience (Darder & Torres, 2002).

Furthermore, others position critical pedagogy as connected to social justice and multicultural education, with an emphasis on teaching values of genuine concern about students from all racial, linguistic and social class backgrounds, as opposed to just focusing on race and the black–white binary (Banks, 1999). This type of critical pedagogy is rooted in holistic curriculum reform through the detection of bias in texts and instruction, and developing a classroom climate that focuses on student achievement through a more critical educational process. Critical pedagogy calls for educators to be agents working for social change and equity in schools and communities.

The aforementioned problems with CRT specifically, and critical theories of race in general, are indeed noted shortcomings when one initially considers it in conjunction with critical pedagogy. These criticisms have merit, yet they have also been discussed in other ways in terms of noting CRT's limitations with respect to providing answers to a host of social class and feminist issues, from lack of proper child care for single mothers on college campuses, to homophobia (see Parker,

1998). However, more recent discussions about critical race theory from a Latino/ Latina perspective have emerged as the LatCrit movement and have engaged in challenging theoretical and practice-based discussions related to the growth of global capitalism and exploitation that has had a profound impact on Latino– Latina populations not only in the U.S. but in Central and South America regarding immigration, language, gay, lesbian and transgendered identity, wealth disparities and political power relations between Latinos–Latinas and other racialized groups (Igleias & Valdez, 1998; Valdez, Culp, & Harris, 2002). But the continual question is, can someone committed to critical pedagogy also find merit in CRT and/or critical studies of race as well? Another question that arises is, how useful is a critical theory of race, when there is an overemphasis on racial identity politics, rather than on attacking capitalism and social class disparities through democratic social justice for all racialized groups?

In this essay we will discuss some of the ways that CRT could be linked to critical pedagogy in order to provide a more comprehensive analytical framework to analyze the role of race–class dynamics. This approach will attempt to address some of the gaps and silences that critical pedagogy has had regarding critical theoretical positions on race and racism and the operation of white supremacy in education. However, we will also point out some of the problems and raise more issues of concern related to critical pedagogy and race in educational research and practice. Handel Wright (2002) articulated insightfully the problems within North American critical pedagogy in terms of its evolution to a rigid dogmatic binary of positions within itself: on the one hand, postmodernist, poststructuralists and feminists argue for a post-critical pedagogy, while post-colonial and neo-Marxist critical pedagogy supporters, on the other hand, argue strongly for the merits of their arguments rooted in class analysis. For the most part, this binary has left race out of the theoretical discussion. More specifically, Wright questions 'where is the black representation in the discussion of the future of critical pedagogy?' (p. 1). This question is important because of the African American/Black ambivalence toward critical pedagogy. Part of the unease and trepidation stems from the fact that although issues such as racism against African American/Black students have been addressed within critical pedagogy, and African American, African Caribbean scholars have borrowed from critical pedagogy to target inequitable schooling practices, critical theories of race have been virtually ignored within the 'generalized theorization of the development and future of critical pedagogy' (Wright, 2002, p. 6).

Given this absence of a theoretical discussion of race within critical pedagogy, we hope this paper performs three initial functions. Since Marvin Lynn has provided an overview of CRT by connecting it to other existing recent work on race, racialism and racism in this collection, we want to connect the tenets of CRT to the current color-blind ideology and discourse in education regarding race studies. Our purpose here is to highlight some of the limitations of critical pedagogy regarding the permanence of racism, and how CRT perspectives have been utilized to analyze the racism, coupled with social class bias, sexism, etc., that still exists in education. Second, we want to present an argument for why there is a need for

CRT and critical race studies (more broadly) to connect with critical pedagogy. Finally, we will speculate about what lies ahead regarding possible points of agreement and conflicts between CRT and critical pedagogy.

White Supremacy, Color-blind Ideology, and Problems with Critical Pedagogy in Education

One of the main problems in critical theory is dealing with the centrality of racism in education and its strong philosophical roots and connections to the political economy. Race has played a major part in shaping the modern and postmodern world (McCarthy & Crichlow, 1993). Even though race is a mythology that has been socially constructed for purposes of control, power and economic exploitation, racialism (e.g., attitudes, actions of stereotyping, discriminatory policies, unequal distribution of resources) is fundamental to everyday life, the shaping of moral character, the formation and implementation of law, policy, and the study of social context in education and other social science fields (Stanfield, 1999). Critical race theory (and its connecting parts, e.g., LatCrit, Asian American poststructural critical legal positions, critical race feminism) argues that race is central in the making of our world. Race has played a fundamental role in: (1) the making of nation–empire that evolves into a system of conquest and enslavement; (2) the creation of capital; and (3) the shaping of culture and identity, especially in the creation of subordinate racialized groups (Winant, 2002). Modern white racism evolved ideologically and philosophically in Europe and North America as a system of human classification based on physical characteristics that were considered fixed (Smedley, 1999; Feagin, 2000). Goldberg (1993) argued that in order to understand modernity and its evolution, one has to understand the ontology of race, racialism, and how each played a fundamental role in shaping major philosophical, political, and scientific thought. Smedley (1999) traced the origins of racial ideology in North America, to British conflicts with other national groups such as the Irish, in order to fully examine how those conflicts over national origin, land, and religion seeded the ideology of British racism and justification of colonialist expansion and domination. As an ideology, white supremacy was imposed in North America, as it was used hierarchically to rank races and justified horrific acts in the form of slavery, colonialist domination of land and populations, and forced assimilation.

The current racialized discourse in the U.S. has taken on a different form through the ideology of color-blind interpretations of law and political, social, and economic relations (Lipsitz, 1998). The core of these racialized arguments posits that there are no fundamental differences between the races based on inequality (Bonilla-Silva, 2001). Overt discriminatory laws have been repealed and there is more popular acceptance of different racial groups within the current conservative multicultural discourse that accepts symbolic individuals such as Colin Powell or Condoleezza Rice, the mainstreaming of Latino popular culture, and Asian Americans' children as 'model minority' students, as evidence of racial and ethnic acceptance in the current conservative U.S. political climate (Dillard, 2001). This ideology of color-blindness and 'racial progress' has also been reflective of an overarching trend in K-12 education for teachers and administrators to ignore race and racism in their schools, by assuming that if attention is not paid to racial implications of problems related to low minority student achievement, school restructuring, or African American teacher disengagement with white staff, then these issues will simply disappear (Lewis, 2001; Lipman, 1997; Madsen & Mabokela, 2000). Another part of this conservative ideology in schools is the open racism that teachers and administrators have toward African Americans, Latinos, Navajos, and other racial groups. This has been illustrated through the case study research on small Midwestern 'liberal' university towns, where the image has belied the reality of white teacher hostility toward African American students and parents (Kailin, 1999). Deyhle (1995) presented evidence of racial warfare in the schools between the Navajo and Anglo population in southern Utah. Her research has been used to demonstrate the illegality of racial tracking practices by the district as well as other inequitable resource distribution issues. Deyhle argued that the role of race and racism has been central in creating 'racial warfare' between Anglos and Navajos (p. 409). Larson (1997) uncovered another aspect of racism that relied on administrative use of rigid policy processes and bureaucratic procedures in attempts to quell racial disturbances and tensions in a Midwestern high school, as African American students, parents, church leaders pressed for increased Black curriculum and representation in the school setting. As the Black student and community protests increased, the administrative staff in the district held on to tighter interpretations of discipline policies to achieve order for whites in the district. Larson found that, in hindsight, some of the administrators saw that they should have relied less on the bureaucratic rules, and more on honest communication and dialogue with the Black community. In the United Kingdom, Sewell (1997) documented a different example of racism regarding white teachers' relationships with Black male youth. On the one hand, there is an acceptance of Black popular culture through music and style. However, Sewell showed how white teachers felt threatened by Black males when they used popular culture behavior to act against unfair treatment in the schools by white authorities.

Given the phenomenon of white backlash toward students of color in predominantly white schools and colleges, critical pedagogy has to address not only the conditions of global capitalist exploitation, but also anti-racist pedagogy, and other commitments to social justice (see special issue of *Educational Theory*, fall 1998). We would argue that one of the main challenges for critical pedagogy has been the intractability of white supremacy in education institutions. This racism ranges from 'microaggressions' toward Latino students on predominantly white college campuses (Villalpando, 2000; Solórzano & Yosso, 2001), to race and social class disparities in financial aid, with college access reserved increasingly for upper-middle-class students (Orfield, 1992), and admission to elite colleges and universities being viewed as an educational 'property right' reserved for whites opposed to affirmative action (Harris, 1993). To be sure, we are in solidarity with one of the main radical purposes of critical pedagogy, which involves a politics of economic and resource distribution as well as a politics of recognition, affirmation, and difference (McLaren, 1998, p. 458). But one of the immediate problems of praxis that also needs to be confronted is the changing shape of racism reflected in the national trends that reveal this white backlash towards African Americans, Latinos–Latinas, Asian American/Pacific Islanders, and Tribal Nation students and communities in many schools. This backlash represents itself through an overwhelmingly white teaching and administrative force having control of, and conflict with, children and parents of color in urban, suburban, and rural communities, an example of which was illustrated in the opening narrative.[2]

The second challenge that race and racism has posed for critical pedagogy has been one of relevance and inclusion in the debate and discussion as to its theoretical underpinnings and practical utility for various racial groups. Appiah (1992), Outlaw (1996) and Mills (1998) have all called for the study and inclusion of African American/Black philosophy as a legitimate contributor to ontological and epistemological debates in the academy. This type of philosophy 'develops out of the resistance to oppression, it is a practical and politically oriented philosophy that, long before Marx was born, sought to interpret the world correctly so as to better change it' (Mills, 1998, p. 17). An African American/Black philosophy counters the 'dehumanization to which people and the ideas of African descent have been subjected through the history of colonialism and of European racism (Hord & Lee, 1995, p. 5). Yet, Wright (2002) posits that critical pedagogy has not been interested in how these race-based philosophic perspectives can inform the general theoretical discourse in the field. The debates between feminist and male respondents, or poststructuralists and post-Marxists, etc., have been 'discussions among white people from which people of color have for the most part been excluded' (p. 6). Wright points out that from its inception at the Frankfurt School, to its principal male theorists, to its mostly feminist critics, the figures involved in theorizing the discourse have been white. Wright raises the issue of representation in critical pedagogy as 'unremarked whiteness' (p. 6), yet sees an ambivalence or caution toward approaching critical pedagogy in terms of questioning the utility of entering the theoretical debate. Grande (2000) voiced skepticism about critical pedagogy, as she noted how its pedagogy of oppression failed to consider the ways that American Indians, as a sovereign tribal people within North America, experience a fundamentally different type of oppression that is incomparable to other minority groups. For example, she noted that the tenet of critical democracy as central in the struggle for liberation for critical pedagogy, fails to recognize tribal nations' struggles against inclusion into the democratic mainstream. Furthermore, the concept of democracy in critical pedagogy has not been seriously questioned regarding how it has been enacted as a lethal colonizing force against tribal nations (p. 468).

Third, critical pedagogy, with its roots centered in social class analysis and critique, can be faulted for not paying enough attention to when class matters, when race matters, and when both areas (along with gender, or areas such as sexual orientation which sometimes conflict) determine the life chances of families in the U.S. Conley (1999) opened his analysis of this issue by pointing out that, for example, in 1994 the median white family held assets worth more than seven times those of the median family of color. Going a step further, when one compares white and racial minority families of similar income levels, whites have more advantages in terms of total wealth and assets:

> For instance, at the lower end of the income spectrum (less than $15,000 per year), the median African American family has no assets, while the equivalent white family holds $10,000 worth of equity. At upper income levels (greater than $75,000 per year), white families have a median net worth of $308,000, almost three times the figure for upper-income African American families ($114,600).[3]

Conley posited that due to past discrimination against African Americans, especially in terms of home ownership, they were not able (until fairly recently) to acquire other wealth assets that they could pass on to their children. This, in turn, compounded the race and social class disparities between themselves and white Americans in areas such as education. Furthermore, whites benefited from racial segregation in terms of wealth accumulation when compared to African Americans. We are in agreement with the criticism of global commercialized capitalism and its influence on education. This is a sharp criticism that needs to be directed toward the current pro-business model that is used to create a community of consumers connected to education, primarily for the purpose of training the majority of low SES (socio-economic status) and racial minority students to become future depoliticized but literate high-tech assembly-line and service-sector workers (Anderson, 2001). However, in connecting this point to critical pedagogy, our concern is that an extreme turn back to rigid class analysis as the fundamental explainer of social position, and potential for democratic emancipation in the political economy primarily through class struggle, once again ignores the fundamental role that race and white supremacy have played in shaping the life chances of other racial groups to pursue educational opportunities and obtain equitable results.[4]

Critical Race Theory and its Links/Conflicts with Critical Pedagogy

Critical race theory emerged from the legal arena as a challenge to the aforementioned ideology of color-blindness, and the accompanying political discourse, viewing it as a pretext for racial discrimination. African Americans, Latinos–Latinas, Asian-American/Pacific Islanders, and various Tribal Nation groups made significant strides in using the law and federal courts to dismantle symbolic racism during the civil rights era of the 1960s and early 1970s. However, critical race theory uses counter-stories or narratives, as well as historical triangulation of facts that have an impact on present-day discrimination, to argue that a color-blind view of race upholds white supremacy in terms of sweeping away racial classifications, but leaves political majorities intact, which in turn uses the power of racism to undermine minority interest (Delgado, 1989; Williams, 1991; Bell, 1992; Crenshaw *et al.*, 1995). At present this is done not so much through legalized measures of overt discrimination; rather, it is through more general everyday racism, where racism and prejudice are embedded in the simple psychological decision-making rules that we use to make inferences and draw conclusions about groups

(Essed, 1991; McMorris, 1996). Critical race theory offers a framework that would attack seemingly neutral forms of racial subordination, while counteracting the devaluation of minority cultural and racial institutions in a color-blind society (Gotanda, 1991). Essentially, the color-blind perspective on race calls for assimilation, while critical race theory calls for the full awareness and critique of the ideology of race as a determining factor in how the law has been used against racialized minority groups and how the law and social action can be used to bring groups together for common interests of racial and class struggle (Yamamoto, 1997).

Our interactions in educational sites of struggles over race (in schools and the academy) have led us to argue for the importance of connecting critical race theory to critical pedagogy. We also acknowledge the limits and possibilities of both at specific points of analysis and action. Critical race theory can move into critical race praxis and pedagogy through the use of critical race theory studies in education, and changes in teacher education through an emphasis on race, racism, and dealing with white supremacy. We posit that there are some salient positions which undergird critical race theory in education (particularly in terms of research and teaching) that in turn have implications for critical pedagogy; they are: (1) the experiences of racial groups merit intellectual pursuit because of the uniqueness of the cultural, historical, and contemporary experiences of persons of color; (2) the historical and contemporary experiences of people of color can prove instructive about human interactions; and (3) one of the most significant tasks of a teacher or scholar who plans to utilize CRT (or LatCrit, etc.) is to develop tools that help generate knowledge designed to describe, analyze and empower people of color and to help change negative social forces into positive social forces as they impact on everyday life. Subsequently, it would be essential for researchers, teachers, or educational administrators steeped in critical pedagogical theory, to know not only the history of race and race relations, but also the connection of race to a community of interest with regard to the group's struggle for power and self-determination.

One of the ways that critical race theory can serve this end is to generate informed perspectives designed to describe, analyze and challenge racist policy and practice in educational institutions. The connection between critical race theory and education would entail linking teaching and research to general practical knowledge about institutional forces that have a disparate impact on racial minority communities. For example, the emphasis on narrative life and perspectives among African American graduate students in the class (mentioned in the opening narrative), would highlight an important aspect of critical race theory's power to illuminate and connect the African American experience of institutional racism as initially documented through the high discipline rates and low achievement of the African American students in these school districts. The narrative or storytelling would not only let the informants speak for themselves, but also deliberately challenge racist assumptions and design the research to be part of the solution and not part of the problem. It is here that CRT differs somewhat from critical pedagogy. Critical theory has been used to provide a lens for seeing and acting upon racial change in order to deal with inequality related to the hidden curriculum and overt schooling practice. Critical theory in education is currently concerned with various forms of critical multiculturalism or anti-racist education, particularly among white European Americans (Derman-Sparks, 1989; Giroux, 1983; 1998; Lewis, 2001). CRT work, presented in the opening narrative, seeks to disrupt the portrayal of the 'problems' with African American education as residing with African American students or parents. Rather, critical race theory in education connects with the experiences, ways of thinking, believing, and knowing the racial communities in their struggle for self-determination and equity in the schools. This is not to completely discount the efforts by critical pedagogy to deal with race. However, from a CRT perspective, racism, its historical dimensions, social construction, and political/social ramifications, become much more central to the debate surrounding power relationships in school policy and practice. So it is also important to make various testimonies of discrimination a part of the legal, social and public record through discourse and demonstration. For example, the actions of the students mentioned at the start of this paper led to them pulling their individual efforts together in the schools and the African American community to document various aspects of the problem of underachievement of African American students in the east-central Illinois public schools (Bartee *et al.*, 2000). In turn, the information has been used in connection with other individual efforts to work with students in the schools, and Black community leaders and parents, to support their efforts to press the districts for equitable remedies.

The current work in critical race theory and education seeks to foster an engagement with praxis and movement toward racial justice in the schools and higher education institutions (Solórzano, 1998; Solórzano & Yosso, 2001). Much of the literature in education related to CRT addresses its origins and links to specific educational issues and policies. Ladson-Billings and Tate (1995) pushed for using CRT in education to deconstruct fundamental assumptions behind seemingly race-neutral policies and ideology about the education of African American children and other students of color. Tate (1997) traced the origins of CRT and elaborated on the positions of founders on the formation of the CRT movement. He also suggested ways in which CRT could be linked to educational research by calling for specificity in using CRT and pinpointing it as the tool used to unmask the effects of racism and how it has been operationalized in educational institutions. Solórzano (1997, 1998) and Solórzano and Yosso (2001) looked at using CRT in higher education settings, first as a theoretical framework to examine teacher education racial discourse about the abilities of children of color, and then to look at its cumulative impact on Chicano–Chicana fellowship students in graduate school settings. Solórzano and Yosso used CRT and LatCrit to analyze the seemingly race-neutral policy language of equal educational opportunity in providing high status education for meritorious minority graduate students. However, the student counternarratives illustrated how they endured the everyday racism of graduate school, as White European American professors and students made these Chicano–Chicana students feel as if they did not deserve to be at elite institutions of graduate study. Building on this theme, Villalpando (2000) used CRT and LatCrit and case study research methods to identify institutional climates related to race in higher education settings and found that some of the campus environments were inhospitable to Chicano–Chicana students. He also used CRT, LatCrit, and critical race praxis to analyze how these students forged racial–ethnic support networks to combat the racism on campus, and take advantage of educational opportunities and serve the local Chicano community. Delgado Bernal (2002), González (1998), Pizarro (1998), and Hidalgo (1998), all discussed how CRT and LatCrit could be linked to Chicano/Latino epistemology, particularly Chicana feminist epistemology and the validation of the experiences of Chicana/Chicano students and Puerto Rican families. Ladson-Billings (1998) discussed CRT's use in analyzing the impact of racism in school policy actions related to curriculum, instruction, and school funding. Lynn (1999) added to this perspective by researching African American teachers who utilized a critical race pedagogical framework when informing African American students as to the importance of their race/culture as a bridge to learning and success. In sum, connections between CRT and critical pedagogy can be forged by using both to examine the origins, development, implementation, and evaluation of educational practices, and both should be useful to help guide this inquiry.

CRT and the Implications for Teacher Education, Educational Leadership, and Critical Pedagogy

We also believe CRT in teacher education and educational leadership could potentially serve as a useful framework with which to explore possibilities of change in both areas. For example, Ladson-Billings (1999) made reference to exemplar programs led by key leaders in the field of teacher education (e.g., Jacqueline Jordan Irvine, Marilyn Cochran-Smith, Joyce King, Martin Haberman), which have all strived to challenge preconceived notions of race and guide new, more critical thinking about race among the teacher education candidates. Some of these programs make an appeal to professionalism regarding the teaching of diverse urban K-12 students. Others stress the generation and development of different thinking about race based on critical reflections and narratives in schools and communities of color. These programs stood out as ones which deliberately prepared new teachers to think and act critically about race and racism in the schools and larger society. Michelle Young, the late Julie Laible, Jim Scheurich, Linda Skrala and others are also seeking to challenge educational leadership in the area of white racism through teaching courses that explore building new foundations of administration knowledge based on more critical perspectives related to race, gender and social justice for children and minority communities of color (Young & Laible, 2000). The work of Annette Henry (1992) and Michelle Foster (1997), which documents the importance of Black teachers' use of critical teaching instruction and role modeling for African American and African Canadian youth in the interest of the Black community, is also important for critical pedagogy to consider with respect to specific critical race perspectives related to Blacks. Similarly, critical pedagogy should take into account various other important aspects of race and critical teaching in the centrality of the theoretical and practice-based discussions about teaching. These range from the review of the literature on the role that minority teachers play in African American and Latino/a student achievement (Quiocho & Rios, 2000), to the importance of African-centered epistemology and culturally appropriate pedagogy for curriculum and instruction with African American students (Hale, 2001; Henry, 2001; Ladson-Billings, 2001; Lee, 2001). The future challenge for CRT in teacher education and educational leadership will also be to link it to anti-racist efforts in teacher education in order to incorporate critical challenges to 'whiteness' in teacher education.[5]

Critical pedagogy should look to specific areas of race-based pedagogy, and examples of successful schools that are comprised of low SES students of color, for ways in which race can be central to achievement in education. Nevelle and Cha-Jua (1998) outline a model of critical pedagogy for Black studies that incorporates many of its fundamental facets but includes race/nationality as a category of analysis in the curriculum and instruction process. Their model for critical pedagogy in Black studies is influenced by Marxist and Black feminist perspectives, and grounded in the accurate documentation of the sociohistorical and cultural realities of African descended people, and a scholarship that advocates the core values of resistance, freedom, self-determination and education (pp. 450–454). Nevelle and Cha-Jua have discussed incorporating knowledge of a variety of learning styles characteristic of the diversity of African American students, and pedagogical choices that provide structure for learners; linking subject matter to students' experiences; and drawing upon cultural roots (pp. 456–459).

The lived experience of success in low SES schools with majority students of color was the focus of Scheurich's (1998) research. The HiPass elementary schools he and his research team evaluated engaged in learning not only met the base-level state standards of achievement. They also encompassed a set of core beliefs and cultural characteristics that emphasized the success of all students with no exceptions, allowed child-centered schooling, children and adults being treated with love and respect, valuing the first language of students and their families, and openness to innovative and experimental ideas. At the center of these schools is a commitment to children and families by the entire staff and community. The schools profiled in Scheurich's study serve to show ways we can look at how race and socioeconomic status do not have to serve as barriers and how high levels of success can be achieved not only on the standardized tests, but also in guiding low SES youth of color towards a different future than what has been stereotyped and scripted for them.

Conclusion

What is the role of race in educational research, teaching and praxis? Critical race theory can hopefully provide some help as we grapple with this question. This paper has introduced the concept of critical race theory and its problematic and potential ways of providing us with openings to theorize and take action in the area of race and education. Furthermore, it holds possibilities for intersection and conjunction with other areas of difference in educational struggles. To be sure, the legal debate surrounding the legitimacy of the theory in relation to the color-blind approach to the law will become even more prominent in education and the social science research circles as well. Yet, we feel that the future of critical race theory is part of a larger on-going power struggle pertaining to the dominant ideological racial context. It is one that concerned researchers, teachers, and activists will discuss and be engaged with in the academy, the schools and the larger community. It is one that will separate camps of concerned scholars by age, class and position. By engaging this new space, the project becomes a contested space with social justice at its center. As we continue to redevelop older positions and bring new perspectives to the table, the responsibility becomes to historicize CRT and embrace its marriage to issues of gender, class and sexuality in education. CRT is not mutually exclusive. Instead, it is the attempt to provide a space for excluded voices in education and the responsibility to produce praxis geared to address the human condition of victimized groups struggling for respect and self-determination through the expansion of their contexts of choice (Moses, 2001).

Culture-centric schools was how Scheurich (1998) described them in his research findings as to how schools in low SES areas, with majority students of color, have been successful in valuing the racial culture and the first language of the child; treating children of color with love, appreciation, care, and respect; believing and proving that all children of color can achieve at the highest academic levels; and focusing on community more than competitive individualism. Community members who work within the school structure as non-teaching and non-administrative professionals embrace these themes with teachers and administrators who share the same sentiment. The work at this level points toward one example of the direction that critical race theory and critical pedagogy could indeed move toward working in various ways to create successful schools that embody the afore-mentioned values and core beliefs, and cultural characteristics. Unfortunately, the former is not easily achieved. As CRT and critical pedagogy converge on this space, it is crucial that proponents of both projects do not envision an adversarial relationship. If we are honest with ourselves about the end of oppression, we must be willing to consider all approaches that do not contribute to the further oppression and marginalization of children of color. The space is not always a safe one, but it is necessary if we profess a commitment to the development of safe spaces for young people to recognize their importance to themselves and the world.

Notes

1. Part of this paper was presented as a symposium session for the *International Journal of Qualitative Studies in Education* at the British Educational Research Association annual conference, University of Leeds, 13–15 September 2001.
2. The problem of white predominance in the teaching force has become more acute over the last few years. For example, Wilder (2000) noted that, over the past thirty years, white teachers comprised approximately 87% of the national teaching force. African Americans only comprised 8%, while the African American student population was at approximately 16% of the total national enrollment. The situation is even worse for Latinos–Latinas, as they only make up 3% to 4% of the national teaching force despite the large increases in Latino–Latina students nationwide.

3. D. Conley, 1999, p. 1.
4. We are not dismissing the crucial role that social class and post-Marxist analysis plays in explaining the disparate treatment of groups in the U.S. and the importance of global capitalist forces in creating these growing inequalities and unequal distribution of power that need to be challenged on multiple fronts. More discussion of this and social action needs to take place in the U.S. and elsewhere to address social class inequality and power, to be sure (McLaren, 1998). However, race does matter in the post-civil rights era and there are times when critical pedagogical theorists need to acknowledge this and specifically tease out when it does matter and when race does indeed act as a stand-in for class analysis (Conley, 1999, p. 1).
5. See Thompson (1999), Cochran-Smith (2000) and Schick (2000) for more discussion on this point, as well as the work by scholars in the UK such as Cecile Wright (1995) and the late Barry Troyna (1995), and various works on anti-racist teaching, policy and research on white teachers and Afro-Caribbean and Pakistani student interactions.

References

Anderson, G. L. (2001) Promoting Educational Equity in a Period of Growing Social Inequity: The silent contradictions of Texas reform discourse, *Education and Urban Society*, 33, pp. 320–332.

Appiah, K. A. (1992) *In my Father's House: Africa in the philosophy of culture* (New York, Oxford University Press).

Banks, J. A. & McGee Banks, C. A. (eds) (1997) *Multicultural Education: Issues and perspectives*, 3rd edn (Boston, Allyn & Bacon).

Bartee, R., Beckham, J., Gill, C., Graves, C., Jackson, K., Land, R., Williams, D. & Parker, L. (2000) Race, Discipline, and Educational Leadership: African American student perspectives on the Decatur, IL incident, *Journal of Special Education Leadership*, 13, pp. 19–29.

Bell, D. (1992) *Faces at the Bottom of the Well: The permanence of racism* (New York, Basic Books).

Bonilla-Silva, E. (2001) *White Supremacy and Racism in the Post-Civil Rights Era* (Boulder, CO, Lynne Reiner).

Cochran-Smith, M. (2000) Blind Vision: Unlearning racism in teacher education, *Harvard Educational Review*, 70, pp. 157–190.

Conley, D. (1999) *Being Black, Living in the Red: Race, wealth, and social policy in America* (Berkeley, CA, University of California Press).

Crenshaw, K., Gotanda, N., Peller, G. & Thomas, K. (eds) (1995) *Critical Race Theory: Key writings that formed the movement* (New York, New Press).

Darder, A. & Torres, R. (2002) Critical Race Theory or a Critical Theory of Race? Symposium conducted at the annual meeting of the American Educational Research Association, New Orleans, LA.

Delgado, R. (1989) Storytelling for Oppositionist and Others: A plea for narrative, *Michigan Law Review*, 87, pp. 2411–2441.

Delgado Bernal, D. (2002) Critical Race Theory, Latino Critical Theory, and Critical Raced-gendered Epistemologies: Recognizing students of color as holders and creators of knowledge, *Qualitative Inquiry*, 8, pp. 105–125.

Delgado Bernal, D. (1998) Using a Chicana Feminist Epistemology in Educational Research, *Harvard Educational Review*, 68, pp. 555–579.

Derman-Sparks, L. & ABC Task Force (1989) Anti-bias Curriculum: Tools for empowering young children (Washington, DC, NAEYC).

Deyhle, D. (1995) Navajo Youth and Anglo Racism: Cultural integrity and resistance, *Harvard Educational Review*, 65, 23–67.

Dillard, A. D. (2001) *Guess Who's Coming to Dinner Now? Multicultural conservatism in America* (New York, New York University Press).

Essed, P. (1991) *Understanding Everyday Racism: An interdisciplinary theory* (Thousand Oaks, CA, SAGE).

Feagin, J. (2000) *Racist America* (New York, Routledge).

Foster, M. (1997) *Black Teachers on Teaching* (New York, New Press).

Giroux, H. (1983) *Theory and Resistance in Education: A pedagogy for the opposition* (South Hadley, MA, Bergin & Garvey).

Giroux, H. (1989) Youth, Memory Work, and the Racial Politics of Whiteness, in: J. Kincheloe, S. Steinberg, N. Rodriguez & R. Chennault (eds), *White Reign: Deploying Whiteness in America* (New York, St Martin's Press, 1997).

Goldberg, D. T. (1993) *Racist Culture: Philosophy and the politics of meaning* (Oxford, Blackwell Press).

Gonzalez, F. E. (1998) Formations of Mexicanness: Trenzas de identidades multiples/growing up Mexicana: Braid of multiple identities, *International Journal of Qualitative Studies in Education*, 11, pp. 81–102.

Gotanda, N. (1991) A Critique of 'Our Constitution Is Color-Blind', *Stanford Law Review*, 44:1, pp. 1–68.

Grande, S. M. A. (2000) American Indian Geographies of Identity and Power: At the crossroads of indigena and mestizaje, *Harvard Educational Review*, 70, pp. 467–498.

Hale, J. E. (2001) Culturally Appropriate Pedagogy, in: W. H. Watkins, J. H. Lewis & V. Chou (eds), *Race and Education: The roles of history and society in educating African American students* (Boston, Allyn & Bacon).

Harris, C. I. (1993) Whiteness as Property, *Harvard Law Review*, 106, pp. 1701–1791.

Henry, A. (1992) African Canadian Women Teachers' Activism: Recreating communities of caring and resistance, *Journal of Negro Education*, 61, pp. 392–404.

Henry, A. (2001) Comment: Researching curriculum and race, in: W. H. Watkins, J. H. Lewis & V. Chou (eds), *Race and Education: The roles of history and society in educating African American Students* (Boston, Allyn & Bacon).

Hidalgo, N. M. (1998) Toward a Definition of a Latino Family Research Paradigm, *International Journal of Qualitative Studies in Education*, 11, pp. 103–120.

Hord, F. L., Lee, J. (eds) (1995) *I Am Because We Are: Readings in black philosophy* (Amherst, MA, University of Massachusetts Press).

Igleias, E. M. & Valdes, F. (1998) Religion, Gender, Sexuality, Race and Class in Coalitional Theory: A critical and self-critical analysis of LatCrit social justice agendas, *Chicano-Latino Law Review*, 19, pp. 504–588.

Kailin, J. (1999) How White Teachers Perceive the Problem of Racism in their Schools: A case study in 'liberal' Lakeview, *Teachers College Record*, 100, pp. 724–750.

Ladson-Billings, G. (1998) Just What Is Critical Race Theory and What's It Doing in a Nice Field Like Education?, *International Journal of Qualitative Studies in Education*, 11, pp. 7–24.

Ladson-Billings, G. (1999). Preparing Teachers for Diverse Student Populations: A critical race theory perspective, in: A. Iran-Nejad & P. D. Pearson (eds), *Review of Research in Education* (Washington, DC, American Educational Research Association).

Ladson-Billings, G. (2001) The Power of Pedagogy: Does teaching matter?, in: W. H. Watkins, J. H. Lewis & V. Chou (eds), *Race and Education: The roles of history and society in educating African American students* (Boston, Allyn & Bacon).

Ladson-Billings, G. & Tate, W. F. (1995) Toward a Critical Race Theory of Education, *Teachers College Record*, 97, pp. 47–63.

Larson, C. L. (1997) Is the Land of Oz an Alien Nation?: A sociopolitical study of school community conflict, *Educational Administration Quarterly*, 33, pp. 312–350.

Lee, C. D. (2001) Comment: Unpacking culture, teaching, and learning: A response to the 'power of pedagogy', in: W. H. Watkins, J. H. Lewis & V. Chou (eds), *Race and Education: The roles of history and society in educating African American students* (Boston, Allyn & Bacon).

Lewis, A. E. (2001). There Is No 'Race' in the School Yard: Color-blind ideology in an (almost) all-white school, *American Educational Research Journal*, 38, pp. 781–811.

Lipman, P. (1997) Restructuring in Context: A case study of teacher participation and the dynamics of ideology, race, and power, *American Educational Research Journal*, 34, pp. 3–38.

Lipsitz, G. (1998) *The Possessive Investment in Whiteness: How white people profit from identity politics* (Philadelphia, Temple University Press).

Lopez, G. R. & Parker, L. (forthcoming) *Research (Im)positions: Interrogating racism in qualitative research methodology* (Baltimore, Peter Lang).

Lynn, M. (1999) Toward a Critical Race Pedagogy: A research note, *Urban Education*, 33, pp. 606–626.

Madsen, J. A. & Mabokela, R. O. (2000) Organizational Culture and its Impact on African American Teachers, *American Educational Research Journal*, 37, pp. 849–876.

McCarthy, C. & Crichlow (eds) (1993) *Race, Identity and Representation in Education* (New York, Routledge).

McLaren, P. (1998) Revolutionary Pedagogy in Post-Revolutionary Times: Rethinking the political economy of critical education, *Educational Theory*, 48, pp. 431–462.

McMorris, G. (1996) Critical Race Theory, Cognitive Psychology, and the Social Meaning of Race: Why individualism will not solve racism, *University of Missouri-Kansas City Law Review*, 67, pp. 695–729.

Mills, C. (1998) *Blackness Visible: Essays on philosophy and race* (Ithaca, NY, Cornell University Press).

Moses, M. S. (2001) Affirmative Action and the Creation of More Favorable Contexts of Choice, *American Educational Research Journal*, 38, pp. 3–36.

Nevelle, H. A. & Cha-Jua, K. S. (1998) Kufundisha: Toward a pedagogy for Black studies, *Journal of Black Studies*, 28, pp. 447–470.

Orfield, G. (1992) Money, Equity, and College Access, *Harvard Educational Review*, 62, pp. 337–351.

Outlaw, L. T. Jr (1996) *On Race and Philosophy* (New York, Routledge).

Parker, L. (1998) Race Is … Race Ain't: An exploration of the utility of critical race theory in qualitative research in education, *International Journal of Qualitative Studies in Education*, 11, pp. 43–57.

Pizarro, M. (1998) Dialogical Praxis-oriented Research: A response to contemporary educational methodological discourse, *International Journal of Qualitative Studies in Education*, 11, pp. 57–80.

Puch, D. (2000) Decatur Ruling Relief for Other School Officials, *Champaign-Urbana News Gazette*, 16 January, pp. A1, A8.

Quiocho, A. & Rios, F. (2000) The Power of their Presence: Minority group teachers and schooling, *Review of Educational Research*, 70, pp. 485–528.

Scheurich, J. H. (1998) Highly Successful and Loving, Public Elementary Schools Populated Mainly by Low-SES Children of Color: Core beliefs and cultural characteristics, *Urban Education*, 33, pp. 451–491.

Schick, C. (2000) 'By Virtue of Being White': Resistance in anti-racist pedagogy, *Race Ethnicity & Education*, 3, pp. 83–102.

Sewell, T. (1997) *Black Masculinities and Schooling: How black boys survive modern schooling* (Staffordshire, UK, Tentham Books).

Smedley, A. (1999) *Race in North America: Origin and evolution of a world view*, 2nd edn (Boulder, CO, Westview).

Solórzano, D. (1997). Images and Words that Wound: Critical race theory, racial stereotyping and teacher education, *Teacher Education Quarterly*, 24, pp. 5–19.

Solórzano, D. (1998). Critical Race Theory, Race and Gender Microaggressions, and the Experience of Chicana and Chicano Scholars, *International Journal of Qualitative Studies in Education*, 11, 121–136.

Solórzano, D. G. & Yosso, T. J. (2001) Critical Race and Latcrit Theory and Method: Counter-storytelling, *International Journal of Qualitative Studies in Education*, 14, pp. 471–497.

Stanfield, J. H. (1999) Slipping Through the Front Door: Relevant social scientific evaluation in the people of color century, *American Journal of Evaluation*, 20, pp. 415–431.

Tate, W. F. (1997) Critical Race Theory and Education: History, theory and implications, in: M. Apple (ed.), *Review of Research in Education* (Washington, DC, American Educational Research Association).

Thompson, A. (1999) Color Talk: Whiteness and off white, *Educational Studies*, 30, pp. 141–160.

Troyna, B. (1995) Can You See the John?: A historical analysis of multicultural and antiracist education policies, in: D. Gill, B. Mayor & M. Blair (eds), *Racism in Education: Structures and strategies* (London, Sage and Open University Press).

Valdez, F., Culp, J. & Harris, A. P. (eds) (2002) *Crossroads, Directions, and a New Critical Race Theory* (Philadelphia, Temple University Press).

Villalpando, O. (2000) *Symposium: Critical race perspectives, interdisciplinary implications and teaching concerns*, paper presented at the meeting of the American Educational Studies Association, Vancouver, CA.

Wilder, M. (2000) Increasing African American Teachers' Presence in American Schools: Voices of students who care, *Urban Education*, 35, pp. 205–220.

Williams, P. J. (1991) *The Alchemy of Race and Rights* (Cambridge, MA, Harvard University Press).

Winant, H. (2002) *The World is a Ghetto: Race and democracy since World War II* (New York, Basic Books).

Wright, C. (1995) Early Education: Multiracial primary school classrooms, in: D. Gill, B. Mayor & M. Blair (eds), *Racism in Education: Structures and strategies* (London, Sage & Open University Press).

Wright, H. (2002) Homes Don't Play Posties, Homies Don't Play Neos: Black ambivalent elaboration and the end(s) of critical pedagogy, Symposium presentation at the annual meeting of the American Educational Research Association, New Orleans, LA.

Yamamoto, E. K. (1997) Critical Race Praxis: Race theory and political lawyering practice in post-Civil Rights America, *Michigan Law Review*, 95, pp. 821–900.

Young, M. D. & Laible, J. (2000) White Racism, Antiracism, and School Leadership Preparation, *Journal of School Leadership*, 10, pp. 374–414.

9

Race, Class, and Gender in Education Research: Surveying the political terrain

MICHÈLE FOSTER

Claremont Graduate University

Introduction

This essay explores the issues of race and prejudice that permeate research. It does so by examining two aspects of educational research on race: conceptual shifts about issues of race, class, and gender, and the politics of citation. Newer alternative research paradigms help free researchers from the racist, sexist, and class baggage from the traditional, positivist approach. The essay concludes with suggestions on how researchers can 'right the wrong' of past and current education research on race.

Critical Theory and Education Research

Critical theory concerns itself with the structures of domination of nations or other systems, examining how these systems exert direct and indirect control over their members. Scholars are attracted to critical theory because it can expose the roots and aspects of inequality that are often hidden. But while education scholars frequently utilize critical theory to examine the conditions in K-12 settings, they rarely turn the critical lens to examine the institutions they themselves inhabit. To paraphrase Gramsci (1971), for too many academics being an intellectual consists merely of eloquent discourse about equity, rights, and social justice, a fleeting appeal to feelings, passions, and intellect, rather than active participation in practical day-to-day life struggles against inequality and oppression. Rarely do academics connect their theory with their own practice. For although much of scholarship academics have undertaken in education over the past thirty years has promoted a sense of social justice as well as an activist narrative, this scholarship merely pays lip service to these ideals. The result is that while academics easily problematize and critique the practices and institutions of others, they do not act in ways that are compatible with their critique nor do they engage in day-to-day actions within their own oppressive sites. Not only does this situation illuminate the elitist nature of the academy, it erodes academia's already waning credibility.

Academics' failure to act to change their own institutions can be seen in the failed attempts at increasing diversity among students and faculty. Although student bodies have become more diverse, the numbers of academics of color remain stagnant[1] (Trower & Chait, 2002). This predominantly White professoriate acts as gatekeeper, and controls the circular process of granting access to faculty positions

at research universities, deciding what gets published, who gets tenured and promoted, and who gets appointed to editorial positions on premier journals.

Over the past several decades, issues of race, class, and gender have become
more prominent in educational research. That these issues are receiving more
attention can be seen in the number of articles published in mainstream journals
that deal with such topics, as well as the funding of national centers and grants by
private foundations, such as the Spencer Foundation, that deal with these issues.
Whereas in 1976–1977, approximately 18 percent of the grants supported by Spencer dealt with these race, class, and gender issues, by 1996–1997 the funding for
research on these same topics had increased to approximately 27 percent.[2] This
essay explores two aspects of educational research on race. First, I consider the
various research trends on this topic, paying particular attention to the major shifts
across different historical periods, illustrating how issues of race, class, and gender
are conceptualized, defined, and analyzed within various research traditions. Second, I examine the politics of citation; that is, whose work on these topics is
acknowledged and cited, offering several reasons for the resulting pattern. Finally,
I close with specific recommendations. A complete analysis of the issues is beyond
the scope of this essay. In an essay of this length, it is possible to provide only a
cursory analysis of any of these issues.

Research and History

The politics of research on issues of race, class, and gender in educational research
cannot be understood independently of the history of educational research in general. The development of educational research as a field of study coincided with
the rise of a community of educational researchers almost all of whom were White,
Protestant, male members of the faculties at such institutions as Harvard, Stanford,
Teachers College, University of Wisconsin, University of Michigan, and Yale. All of
these institutions except the last still maintain schools of education and are currently considered among the top schools of education (Langemann, 1997; America's Best graduate schools, 1997). It was during this period that quantitative
analyses and psychological approaches came to predominate in the educational
research community, gradually displacing historical approaches that had once held
sway (Langemann, 1997).

Developing as it did alongside psychometrics and the statistical tests that made
this field possible, the field of educational research came to be dominated by
research methodologies such as large-scale surveys or other investigations that
relied on empirical science and quantitative measurement. Distant and hierarchical
relationships between researcher and researched, as well as unequal and dominant
gender relationships, came to characterize much of the educational research. Most
educational researchers, like most school administrators, were male, whereas the
majority of classrooms they studied had female teachers. Last, the stratification of
society according to race and class lines, as well as the racist pseudoscientific
discourse of the period, gave rise to racist and sexist ideologies that are evident in
today's research (Langemann, 1997). These patterns—the traditional positivist

research methodologies undergirded by empirical science and quantitative measurement; racist, sexist, and class-based ideologies; and an overwhelmingly male research community—characterized educational research well past the middle of this century.

Psychological, Policy, and Interpretive Paradigms in Educational Research

Much of the social and behavioral science on which educational research has traditionally rested has been grounded in psychology, a field that has measured persons of color, women, and those from working classes against a standard of White middle-class males. Until criticized by other scholars, research in child and human development considered males the standard against which women were measured (Gilligan, 1982). Reifying concepts of cultural deprivation, cultural deficit, and of being disadvantaged, psychological research asserted that, because of linguistic and cognitive deficits, certain groups of children (especially those of color and from working-class backgrounds) were incapable of high academic achievement (Bernstein, 1960; Gray & Klaus, 1965; Hess & Shipman, 1965; Jensen, 1969) These ideas bolstered and reinforced the idea of White racial superiority permeating the educational journals of the 1950s and 1960s.

Although these concepts were forcefully challenged by scholars working within the anthropological and linguistic traditions (Baratz & Baratz, 1970; Labov, 1972), this 'academic supremacy' research paradigm still holds sway, having been reinvented in the language of 'at risk' in the 1980s and revived in the neoconservative theories of genetic inferiority of the 1990s (Hernnstein & Murray, 1994). Some scholars working within a psychological framework, including many but not all scholars of color, have challenged the hegemony of White racial superiority, an ideology that suffuses much of the psychologically based research (e.g. Allen & Boykin, 1997; Boykin, 1984; Boykin *et al.*, 1997; Cross, 1989; Helms, 1989, 1992, 1997; Steele, 1992, 1997; Tatum, 1992). However, despite these criticisms, much of the research informed by a psychological paradigm furthers the ideology of White racial superiority.

Ethnography and Critical Theory

Interpretive research has a long tradition in the philosophy of science, but, except for the tradition of historical research in education, it was not until the 1980s that qualitative, ethnographic, feminist, and critical approaches began to gain a foothold in educational research as alternative conceptions of educational research. Some general education journals, such as the *American Journal of Education* and the *Harvard Educational Review*; discipline-based education journals, such as *Anthropology of Education Quarterly* and *Linguistics and Education*; and educational journals that deal with specific topics, such as *English Education* and *Reading Research Quarterly*, have consistently published interpretive research. However, not until the late 1980s did the *American Educational Research Journal* (*AERJ*), the official journal of

the American Educational Research Association (AERA), begin publishing interpretive research on a consistent basis.

Concerned as they are with capturing the meanings, interpretations, and intentions of the actors (Geertz, 1976), interpretive approaches are often the choice of
scholars concerned with challenging the status quo. Likewise, critical theory is
concerned with exposing and analyzing the explicit and covert control that institutions exert on the political, social, cultural, and economic manifestations, expressions and interests of the populace. But employing interpretive or critical
approaches does not guarantee that the resulting research will not foster racial,
gender, or class biases. Too often, mainstream research—including interpretive and
critical approaches—investigates topics without sufficient attention to issues of
race, class, and gender, with the results of this research often used to argue the
efficacy of particular approaches for all groups of students, irrespective of race,
class, or gender. Moreover, critical approaches highlight the interplay between
power and race, class, and gender, because those undertaking this mode of research
are frequently oblivious to the ways in which their own racial, class, and gender
positions affect the conduct and interpretation of the data, and normalize White,
male, colonialist discourses. For instance, research that adopts a sociocultural
approach to studies of learning in classrooms often glosses over student characteristics, making it difficult to ascertain what effect these changed classroom practices
have on the achievement of students from different backgrounds (Cazden, 1998).
Similarly, educational research representing teachers' voices often privilege the
'voices of predominantly humanistic, child-centered teachers, then condensing
them into a singular voice, the teacher's voice, which becomes representative of all
teachers' (Hargreaves, 1996), even though African American and Latino teachers,
and others are otherwise marginalized and disaffected (Foster, 1990, 1993). And,
despite the large body of research on school reform and change, until recently
gender has not figured prominently in these analyses (Datnow, 1998). Lastly, feminists have pointed out how policy analysis not only privileges White males while
excluding women, but also creates a gender regime that is institutionalized and
appears natural and normal (Marshall, 1997).

The male-dominated educational research community was firmly entrenched
more than a half-century later, and its presence was unmistakable in educational
journals of the mid-1960s. Only a dozen women contributors can be found in
volumes 35 and 36 of the *Harvard Educational Review* published in 1965 and
1966, most represented as coauthors or book reviewers, or single authors of topics
that are more in keeping with research topics suitable for women, such as language
arts. Since 1987, however, women have steadily gained an increasing presence both
as authors and as members of editorial boards. For example, in 1987–1988, women
made up 31 percent of AERA-sponsored journal editorial board members but only
23 percent of the authors. However, within a decade, their numbers would reach
a high of 50 percent of editorial board members and 41 percent of authors, figures
that have never dropped below the 1987–1988 percentages. The presence of scholars of color, by contrast, has not grown as steadily, and we remain woefully underrepresented, especially in the more prestigious journals. Whereas scholars of color

constituted 13 percent of editorial board members in 1987–1988, in 1996–1997 they constituted 16 percent. Although it reached 18 percent for two consecutive years, unlike the percentages of women, the percentage has dropped below its 1987–1988 figure. In 1987–1988, only 4 percent of AERA journals had authors of color. In 1996–1997, the percentage was 5 percent and, except for one year where the authorship reached 11 percent, the percentages have remained in the single digits. Between 1990 and 1994, not one African American researcher published an article in *AERJ*. During the same period, only two Latinos published in *AERJ*. The other AERA publications show a similar pattern. More than a decade ago, in 1985, trying to solicit more authors of color to contribute to a special issue on race, racism, and American education, the editorial board of the *Harvard Educational Review* noted the limited presence of scholars of color in mainstream academic journals (Editorial, 1987).

There are several reasons for these low numbers. In part, the paucity can be attributed to the low number of researchers of color being trained and graduating from the top colleges and schools of education; the exclusion of doctoral students of color from participation on externally funded research projects; exclusion from informal networks in graduate school, as coauthors of research papers and articles with established faculty researchers; or the low number employed in research universities where publishing in educational journals is expected as a condition for continued employment (Frierson, 1990; Hood & Freeman, 1995; Moses, 1989; Willie *et al.*, 1991). It is the case, moreover, that even if they successfully join the ranks of the academy, scholars of color often find themselves outside of the formal research networks (Moses, 1989). A recent analysis of the families of researchers who conduct research on teaching found that only one scholar of color was a member of a network not comprised entirely of scholars of color (Morine-Dershimer, 2001).

Scheurich and Young (1997) argue that social science research is plagued by 'epistemological racism,' an unconscious form that stems from White culture's historical domination of society and of its philosophers, all White, who created the basis for the way knowledge is pursued. Noting the rise of the culture of race-based epistemologies, they point to Asante's Afrocentric paradigm, Patricia Hill Collins's Black feminist approach or the native anthropology approach of John Langston Gwaltney (1980, 1981). Scheurich and Young (1997) observe that some scholars of color have made explicit their choice of race-based epistemologies. But others whom they overlook have deliberately adopted varieties of interpretive research, not only because of a commitment to challenging the culture of poverty hypothesis, theories of cultural deprivation, and resurgent theories of genetic inferiority, and establishing new educational discourses that stress the linguistic, cultural, intellectual strength, and sense of agency of oppressed groups, but also because of their desire to present their groups' perspectives. Interpretive research makes a commitment to understanding the actors from their own point of view (Geertz, 1976).

One result of this commitment, however, is that many scholars of color often find that mainstream journals are not receptive to publishing their scholarship, especially if it uses unfamiliar paradigms or methodologies (Padilla, 1994). This bias forces them to publish in race-based journals such as the *Journal of Negro Education*, the *Hispanic Journal of the Behavioral Sciences,* or the *Journal of Black Psychology,* which are rarely counted in awarding tenure. It is also worth noting, however, that many scholars of color who have been published in mainstream journals have also chosen to publish their work in race-based journals, which may suggest a commitment to reaching a wider, more diverse audience than that of the main-stream educational journal. and even when scholars of color do publish in AERA journals, occasionally their work is introduced in a manner that many, scholars believe denigrates the scholarship and the scholar's capability (Gordon, 1997; Levin, 1993). Although the perception of mistreatment can be limited to this one situation, a significant number of scholars of color have expressed concerns about the way we are treated, allowed to participate in our professional organizations, and represented in the scholarly organizations' (Edirisooriya, 1996; Gordon, 1997). Finally, although rarely discussed in mainstream, majority educational circles, in private, scholars of color frequently comment that when it comes to research that addresses race, the perspectives of White scholars are privileged over those of scholars of color. They remark that, except for a few 'stars,' the research of citation patterns routinely exclude the work of scholars of color (Irvine & Walker, 1998). These topics were publicly addressed in New Orleans at the 1994 AERA symposia.[3]

Righting the Wrong

While engaging in social change is the ideal form of progressive education, within their own academic contexts most academics fail miserably. Even more important than manipulating the language of critique, is acquiring the will and the tools with which to transform social context within which academics move, with the ultimate goal of substantially increasing the numbers of scholars of color in the academy. To that end, the last section of this essay describes some of the small, practical steps, both political and personal, that academics can undertake to make some difference in their academic settings. One action is to appoint more editors of color and more scholars of color to the editorial boards of scholarly journals, a necessary but insufficient condition for increasing the number of scholars of underrepre-sented groups who publish in journals. In 2001 and 2002, for example, under the tenure of editors of color, scholars of color authored more than 50 percent of the twenty book reviews published in *Educational Researcher,* an accomplishment unri-valed in the history of AERA journals. First, academics can familiarize themselves with the wide range of educational research that addresses issues of race, class, and gender, particularly research undertaken by scholars of color as well as research that employs new epistemologies. This awareness will mean extending habitual read-ing habits to include race-based journals and other publications where such schol-arship can be found. In addition, academics must familiarize themselves not only with the research of acknowledged, accepted, and famous, scholars of color, but also with others whose work (not heralded) may yield important insights.

The canon of scholarship in most fields of educational research is overwhelm-ingly composed of White researchers with only a few scholars of color, who achieve honorary status as 'whites,' represented as tokens. For example, although Scheurich and Young (1997) are to be commended for their critical analysis of the race-based methodologies, they included only the work of those authors of color that have been highlighted in the prestigious journals, often overlooking the critical work of others. Second, academics can make it a practice to include this scholarship in their classes. A few academics from mainstream backgrounds have already begun this work. Some have publicly acknowledged the growth of a new generation of African American and Latino scholars (Foley, 1998). Others make it a point to include scholars of color in their research methods class, invite their students to locate this scholarship and use it in their own work, and discuss why these authors are important in terms of the contribution they have made in the field (Bloome, 1997; Noblit, 1997; Scheurich & Young, 1997). Finally, academics can interrupt the process by which certain scholars become tokens, routinely and ritualistically cited, whereas the vast majority go unrecognized unless their work happens to appear in a collection edited by a prominent White scholar. As scholars, they can cite a wider range of scholarship in their own research, being careful not to cite the research of scholars whose work or ideas may not be relevant in favor of those whose work is. And researchers, reviewers, and editors can encourage others to do the same. Failure to take these affirmative steps will result in perpetuating the phenomenon Carter (1991) has dubbed 'the best black syndrome,' a form of academic tokenism whereby African Americans and, by extension, other people of color are assessed and valued only when they are 'first black, only black, best black' (p. 50). Academics must get beyond this colonial mentality of citation where only the accepted natives are deemed as known, let alone worthy of citation, by the colonials. This change will require that academics become familiar with a wider range of scholarship than the diet typically served up in graduate school. It is not enough to theorize about social justice without taking affirmative action to begin to make it a reality in our practice, scholarship, and actions as academics.

Notes

1. Between the decades of the 1970s and 1990s, the percentages of African Americans, Latinos, and Asian American undergraduates has increase from 8.4 to 11, 2.8 to 8 and 1.8 to 6 percent respectively. In contrast, however, the percentage of faculty of color has not grown proportionately. In the same period, Asian American faculty has grown from 2.2 to 4.5 percent, Latino faculty from 1.4 to 2.8 percent, African American faculty from 4.4 to 5 percent, with almost half of all Black faculty teaching at historically Black colleges. In 1997 Whites constituted 83 percent of all faculty members, down from 95 percent in 1972.
2. The data are derived from the titles of the Major Research Grants and the Spencer Small Grants, which until 1987 were not named, but were listed under 'Other Grants' in two Spencer Reports: *Twenty-Five Years of Grant Making: The Spencer Foundation 1998 Annual Report* and *The Spencer Foundation Annual Report for the Year Ended March 31, 1997*. Information about the National Academy of Education Postdoctoral Fellowships, the Dissertation Fellowships, and the AERA/Spencer Fellowships is not included. If it were, the trend toward including issues of race, class, and gender in educational research would be even stronger.
3. There were two symposia dealing with this topic (see Private Lives in Public Conversations, 1994).

References

Allen, B. A. & Boykin, A. W. (1997) African American Children and the Educational Process: Alleviating cultural discontinuity through prescriptive pedagogy, *School Psychology Review*, 21:4, pp. 586–596.

America's Best graduate schools (1997) *US News & Word Report*, Special Supplement (March).

Baratz, S. S. & Baratz, J. C. (1970) Language and Social Class, *British Journal of Sociology*, 11:2, pp. 271–276.

Bernstein, B. (1960) Language and Social Class, *British Journal of Sociology*, 11:2, pp. 271–276.

Bloome, D. (1997) Personal communication.

Boykin, A. W. (1984) Reading Achievement and the Social-Cultural Frame of Reference of Afro-American Children, *Journal of Negro Education*, 53:4, pp. 464–473.

Boykin, A. W., Jaggers, R. J., Ellison, C. M. & Albury, A. (1997) Communalism, Conceptualization and Measurement of an Afrocultural Social Orientation, *Journal of Black Studies*, 27:3, pp. 411–418.

Carter, S. L. (1991) *Reflections of an Affirmative Action Baby* (New York: Basic Books).

Cazden, C. (1998) Future Directions for the Study of Classroom Discourse: A conversation with Courtney Cazden, paper presented at the American Educational Research Association Conference, San Diego, CA (April).

Cross, W. E. (1989) Nigrescence: A Nandiaphanous phenomenon, *Counseling Psychologist*, 17:2, pp. 273–276.

Datnow, A. (1998) *The Gender Politics of Educational Change* (Bristol, PA, Falmer)

Edirisooriya, G. (1996) Research Presentation in a Democratic Society: A voice from the audience, *Educational Researcher*, 25:6, pp. 26–30.

Editorial (1987) *Harvard Educational Review*, 57:2, pp. vii–viii.

Foley, D. (1998) Review Symposium, *Race Ethnicity and Education*, 1:1 (March), p. 131.

Foster, M. (1990) The Politics of Race through African-American Teachers' Eyes, *Journal of Education*, 172:3, pp. 123–141.

Foster, M. (1993) Educating for Competence in Community and Culture: Exploring the views of exemplary African American teachers, *Urban Education*, 27:4, pp. 370–394.

Foster, M. (1999) Race, Class, and Gender in Education Research: Surveying the political terrain, *Educational Policy*, 13 (January), pp. 77–85.

Frierson, H. T. (1990) The Situation of Black Educational Researchers: Continuation of a crisis, *Educational Researcher*, 1992, pp. 12–17.

Geertz, C. (1976) From the Native's Point of View: On the nature of anthropological understanding, in: K. Basso & H. Shelby (eds), *Meaning in Anthropology* (Albuquerque, University of New Mexico Press).

Gilligan, C. (1982) *In a Different Voice: Psychological theory and women's development* (Cambridge, MA, Harvard University Press).

Gordon, E. W. (1997) Task Force on the Role and Future of Minorities, American Educational Research Association, *Educational Researcher*, 26:3 (April), pp. 44–52.

Gramsci, A. (1971) Selections from the Prison Notebooks, ed. and trans. Q. Hoare & G. Nowell Smith (London, Lawrence & Wishart).

Gray, S. W. & Klaus, R. A. (1965) An Experimental Preschool Program for Culturally Deprived Children, *Child Development*, 36:3, pp. 887–898.

Gwaltney, J. L. (1980) *Drylongso: A self-portrait of Black America* (New York: Random House).

Gwaltney, J. L. (1981) Common Sense and Science: Urban core black observation, in: D. Messerschmidt (ed.), *Anthropologists at Home in North America: Methods and issues in the study of one's own society* (New York, Cambridge University Press), pp. 46–61.

Hargreaves, A. (1996) Revisiting Voice, *Educational Researcher*, 25:1, pp. 12–19.

Helms, J. E. (1989) Eurocentricism Strikes in Strange Ways and in Unusual Places, *Counseling Psychologist*, 17:4, pp. 643–647.

Helms, J. E. (1992) Why Is There No Study of Cultural Equivalence in Standardized Cognitive Ability Testing?, *American Psychologist*, 47:9, pp. 1083–1101.

Helms, J. E. (1997) How Multiculturalism Obscures Racial Factors in the Therapy Process: Comment on Ridley *et al.* (1994), Sodowsky *et al.* (1994), Ottavi *et al.* (1994), *Journal of Counseling Psychology*, 39:2, pp. 1246–1247.

Hernstein, R. & Murray, C. (1994) *The Bell Curve: Intelligence and class structure in American life* (New York: Free Press).

Hess, R. E. & Shipman, V. (1965) Early Experience and Socialization of Cognitive Modes in Children, *Child Development*, 36:3, pp. 369–386.

Hood, S. & Freeman, D. (1995) Where Do Students of Color Earn Doctorates in Education? The 'Top 25' colleges and schools of education, *Journal of Negro Education*, 64:4, pp. 423–436.

Irvine, J. J. & Walker, V. S. (1998) Treatment Does Not Confer Status, *Black Issues in Higher Education*, 15:5 (6 April), p. 72.

Jensen, A. R. (1969) How Much Can We Boost IQ and Scholastic Achievement, *Harvard Educational Review*, 39:1, pp. 1–123.

Labov, W. (1972) Academic Ignorance and Black Intelligence, *Atlantic Monthly*, 17:6 (June), pp. 50–67.

Langemann, E. C. (1997) Contested Terrain: A history of educational research in the United States, 1890–1990, *Educational Researcher*, 26:9 (December), pp. 5–17.

Levin, H. (1993) Editor's Comments, *Review of Educational Research*, 63:2, p. 113.

Marshall, C. (1997) Undomesticated Gender Policy, in: B. J. Bank & P. M. Hall (eds), *Gender Equity, and Schooling: Policy and practice* (New York, Garland), pp. 63–91.

Morine-Dershimer, G. (2001). 'Family Connections' as a Factor in the Development of Research on Teaching, in: V. Richardson (ed.), *Handbook of Research on Teaching* (4th edn; Washington, DC, American Educational Research Association), pp. 47–68.

Moses, Y. T. (1989) *Black Women in Academe Issues and Strategies* (Washington, DC, Association of American Colleges).

Noblit, G. (1997) Personal communication, October.

Padilla, A. M. (1994) Ethnic Minority Scholars, Research, and Mentoring Current and Future Issues, *Educational Researcher*, 23:4, pp. 24–27.

Private Lives in Public Conversations: The ethics of research across cultural communities (1994), symposium presented at the American Educational Research Association, New Orleans, LA.

Scheurich, J. & Young, M. (1997) Coloring Epistemologies: Are our research epistemologies racially biased?, *Educational Researcher*, 26:4, pp. 4–16.

Steele, C. M. (1992) Race and the Schooling of Black Americans, *Atlantic Monthly*, 169:4 (April), pp. 68–78.

Steele, C. M. (1997) A Threat in the Air: How stereotypes shape intellectual identity and performance, *American Psychologist*, 52:6, pp. 613–629.

Tatum, B. D. (1992) African-American Identity Development, Academic Achievement, and Missing History, *Social Education*, 56:6, pp. 331–334.

Trower, C. A. & Chait, R. P. (2002) Faculty Diversity: Too little, for too long, *Harvard Magazine*, 33–37 (April–May), p. 98.

Willie, C. V., Grady, M. K. & Hope, R. O. (1991) *African-American and the Doctoral Experience: Implications for policy* (New York, Teachers College Press).

10

An Apartheid of Knowledge in Academia: The struggle over the 'legitimate' knowledge of faculty of color

DOLORES DELGADO BERNAL & OCTAVIO VILLALPANDO
University of Utah

> The University as an institution is a key arena where 'legitimate' knowledge is established. While discourses of power may have qualities of constraint and repression, they are not, nor have they ever been, uncontested. Indeed, the process of determining what is 'legitimate knowledge' and for what purpose that knowledge should be produced is a political debate that rages in the University. Our presence, as working-class people of color (especially women of color), in an institution which values itself on its elitist criteria for admission, forces the debates and challenges previously sacred canons of objective truth. ... It is probably for this reason that our presence here is so complex—and so important.
>
> —Córdova, 1998, p. 18

In the Afrikaans language, 'apartheid' has been most commonly used to refer to the historical, rigid racial division between the governing white population and the non-white majority population in South Africa. The term not only describes the physical separation imposed by the white population, but also represents the subordination and marginalization of the cultural norms, values, and knowledge of the non-white majority in South Africa. In this essay, we apply the concept of apartheid to the separation of knowledges that occur in the American higher education context.[1] We believe that an 'apartheid of knowledge' (Villalpando & Delgado Bernal, 2002) is sustained by an epistemological racism that limits the range of possible epistemologies considered legitimate within the mainstream research community (Scheurich & Young, 1997). Too frequently, an epistemology based on the social history and culture of the dominant race has produced scholarship which portrays people of color as deficient and judges the scholarship produced by scholars of color as biased and non-rigorous.

We apply a Critical Race Theory (CRT) lens to analyze how an apartheid of knowledge that marginalizes, discredits, and devalues the scholarship, epistemologies, and other cultural resources of faculty of color[2] is embedded in higher education. We draw from two specific CRT themes in this analysis. The first theme questions dominant claims of objectivity, meritocracy, and individuality in United States society, and the second affirms the importance of drawing from the experiential knowledge of people of color and our communities of origin (Ladson-Billings & Tate, 1995; Solórzano, 1997). These themes parallel some of the conceptual tools and ideas of critical pedagogy. And while both CRT and critical pedagogy view schooling as 'contradictory social sites' (Giroux, 1983, p. 115), CRT argues for a deeper engagement of the question of race. Therefore, unlike much of the critical pedagogy scholarship, the CRT analysis that follows places race at the forefront and confronts racism in higher education.

The first part of our analysis draws from national trend data on the representation of faculty of color across different types of post-secondary institutions, academic ranks, and departments. The second part of our analysis presents the tenure story of a faculty member of color. The story is told twice, from a majoritarian and a counter perspective (Delgado, 1989). The quantitative data, along with the story, reveal how the structural segregation of faculty of color and the racialized discourse and double standards in higher education combine to create an apartheid of knowledge. Both the quantitative data and the story help to provide a context for the struggle over 'legitimate knowledge' and illuminate how faculty of color challenge sacred canons of objective truth (Córdova, 1998). In addition, the story told from a majoritarian and marginalized perspective serves as a pedagogical tool by allowing us to challenge the stories of those in power and also tell the stories of those experiences that are not often told (Delgado, 1989). If critical pedagogy explores 'how pedagogy functions as a cultural practice to produce rather than merely transmit knowledge within asymmetrical relations of power' (Giroux, 1992, p. 98), then CRT work in storytelling certainly provides a rich way of conceptualizing critical pedagogy in ways that address structures of race and race relations in higher education.

The De Facto Segregation of Faculty of Color[3]

> Malcolm X stressed that the United States differed from South Africa only in that they practiced what they preached, while we preach integration and deceitfully practice segregation
>
> —Kushner, 1980

Despite an official end to *de jure* racial segregation and the current discourse surrounding integration and equality in education, higher education continues to reflect a state of *de facto* racial and gender segregation. Faculty of color are stratified along institutional type, academic ranks, and departments. In this section, we review national trend data to illustrate the *de facto* segregation of faculty of color.

The Segregation of Faculty of Color Across Different Institutions

Since the early 1970s, faculty of color have increased our[4] representation in all of American higher education by less than 6 percent (Astin & Villalpando, 1996; Sax et al., 1999). The smaller and more prestigious institutions, like private four-year colleges and universities, have had the smallest percentage of faculty of color. Indeed, less than 8 percent of the faculty at private four-year institutions self-identified as members of an underrepresented ethnic/racial group in 1998 (Milem and Astin, 1993; Sax *et al.*, 1999). In contrast, the larger and less elite two-year institutions have had among the highest percentage and growth of faculty of color during the same period. In 1998 approximately 12 percent of the faculty at these institutions self-identified as persons of color.

These patterns also hold true for women, regardless of race. Since 1989, women have only increased their representation as a percentage of all faculty by approximately 7 percent (Milem and Astin, 1993; Sax *et al.*, 1999). Women of color held the largest proportional representation in public two-year institutions, and the smallest representation in private universities (Astin, Antonio *et al.*, 1997).

Faculty of color are not only concentrated in institutions of lesser prestige with fewer resources, but can also expect to achieve lower levels of lifetime earnings and social mobility as a result of working in these types of institutions (Karabel, 1977; Astin, 1982; Astin, 1993; Carnevale, 1999). The popular claims that higher education is objective, meritocratic, color-blind, race-neutral, and provides equal opportunities for all (Bennet, 1982; Bloom, 1987; D'Souza, 1991; Shlesinger, 1993) clearly do not hold up in an analysis of the racial segregation and gender stratification of faculty in American colleges and universities. These claims, interpreted through a critical race lens, camouflage the self-interest, power, and privilege of dominant groups in U.S. society who in turn exert significant influence over higher education (Delgado, 1984; Calmore, 1992).

The Segregation of Faculty of Color Across Academic Ranks

In addition to our segregation along types of higher education institutions, faculty of color are also stratified by academic rank—and the disparities appear to have remained relatively unchanged in nearly twenty-five years. Between 1972 and 1989, faculty of color improved our representation within the rank of *professor* by less than 4 percent (Milem & Astin, 1993). This rank continues to be most elusive for women of color as a group. For example, only 9 percent of all Latina faculty and only 12 percent of all American Indian women faculty hold the rank of *professor* (Astin *et al.*, 1997).

The largest representation of faculty of color has consistently been in the lower and less prestigious academic ranks of *lecturer* and *instructor*, both of which are non-tenure track positions. Between 1972 and 1989, African Americans, Chicana(o)s/Latina(o)s, American Indians, and Asian Americans comprised between 7 percent and about 12 percent of all *lecturers* and *instructors*. This representation constituted the largest and most stable presence of faculty of color among all academic ranks, suggesting that the minimal growth of faculty of color occurred only in the lower ranks of the professoriate (Milem & Astin, 1993). And again, women, regardless of race, occupy the lowest academic ranks *(lecturer and instructor)* in larger proportions than men. Among faculty of color, this pattern is repeated, with women of color representing a larger proportion than men in these ranks. For example, 37 percent of all Latina faculty, and 41 percent of all American Indian women faculty, hold the ranks of *lecturer and instructor* (Astin *et al.*, 1997).

The Segregation of Faculty of Color Across Academic Departments
In addition to our disproportionate stratification along types of higher education institutions and academic ranks, faculty of color are also unevenly represented across different types of academic departments. Faculty of color are concentrated in departments, such as humanities, ethnic studies, women studies, education, and the social sciences, which often have fewer resources and are considered less prominent and prestigious within higher education (Allen *et al.*, 2000). Garza (1993) termed this phenomenon the 'ghettoization' and 'barrioization' of faculty of color and our scholarship. The data appear to support these assertions. For example, in 1995, 32 percent of African American faculty had appointments in the humanities or in education, while less than 2 percent were in the physical sciences (Astin *et al.*, 1997). Similarly, almost 37 percent of all Chicana/o faculty held appointments in the humanities or in education while only 2 percent taught in the physical sciences. Women of color follow an equally disproportionate representation in these fields, with 34 percent teaching in the humanities or in education, and 3 percent in the physical sciences (Astin, Antonio *et al.*, 1997).

Faculty of color have a high concentration in the humanities, social sciences, and education for reasons related to opportunity structures and to personal choice. First, as a result of K-12 tracking, students of color are often placed in vocational tracks or academic tracks that do not prepare them for science-based fields (Oakes, 1985). At every educational level from K-12 through graduate schools, the schooling process lacks the commitment, skills, and resources to support and develop talent among students of color who are interested in the natural or physical sciences or in other science-based fields. Few students of color have an opportunity to benefit from adequate resources and academic support to pursue our interests in these fields, and many are consequently ineligible for graduate programs and for the academic profession.

The second reason why faculty of color are concentrated in these fields is often related to our sense of responsibility to our community (Villalpando, 1996; Villalpando, 2003). We often enter fields where we can work toward achieving social justice for our communities through teaching and research on issues that address the status of our politically and socioeconomically disenfranchised communities (Garza, 1993; Villalpando, 2003). We produce scholarship that addresses different forms of social inequality, often through the fields of humanities, education, social sciences, and ethnic studies.

Scholarship produced by faculty of color in these fields, however, is often undervalued by the academic profession, even though, as Garza (1993) notes:

> Most of the national and international politics and principal movements for change of at least the last quarter century centered on racial and ethnic group matters. Therefore, this kind of scholarship and the scholars who do it should be accorded the necessary respect and legitimacy it and they deserve. (p. 40)

Rather than receiving respect, this kind of scholarship is regarded as illegitimate, biased, or overly subjective (Turner *et al.*, 1999; Turner & Myers, 2000).

The representation of faculty of color across all institutions, academic ranks, and departments has remained relatively unchanged since the early 1970s, resulting in our current *de facto* segregation in higher education. We contend that our under-representation and disproportionate stratification in academia also isolates our contributions and scholarship, rendering our knowledge to the margins.

Challenging a Dominant Eurocentric Epistemology

Higher education in the United States is founded on a Eurocentric epistemological perspective based on white privilege and 'American democratic' ideals of meritocracy, objectivity, and individuality. This epistemological perspective presumes that there is only one way of knowing and understanding the world, and it is the natural way of interpreting truth, knowledge, and reality. For example, the notion of meritocracy allows people with a Eurocentric epistemology to believe that all people—no matter what race, class, gender, or sexual orientation—get what they deserve based solely on their individual efforts. Those who believe that our society is truly a meritocratic one find it difficult to believe that men gain advantage from women's subordination or that whites have any advantage over people of color.

This epistemology, or system of knowing, is at least partially based on an ideology of white supremacy and white privilege (Harris, 1993). By white supremacy we adhere to a definition that goes beyond the overt racism of white supremacist hate groups and includes:

> [a] political, economic, and cultural system in which whites overwhelmingly control power and material resources, conscious and unconscious ideas of white superiority and entitlement are widespread, and relations of white dominance and non-white subordination are daily reenacted across a broad array of institutions and social settings. (Ansley, as cited in Harris, 1993)

By white privilege, we refer to 'an invisible package of unearned assets' and a system of opportunities and benefits that are bestowed on an individual simply for being white (McIntosh, 1997). Tatum writes about the power of white supremacy and the invisibility of white privilege, and points out their very real effects by stating that 'despite the current rhetoric about affirmative action and reverse discrimination, every social indicator, from salary to life expectancy, reveals the advantages of being White' (Tatum, 1999, p. 8).

Because it is invisible, white privilege and an ideology of white supremacy are legitimized and viewed as the norm, the point of departure within a Eurocentric perspective (Thompson, 1998). Practices, standards and discourses, like those adopted in higher education, are based on this Eurocentric norm and faculty of color and/or knowledges that depart from this norm are devalued and subordinated (Parker, 1998; Aguirre, 2000). Certainly, the discourse within higher education works in a very material way 'to construct realities that control both the actions and bodies of people' (St. Pierre, 2000).

A Eurocentric epistemological perspective can subtly—and not so subtly—ignore and discredit the ways of knowing and understanding the world that faculty of color often bring to academia. Indeed, this Eurocentric epistemological perspective creates racialized double standards that contribute to an apartheid of knowledge separating from mainstream scholarship the type of research and teaching that faculty of color often produce (Villalpando & Delgado Bernal, 2002). This apartheid of knowledge goes beyond the high value society places on the positivist tradition of the 'hard sciences' and the low regard for the social sciences; it ignores and discredits the epistemologies of faculty of color.

An apartheid of knowledge ignores and excludes the 'cultural resources' that are based on the epistemologies that many faculty of color bring to academia. Our concept of cultural resources is similar to the community 'funds of knowledge' concept that addresses how Mexicano school-aged children draw on their diverse linguistic resources and family knowledge to function in schools and society (Velez-Ibanez & Greenberg, 1992; González *et al.*, 1995). It is also similar to the concept of 'pedagogies of the home' that allows Chicana college students to draw upon their bilingualism, biculturalism, commitment to communities, and spiritualities in their academic pursuits (Delgado Bernal, 2001). We believe that cultural resources include the knowledge, practices, beliefs, norms, and values that are derived from culturally specific lessons within the home space and local communities of people who have been subordinated by dominant society. Cultural resources are often shaped by collective experiences and community memory and passed on from one generation to the next. These resources can be empowering and nurturing while also helping us survive in everyday life by providing strategies and skills to confront and overcome oppressive conditions.

CRT challenges a Eurocentric epistemological perspective by recognizing people of color as creators and holders of knowledge that may challenge and critique mainstream traditions (Solórzano, 1998; Ladson-Billings, 2000; Delgado Bernal, 2002). It calls for epistemologies in higher education that acknowledge the racialized history and present social realities of people of color. We use a CRT epistemology to frame the following story. The story demonstrates how the Retention, Promotion, and Tenure (RPT) process is grounded in a Eurocentric standard of knowledge that devalues and separates the worldviews and cultural resources that scholars of color often bring to academia.

One Story: A majoritarian and counter perspective

In this essay, we adopt the CRT storytelling method to demonstrate how a dominant Eurocentric epistemology leads to an apartheid of knowledge that impacts the lives and success of faculty of color in the academy. Storytelling in CRT provides a rich way of understanding knowledge from communities of color (Bell, 1987; Williams, 1991; Bell, 1995). It is a type of narrative that challenges preconceived notions of race, class, and gender and confirms that we must listen to those who experience and respond to racism, sexism classism, and heterosexism (Parker & Lynn, 2002; Solórzano & Yosso, 2002). Critical race scholars view experiential knowledge as a strength and draw explicitly on the lived experiences of people of color to counter the dominant educational discourse about people of color.

Storytelling has a rich legacy and continuing tradition in African American, Chicana/o, Asian American, and American Indian communities (Olivas, 1990). Indeed, Delgado (1995) asserts that many of the 'early tellers of tales used stories to test and challenge reality, to construct a counter-reality, to hearten and support each other and to probe, mock, displace, jar, or reconstruct the dominant tale or narrative' (p. xviii).

The storytelling method and the development of composite characters that emerge from research and experience is also a way for education scholars to put 'a human and familiar face to educational theory and practice' (Solórzano & Delgado Bernal, 2001, p. 337). This work builds on the scholarship of Bell (1987, 1995), who tells stories of society's treatment of race through his protagonist and alter ego Geneva Crenshaw, and Delgado (1995, 1999), who discusses race, class, and gender issues through Rodrigo Crenshaw, the half-brother of Geneva. Sleeter and Delgado Bernal (2004) point out that there is a web of composite characters of professors, graduate students, and undergraduates whose interconnected lives have recently appeared in the educational literature (Solórzano & Villalpando, 1998; Delgado Bernal, 1999; Solórzano & Yosso, 2000, 2001; Solórzano & Delgado Bernal, 2001; Villalpando, 2003). These characters illustrate the educational system's role in reproducing and sustaining racial, gender, and class oppression, as well as the myriad ways in which people of color respond to different forms of oppression. We add to this body of literature by introducing Patricia Avila, a Chicana assistant professor.[5]

The storytelling method enables us to challenge reality by offering one story that includes both the stock story from a majoritarian perspective and a counterstory from a non-majoritarian perspective (Delgado, 1989). A 'story' can refer to a majoritarian story or a counterstory; it becomes a counterstory when it incorporates elements of critical race theory (Solórzano & Yosso, 2002). In other words, a counterstory counters a set of unexamined assumptions made by the dominant culture. The first part of our story, the majoritarian story, is from the perspective of white faculty members. It conveys how unexamined assumptions seemingly objectively guide the tenure process. The second part of our story is presented as a counterstory from the perspective of Patricia Avila, and it illuminates just how biased and partial these unexamined assumptions can be. Both parts of the story revolve around the Retention, Promotion, and Tenure (RPT) process for faculty of color by looking at how a decision for tenure is made at the academic department level.

The setting is at an urban, public four-year teaching college, in a small curriculum studies department. Patricia Avila's file is being reviewed by her department for consideration of promotion to associate professor with tenure. She is the only Chicana in her department, but there is a new African American assistant professor, Ronald Lindsay, in her department of eight faculty. Ronald is an ally and has his own tenure process to face in the near future. Patricia has been with the department for six years, and her file is being reviewed in the fall term of her seventh year.

The majoritarian part of the story begins with a meeting of her department's four tenured RPT committee members, all of whom are white and female, except for the chair of the committee who is male. The committee members have read Patricia Avila's published work and reviewed her file in advance of the meeting. Dale, the RPT chair begins the meeting.

***

'Well, Patricia's file is complete. She submitted a pretty well-developed professional statement, copies of her publications, teaching evaluations, and syllabi. We also received three letters from her external reviewers. Let me begin with a summary of her publications.

'As you noticed in her personal statement, she describes her scholarship as focusing on the sociocultural and educational experiences of Chicana and Chicano students. Most of her publications seem to address some dimension of schooling and curricular issues for Chicanos or other minority students. In the past six years, she's had six articles published in refereed journals, four chapters in edited books by university presses, two technical reports, one published as a monograph by the college and the other by the district, and three articles forthcoming or in press by refereed journals.'

Catherine, a senior professor in the department, who considers herself an unofficial mentor to Patricia and views her role during this meeting as an objective supporter of her tenure, is the first committee member to speak after the chair: 'I have to say that I really appreciate Patricia's positive nature. You know, even though her scholarship addresses somewhat controversial issues—maybe even a bit militant— unlike some other minority faculty, she doesn't carry around any anger that is misdirected at us or at students. I really like the fact that she can be objective and positive in her relationships with her colleagues and students in the department.

'I also have to say that Patricia has what would appear to be an impressive file. In fact, I'm a bit surprised by it. When she first got here, I really wasn't sure whether she would get to this point. She came highly recommended as a skilled former elementary school teacher, and came from a good doctoral program, but I wasn't sure how she'd do in her writing and publications. So, to see that she's published six articles in refereed journals is very exciting to me.'

Sarah, an associate professor and one of the most outspoken faculty in the department offers a different perspective on Patricia's publications, 'Well Catherine, I can see where her six refereed articles may seem impressive if we're only looking at quantity, but I think that we also have to look at *where* she's published them.

'For example, she has one publication in *Aztlan*, an ethnic studies journal that sometimes publishes poems and short stories. I don't think that Patricia would misstate that the journal was refereed, but I would question who the people were who reviewed her articles? And, the more important questions—who really reads her articles in these journals and how do the articles inform practice or theory in the field of education? She's not an ethnic studies professor; she's an education professor. The same issues apply for her article in *Frontiers: A Journal of Women's Studies*. She's not a women's studies professor, so why publish an education article in a women's studies journal?

'So, for me, the fact that she has six refereed articles is less important than where these pieces were published and how they inform her field. And, by the way, I should add that the fact that three of these articles are co-authored makes me wonder what her contributions were to each piece.'

'You have a good point, Sarah,' says Dale, 'Our RPT department policy does state that our scholarship must inform educational practice, theory, or research. So, I would also wonder how these outlets in which she's published advance educational theory or practice. Why didn't she just publish in education journals?'

Catherine, attempting to be supportive, points out, 'Patricia has articles in *Equity and Excellence in Education, Urban Education, Curriculum Inquiry*, and the other pieces in press are in more practitioner-oriented education journals.'

'Well, she showed poor judgment by not submitting *everything* to education journals,' says Dale. 'I wish she'd consulted with us before submitting her work. Now, she may have put herself in a bind.'

Jeannie, another member of the committee refers everyone back to Patricia's personal statement and says 'Patricia actually indicates that she purposely sent some of her work to outlets outside of education because her scholarship is interdisciplinary. As she states, her work "focuses on eliminating racial and social inequality in education by examining the sociocultural experiences of Chicanas and Chicanos." But, as you say Dale, the question is why didn't she choose education journals for *all* of her work?'

'I wondered the same thing,' says Sarah. 'Maybe the ethnic and women's studies journals she chose were more open to some of the inherent biases in her work?'

Dale then redirects the conversation toward Patricia's teaching by asking, 'OK, publications are important, but remember that teaching is equally significant in this department. In the last six years, she's developed four new classes for the department and taught the core graduate multicultural seminar every term during each of the last five years. She's also volunteered to teach our methods class on three different occasions. Her teaching evaluations were a little above the department average, although her lowest scores and strongest criticisms seemed to come from her multicultural education courses. She really got hammered hard by some students in these courses.'

Jeannie explains that the scores from students' teaching evaluations have never been of much value to her. 'To tell you the truth, I've never really trusted those numbers much,' she says. 'The questions aren't worded very clearly and I think that students are confused by them. I find students' written comments to be much more helpful and valuable. So, the fact that Patricia's scores were this or that doesn't mean much to me. I want to know what the students *stated in their own words* about her teaching.'

'Well, I agree with you to an extent,' says Sarah. 'These teaching evaluation scores aren't very important to me either, but I think that we have to pay attention to patterns. In Patricia's case, she's had a pattern of low scores in her multicultural education courses. Every time she's taught it, she gets lower scores than she does on all of her other courses. But, as you say Jeannie, the more important issue is the students' comments. Dale, can you read some of the written comments that students have made in their evaluations of her multicultural education classes?'

'Sure,' he begins, 'many of the comments in this class were positive, but there were also many that were very critical. For example:

- The instructor was very biased; she only presented one-sided views of minority students' educational experiences.
- The professor didn't invite differing viewpoints that countered her viewpoint. She blamed the schools for all of the minority students' problems and didn't want to place any responsibility on the students or their families.
- This class focused too much on the needs of ethnic minority students. I expected a multicultural education class to also focus on the needs of students with learning disabilities.
- One of the main goals of this instructor seemed to be to make us Caucasians feel guilty and responsible for all of the minorities' educational problems and lack of success.
- This professor supports reverse discrimination and doesn't believe in merit.'

'Well,' says Sarah, 'there you have it. It seems that Patricia's lack of objectivity in her teaching is isolating and silencing students. We can't take this issue lightly. Our department has always placed a very high value on good teaching. I seem to remember that we brought these same issues to her attention during her third-year review, so obviously she hasn't taken them seriously.'

Catherine tries to offer a sympathetic response to Sarah, 'You're right, teaching has always been very important in this department. In the seventeen-plus years that I have been here, I don't recall that we ever recommended a professor for tenure who was a poor teacher. If indeed Patricia is struggling with being an effective teacher, then we need to be concerned. I know that minority students really like her and her teaching, and ...'

'But that's exactly the point,' interrupts Sarah, 'minority students love her but mainstream non-minority students appear to be challenging her biased favoritism. The question is, what do we do with a faculty member who silences students?'

Catherine continues, 'I was about to say that the fact that so many of our minority students like her is a very good thing, given that our minority student enrollment has and continues to increase. And I'm not convinced that all white students feel silenced by her. In fact, look at Mary Baker, probably one of our best master's students ever. She constantly says how indebted she is to Patricia for her guidance. She's not even her formal advisor, but Mary goes to her for academic and professional advice. Mary attributes much of her intellectual development to Patricia's courses and mentoring. She is very indebted to Patricia, and credits her for being admitted to UCLA's education doctoral program next year.'

Referring to Patricia's professional statement, Dale reminds everyone that 'she states that she's become the "unofficial" advisor to about eight master's students in the department, and the assigned advisor for another twelve—and I don't think they're all minority students. She's directed seven theses and is currently on 11 other thesis committees. So, she has her share of students to advise. She's no slouch there. In fact, you may have read the three unsolicited letters of support from our students in her file. They were all very positive, and were especially complimentary about her mentoring.

'With respect to her service, she's been a member of six department committees and chaired four of them, including the admissions, scholarships, and curriculum committees, as well as the faculty search committee for Ronald's position. She's also been a member of three college-wide committees and three university committees, including the academic senate and the diversity committee. She has a long list of outside groups she's participated in and led, four of which alone were somehow related to Chavez Elementary School.'

Jeannie observes that 'Patricia has a very good service record. She's really been involved with many department, college, and university committees, and her participation in community groups, especially at Chavez Elementary is very commendable. I wonder how she found the time to stay so involved with so many community organizations and projects.'

'Well,' says Sarah, 'I agree that her service record is very long, but she would have been better-served by being more selective about her involvement in some of the community groups. You know, some of those organizations were more political in nature than educational. At times she seemed to cross over into political activism instead of educational leadership.'

Catherine looks confused and asks, 'Sarah, I'm not sure I see in her CV where she lists her involvement in political organizations.'

Sarah replies, 'Well, look at her involvement with the Chavez Elementary Parents Against the English Only Initiative, her consultation work with the Consortium to defeat the Anti-Bilingual Education Proposition, and some of the volunteer work she's done with the Immigration Center. In my book, she would have been a more productive role model by participating in in-service presentations related to education instead of getting into political activism.'

'Nevertheless, she's done what she's done and there you have it,' says Dale. 'That's her file.'

***

Rather than provide an analysis of the first part of our story here, we ask you to listen for the story's points and compare and contrast the reality in the first half of the story with the reality in the next part of the story. The next part of the story is the counterstory, which takes place at the same time that the RPT committee is meeting. Patricia and Ronald are having lunch together in the Faculty Center. This is only Ronald's second year in the department and he is interested in supporting Patricia and knowing how she feels about the department's review of her candidacy for tenure and promotion to associate professor.

***

Ronald asks, 'Does this feel kind of eerie for you Patricia? How do you feel about the fact that at this exact moment our colleagues are reviewing the last six years of your life's work and debating whether you're worthy of joining "the club." You don't seem very anxious about it.'

'Anxious?' asks Patricia. 'I'm not sure that I feel anxious any more. I'm more curious than anxious about knowing how our colleagues are interpreting my scholarship. I am pretty confident about my record; it's solid for achieving tenure at this institution.'

Ronald interrupts, 'Well, it may be solid, but you and I know that the tenure process is very subjective, especially for faculty of color and the type of scholarship that many of us do. How can you be so confident that you'll be reviewed fairly?'

'Well,' replies Patricia, 'you're right. The process is hardly ever "objective," but they would have a lot of explaining to do if I got rejected. I compared my record and productivity with that of most of our colleagues sitting around the RPT tenure table right now, and I know that it stands on its own.

'What I'm most curious about is knowing how they are interpreting the focus of my scholarship on social and racial inequality in education. Most of my teaching, publications, and service have addressed the intersection of race, class, and gender, and I've been especially focused on the experiences of Chicana and Chicano students. Our colleagues have never had someone like you and me in the department, with our type of scholarly agenda. Even though they've never told me explicitly that my scholarship might be a little too controversial for them, I've always had the sense that I was on my own, especially since no other colleagues shared a similar interest until you arrived.'

'But they really can't do anything about the focus of your scholarship,' says Ronald. 'Your work is getting published in good journals and you're making contributions to your field. How can they challenge that?'

'Yes,' Patricia says, 'I'm getting published, but I wonder how my colleagues will respond to some of the journals where my work is being published. I have stuff in good education journals, but I also explained in my professional statement that I'm deliberately placing some of my work in Chicana/o studies and women's studies journals.'

'So, it sounds like the issue isn't just where you're publishing but what you're publishing and why you're publishing it in these journals, isn't it?' asks Ronald.

'That's right,' replies Patricia. 'For example, I did some work on how Chicana/o students interpret their familial knowledge as assets in their formal schooling experiences. I interviewed Chicana/o high school students who came from working-class families, like me, and asked about their family and cultural practices. I thought it was a good piece that would help Chicanas/os reinterpret how their family's cultural resources may have shaped their educational experiences, despite the often poor schooling conditions that they had to endure. I also wanted to counter the cultural deficit discourse about Chicanas/os and their families. I purposely sent the manuscript to *Aztlan*, the premier Chicano/a Studies journal, and it received excellent reviews. The journal published the article and I feel very good about the audience who will read it. Yet, I'm wondering whether my colleagues will value this journal in the same way that they value mainstream education journals?

'This is what I mean about feeling curious, and maybe even a bit concerned. I wonder if my colleagues really value my scholarship and my potential contributions, or whether they will conclude that somehow my work is less important because it's based on the experiences and voices of working-class Chicanas.'

Ronald says, 'Of course, they would never say this explicitly, would they?'

'No,' answers Patricia, 'but they may instead focus on the publication outlets as the substitute issue. In other words, they may explicitly question why I published in *Frontiers* and *Aztlan* since these are not education journals, but implicitly suggest that ethnic and women's studies journals are second-class and less rigorous outlets.

'However, the real issue is that the knowledge "created" by, for, and about women and people of color is considered by the academy as biased or illegitimate. Not only are we often unsuccessful in publishing much of our work in "mainstream" journals, but then we're penalized for publishing it in ethnic and women's related journals. To everyone's detriment, our knowledges and epistemologies are separated from and subordinated to "mainstream" Eurocentric knowledge.'

Ronald responds, 'So you're somewhat confident about your publication record, but a bit concerned about how they will interpret it. What are they likely to do about your teaching. Surely there isn't a lot of room for misinterpreting your strong contributions around teaching, is there?'

'No,' says Patricia, 'there shouldn't be. My classes have always had among the highest enrollments. I've taught the most demanding courses in the department, have created several new classes at the department's request, and my teaching evaluations have consistently been above the department average.

'My only question revolves around the multicultural education course that I've taught every term since coming here. You and I know, and the literature bears this out, that courses with a focus on race, ethnicity, gender, sexual orientation, class, power, and privilege touch on very personal issues for students. These courses often make white students very uncomfortable and they frequently take their frustrations out on the instructor through negative course evaluations. I've yet to meet a colleague—and especially a woman of color—who teaches these types of courses and hasn't been burned by some white students in the teaching evaluations. I guess that my hope is that my colleagues understand this and place any of the negative evaluations I received in context. I've had some very assertive white students in these courses who have threatened to write letters to the department chair and college dean because they feel "marginalized" in my multicultural education classes. The irony is that students of color routinely tell me that they feel silenced in most of their courses with our white faculty colleagues when issues of racial inequality come up in class discussions, yet they aren't writing letters to the chair or writing negative comments on teaching evaluations.'

Ronald tries to reassure her, 'They really can't ding you on teaching, Patricia. They have to recognize that you're been a workhorse and understand that you are bound to get a few critical evaluations for teaching a course that pushes students to examine their own privileged positions in society.'

'Yeah, I hope you're right,' answers Patricia. 'I would hope that our colleagues understand the impact that I have as a teacher, advisor, and mentor to the many students who seek me out. I have never turned a student away and, like you, I feel a special commitment to our students of color. I've been very careful to make sure that I'm available for students of color—and for communities of color outside of the campus. In fact, I've always been careful to try to balance my university service with my outside service so that I'm able to stay connected to the local Latina/o community.'

Ronald says, 'Again, hopefully the committee will understand how your presence benefits the department by linking us a little more to the educational issues in the Latina/o community.'

'Well Ronald,' says Patricia, 'whether the committee understands my work is important for my tenure, but what's most important for me is knowing that I will continue to have an opportunity to stay at this campus and continue to represent the educational needs of Chicana/o and Latina/o communities.'

***

What Does the Story Tell Us?

> My story is about real experience, an experience that is as real as my social reality. It is an experience that is representative of the practices, rules, and customs that minority persons like myself encounter inside and outside of academia. I tell my story to bring to light an alternative interpretation of institutional practices in academia that support the majority stock story. (Aguirre, 2000, p. 319)

Our story, told from both a majoritarian and counter perspective, adds to the collection of scholarship that provides alternative interpretations of higher education practices and documents the challenges that faculty of color face in academia (Olivas, 1988; Altbach & Lomotey, 1991; Padilla & Chavez, 1995; Valverde & Castenell, 1998; Turner & Myers, 2000; Smith *et al.*, 2002). It does so by offering competing interpretations and perspectives of the RPT process, and unveils at least two important issues that are usually not discussed in traditional analyses of higher education practices.

First, the story illustrates how the dominant Eurocentric epistemology is embedded in the formalized RPT practices and procedures that guide the committee's tenure review. The committee's Eurocentric worldview is a very important issue, given how it influences the academic choices of all tenure-track faculty members, and especially those who draw upon cultural resources as does Patricia Avila. In previous work, we provided an in-depth review and discussion of racialized double standards in higher education and how they impact faculty of color (Villalpando & Delgado Bernal, 2002). The story in this essay points to how a Eurocentric epistemology creates racialized double standards that are firmly embedded in the whiteness of the academy and facilitate an apartheid of knowledge.

The committee cannot find much value in Patricia Avila's scholarship partially because their discourse and the RPT process they follow are based on a particular set of standards that are believed to be neutral, meritocratic, and objective. Even the rules of their discourse 'allow certain people (usually white and tenured) to be the subjects of statements and others (often untenured scholars of color) to be objects' (St.Pierre, 2000, p. 485). Individual members of the committee who consider themselves supportive of Patricia do not have the insights or necessary perspectives to adopt a discourse or epistemological stance that can help them recognize her scholarship, teaching, and service as important and valuable. Their situated realities frame the evaluation of her work.

Their inability to adopt a non-Eurocentric epistemology gives rise to the second issue highlighted in this story; that is, the ways in which the knowledge and cultural resources of a scholar of color are overlooked and devalued in the RPT process. Among many faculty of color, cultural resources are often revealed in academia through a personal and scholarly commitment to improving the socioeconomic, political, and educational conditions of our own or other similarly disenfranchised community. Faculty of color often draw from cultural resources to inform our work, most often apparent through the content of our teaching, publications, service, and student advising and mentoring. The cultural resources and epistemologies that many faculty of color bring to academia contribute to the goals of higher education and to the overall knowledge base in academia, yet these resources and epistemologies are often unrecognized or devalued.

The RPT committee members in the majoritarian story suggest that the focus and content of Patricia's work is suspect and biased, rather than valuable and relevant to important social issues. Even though she has a record that includes both quantity and quality, the committee openly questions the rigor and worthiness of the ethnic and women's studies journals in which she has published. In addition, Patricia experiences a devaluation of her teaching as students and the committee discount the legitimacy of what she teaches and accuse of her of being biased. Research shows that issues of authority and legitimacy in the classroom are especially complicated for faculty of color who teach multicultural or social justice classes (Bell *et al.*, 1997). For example, 'A professor of color and a white professor teaching about racism … are likely to be perceived quite differently by students of color and white students' (p. 308). Finally, Patricia's community service is viewed as 'political activism instead of educational leadership' even though (and probably as a result of the fact that) it is directly related to improving the educational conditions of the local Latina/o community. Despite the significance of her publications, teaching, and community service that address social justice issues related to the educational needs of an underserved and disenfranchised racial/ethnic community, her work is characterized as lacking academic rigor and being inherently biased.

Summary

In this essay we have proposed that, by marginalizing the knowledges of faculty of color, higher education has created an apartheid of knowledge where the dominant Eurocentric epistemology is believed to produce 'legitimate' knowledge, in contrast to the 'illegitimate' knowledge that is created by all other epistemological perspectives. Scheurich and Young (1997) describe the process that leads to this form of racial division as epistemological racism. The CRT counterstory-telling method we adopt in this essay serves as a critical pedagogical tool that helps to illustrate how epistemological racism and the apartheid of knowledge continue to exist. As such, we believe that CRT counterstory-telling provides critical pedagogy with a place for the interrogation of race and racism and a way to incorporate the voices and unique experiences of faculty of color into higher education.

The apartheid of knowledge in the academy is sustained by the *de facto* racial segregation that exists in higher education institutions, across academic ranks, and within departments. Our analysis of national data on faculty over the last thirty years reveals that there has been very little to almost no change in the representation of faculty of color in higher education. Faculty of color continue to be severely underrepresented in American higher education. When viewed through the CRT theme that challenges dominant claims of meritocracy and objectivity in U.S. institutions, the pernicious underrepresentation of faculty of color along with the apartheid of knowledge that exists in academia underscore the pressing need to eliminate the racialized barriers that exist in higher education.

By analyzing the decision-making process of one of the most important gate-keeping practices for faculty in higher education, our story twice-told reveals how the cultural resources and experiential knowledge that faculty of color can contribute to the learning environment is devalued and dismissed by academia. To value our experiential knowledge, higher education must recognize the cultural resources that we bring to academia and must welcome, engage, and encourage our perspectives and our scholarship, for the benefit of all students. As Matsuda (1988) states, 'human beings learn and grow through interaction with difference, not by reproducing what they already know. A system of ... education that ignores outsiders' perspectives artificially restricts and stultifies the scholarly imagination' (p. 3). Critical race theory suggests that the experiential knowledge of faculty of color brings different perspectives about how to move toward eliminating all forms of subordination and creating a more just society. Until higher education fully recognizes and places greater value on our epistemologies and scholarship, the struggle over 'legitimate knowledge' in academia will continue.

Acknowledgements

We would like to thank Marvin Lynn and Maurianne Adams for their important comments and insightful suggestions on this manuscript. We also thank Mary DeLaRosa for her much appreciated assistance in the final version of this manuscript. Both authors contributed equally to it.

Notes

1. In adopting the term apartheid, we recognize that there are very significant material differences between the context of South Africa and that of American higher education, and we are in no way equating the two contexts. Rather, we use the term to help us convey the racial divisions between a dominant Eurocentric epistemology and epistemologies that stand in contrast to it, and to illustrate the climate of separation

between what is considered 'legitimate' knowledge and 'illegitimate' knowledge in academia. By doing this, we also extend Padilla and Chavez's (1995) notion of 'academic apartheid' which refers to the climate of academia that keeps faculty of color on the margins.

2. We use the term people of color to refer to persons of African American, Chicana(o)/ Puerto Rican/Other Latina(o), American Indian, and Asian American ancestry.

3. This section builds upon material that we discuss in greater detail in our chapter 'A Critical Race Theory Analysis of Barriers that Impede the Success of Faculty of Color,' that appears with the important collection of works found in Smith, Altbach, and Lomotey (2002).

4. We use 'our' and 'we' to include ourselves among faculty of color throughout this article, rather than the detached 'their' or 'they.' Our intent is not to essentialize the experiences or scholarship of faculty of color, but to collectively address the nature of many of our experiences and those of our colleagues of color.

5. Patricia Avila and the other persons in this story are composite characters who represent authentic experiences based on biographical narratives in the humanities, education, and social science literature, dialogues with colleagues, and our own personal experiences. As Solórzano and Yosso (2002) state, 'We are not developing imaginary characters that engage in fictional scenarios. Instead, the "composite" characters we develop are grounded in real-life experiences and actual empirical data and are contextualized in social situations that are also grounded in real life, not fiction' (p. 36).

References

Aguirre, A. (2000) Academic Storytelling: A critical race theory story of affirmative action, *Sociological Perspectives*, 43:2, pp. 319–321.

Allen, W. R., Epps, E. G., Guillory, E., Suh, S., Bonous-Hammarth, M. & Stassen, M. (2000). Outsiders Within: Race, gender, and faculty status in U.S. higher education, in: K. Lomotey, *The Racial Crisis in American Higher Education* (New York, SUNY).

Altbach, P. & Lomotey, K. (eds) (1991) *The Racial Crisis in American Higher Education* (Albany, State University of New York Press).

Astin, A. W. (1982) *Minorities in American Higher Education: Recent trends, current prospect, and recommendations* (San Francisco, Jossey-Bass Publishers).

Astin, A. W. (1993) *What Matters in College? Four critical years revisited* (San Francisco, Jossey-Bass Publishers).

Astin, A. W. & Villalpando, O. (1996) A Demographic Profile of Today's Faculty, in: *Integrating Research on Faculty: Seeking new ways to communicate about the academic life of faculty. Results from the 1994 forum sponsored by the National Center for Education Statistics (NCES), the Association for Institutional Research (AIR), and the American Association of State Colleges and Universities* (Washington, DC, Department of Education, Office of Educational Research and Improvement), pp. 96–849.

Astin, H., Antonio, A., Cress, C. & Astin, A. W. (1997) *Race and Ethnicity in the American Professoriate, 1995–96*, (UCLA Higher Education Research Institute, Los Angeles, CA).

Bell, D. A. (1987). *And We Are Not Saved : The elusive quest for racial justice* (New York, Basic Books).

Bell, D. A. (1995) Who's Afraid of Critical Race Theory, *University of Illinois Law Review*, pp. 893–910.

Bell, L. A., Washington, S., Weinstein, G. & Love, B. (1997) Knowing Ourselves as Instructors, in: P. Griffin, *Teaching for Diversity and Social Justice: A sourcebook* (New York, Routledge), pp. 299–310.

Bennet, W. (1982). *To Reclaim a Legacy* (Washington, DC, National Endowment for the Humanities).

Bloom, A. (1987) *The Closing of the American Mind: How higher education has failed democracy and impoverished the souls of today's students* (New York, Simon and Schuster).

Calmore, J. (1992) Critical Race Theory, Archie Shepp, and fire music: Securing an authentic intellectual life in a multicultural world, *Southern California Law Review*, 65, pp. 2129–2231.

Carnevale, A. (1999) *Education=Success: Empowering Hispanic youth and adults* (Princeton, NJ, Educational Testing Service).

Córdova, T. (1998) Power and Knowledge: Colonialism in the academy, in: C. Trujillo, *Living Chicana Theory* (Berkeley, CA, Third Woman Press).

Delgado, R. (1984) The Imperial Scholar: Reflections on a review of civil rights, *University of Pennsylvania Law Review*, 132, pp. 561–578.

Delgado, R. (1989) When a Story Is Just a Story: Does voice really matter?, *Virginia Law Review*, 76, pp. 95–111.

Delgado, R. (1995) *Critical Race Theory: The cutting edge* (Philadelphia, Temple University Press).

Delgado, R. (1999) *When Equality Ends: Stories about race and resistance* (Boulder, CO, Westview Press).

Delgado Bernal, D. (1999) Chicana/o Education from the Civil Rights Era to the Present, in: J. F. Moreno, *The Elusive Quest for Equality: 150 Years of Chicano/Chicana education* (Cambridge, MA, Harvard Educational Publishing Group), pp. 77–108.

Delgado Bernal, D. (2001) Learning and Living Pedagogies of the Home: The mestiza consciousness of Chicana students, *International Journal of Qualitative Studies in Education*, 14:5, pp. 623–639.

Delgado Bernal, D. (2002) Critical Race Theory, LatCrit Theory, and Critical Raced Gendered Epistemologies: Recognizing students of color as holders and creators of knowledge, *Qualitative Inquiry*, 8:1, pp. 105–126.

D'Souza, D. (1991) *Illiberal Education: The politics of race and sex on campus* (New York, Free Press).

Garza, H. (1993) Second-class Academics: Chicano/Latino Faculty in U.S. Universities, *New Directions for Teaching and Learning*, 53, pp. 33–41.

Giroux, H. A. (1983) *Theory and Resistance in Education* (South Hadley, MA, Bergin & Garvey).

Giroux, H. A. (1992) *Border Crossings* (New York, Routledge).

González, N., Moll, L. C., Tenery, M. F., Rivera, A., Rendón, P., Gonzáles, R. & Amanti, C. (1995) Funds of Knowledge for Teaching Latino Households, *Urban Education*, 29:4, pp. 443–470.

Harris, C. (1993) Whiteness as Property, *Harvard Law Review*, 106.

Karabel, J. (1977) Community Colleges and Social Stratification: Submerged class conflict in American higher education, in: A. H. Halsey, *Power and Ideology in Education* (need city and publisher), pp. 232–254.

Kushner, J. A. (1980) *Apartheid in America: An historical and legal analysis of contemporary racial segregation in the United States* (Fredrick, MD, University Publications of America).

Ladson-Billings, G. (2000) Racialized Discourses and Ethnic Epistemologies, in: Y. S. Lincoln, *Handbook of Qualitative Research* (Thousand Oaks, Sage Publications Inc.).

Ladson-Billings, G. & Tate, W. (1995) Toward a Critical Race Theory of Education, *Teacher College Record*, 97, pp. 47–68.

Matsuda, M. (1988) Affirmative Action and Legal Knowledge: Planting seeds in plowed-up ground, *Harvard Women's Law Journal*, 11, pp. 1–17.

McIntosh, P. (1997) White Privilege: Unpacking the invisible knapsack, in: B. Schneider, *An Anthology: Race in the first person* (New York, Crown Trade Paperbacks).

Milem, J. & Astin, H. (1993) The Changing Composition of the Faculty, *Change*, 25:2.

Oakes, J. (1985) *Keeping Track: How schools structure inequality* (New Haven, MA, Yale University Press).

Olivas, M. (1988) Latino Faculty at the Border, *Change*, 20, pp. 6–9.

Olivas, M. (1990) The Chronicles, My Grandfather's Stories, and Immigration Law: The slave traders chronicle as racial history, *Saint Louis University Law Journal*, 34, pp. 425–441.

Padilla, R. & Chavez, P. (eds) (1995) *The Leaning Ivory Tower: Latino professors in American universities* (Albany, State University of New York Press).

Parker, L. (1998). 'Race Is ... Race Ain't': An exploration of the utility of critical race theory in qualitative research in education, *Qualitative Studies in Education*, 11:1, pp. 43–55.

Parker, L. & Lynn, M. (2002) What's Race Got to Do With It? Critical race theory's conflicts with and connections to qualitative research methodology and epistemology, *Qualitative Inquiry*, 8:1, pp. 7–22.

Sax, L., Astin, A., Korn, W. S. & Gilmartin, S. K. (1999) National Norms for the 1998–99 HERI Survey, *American College Teacher*.

Scheurich, J. & Young, M. (1997) Coloring Epistemologies: Are our research epistemologies racially biased?, *Educational Researcher*, 26:4, pp. 4–16.

Shlesinger, A. (1993) *The Disuniting of American: Reflections on a multicultural society* (New York, W. W. Norton & Co).

Sleeter, C. & Delgado Bernal, D. (2004) Critical Pedagogy, Critical Race Theory, and Antiracist Education: Implications for multicultural education, in: J. A. Banks & C. M. Banks (eds), *The Handbook of Research on Multicultural Education* (New York, Macmillan), pp. 240–258.

Smith, W., Altbach, P. & Lomotey, K. (eds) (2002) *The Racial Crisis in American Higher Education: Continuing challenges for the twenty-first century* (New York, SUNY).

Solórzano, D. (1997). Images and Words that Wound: Critical race theory, racial stereotyping, and teacher education, *Teacher Education Quarterly*, 24, pp. 5–19.

Solórzano, D. (1998) Critical Race Theory, Race and Gender Microaggresions, and the Experience of Chicana and Chicano Scholars, *Qualitative Studies in Education*, 11:1, pp. 121–136.

Solórzano, D. & Delgado Bernal, D. (2001) Examining Transformational Resistance Through a Critical Race and LatCrit Theory Framework: Chicana and Chicano students in an urban context, *Urban Education*, 36:3, pp. 308–342.

Solórzano, D. & Villalpando, O. (1998) Critical Race Theory, Marginality, and the Experience of Students of Color in Higher Education, in: T. Mitchell & R. Albany, *Sociology of Education: Emerging perspectives* (State University of New York Press), pp. 211–224.

Solórzano, D. & Yosso, T. J. (2000). Toward a Critical Race Theory of Chicana and Chicano Education, in: C. Tejeda, C. Martineze, Z. Leonardo (eds), Charting New Terrains of Chicana(o)/Latina(o) Education, *Demarcating the Border of Chicana(o)/Latina(o) Education* (Cresskill, NJ, Hampton), pp. 35–65.

Solórzano, D. & Yosso, T. J. (2001) Critical Race and LatCrit Theory and Method: Counter-storytelling, *Qualitative Studies in Education*, 14:4, pp. 471–495.

Solórzano, D. & Yosso, T. J. (2002) Critical Race Methodology: Counter-storytelling as an analytical framework for education research, *Qualitative Inquiry*, 8:1, pp. 23–44.

St.Pierre, E. A. (2000) Poststructural Feminism in Education: An overview, *Qualitative Studies in Education*, 13:5, pp. 477–515.

Tatum, B. (1999) *Why Are All the Black Kids Sitting Together in the Cafeteria? And other conversations about race* (New York, Basic Books).

Thompson, A. (1998) Not the Color Purple: Black feminist lessons for educational caring, *Harvard Educational Review*, 68:4, pp. 522–554.

Turner, C. S. V. & Myers, S. L. Jr. (2000) *Faculty of Color in Academe: Bittersweet success* (Boston, Allyn and Bacon).

Turner, C. S. V., Myers, S. L. Jr. & Cresswell, J. W. (1999) Exploring Underrepresentation: The case of faculty of color in the midwest, *Journal of Higher Education*, 70:1, pp. 27–59.

Valverde, L. & Castenell, L. (eds) (1998). *The Multicultural Campus: Strategies for transforming higher education* (Walnut Creek, CA, AltaMira Press).

Velez-Ibanez, C. G. & Greenberg, J. B. (1992) Formation and Transformation of Funds of Knowledge among U.S. Mexican Households, *Anthropology and Education Quarterly*, 23:4, pp. 313–335.

Villalpando, O. (1996) The Long Term Effects of College on Chicana and Chicano Students: 'Other oriented' values, service careers, and community involvement PhD dissertation (Los Angeles, University of Los Angeles).

Villalpando, O. (2003) Self-segregation or Self-preservation?: A critical race theory and Latina/o critical theory analysis of a study of Chicana/o college students, *Qualitative Studies in Education*, 16:5, pp. 619–646.

Villalpando, O. & Delgado Bernal, D. (2002) A Critical Race Theory Analysis of Barriers that Impede the Success of Faculty of Color, in: K. Lomotey, *The Racial Crisis in American Higher Education* (New York, SUNY Press: 243–269).

Williams, P. J. (1991). *The Alchemy of Race and Rights* (Cambridge, Harvard University Press).

11

Postcolonial Literature and the Curricular Imagination: Wilson Harris and the pedagogical implications of the carnivalesque

CAMERON MCCARTHY & GREG DIMITRIADIS

University of Illinois at Urbana; University at Buffalo, the State University of New York

Introduction

We are indeed living in new times—times in which the radical rearticulation and reconfiguration of identity and belonging are taking place as a part of the complex, many-sided effects of the rapid movement of people and cultural and economic capital across national borders. As a consequence, dynamic heterogenous cultures are being spawned everywhere confounding traditional understandings of center–periphery relationships as well as purist or atavistic notions of a singular or homogenous basis of group affiliation. While contemporary educational theorists are just beginning to inquire into these developments, artists, particularly third world postcolonial artists, have been grappling with these cross-cultural worlds for some time now. These artists have offered up important spaces for educators grappling with new and generative interconnections between critical pedagogy and race studies—the subject of this important collection of *Educational Philosophy and Theory*. In particular, these artists give us a way to reconceptualize a 'critical pedagogy of difference' that avoids staid conceptions of 'multiculturalism.' This is critical. Contemporary debates around multiculturalism have typically been driven by notions of 'inclusion,' quite often over the literary canon or historical record. Like many aspects of critical pedagogy, these debates have come to rest perhaps too comfortably and easily in and within dominant educational and curricular reform movements. Postcolonial artists, however, give us no such easy referents. They evoke complex polyglot worlds of negotiation that cannot be so easily contained. These worlds of negotiation are best captured, we argue, in the concept of the 'carnivalesque,' or the notion of unpredictable patterns of association, inversions of hierarchies of powers, and the playful, uncontrollable, rhizomatic flourishing of multiplicity that has taken over the modern city and metropolis.

Many social, cultural and literary theorists, such as Tony Bennett (1995), Peter Stallybrass and Allon White (1986), Michael Holquist (1985), and of course Mikhail Bakhtin (1984), have written about the carnivalesque—its significant contributions to the rise of the public sphere, its celebration of anti-hierarchical peasant world views, its anti-modernist and anti-capitalist moment, its sublimation in literature, and its associated participation in the rise of a heterological literary voice. In talking about 'the characteristics of genre' in his *Problems of Dostoevsky's Poetics*, Bakhtin (1984) maintains the following about the carnivalesque as a cultural and political form:

> Carnival is a pageant without footlights and without a division into performers and spectators. In carnival everyone is an active participant, everyone communes in the carnival act ... The laws, prohibitions, and restrictions that determine the structure and order of the ordinary, that is noncarnival, life are suspended during carnival: what is suspended first of all is hierarchical structure and all the forms of terror, reverence, piety, and etiquette connected with it—that is, everything resulting from socio-hierarchical inequality or any other form of inequality among people ... All *distance* between people is suspended, and a special carnival category goes into effect: *free and familiar contact among people*. (pp. 122–123)

For Bakhtin, the carnival inverts the hierarchies, structures, prohibitions, and restrictions that atomize public life. In the carnival, the 'order of the ordinary' is suspended. New social orders and modes of association proliferate and 'free and familiar contact among people' reigns.

But, Bakhtin's insights included, the writing on the carnivalesque has focused overwhelmingly on the cultural dynamics of European contexts and cultural practices. Less intellectual energy has been directed toward carnivalesque practices operating in the postcolonial setting. Neither have theorists sought to connect the carnivalesque in postcolonial writing to the challenges of classroom pedagogy and education in our modern times. In this essay, we join with an emergent set of voices shifting intellectual focus to postcolonial carnivalesque practices. Here, we refer to writers such as Paget Henry (2000), Hommi Babha (1994), Michael Dash (1990), Sandra Drake (1989), and Russell McDougall (1989). We are particularly interested in the carnivalesque as manifested in the literary works of third world writers and the extent to which the carnivalesque discourse within third world fiction is an enabling system of representation that generates a new, subaltern subjectivity at the epicenter of the novel form. We will use as an exemplar of these developments the work of the Guyanese novelist, Wilson Harris. We will discuss his novels *Carnival*, *Palace of the Peacock*, and *Companions of the Day and Night*—three novels that herald the age of multiplicity that now defines the terms of existence for modern subjects attempting to negotiate contemporary social institutions such as schooling. Contemporary school practice seems paralyzed when confronted with the new developments in world cultures toward hybridity, falling back, instead, on a default curriculum that privileges monoculturalism or a diluted form of multiculturalism. These dominant curriculum models preserve the imperialist disciplinary core of the organization of school knowledge and pedagogy. The carnivalesque postcolonial writing of novelists such as Harris offers pedagogues new models of thoughtfulness that challenge the tendency toward intellectual isolationism and cultural insularity in the educational enterprise.

Wilson Harris, School Life and the Fractured Self

Harris, like many artists coming out of the postcolonial tradition, has a complex family history. He was born in New Amsterdam, British Guyana, in 1921, of mixed parentage—Amerindian, European, and African. Such diversity was not uncommon in Guyana, where, like many other parts of the Caribbean the familial, ancestral and cultural tributaries of the continents of Africa, Asia and Europe meet with terrific force. Harris would be deeply influenced by Guyana's multiracial and multi-ethnic make up. His work would fundamentally define itself, against all manner of social and intellectual parochialism and essentialism. According to the *Cambridge Guide to Literature in English*, Harris's 'free-ranging, non-logical, highly metaphoric, associative techniques in prose derive from a poetic imagination fired intellectually by extensive reading' in philosophy, anthropology, and folk-mythology (Ousby, 1988, p. 437). Harris attended Queen's College, Georgetown. After leaving school, he worked as a surveyor for the Guyanese government, often traveling to the interior of Guyana to construct maps and conduct geological studies. The experience was formative. Visually, Harris's writing is energized by the Guyanese savannahs, the powerful river currents, and the swirling rock strata of Guyana. In novels such as *Palace of the Peacock* (1960), *The Far Journey of Oudin* (1961), *The Whole Armour* (1962), and *The Secret Ladder* (1963), published as the *Guyana Quartet* (1985b), Harris uses the physical landscape as metaphor in allegorical tales that serve to dramatize the workings of the human psyche and to establish insights about its capacity to resist ossification by the categorical and the static.

In what follows, we focus on a new subject identity at the epicenter of Harris's novels—a twin or double figure of reversible sensibility and feeling, neither colonizer nor colonized but both—a shadow and a mask rising from the flotsam, detritus and ruins of colonial historical realities—an allegorical trope and carrier of the new society, the new dispensation, the new epiphany. How might we understand this new subject in light of the carnivalesque? And what broad implications does Harris's deployment of the same have for curriculum and educational change?

We see Harris's work as profoundly important for thinking through contemporary trends and pressures in education and multicultural education today. As Michael Apple (1993), among others, has made so very clear, educators are facing accelerating pressures of standardization and professionalization. 'At the local, state, and national levels,' he writes, 'movements for strict accountability systems, competency-based education and testing, management by objectives, a truncated vision of the "basics," mandated curricular content and goals, and so on are clear and growing' (pp. 121–122). The role of the teacher as a transformative intellectual has been increasingly circumscribed by these imperatives. Apple relates these concerns to a broader and longer history of management's rationalizing and standardizing people's work (p. 120). He sees two major consequences of these twin imperatives, both of which have come to mark the field of education in our times:

> The first is what we shall call the *separation of conception from execution*. When complicated jobs are broken down into atomistic elements, the person doing the job loses sight of the whole process and loses control

over her or his own labor since someone outside the immediate situation now has greater control over both the planning and what is actually to go on. The second consequence is related, but adds a further debilitating characteristic. This is known as *deskilling*. As employees lose control over their own labor, the skills that they have developed over the years atrophy. They are slowly lost, thereby making it even easier for management to control even more of one's job because the skills of planning and controlling it yourself are no longer available. (p. 121)

The role of the teacher has been increasingly narrowed and circumscribed by these emerging processes, less and less tied up with individual student and teacher biographies, interests, dispositions, and so forth. Education becomes a kind of normative science on this logic, one that aims for a totalizing vision and control over knowledge, and that robs teachers of their calling as transformative intellectuals.

Apple's analysis regarding the loss of teacher autonomy is extended in the work of John Schmidt (2000), who sees teachers as a part of a general class of professionals of the 'disciplined mind' who have sold their souls to modern institutions for a salary. They live a double life in which their humanity is repressed and a hard calculating nature now dominates them and the work they do, as a matter of survival. Schmidt maintains that educational professionals, especially, have lost control over the nature of their work and are rendered as mere functionaries, hostile to difference and creativity in the educational setting. He further insists that educators are disciplined by the whole process of educational preparation and a hierarchical structure that regulates the use of their labor power. Professors, he maintains, symbolize the tragedy of all employed professionals who started out as students loving their subjects. Such students submit themselves to the process of professional training in an effort to be free of the marketplace, but instead of being strengthened by the process they are crippled by it. Deprived of political control over their work, they become alienated from their subjects and measure their lives by success in the marketplace (p. 146).

As we have argued elsewhere (McCarthy & Dimitriadis, 2000), multicultural education today has become just such a science of professional training—a form of disciplinarity of difference in which the matter of cultural alterity has been effectively displaced as a supplement—and dovetails similarly with corporate logics. Frustrated by the professionalization of multicultural education, we look to postcolonial literature for new ways of mediating the complexity and plurality that now define modern life, but that are subordinated in schools and other contemporary institutions. In this emergent literature, we seek out sources of alterity that might work against the grain of educational normalization. Harris elaborates an aesthetics of existence that strives toward a broader and more invested kind of encounter between human actors. Such an encounter is a paradigm for a new pedagogical model that involves teachers and students in authentic dialogue across difference, which does not aim at competency, control, and ossification but makes each member of the dialogue, in Paulo Freire's sense, responsible for the humanity of the others. We see the notion of the 'carnival' as having some purchase here, in foregrounding the decentered and porous subject necessary for such an encounter.

Beyond Realism: Wilson Harris and the Postcolonial Novel

Drawing on Bakhtin's insights, Russell McDougall (1989) focuses attention on the literary appropriation of the carnivalesque and its radical effects on the novel. For McDougall, carnivalesque fiction tends to be distinguished by the following features: (1) satire, parody, laughter, and extraordinary inventiveness of plot; (2) Socratic settings of truth and discovery in dialogue; (3) inserted genres of philosophical speculation, oratorical speeches and other normatively 'non-fictional' discourses; (4) a mock-heroic protagonist whose experiences and adventures are presented as an allegorical exploration of a larger system of political or cosmic forces; (5) characters who are in a constant state of flux, fragmentation, or decomposition; (6) reversibility of fiction in which characters' fortunes and roles are as interchangeable as a set of masks; (7) cumulatively, a peculiar sense of doubling or mirror distortion of the polyglot characters that inhabit the novel.

All of these elements of the carnivalesque literary genre are substantively present in Wilson Harris's work. Harris's own writing proceeds from an acute desire to decode, disassemble, and reconstruct the classical realist nineteenth-century novel genre. His is a radical impulse to shatter the nineteenth-century novel's self-security, its privileged discourse, and its pretensions to objective or foundational truth. The classical realist novel, as Harris (1967) notes in his *Tradition, the Writer, and Society*, proceeds along a path of consolidated biases and prerogatives. It insists on a free-standing individual character or protagonist at the center of events, conflicts, tradition or change. Harris indicates his own departure from the realist novel in the following:

> The consolidation of character is, to a major extent, the preoccupation of most novelists who work in the twentieth century within the framework of the nineteenth-century novel. Indeed the nineteenth-century novel has exercised a very powerful influence on reader and writer alike in the contemporary world. And this is not surprising after all since the rise of the novel in its conventional and historical mould coincides in Europe with states of society which were involved in consolidating their class and other vested interests. As a result, 'character' in the novel rests more or less on the self-sufficient individual—on 'elements of persuasion' (a refined or liberal persuasion at best in the spirit of the philosopher Whitehead) rather than 'dialogue' or 'dialectic,' in the profound and unpredictable sense of person which Martin Buber, for example, evokes. (pp. 28–29)

Harris goes on in the same essay to make an even more specific indictment of the realist novel:

> The novel of persuasion rests on grounds of apparent common sense: a certain 'selection' is made by the writer, the selection of items, manners,

uniform conversation, historical situations, etc., all lending themselves to build and present an individual span of life which yields self-conscious and fashionable moralities. The tension which emerges is the tension of individuals—great or small—on an accepted plane of society we are persuaded has inevitable existence. (p. 29)

Harris believes that the freedom that the individual is allowed in the realist novel is ultimately illusory—an elaborate form of what the Frankfurt School critic Theodor Adorno calls 'false clarity.' The novel of consolidation or persuasion is an inadequate aesthetic vehicle for the hybrid form of postcolonial subjectivity. As Harris argues, 'What in my view is remarkable about the West Indian [or the postcolonial subject] in depth is a sense of subtle links, the series of subtle and nebulous links which are latent within him, the latent ground of old and new personalities' (p. 28). Harris argues for a revolution in the form of the novel that would connect existing postcolonial communities to 'their variable pasts' (p. 31). These variable pasts are neither the separated historical origin stories of particular ethnic groups nor the fixed cultural property of twenty-first-century nations and races. Instead, Harris insists that cultural traditions are gateways of unsuspected association and cultural connection between all past and contemporary peoples.

Instead of the strategy of 'consolidation' or persuasion, then, Harris foregrounds a new task or orientation for the postcolonial novel. He offers one word to describe the new career of the carnivalesque novel—'fulfillment.' In his artistic imagination, the novel of 'fulfillment' is a polysemic text that privileges contradiction and incompleteness. Yet, for Harris, incompleteness is more than the narcissistic desire of the self for the other, in which both self and other remain discrete. Instead, Harris breaks down any unity of position by producing a kind of fiction that 'seeks to consume its own biases through the many resurrections of paradoxical imagination' (1960, p. 9). This self-consuming and re-generating novel inaugurates an alternative to the Hegelian dialectic of master and slave, dominator and dominated—an ultimately one-dimensional model of power and communication.

We have moved beyond what Hommi Bhabha calls 'the transparency of power,' and we have now entered the twilight zone of the hybrid. Hybridity is not cultural diversity or some racial admixture of some fortuitously agreeable elements. Hybridity, instead, is a radical disturbance of both 'self' and 'other,' an encounter that leads ultimately to unanticipated, maybe even unspeakable, transgressions. Bhabha (1984) is helpful here:

Hybridity is the sign of the productivity of colonial power, its shifting forces and fixities; it is the name for the strategic reversal of the process of domination through disavowal (that is the production of discriminatory identities that secure the 'pure' and original identity of authority). Hybridity is the revaluation of the assumption of colonial identity through the repetition of discriminatory identity effects. It displays the necessary deformation and displacement of all sites of discrimination and domination. It unsettles the mimetic or narcissistic demands of colonial power but reimplicates its identifications in strategies of subversion that turn the gaze of the discriminated back upon the eye of power. (p. 112)

What Bhabha suggests is that the colonial encounter is not repressive but productive of all kinds of effects the colonizer did not anticipate, such as lively distortions of the colonizing culture that leave their traces in skin tones, colloquialisms, hybrid musics, spiritual practices, and foods. The postcolonial novel is born in the crucible of cultural modernization, not in the purported pure space of pre-modern folk origins and the associated auratic art before the advent of cultural commodification.

Harris tells the story of the hybrid postcolonial subjects of the New World: the half-made, broken individuals strewn among the melancholy historical ruins of empire, who mediate the gateway between the Old World and the New, the West and the non-West. Harris is interested in exploring the palpable tensions between overlordship and dependency, the mutual desires and transgressions of the self and the other, and the very fragility of normative structures as they are inscribed in society and in the novel. He is interested in the reversal of hierarchical systems and in the subversion of absolute powers in the production of meaning—in the novel form and, by extension, the classroom. Harris mines the subversive capacities boiling underneath the surface of language itself. He puts into play new categories of meaning that allow his characters to cross the zones of confinement, alienation and difference. His characters are Old World and New World, female and male, ethnically ambiguous and androgynous. They are the half-made apostles of a new dispensation—the traumatized inhabitants of a postmodern/postcolonial world, somehow thriving after the holocaust of colonization.

Carnival and the Life and Death of Everyman Masters

We now turn to a more detailed discussion of Harris's novels. The principal protagonists in Harris's *Carnival* and *Palace of the Peacock* are Everyman Masters and Captain Donne, respectively. They are paired with narrator-biographers who seem to be so compelled by the lives, adventures and associative worlds of their elusive subjects that the narrators lose themselves again and again in the stories that they seek to record. In *Carnival*, it is difficult to tell Everyman Masters at times from John Weyl, his narrator, who becomes Masters' double and ultimately lives out the implications of Masters' early seemingly aborted life. In *Palace of the Peacock*, the 'I' narrator is Donne's brother, his shadowy alter ego. Like Harris himself, these narrators become the subjects of the stories they tell. In both novels the principal characters derive their energies from their associations with their opposites and antagonists. Individual characters literally flow into the lives of their fellow inhabitants in these novels. Within this fluid fictive framework, there is no attempt at consolidation of character: the characters' self-constitutions and egos keep dissolving before our eyes.

Carnival (1985a) is the story of the life and death of Everyman Masters. The name itself is an allegorical trope that binds the colonizer and colonized in the same life, in the same time, space and historical fortune. Everyman Masters is a colonial subject reared and educated in the South American and Caribbean state of New Forest, where he rises to the status of plantation overseer. Everyman is paradoxically, then, an oppressor. He is 'Masters' after all. But in this role Everyman Masters has to submit himself to what Harris calls 'the therapy of justice.' He pays with his life for his oppression of the plantation women who make up his labor force. Masters experiences what the narrator calls 'his first death' when the wife of a fisherman, Jane Fisher the First, invites him to her home, on the understanding that her husband is away fishing, and stabs Masters to death.

But, as always with Harris, the act itself is not an act of definitiveness or finality: it merely opens a doorway for the shadow of irony to cast its suspicions on both Masters and Jane the First herself. Jane the First mistakes Masters for a past lover, who deceived her. Masters therefore enters a purgatorial cycle in which he must shoulder the guilt of the 'sovereign demon' who 'borrowed his face' (p. 156) to deceive Jane the First. Thus Masters is allowed a second life, this time in the imperial center in England. In his second life, Masters becomes an Everyman—one among the many West Indian and Asian immigrant minorities working in the factories of industrial England—a man, like Johnny the Plantation Czar and Carnival King of New Forest, carrying 'a globe on his back.' Masters is a postmodern Atlas, uprooted, deracinated, a hybrid of all dislocated subcultures—a folk hero with a partly malignant, partly redemptive history. When we first encounter Masters in the beginning of the novel, we meet him at the end of the second cycle of his life, mounting the stair to his London apartment for a final rendezvous with Jane Fisher the Second. Masters is a latter-day Sweeney Erectus, driven by guilty desire to his untimely exit from this divine comedy of postcolonial life.

The second death takes place under shadowy circumstances. It is an apparent assassination by an intruder who enters through a door left ajar by the mercurial Jane Fisher the Second. But Masters' death is also a final reconciliation with both Jane Fishers and the reintegration of his psyche and tortured soul. In his dying moments, Masters finds expiation and release in the self-surrender of love: 'A first and second death dying now as I embrace you my dearest enemy, my dearest love' (p. 14). Masters' final transformation has implications beyond their individual relationship to the new relations in the post-plantation society. Harris (1983) describes this transformation as the psychic integration of self and other, a dramatization of the fissuring of those ' "object" or "slave" functions consolidated in plantation psychologies' (p. 120).

Masters, like most of the characters in *Carnival*, wears the twin masks of slave and overlord, plaintiff and accused, subject and object of history. There is also Johnny the Czar and Carnival King, a petty plantation bureaucrat by day and a village radical by night. There are, of course, Jane Fisher the First and Jane Fisher the Second, Amerindian wife of a fisherman of New Forest, English paramour to Masters. There is Doubting Thomas whose origins and parents the narrator cannot trace. He is the protector of the young Masters and heroic savior of Charlotte Bartleby, the Market woman whom the racketeer Johnny the Czar attacks. Through these double characters, *Carnival* pursues its themes of transgression and reconciliation beyond life's stalemate of one-dimensional power. For Harris, the postcolonial relations to Empire can best be understood from the standpoint of a peculiar doubling of psyche, performance and experience. The circulation of power and agency proceeds along a circuitous path, and no one, not even the oppressed, can return to the state of innocence before the fall. As Everyman Masters puts it at the beginning of *Carnival*:

> Their [oppressed] lives and deaths accumulate into statistics of motiveless or meaningless crime. How to identify those who are guilty, acquit those who are innocent! How to perceive the morality of *Carnival* within a universal plague of violence! That is our play. (p. 14)

Here, as Harris suggests, power relations run through the entire social body. And, to use the language of the postcolonial policy critic Uma Kothari (2001), 'these relations are not confined to particular central sites nor located solely amongst the elite' (p. 20). In the role reversal and the exchange of hidden masks of colonial domination highlighted in *Carnival* lay the groundwork for hope and possibility that reside in new structures of feeling, new terms of association and being unleashed in the carnival of history. Here in these acts of free association lies the possibility of what Harris (1983) calls 'the comedy of freedom masking itself in claustrophobic ritual or vehicle' (p. xv).

Hybrid Subjects in *Palace of the Peacock* and *Companions of the Day and Night*

In *Palace of the Peacock*, the counterpart to Everyman Masters is Donne (a creole cattle rancher with a reputation for cruelty and hard-nosed efficiency). Even more directly than Masters, Donne represents the survival of a colonizing, adventurist and instrumentalist spirit within the postcolonial setting. He is the colonizer in the colonized. When we encounter him, he is also dead, shot by Mariella, the colonized shaman woman, whom Donne has abused. *Palace of the Peacock* is set in the interior of Guyana. The story is that of a journey made in an open pontoon or boat by Donne and a motley crew of racially ambiguous underlings. Their mission is to repossess an Amerindian settlement or maroon colony established deep in the forest by runaway members of Donne's Amerindian workforce. This cross-cultural crew has a hard time of it. Because of the rugged nature of the terrain, many times they must disembark and haul their precarious boat over land through portages in the forest. At each point of their journey they are eluded by the Amerindian renegades. When they finally arrive at the Mission there is nobody there. They set off again, this time with an old Amerindian woman who has been left behind by the people. On their second voyage out, the crew runs into a number of misfortunes. Some fall overboard. Others are killed in duels precipitated by the stress of the trip. Ultimately, the remainder of Donne's expeditionary party meet their deaths as they plunge over a waterfall to their perilous end.

These deaths are deeply symbolic. They represent a necessary dissolution of ego—the frustration and subversion of crass materialism. In Harris's novels, death often demarcates a transition—a doorway to a new experience of life and a necessary condition for psychic and social reintegration and regeneration. After one of the many deaths on board, the crew members discover their deeper association beyond the petty differences that had divided them all along. The reality of shared experience, shared history, and shared identity is revealed in a vision that the I-narrator experiences as Donne's crew approaches and finally enters the palace of the peacock— the mythical place of redemption and transformation at the top of a waterfall:

> The wall that had divided him from his true otherness and possession was a web of dreams. His feet climbed a little and they danced again, and the music of the peacock turned him into a subtle step and waltz like the grace and outspread fan of desire that had once been turned by the captain of the crew into a compulsive design and blind engine of war. His feet marched again as a spider's towards eternity, and the music he followed welled and circumnavigated the globe ... This was the inner music of the peacock I suddenly encountered and echoed and sang as I had never heard myself sing before. I felt the faces before me begin to fade and part company from me and from themselves as if our need of one another was now fulfilled, and our distance from each other was the distance of a sacrament, the sacrament and embrace we knew in one muse and one undying soul. Each of us now held at last in his arms what he had been forever seeking and what he had eternally possessed. (pp. 114–117)

This 'discovery' of vital links and connections between the self and other in *Palace of the Peacock*, and in *Carnival*, reminds one of a similar reintegrative motif that Harris pursues in another of his novels, *Companions of the Day and Night* (1975). On a sojourn to Mexico City, which lasts for centuries, *Companions'* apparently European/Everyman narrator, Idiot Nameless, finds himself inexplicably falling though passageways of historical ruins to the pre-Columbian past of Aztec and Toltec cultures. Harris links Idiot Nameless's 'falling sickness' to the Aztec fear of the sun's irretrievable fall into darkness. Again and again in his wandering through post-revolutionary Mexico, Idiot Nameless enters, like a new millennial archeologist, into fields of unsettling contrasts and unexpected associations. In his touristic travels through the city, for example, Nameless encounters hidden Catholic convents buried alongside sunken, pre-conquest Toltec shrines. What was obviously a Spanish colonial effort to deploy Catholicism against the native religion is recorded in a fossilized inventory that exposes the limits of colonial power, while affirming the rich cultural hybridity that is contemporary Mexico. The juxtaposition of these two erstwhile hostile cultures exemplifies Harris's insistence on cross-cultural interrogation and dialogue, his insistence on the radical interpretations of all cultures and the growing interdependence of contemporary peoples.

Harris experiments in all of these novels with a radical subversion of the structure and deployment of characterization in the nineteenth-century novel genre. The characters that inhabit these postcolonial texts are peculiarly fragile: they flow into each other, they decompose and crumble like ancient masks recovered from an archeological digging. They are parodies of any certifiable identity. Their claim to truth, to objectivity, is ridiculed and imperiled. Like *Companions of the Day and Night*, *Carnival* and *Palace of the Peacock* foreground a decentered, hybrid subject, alienated from any sense of predictable origins, constantly reassembling, like a bricoleur, the discontinuous elements of subordinate history.

Conclusion: The Rendezvous with Pedagogy

To return to our earlier questions: what do Harris's novels offer us as educators facing an increasingly delimited and circumscribed field of activity and influence? What might his insights provoke in the curriculum field in these times of crass localism, ethnic chauvinism, and its converse, multicultural appeasement? We see Harris's novels as an extended series of parables on the fate of the intellectual, of the educator—a kind of tragi-comedy of the perils of fundamentalism and its corporate logics. The lesson is an apt one. As educators, we grow more wary as the critical space in the field continues to collapse and a normative regime of truth inhabits not only our schools but academic life itself. The great struggle of our times is the struggle to regenerate a public sphere when the spheres of culture and education are increasingly being colonized. Such a struggle necessitates giving up something, giving up our certainties and our illusions of control over knowledge. It means a powerful and painful kind of rapprochement.

Thus we may learn from the way Harris, in *Carnival* and *Palace of the Peacock*, maps out the field of encounter of opposites in a disoriented world in which the paths to change re-open the old wounds of our colonizing histories, those unspeakable moments that Toni Morrison regards as the shared secrets of repressed memory and desire. Over time, the classroom has become the burial ground of genuine conversation and engagement—the place of perpetual avoidance of the combustible world outside. This avoidance is the Old World dispensation that inflects recent discourses in the educational arena of localism, centricities, panethnicities, practice versus theory, and so forth. We are lost in the world of ourselves, our group, our neighborhood, writing the world from our suburban home—Sweeney Erectus's last stand. Perhaps no one has put it more bluntly than bell hooks (1994) in her book *Teaching to Transgress*:

> In the weeks before the English Department at Oberlin College was about to decide whether or not I would be granted tenure, I was haunted by dreams of running away—of disappearing—yes, even of dying. These dreams were not a response to the fear that I would not be granted tenure. They were a response to the reality that I *would* be granted tenure. I was afraid that I *would* be trapped in the academy forever. (p. 1)

But ultimately, in *Teaching to Transgress*, hooks plows her way out of this fog and discovers the act of teaching to transgress, teaching as a performative act in which 'each class is different from the other.' Finding and sustaining these ex-centric, marginal spaces in education is the great challenge of teaching in our time. In the world of Harris, it means a willing death of authority over knowledge production, the quiet embrace of the fluidity of persons and identities that now people our classrooms and the world, and the pursuit of the loose ends of connectedness and association across disparate fields of inquiry, humanity and feeling wherever they may lead. This is our new-century challenge, carnival, and play. It is also our great responsibility. As we enter the carnival, as we give up our certainties, our prescribed and circumscribed roles, we must be prepared to answer to our social others for our effects, intentional and otherwise.

We return, then, in the manner of Harris's 'infinite rehearsal,' back to the concerns raised at the beginning of this essay by Apple and Schmidt, about the loss of the soul of teaching. These concerns are also raised by school critics such as Thomas Popkewitz in his *Struggling for the Soul* (1998) and John Devine in his *Maximum Security* (1996). The daily grind of schooling has led us down a corridor of serial disinvestments. According to these writers, we have given over our bodies and the bodies of our students to an impersonal educational regime of disciplinary surveillance, security systems, time on task, standardized testing, and curricular formulas of knowledge insulation and ability grouping. By performing the carnivalesque play in his novels, Harris challenges us with the task of an existential problematization of our daily lives as educators. Transformation in schooling must involve a pedagogy that reintroduces all those endangered and discarded philosophies and pragmatics of living to each other, within the context of material and cultural constraint and possibility.

The great challenge in the postcolonial environments in which we live is to rebuild the human community after the trauma of colonial administration and imposition. The great task set before teachers and educational practitioners today is the challenge of constructing a pragmatic process of meaningful, reciprocal communication that would help us reconnect our emotional and ethical investments with our work, our students and each other. Borrowing from Harris, we argue that the quest for change in education must be linked to a deepening investment in community—a sense of community that must be built from the charred remains of modernization and colonization. We will build this community by re-infusing difference, plurality, heterogeneity, and intellectual problematization into the daily lives of our school children and into our lives as brokers of cultural knowledge and social change.

References

Apple, M. (1993) *Official Knowledge: Democratic education in a conservative age* (New York, Routledge).

Bakhtin, M. (1984) *Problems of Dostoevsky's Poetics* (Minneapolis, University of Minnesota Press).

Bhabha, H. K. (1994) *The Location of Culture: Literature related to politics* (London, Routledge).

Bennett, T. (1995) *The Birth of the Museum* (New York, Routledge).

Dash, M. (1990) Ex-centric Spaces: Marronnage and metissage in the Caribbean imagination (unpublished paper presented at 'Plantation Societies' Conference, Louisiana State University, Baton Rouge).

Devine, J. (1996) *Maximum Security: The culture of violence in inner-city schools* (Chicago, University of Chicago Press).

Drake, S. (1989) Language and Revolutionary Hope, in: M. Gilkes (ed.), *The Literate Imagination* (London, Macmillan).

Harris, W. (1960) *Palace of the Peacock* (London, Faber).

Harris, W. (1961) *The Far Journey of Oudin* (London, Faber).

Harris, W. (1962) *The Whole Armour* (London, Faber).

Harris, W. (1963) *The Secret Ladder* (London, Faber).

Harris, W. (1967) *Tradition, the Writer, and Society: Critical Essays* (London, New Beacon).

Harris, W. (1975) *Companions of the Day and Night* (London, Faber).

Harris, W. (1983) *The Womb of Space* (Westport, CT, Greenwood Press).

Harris, W. (1985a) *Carnival* (London, Faber).

Harris, W. (1985b) *The Guyana Quartet* (London, Faber).

Henry, P. (2000) *Caliban's Reason: Introducing Afro-Caribbean philosophy* (New York, Routledge).

hooks, b. (1994) *Teaching to Transgress: Education as the practice of freedom* (London, Routledge).

Holquist, M. (1985) The Carnival of Discourse: Bakhtin and simultaneity, *Canadian Review of Comparative Literature*, 12:2, pp. 220–234.

Kothari, U. (2001) Participatory Development: Power, knowledge, and social control (unpublished manuscript, Institute of Development Policy and Management, University of Manchester, UK).

McDougall, R. (1989) Native Capacity, Blocked Psyche: 'Carnival' and 'Capricornia', in: M. Gilkes (ed.), *The Literate Imagination* (London, Macmillan).

McCarthy, C. & Dimitriadis, G. (2000) Globalizing Pedagogies: Power, resentment and the re-narration of difference, *World Studies in Education*, 1:1, pp. 23–39.

Ousby, I. (ed.) (1988) *The Cambridge Guide to Literature in English* (Cambridge, Cambridge University Press).

Popkewitz, T. (1998) *Struggling for the Soul: The politics of schooling and the construction of the teacher* (New York, Teachers College Press).

Schmidt, J. (2000) *Disciplined Minds: A critical look at salaried professionals and the soul-battering system that shapes their lives* (Lanham, Rowman and Littlefield).

Stallybrass, P. & White, A. (1986) *The Politics and Poetics of Transgression* (Ithaca, NY, Cornell University Press).

Notes on Contributors

Zeus Leonardo is an Associate Professor in the College of Education at California State University, Long Beach and a Visiting Associate Professor and Acting Director of the Center for Multicultural Education during 2005–2006 at the University of Washington, Seattle. He is the author of *Ideology, Discourse, and School Reform* (2003) and has published articles and book chapters on critical education and social theory with special attention to issues of race, class and gender. His essays have appeared in *Educational Researcher*, *Race Ethnicity and Education*, and *Studies in Philosophy and Education*.

Eduardo Bonilla-Silva is an Associate Professor of Sociology at Texas A&M University. He is best known for his 1997 *American Sociological Review* article 'Rethinking Racism: Toward a structural interpretation'. Apart from his many articles in journals, he has published three books: *White Supremacy and Racism in the Post-Civil Rights Era* (2001), co-winner of the 2002 Oliver Cromwell Cox Award; *Racism Without Racists: Color blind racism and the persistence of racial inequality in the United States* (2003), winner of a 2004 CHOICE Award, and *Whiteout: The continuing significance of racism,* with Ashley Doane, Jr (2003).

Ricky Lee Allen is an Assistant Professor of Educational Thought and Sociocultural Studies at the University of New Mexico. His scholarship focuses on the sociology of education, critical studies of whiteness, critical race theory, and critical pedagogy. More specifically, his primary interest is the racial identity politics of critical theories.

Daniel G. Solórzano is a Professor in the Graduate School of Education and Information Studies at the University of California, Los Angeles. His teaching and research interests include critical race and gender studies on the educational access, persistence, and graduation of underrepresented minority undergraduate and graduate students in the United States.

Tara J. Yosso is an Assistant Professor in the Department of Chicana and Chicano Studies at the University of California, Santa Barbara. Her research and teaching address issues of educational access and equity through the frameworks of critical race theory, LatCrit theory, visual sociology, and critical media literacy.

James A. Banks is Russell F. Stark University Professor and Director of the Center for Multicultural Education at the University of Washington, Seattle. His books include *Teaching Strategies for Ethnic Studies, Educating Citizens in a Multicultural Society*, and *Diversity and Citizenship Education: Global Perspectives*. He is the editor of the *Handbook of Research on Multicultural Education* and of the Multicultural Education Series of books published by Teachers College Press. During the 2005–6 academic year, he will be a Fellow at the Center for Advanced Study in the Behavioral Sciences at Stanford University.

David Gillborn is Professor of Education and Head of the School of Educational Foundations and Policy Studies at the Institute of Education, University of London. In addition to examining the consequences of current educational practices, he is also involved in attempts to improve future policy. He is founding editor of the journal *Race Ethnicity & Education*, and his most recent book, *Rationing Education* (with co-author Deborah Youdell), was judged the best book in the field of educational studies (2000) by the Standing Conference on Studies in Education / Society for Educational Studies.

Marvin Lynn is an Assistant Professor and Coordinator of Minority & Urban Education within the Department of Curriculum and Instruction at the University of Maryland, College Park. In his research, he uses Critical Race Theory as the lens through which he examines the work and lives of Black men who teach in K-12 urban schools.

Valerie Scatamburlo-D'Annibale, an award-winning author and educator, is an Associate Professor in the Department of Communication Studies and chairs the Graduate Program in Communication and Social Justice at the University of Windsor, Ontario, Canada.

Peter McLaren is a Professor in the Graduate School of Education and Information Studies, University of California, Los Angeles. He is the author and editor of forty books on topics that include the sociology of education, Marxist theory, critical pedagogy, critical multiculturalism and critical ethnography. His writings have been translated into twelve languages. Professor McLaren is the inaugural recipient of the Paulo Freire Social Justice Award presented by Chapman University.

Laurence Parker is an Associate Professor in the Department of Educational Policy Studies at the University of Illinois at Urbana-Champaign. His areas of teaching and research focus on critical race theory and educational policy analysis and leadership for social justice and equity. Laurence Parker's most recent publication is an edited book (2003) with Gerardo Lopez, entitled *Research Impositions: Interrogating Racism in Qualitative Research Methodology*, published by Peter Lang.

David Stovall is an Assistant Professor of Policy Studies in the College of Education at the University of Illinois at Chicago. His research interests include critical race theory, social justice education and school–community relationships.

Michèle Foster is an educational anthropologist and sociolinguist whose research focuses on the social, cultural, and linguistic contexts of education, particularly of African Americans. Prior to working at Claremont Graduate University, she was on the faculty of the University of Pennsylvania and the University of California at Davis. During 2004–5 she was Distinguished Visiting Research Scholar at Mills College in Oakland, California. Her articles appear in *Teachers College Record*, *Journal of Education, Language in Society, Theory into Practice, Phi Delta Kappa, Educational Theory*, and *Anthropology of Education Quarterly*.

Dolores Delgado Bernal is an Associate Professor at the University of Utah in the Department of Education, Culture, and Society and the Ethnic Studies Program. Her research draws from critical race theory and US Third World feminist theories to examine and improve the educational experiences of students of color. She is the author of numerous chapters and articles, some of which appear in *Harvard Educational Review, International Journal of Qualitative Studies in Education, Urban Education*, and *Frontiers: A Journal of Women Studies*.

Octavio Villalpando is Associate Professor of Educational Leadership and Policy at the University of Utah. He received his PhD at UCLA, and engages in scholarship that contributes to the field of higher education around questions of how colleges and universities shape the experiences and educational outcomes of Chicanas/os and other students and faculty of color. He draws from Critical Race Theory (CRT) and Latina/o Critical Theory (LatCrit) and utilises a mixed method approach in his research. He teaches courses in the areas of CRT, diversity and multiculturalism in higher education, student development, and ethnic studies.

Cameron McCarthy is Research Professor and University Scholar in the Institute of Communications Research at the University of Illinois at Urbana-Champaign. He has authored numerous books including *The Uses of Culture, Reading and Teaching the Postcolonial* and *Foucault, Cultural Studies and Governmentality*.

Greg Dimitriadis is an Associate Professor in social foundations of education at the University at Buffalo, the State University of New York.

Index

CPSIA information can be obtained
at www.ICGtesting.com
Printed in the USA
FSHW021053010921
84345FS